BBC

Bitesize

Bitesize AQA GCSE (9-1) COMBINED SCIENCE TRILOGY

REVISION WORKBOOK

FOUNDATION

Series Consultant:
Harry Smith

Authors:
Amani Leslie
Aidan Gill
Nigel Saunders

Published by BBC Active, an imprint of Educational Publishers LLP, part of the Pearson Education Group, 80 Strand, London, WC2R 0RL.

www.pearsonschools.co.uk/BBCBitesize

Typeset by Newgen KnowledgeWorks Pvt. Ltd., Chennai, India
Produced and illustrated by Newgen Publishing UK
Cover design by Andrew Magee & Pearson Education Limited 2019
Cover illustration by Darren Lingard / Oxford Designers & Illustrators

First published 2019

22 21 20 19
10 9 8 7 6 5 4 3 2 1

British Library Cataloguing in Publication Data
A catalogue record for this book is available from the British Library

ISBN 978 1 406 68612 8

Printed and bound in Slovakia by Neografia.

The Publisher's policy is to use paper manufactured from sustainable forests.

Acknowledgements
Text
p21: Measles in England and Wales between 1998 and 2008, Health Protection Agency. © Crown copyright, 2008. Contains public sector information licensed under the Open Government Licence v3.0; **p23:** Chan, J. M., Rimm, E. B., Colditz, G. A., Stampfer, M. J., & Willett, W. C. (1994). Obesity, Fat Distribution, and Weight Gain as Risk Factors for Clinical Diabetes in Men. Diabetes Care, 17(9), 961–969. doi:10.2337/diacare.17.9.961. © 1994 American Diabetes Association; **p27:** Data from Lane CR, LeBaigue S, Esan OB, Awofisyo AA, Adams NL, Fisher I, et al. Salmonella enterica Serovar Enteritidis, England and Wales, 1945–2011. Emerg Infect Dis. 2014;20(7):1097–1104. https://wwwnc.cdc.gov/eid/article/20/7/12-1850_article. Centers for Disease Control and Prevention; **p30:** Data from The Pink Book: Course Textbook – 13th Edition, 2015, https://www.cdc.gov/vaccines/pubs/pinkbook/downloads/meas.pdf. Centers for Disease Control and Prevention; **p31:** Data from Achievements in Public Health, 1900-1999: Control of Infectious Diseases, MMWR, CDC, Weekly, July 30, 1999 / 48(29);621–629, https://www.cdc.gov/mmwr/preview/mmwrhtml/mm4829a1.htm#fig1. Centers for Disease Control and Prevention; **p59:** Deaths involving MRSA: 2008 to 2012, 22 August 2013. The Office for National Statistics (ONS). © Crown copyright, 2013. Contains public sector information licensed under the Open Government Licence v3.0; **p217:** Data from Measles (Rubeola), Cases and Outbreaks. https://www.cdc.gov/measles/cases-outbreaks.html. Centers for Disease Control and Prevention.

BBC: pp1–212 © 2019

Photographs
Alamy Stock Photo: Bill Coster In 54t, Blickwinkel/Baesemann 64b, Sanjay Thakur/Ephotocorp 66, David Paterson/Picade LLC 160b, Lev Radin 161, PictureLux/The Hollywood Archive 229, **Getty Images:** Ed Reschke/Photolibrary 5, Morsa Images/DigitalVision 25, Sharply_done/E+ 55, Johan63/iStock 58, Make_Video_Company/ iStock 64t, **Science Photo Library:** Alvin Telser 19,233,234, **Shutterstock:** Dewin Indew 34, Teekayu 54b, Frantic00 57, Anton_Ivanov 69, DrimaFilm 71t, Kusska 71b, Bixstock 158, Steve Meese 160t, Francois Boizot 160c, IndustryAndTravel 161, Olinchuk 163, Ruslan Ivantsov 170, Serghei Starus 171, ForeverLee 173, Brent Hofacker 178, Sathienpong Prempetch 179, Lzf 200, Olga Popova 208, Medwether 210t, Suttha Burawonk 210b, Nkjn22 216.

Contents

Tick off each topic as you go.

Each bite-sized chunk has a **timer** to indicate how long it will take. Use them to plan your revision sessions.

Scan the **QR codes** to visit the BBC Bitesize website. It will link straight through to revision resources on that subject. You can also access these by visiting www.pearsonschools.co.uk/BBCBitesizeLinks.

Grades have been assigned to most questions in this workbook. These are intended to show you the level of challenge of those questions, and to help you track your progress. In your exam, your grade will be based on your overall mark, and not on your responses to individual questions.

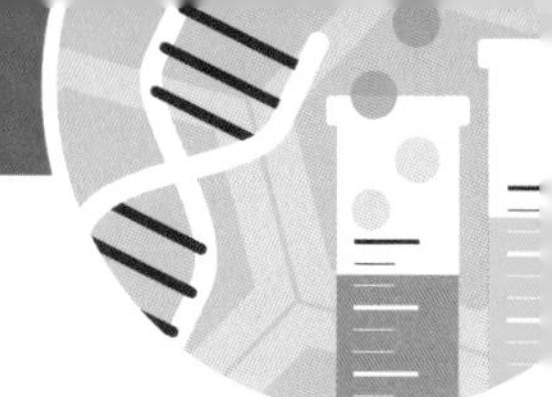

Levels of organisation

2 Quick quiz

Put the parts in order of size from smallest to largest. One has been done for you.

cell	organ	organ system	organism	tissue

.... → .... → .... → organ system → ....

smallest — largest

5 Tissues, organs and organ systems — Grade 3

1. Draw **one** line from each key word to its definition. **[3 marks]**

Key word
tissue
organ
organ system

Definition
group of tissues that performs a specific job
subcellular structure that performs special functions within the cell
group of organs
group of specialised cells with similar structures and functions

2. Name **two** organs in the central nervous system. **[2 marks]**

1 spinal cord

2 ....

15 Organisation of the human body — Grade 3

3. Which of these is an example of an organ. Tick **one** box. **[1 mark]**

mitochondria ☐ lung ☐

nerve cell ☐ digestive system ☐

4. Name **two** examples of organ systems. **[2 marks]**

1 ....

2 ....

5. Complete **Table 1** to show examples of the levels of organisation in the circulatory system. Use words from the box. **[4 marks]**

muscle cell	heart	cardiac tissue	circulatory system	mitochondria

Table 1

Level of organisation	Example
cell	
tissue	
organ	
organ system	

The levels of organisation in the table go from smallest to largest.

 Made a start  Feeling confident  Exam ready

Prokaryotic and eukaryotic cells

2 Quick quiz

Are these statements about prokaryotic and eukaryotic cells true or false?

Bacteria are eukaryotes.	**True / False**
Prokaryotic cells are usually bigger than eukaryotic cells.	**True / False**
Prokaryotic cells have cell walls.	**True / False**
Both prokaryotic and eukaryotic cells have ribosomes.	**True / False**
Eukaryotic cells have a nucleus.	**True / False**

10 Using prefixes — Grade 3

1. Draw **one** line from each measurement to its unit. **[3 marks]**

centimetre	mm
millimetre	cm
micrometre	nm
nanometre	µm

2. Calculate these conversions.

(a) 1 cm into mm 1 cm × 10 = ... mm **[1 mark]**

(b) 50 cm into m .... **[1 mark]**

(c) 150 mm into cm .... **[1 mark]**

(d) 2200 mm into m .... **[1 mark]**

(e) 200 mm into µm. Give your answer in standard form. .... **[1 mark]**

100 cm = 1 m; 1 cm = 0.01 m;
1 mm = 0.001 m; 1 µm = 1×10^{-6} m

Standard form lets you write very large or very small numbers more easily. Use the formula $A \times 10^n$ where A is a number between 1 and 10 and n is the number of powers of ten that A is multiplied by, e.g. $50\,000 = 5 \times 10^4$

10 Eukaryotic and prokaryotic cells — Grade 4

3. Figure 1 shows a diagram of a prokaryotic cell.

(a) What is the structure labelled **A**? Tick **one** box. **[1 mark]**

cell membrane ☐

plasmid ☐

flagella ☐

(b) Name structure **B**. .... **[1 mark]**

A
B

Figure 1

4. Give **one** similarity and **one** difference between prokaryotic cells and eukaryotic cells. **[2 marks]**

....

5. Which part of a prokaryotic cell contains DNA? Tick **one** box. **[2 marks]**

cell wall ☐ flagella ☐ plasmid ☐

Made a start

Feeling confident
Exam ready

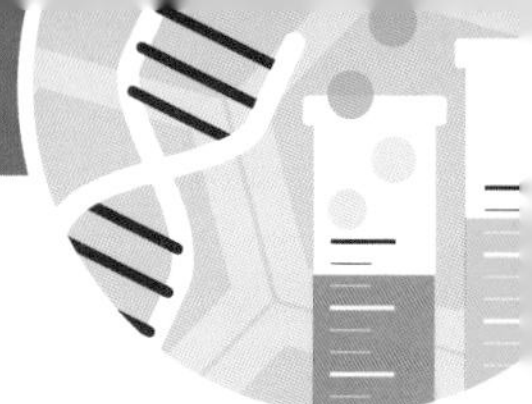

Animal and plant cells

2 Quick quiz

(a) Tick the boxes to show if the organelles are found in animal cells and/or plant cells.

(b) Write down **one** organelle that is found in both animal cells and plant cells.

....

(c) Write down **one** organelle that is found only in plant cells.

....

Organelle	Animal cell	Plant cell
cell membrane		
cell wall		
chloroplast		
mitochondria		
nucleus		
ribosomes		

5 Plant cells — Grade 2

1. Figure 1 shows a diagram of a plant cell.

What is the structure labelled **A**? Tick **one** box. **[1 mark]**

cell membrane ☐

cell wall ☐

chloroplast ☐

nucleus ☐

Exam focus
You must be able to interpret images of plant and animal cells and recognise their identifying structures.

A

B

Figure 1

2. Name structure **B**. .... **[1 mark]**

5 Functions of organelles — Grade 3

3. Draw **one** line to link each organelle with its function. **[3 marks]**

Organelle
chloroplast
cellulose cell wall
cell membrane
nucleus
ribosome

Function
controls what enters and exits the cell
contains chlorophyll for photosynthesis
contains the genetic material
gives the cell protection, strength and structure
where proteins are made

Think about the functions that need to happen in plant cells and animal cells.

5 Cell size — Grade 4

4. An animal cell is 20 μm in diameter. A plant cell is 80 μm in diameter.

(a) Calculate how many times bigger the plant cell is compared to the animal cell. **[1 mark]**

(b) Suggest, in terms of cell structure, why plant cells are usually larger than animal cells. **[1 mark]**

....

Exam focus
The command word 'suggest' means you need to apply your knowledge and understanding to a new situation.

 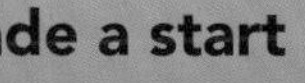   

Made a start | Feeling confident | Exam ready

Microscopy

2 Quick quiz

Complete the sentences using the words in the box.

magnification	resolution	scale	size

.... is a measure of how many times bigger the image is than the object.

.... is a measure of how well a microscope can distinguish between two very close objects.

5 Calculating magnification — Grade 3

1. (a) Calculate the total magnification if the eyepiece lens magnification is ×10 and the objective lens magnification is ×40. **[1 mark]**

total magnification = 10 × 40 = ...

total magnification = eyepiece lens magnification × objective lens magnification

(b) What is the total magnification if the eyepiece lens magnification is ×20 and the objective lens magnification is ×4? Tick **one** box. **[1 mark]**

×5 ☐ ×20 ☐ ×80 ☐ ×40 ☐

5 Cell size and magnification — Grade 5

2. A scientist observed a plant cell under a light microscope.
The magnification used was ×100. The size of the image was 2000 µm.

(a) Calculate the actual size of the cell. Give the unit. **[3 marks]**

Size = ... Unit ....

$$\text{magnification} = \frac{\text{size of image}}{\text{size of real object}}$$

(b) Suggest if the scientist could see the cell nucleus and the chloroplasts. **[2 marks]**

....

....

5 Light and electron microscopes — Grade 5

3. (a) Describe **three** differences between light microscopes and electron microscopes. **[3 marks]**

1 ....

2 ....

3 ....

Think about when both types of microscopes were first made and their magnification and resolving powers.

(b) A scientist wants to look at ribosomes in a cell. Explain which type of microscope should be used. Give a reason for your answer. **[2 marks]**

....

Made a start

Feeling confident
Exam ready

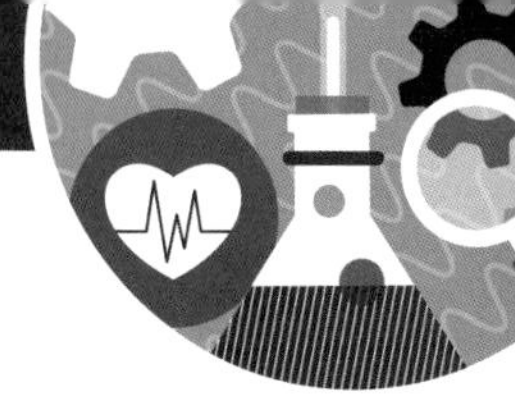

Using microscopes

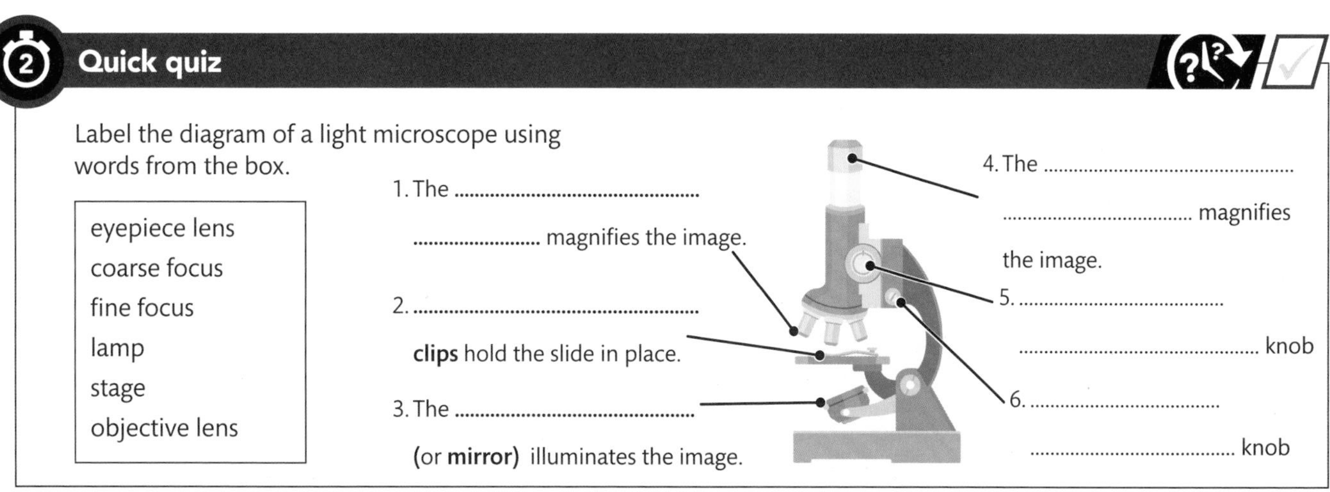

Quick quiz

Label the diagram of a light microscope using words from the box.

eyepiece lens
coarse focus
fine focus
lamp
stage
objective lens

1. The .... magnifies the image.

2. .... **clips** hold the slide in place.

3. The .... (or **mirror**) illuminates the image.

4. The .... magnifies the image.

5. .... knob

6. .... knob

Parts of a light microscope

Grade 3

1. Draw **one** line to match each function to a part of the microscope. **[2 marks]**

Function	**Part of the microscope**
magnifies the image	coarse focus knob
adjusts the focus of the image	eyepiece / objective lens
illuminates the image	lamp

2. The statements explain how you would view a slide underneath a microscope. They are not in the correct order. Write numbers next to the statements to show the correct order. **[3 marks]**

Use the coarse focus knob to lower the low power objective lens to just above the slide.	
Look through the eyepiece lens and raise the lens until the image is nearly in focus.	
Place the prepared slide under the stage clips of the microscope.	1
Use the fine focus knob to get a clear sharp image.	

Viewing cells with a microscope

Grade 5

3. **Figure 1** shows an animal cell.

(a) Identify the cell part labelled **A**. .... **[1 mark]**

(b) Identify the cell part labelled **B**. .... **[1 mark]**

(c) The cell was stained before viewing. Suggest why. **[1 mark]**

....

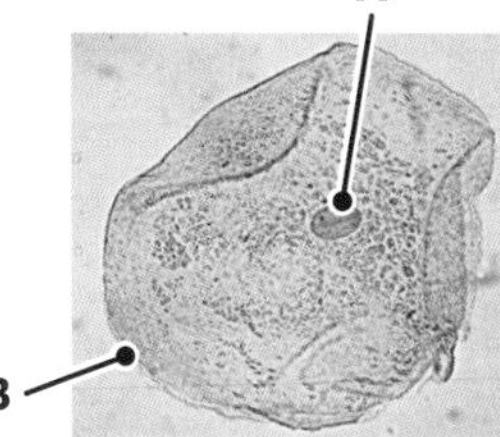

Figure 1

Exam focus

You must be able to interpret images of plant and animal cells and recognise their identifying structures.

 Made a start  Feeling confident  Exam ready

Specialised cells

2 Quick quiz

Complete the table to show if the specialised cells are animal cells or plant cells.

Specialised cell	muscle cell	nerve cell	phloem	root hair cell
Animal or plant cell				

5 Specialised cells — Grade 3

1. Describe the functions of nerve cells and root hair cells. **[2 marks]**

Nerve cells carry ....

Root hair cells absorb ....

Think about what is carried around the body by nerve cells and what plants need to absorb to be healthy.

2. Draw **one** line to match each adaptation of sperm cells to its correct function. **[3 marks]**

Adaptation
acrosome containing enzymes
haploid nucleus
tail

Function
to form a complete set of chromosomes after fertilisation
digest the outer layer of the egg cell
to swim to the egg cell
to provide energy from respiration

5 Xylem cells — Grade 3

3. Xylem is a tissue that is specialised for transport of materials in plants.

(a) Name **two** materials transported by xylem. **[2 marks]**

1 .... 2 ....

(b) Which **two** of the following are adaptations of xylem? Tick **two** boxes. **[2 marks]**

- lignin walls ☐
- dendrites ☐
- sieve plates ☐
- hollow centre (lumen) ☐
- large vacuole ☐

Exam focus

For extra revision once you have answered the question, try to identify which specialised cells have the other adaptations.

(c) Name **one** other tissue used for transport in plants. .... **[1 mark]**

5 Muscle cells — Grade 5

4. **Figure 1** shows part of a muscle cell. Explain why muscle cells have many mitochondria. **[3 marks]**

....

....

....

Think about what mitochondria do in a cell.

mitochondria

protein filaments that can shorten the cell

Figure 1

 Made a start 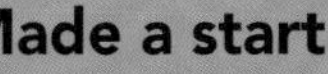  Feeling confident  Exam ready

Cell differentiation

2 Quick quiz

Circle the correct words in bold to complete the sentences about cell differentiation.

Cells differentiate to form **specialised / non-specialised** cells.

Stem / muscle / nerve cells can form any type of cell.

Cell differentiation happens **early in / throughout** an animal's life.

Cell differentiation happens **early in / throughout** a plant's life.

10 Cell differentiation in animals — Grades 3–4

1. Where do human stem cells come from? Tick **two** boxes. **[2 marks]**

bone marrow ☑ liver ☐ lung tissue ☐

muscle ☐ embryos ☐

Exam focus
Read instructions carefully. If the question asks you to tick two boxes make sure you only tick two boxes.

2. Name **two** specialised cells in humans. **[2 marks]**

1 muscle cells .... 2 ....

3. Give **three** examples of repair and replacement in humans. **[3 marks]**

1 healing broken bones ....

2 ....

3 ....

10 Cell differentiation in plants — Grade 5

4. Where are the cells that can differentiate into any type of cell found in plants? Tick **one** box. **[1 mark]**

meristem ☐ leaf ☐ stem ☐

5. Name **one** type of specialised plant cell. **[1 mark]**

....

6. Explain how plants can regrow branches after the branches have been cut off. **[3 marks]**

....

....

....

Think about at what phase in a plant's life its cells can differentiate.

Exam focus
Include keywords in longer response type questions, for example, meristems and differentiation.

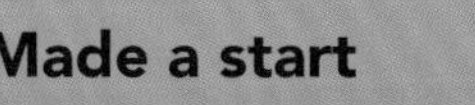

Made a start ☐ Feeling confident ☐ Exam ready ☐

Chromosomes, mitosis and the cell cycle

2 Quick quiz

Are these sentences about mitosis true or false?

Chromosomes contain many genes. **True / False**

Mitosis always produces haploid cells. **True / False**

Mitosis can produce clones. **True / False**

Humans have 46 pairs of chromosomes. **True / False**

Mitosis can be used for asexual reproduction. **True / False**

10 Cell cycle — Grade 3

1. Put these parts of a cell in order of size starting with the smallest. | cell | chromosome | gene | nucleus | **[3 marks]**

gene → .... → .... → cell

smallest — largest

2. Figure 1 shows the first stage of the cell cycle. Use **Figure 1** to describe what happens. **[3 marks]**

The DNA inside the nucleus ....

The number of subcellular structures ....

There are now .... copies of each chromosome.

Figure 1

Exam focus
If the question tells you to use the figure, there will be information to help you answer the question.

3. Figure 2 shows part of the cell cycle. What is happening in this part of the cell cycle? Tick **two** boxes. **[2 marks]**

cell membrane is dividing ☐

chromosomes are separating ✓

DNA is replicating ☐

nucleus is splitting ☐

Figure 2

Look at what is actually happening to the components of the cell in the diagram.

10 Mitosis — Grade 5

4. Give **two** purposes of mitosis in multicellular organisms. **[2 marks]**

1.. 2..

5. In mitosis, a parent cell produces daughter cells. Compare the daughter cells to the parent cell. **[2 marks]**

....

....

Think about how the cells are the same and different in terms of quantity and genetics.

Made a start | Feeling confident | Exam ready

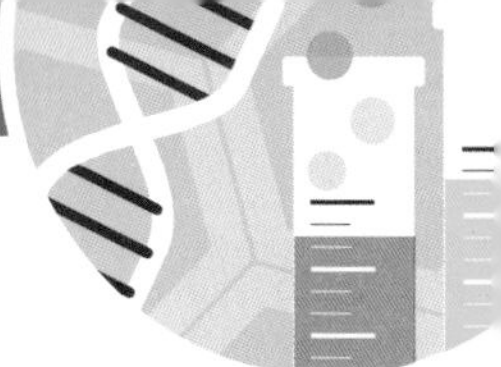

Stem cells

Quick quiz

Match the type of stem cell to where it is found.

Type of stem cell
adult stem cell
embryonic stem cell
plant stem cell

Where it is found
embryo
meristem
bone marrow

Some types of stem cell are found in more than one place.

Human stem cells

Grade 4 

1. Table 1 shows some features of adult and embryonic stem cells. Complete the table by ticking the boxes to show the correct features. **[4 marks]**

Table 1

Feature	Adult stem cell	Embryonic stem cell
can form any type of cell		✓
when used, life is destroyed		
comes from living organisms		
can be used to treat disease		

Think about the similarities and differences between adult and embryonic stem cells. Some features belong to both adult and embryonic stem cells.

Plant stem cells

Grade 3 

2. Define the term 'clone'. **[1 mark]**

A clone is an organism that is genetically ....

Exam focus

The command word 'define' means that you need to write what the word means.

3. Give **two** advantages of cloning plants. **[2 marks]**

1 Taking cuttings produces cloned plants quickly and ....

2 Rare plants can be grown to protect them from ....

Cloned plants are also identical, which can be an advantage.

Using stem cells

Grades 3–5 

4. Name **two** places where adult stem cells are found. **[2 marks]**

1 .... 2 ....

5. Give **one** argument for and **one** argument against using adult stem cells to treat disease. **[2 marks]**

For ....

Against ....

Exam focus

You are expected to be able to look at other people's opinions and discuss the arguments for and against different scenarios.

Adult stem cells come from adults who are able to choose to donate their stem cells.

 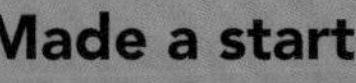
Made a start
 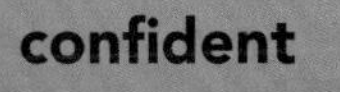
Feeling confident

Exam ready

Diffusion

2 Quick quiz

Draw an arrow on the diagram to show the net movement of the particles across the cell membrane.

cell membrane
high concentration | low concentration

5 The role of diffusion

Grade 4

1. Complete the definition of the term 'diffusion'. Use words from the box. **[2 marks]**

higher	lower	net

Diffusion is the ....net......... movement of particles of gas or particles in solution down a concentration gradient from an area of their .... concentration to an area of their .... concentration.

5 Surface area to volume ratio

Grade 4

2. (a) Complete **Table 1** to show the surface area of the two cubes shown in **Figure 1**. **[4 marks]**

Table 1

Cube	Length of one side in cm = *a*	Area of one side in cm² = *a* × *a* = *b*	Number of sides = *c*	Surface area in cm² = *b* × *c*
1	2	4	6	24
2	3		6	

2 cm   cube 1   3 cm   cube 2

Figure 1

(b) Complete **Table 2** to show the surface area to volume ratio of the two cubes. **[4 marks]**

Table 2

Cube	Surface area in cm²	Volume in cm³ (*a* × *a* × *a*)	Surface area to volume ratio
1	24	8	3 : 1
2		27	

Divide the surface area by the volume to get the smallest ratio.

10 Gas exchange surfaces

Grades 3–5

3. Name **two** factors that affect the rate of diffusion. **[2 marks]**

1 .... 2 ....

4. Which are **two** features of gas exchange surfaces in animals? Tick **two** boxes. **[2 marks]**

small surface area ☐ well ventilated ☐ efficient blood supply ☐

thick membrane ☐ lots of mitochondria ☐

5. Give **two** ways that a plant leaf is adapted to be an efficient gas exchange surface. **[2 marks]**

1 .... 2 ....

Think about what is important about gas exchange surfaces in general, animals as well as plants.

 Made a start  Feeling confident  Exam ready

Osmosis

2 Quick quiz

Label the diagram using the words in the box.
For the net movement of water molecules, indicate direction using an arrow.

dilute sucrose solution net movement of water molecules concentrated sucrose solution partially permeable membrane

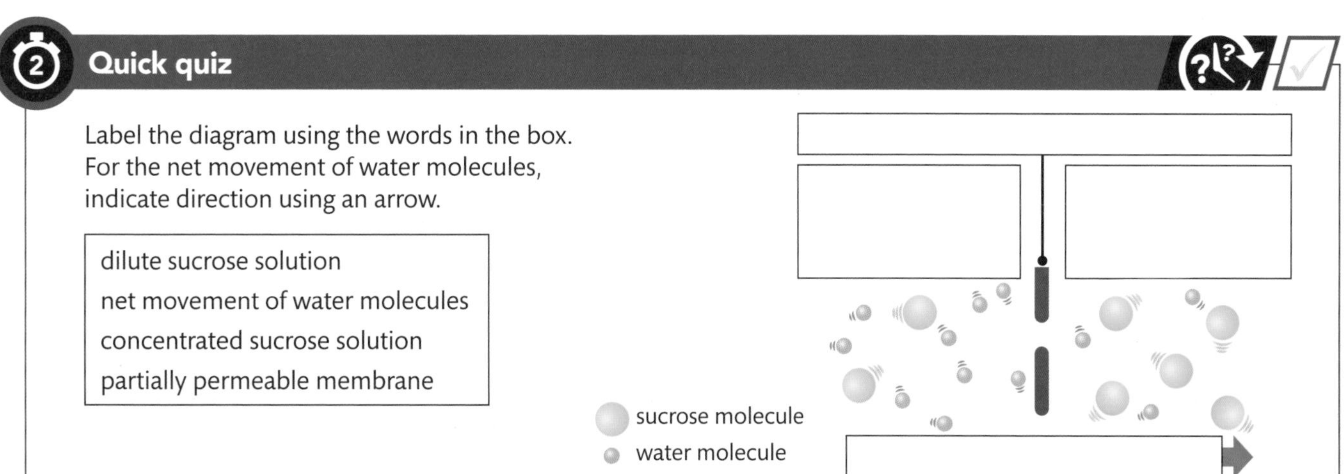

5 Diffusion — Grade 3

1. Name **two** substances that can diffuse through a partially permeable membrane. **[2 marks]**

1 water .... 2 ....

Only small molecules can diffuse through a partially permeable membrane. Large molecules, such as starch, cannot.

2. Explain the difference between a dilute and a concentrated solution. **[2 marks]**

A dilute solution contains high concentrations of ....

A concentrated solution contains ....

10 Osmosis — Grade 5

3. A plant cell was placed in different solutions of sucrose. Draw **one** line to link each solution with its effect on the plant cell. **[2 marks]**

Solution	Effect on plant cell
a more dilute solution	the cell decreases in size
a more concentrated solution	the cell increases in size
a solution with the same concentration	the cell stays the same size

A more dilute solution has a higher concentration of water.
A more concentrated solution has a lower concentration of water.

4. Red blood cells only have a cell membrane and contain many solute molecules. Explain why red blood cells burst when they are placed in distilled water. **[3 marks]**

....

....

....

What does a cell wall do in a plant? Think about what happens to the size of a cell if you put it in distilled water and why it happens.

Exam focus

Remember to include keywords in your answer. In this question, you should include the words osmosis and concentration as well as ideas about the movement of water.

Investigating osmosis

2 Quick quiz

Osmosis involves the net movement of which substance?

carbon dioxide ☐ oxygen ☐ sugar ☐ water ☐

10 Calculating percentage change — Grade 5

1. A student measured the masses of five equal-sized potato cubes. Each cube was placed in a beaker of distilled water for 30 minutes before being dried and reweighed. The student recorded the initial and final masses of the potato cubes and calculated the mean initial mass and mean final mass:

mean initial mass = 1.13 g, mean final mass = 1.25 g

Calculate the percentage change in the mean mass of the potato cubes. **[2 marks]**

> percentage change in mass = $\frac{\text{(final mass – initial mass)}}{\text{initial mass}} \times 100\%$

final mass − initial mass = ... − .... = ... g

percentage change = $\left(\frac{\text{..........................}}{1.13\text{g}}\right) \times 100 =$ .... %

10 Osmosis and concentration of sugar solution — Grades 2–5

2. An investigation was carried out to determine the effect of concentration of sugar solution on osmosis. Potato cubes were placed in beakers containing different concentrations of sugar solution.

(a) Complete **Table 1** by ticking the correct boxes to show which variable is the independent variable, dependent variable and control variable in this investigation. **[3 marks]**

Table 1

Variable	Independent variable	Dependent variable	Control variable
mass of potato			
concentration of sugar solution			
volume of sugar solution			

> The independent variable is the variable you change. The dependent variable is the one that you measure. Control variables are those that are kept constant so that they do not affect the results.

(b) (i) Predict what would happen to the mass of a potato cube if it were placed in a concentrated sugar solution. **[1 mark]**

....

> This is a required practical so think back to how you carried out the experiment.

(ii) Explain your answer. **[4 marks]**

....

....

....

....

> Osmosis is the movement of water from its higher concentration to its lower concentration. Water will move from a more dilute to a more concentrated solution.

Exam focus

This question has the command word 'explain' and 4 marks. You need to give reasons for your answer and make at least four valid points including what is happening to the water molecules, why it happens and how it happens.

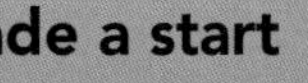

Feeling confident

Exam ready

Active transport

2 Quick quiz

Which statements about active transport are true and which are false?

Active transport is the movement of water. **True / False**

Active transport requires energy. **True / False**

Root hair cells absorb mineral ions by active transport. **True / False**

Materials are moved down a concentration gradient. **True / False**

5 Types of transport — Grade 3

1. Draw **one** line to match each type of transport with its definition. **[2 marks]**

Type of transport	Definition
diffusion	the movement of substances against a concentration gradient using energy from respiration
osmosis	the movement of particles from higher to lower concentration
active transport	the movement of water from a dilute to a more concentrated solution through a partially permeable membrane

5 Absorption in root hair cells — Grades 2–4

2. (a) Which **two** substances are absorbed by root hair cells? Tick **two** boxes. **[2 marks]**

water ☐ carbon dioxide ☐ glucose ☐ mineral ions ☐

(b) Describe how these **two** substances are absorbed by the root hair cell. **[2 marks]**

1 ....

2 ....

5 Active transport in the small intestine — Grade 5

3. Figure 1 shows a cell that lines the small intestine. This cell absorbs glucose. It contains many mitochondria. Explain why this cell needs mitochondria to transport glucose. **[4 marks]**

....

....

....

....

Think about what mitochondria do in a cell and how glucose is transported.

Exam focus

This question is 4 marks so you need to make at least four points. Include the name of the process, how and why it happens, and what is needed.

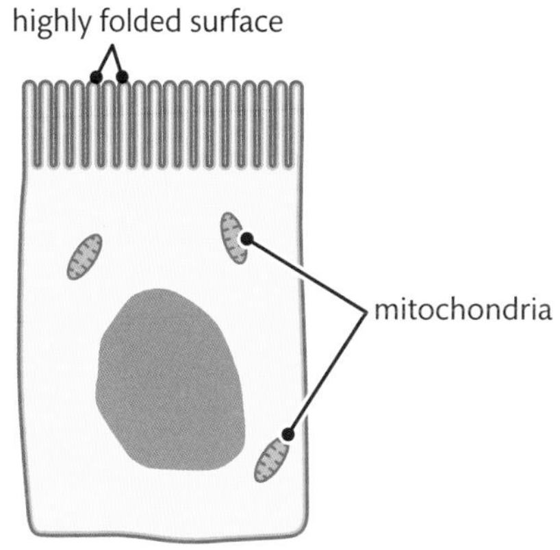

Figure 1

Plant tissues

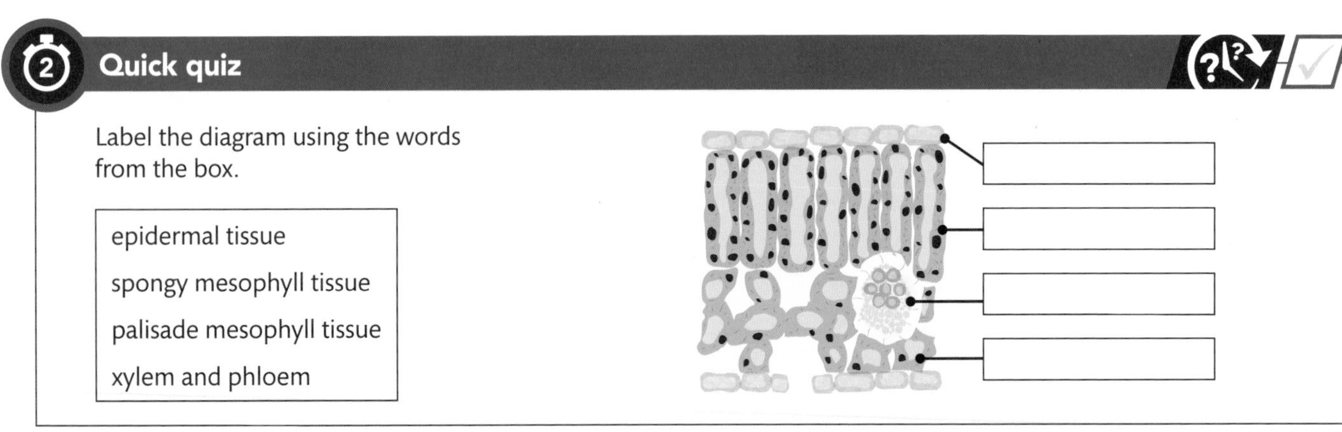

5 Functions of leaf tissues — Grade 3

1. Draw **one** line from each leaf tissue to its function. **[3 marks]**

Leaf tissue	Function
epidermal tissue	contains many chloroplasts for photosynthesis
palisade mesophyll tissue	has a large surface area for gas exchange
phloem tissue	secretes a waxy cuticle for protection
spongy mesophyll tissue	transport of dissolved sugars
xylem	transport of water and mineral ions

5 Stomata and guard cells — Grade 3

2. Complete the sentences to describe the functions of stomata and guard cells in a leaf. Use words from the box. **[5 marks]**

carbon dioxide	guard cells	photosynthesis	pores	protrusions	water

Stomata are small .... on the underside of a leaf.

They are open during the day to allow .... and oxygen to enter and leave the leaf for photosynthesis.

During transpiration, ... also leaves the plant.

At night, ... close the stomata because there is no ....photosynthesis.... at night.

5 Adaptations for photosynthesis — Grade 5

3. Explain how the following parts make a leaf efficient for photosynthesis.

(a) transparent upper epidermis **[2 marks]**

....

(b) air spaces in the spongy mesophyll tissue **[2 marks]**

....

Exam focus

The command word 'explain' means you need to give a reason for why each of these parts helps to make photosynthesis efficient in a plant.

 Made a start  Feeling confident  Exam ready

Plant transport

2 Quick quiz

Tick the boxes to show the substances each plant part transports.

	Phloem	Root hair cell	Xylem
dissolved sugars			
mineral ions			
water			

5 Transpiration — Grades 3–4

1. (a) Define the term 'transpiration'. **[1 mark]**

Transpiration is the movement of water from the roots ....

....

Exam focus
You will be expected to be able to give definitions for important biological terms and processes.

(b) Complete the sentence about transpiration. Use words from the box. **[3 marks]**

leaves	stomata	water	xylem cells	oxygen

.... evaporates from the surface of mesophyll cells in the .... and diffuses out through open ....

15 Transpiration rates — Grade 5

2. A student measures the rate of transpiration at different humidity levels. **Figure 1** shows a graph of the results.

(a) Describe the relationship between humidity and the rate of transpiration. **[1 mark]**

As the humidity increases ....

Exam focus
If a figure or a graph is provided in the question you will be expected to use it and refer to it in your answers.

Transpiration rate

Relative humidity

Figure 1

(b) Explain the reasons for the shape of the graph. **[3 marks]**

As air humidity increases the .... between the water vapour inside the air spaces of the leaf and the outside air so the rate of diffusion ....

If the humidity increases, there will be more water vapour in the air, reducing the concentration gradient.

(c) Name **three** other factors that affect the rate of transpiration. **[3 marks]**

1 temperature .... 2 .... 3 ....

5 Transport in plants — Grades 4–5

3. (a) Which of the following are ways that xylem is specialised for its function? Tick **one** box. **[1 mark]**

hollow tubes ☐ sieve plates ☐ lots of chloroplasts ☐ pits ☐

(b) Explain **two** ways that root hair cells are adapted for their function. **[4 marks]**

1 ....

2 ....

 Made a start  Feeling confident  Exam ready

Digestion in humans

Quick quiz

Label the diagram of the lock and key model using words from the box.

active site	enzyme	products	substrate

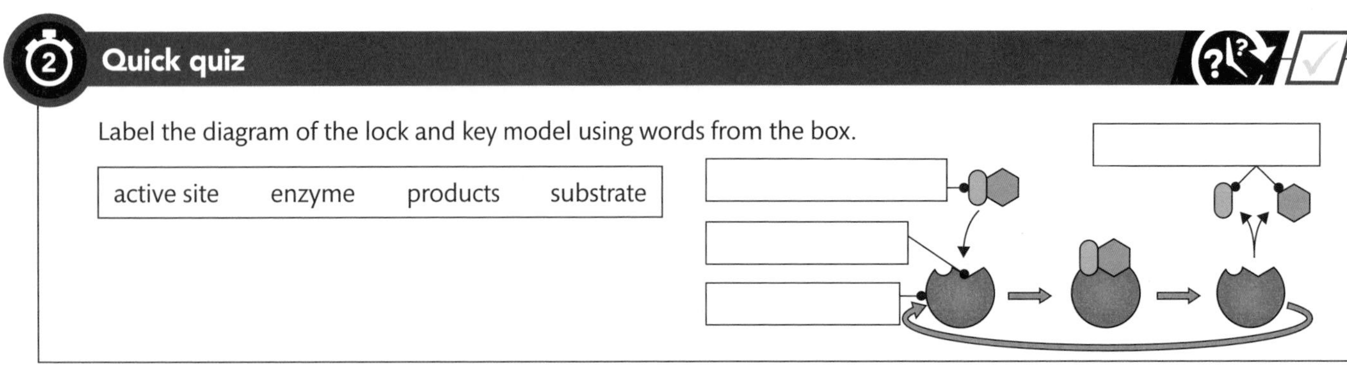

Digestive enzymes

Grades 3–4

1. Complete **Table 1** which shows three digestive enzymes, the substances they break down into and the products they form. **[3 marks]**

Exam focus

You will be expected to be able to state where each digestive enzyme is produced and what they do.

Table 1

Digestive enzyme	Substance	Products
lipase	fats and oils	
protease	proteins	amino acids
carbohydrase		

2. Explain why an increase in temperature can decrease the rate of digestion. **[4 marks]**

Digestion involves the use of digestive ....

High temperatures affect the shape of ....

So the enzyme and substrate can no longer ....

So the food substances cannot be ....

Digestion involves enzymes that are affected by high or low pH and temperature.

Exam focus

The command word 'explain' requires a detailed response. You need to be able to say what is happening as well as why it happens and the effect of it.

Bile

Grades 4–5

3. Bile is a substance found in the digestive system.

(a) Draw **one** line from each word on the left to a word on the right to show where bile is produced, stored and released. **[2 marks]**

produced		gall bladder
stored		liver
released		small intestine

(b) Describe **two** ways that bile helps digestion. **[2 marks]**

1 ....

2 ....

Think about the pH of stomach acid and at what pH enzymes work best. How does bile help this? Other factors such as surface area will also affect enzyme activity.

Exam focus

The command word 'describe' means you write about what happens but you do not need to give a reason why. Here, you need to give two ways that bile helps digestion but you do not need to explain how bile does this.

 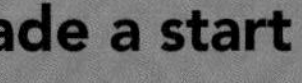 Made a start   Feeling confident  Exam ready

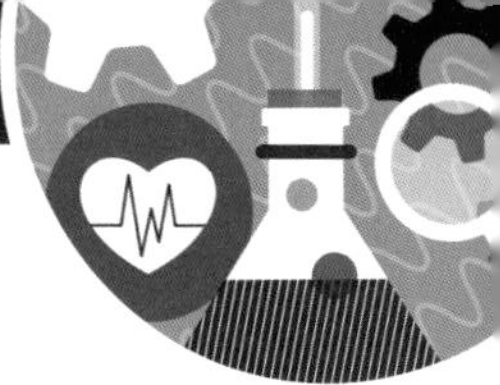

Food tests

2 Quick quiz

Which reagents are used to test for the following foods? Use the reagents in the box.

lipids .... proteins ....

sugars .... starch ....

Benedict's solution	biuret reagent
ethanol	iodine solution

10 Food tests — Grade 4

1. Draw **one** line from each type of food to the positive result of its test. **[3 marks]**

Type of food
lipids
proteins
sugars
starch

Positive result
turns from amber to black
forms a milky white emulsion
turns blue to purple
turns red-orange or green depending on the amount present

2. Describe how you would test a food for lipids. **[3 marks]**

Add .... to the sample of food. Shake the mixture.

Add .... to the mixture.

You need to add two substances in order to test for fats.

Exam focus
If you're asked to describe a method, make sure you cover each step. This is a required practical so think back to how you tested for different types of food.

10 Testing food — Grades 4–5

3. A student tests some food to see what it contains. **Table 1** shows the results.

Table 1

Reagent	Colour
iodine solution	brown
biuret reagent	purple
Benedict's solution	blue

(a) Which type of food does iodine solution test for? Tick **one** box. **[1 mark]**

protein ☐ simple sugar ☐ starch ☐

(b) Give the colour of the positive result for simple sugars. **[1 mark]**

....

(c) Name **one** type of food in this food sample. **[1 mark]**

....

Think about the colours of the positive results. If a reagent does not change colour, then the type of food it is testing for is not present.

(d) Explain whether the student can conclude that this food contains fat. Give a reason for your answer. **[2 marks]**

....

....

Exam focus
Think back to the results you got in your required practical to help you answer questions based on a practical task.

Exam focus
You will be expected to use your own knowledge to analyse practical results given to you in the exam.

 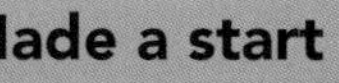 Made a start  Feeling confident  Exam ready

Investigating enzymes

2 Quick quiz

Circle the correct words in the sentences about testing the effect of amylase on starch.

The reagent used to test for starch is **Benedict's solution / ethanol / iodine solution**.

If starch is present the colour will turn **black / purple / yellow**.

If there is no starch present the colour will stay **black / purple / yellow**.

10 Investigating the effect of pH — Grade 4

1. A student investigated the effect of pH on the activity of the enzyme amylase.

(a) Which are **two** pieces of equipment they would use during this investigation? Tick **two** boxes. **[2 marks]**

1M hydrochloric acid	☐	Bunsen burner	☐
pipettes	✓	thermometer	☐
crocodile clips	☐		

Exam focus
This is a required practical. Think back to what equipment you used during the practical.

(b) These statements describe the method that could be used to investigate the effect of pH on the activity of amylase. They are not in the correct order. Write a number next to each statement to show the correct order. **[2 marks]**

Pour one test tube of amylase into one test tube of starch.	4
Take a drop from each test tube every 30 seconds and add it to the iodine solution.	
Add one drop of iodine solution to each well of the spotting tile.	
Place beakers in the water bath.	
Make up three beakers containing a test tube of starch, and three test tubes of amylase in different buffer solutions.	

10 pH and rate of reaction — Grades 4–5

2. A student measured the effect of pH on the rate of reaction of amylase. **Figure 1** shows the results.

(a) Give the pH that resulted in the fastest rate of reaction.............. **[1 mark]**

(b) Which equation did the student use to calculate rate of reaction? Tick **one** box. **[1 mark]**

$\text{rate} \propto \dfrac{1}{\text{time taken for solution to turn black (s)}}$ ☐

$\text{rate} \propto 1 \times \text{time taken for solution to turn black (s)}$ ☐

$\text{rate} \propto \dfrac{\text{time taken for solution to turn black (s)}}{1}$ ☐

Figure 1

Exam focus
Make sure that you know how to calculate the rate of reaction.

(c) Suggest **two** sources of error in this practical. **[2 marks]**

1 .... 2 ....

A source of error is an error that may occur due to inaccuracies of your equipment or your method.

Made a start | Feeling confident | Exam ready

The blood

Quick quiz

The diagram shows a photograph of blood seen under a microscope. Label the parts using the words in the box.

red blood cell	white blood cell	plasma

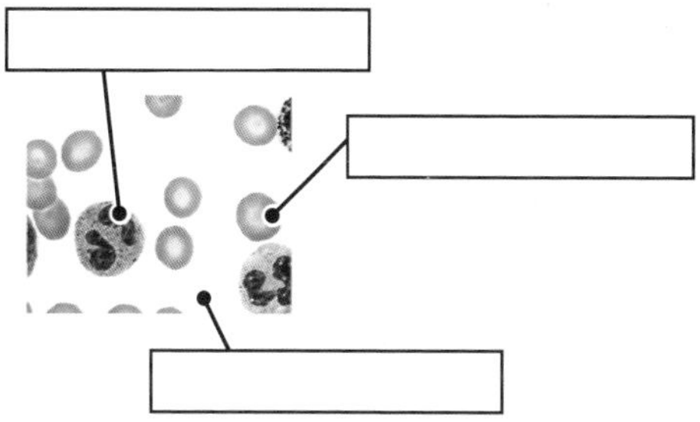

Parts of the blood

Grades 2–4

1. Name **two** substances carried by the plasma. **[2 marks]**

1 carbon dioxide ....

2 ....

What other substances are either waste products or needed by the body? The body will need to transport these in the blood.

2. Give the function of platelets. **[1 mark]**

....

Blood cells

Grades 4–5

3. One way that red blood cells are adapted for their function is that they have no nucleus.

(a) What **two** other ways are red blood cells adapted for their function? Tick **two** boxes. **[2 marks]**

- are small ☐
- contain chlorophyll ☐
- contain valves ☐
- have a biconcave shape ☐
- have lots of mitochondria ☐

Red blood cells transport oxygen. Which of these ways would help a red blood cell to do its job?

(b) Describe how a lack of nucleus helps red blood cells perform their function. **[3 marks]**

....

....

Think about the amount of space different parts of the cell take up.

4. Describe **three** ways that white blood cells help defend the body from disease. **[3 marks]**

1 ....

2 ....

3 ....

Exam focus

For this question you need to write about three different ways that white blood cells help defend against disease. Try not to just write about the same thing (for example, phagocytosis) in three different ways.

 Made a start  Feeling confident  Exam ready

The heart and lungs

2 Quick quiz

Are these statements about the heart and lungs true or false?

The main function of the heart is gas exchange.	**True / False**
There are two types of blood vessels.	**True / False**
The heart contains oxygenated and deoxygenated blood.	**True / False**

5 The lungs — Grades 2–4

1. The alveoli are the gas exchange surface (**Figure 1**).

(a) Name **two** parts that air travels through on the way to the alveoli. **[2 marks]**

1 trachea .... 2 ....

(b) Explain **two** ways that alveoli are adapted for gas exchange. **[4 marks]**

1 They have thin membranes so ....

2 There are millions of them, which provides ....

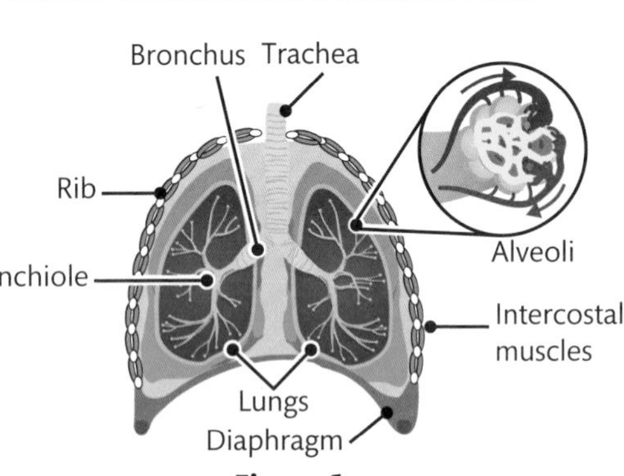

Figure 1

Exam focus

To explain a feature of something, you need to say what the feature is then why it is important for its function.

Gases are exchanged by diffusion. Think about which factors affect the rate of diffusion.

15 The heart — Grades 4–5

2. Figure 2 shows a diagram of the heart.

(a) (i) Give the **two** parts of the heart that carry oxygenated blood. **[1 mark]**

1 .... 2 ....

Think about which side of the heart has blood coming from the lungs.

(ii) Which part of the heart contains the pacemaker? Tick **one** box. **[1 mark]**

A ☐ **B** ☐ **C** ☐ **D** ☐

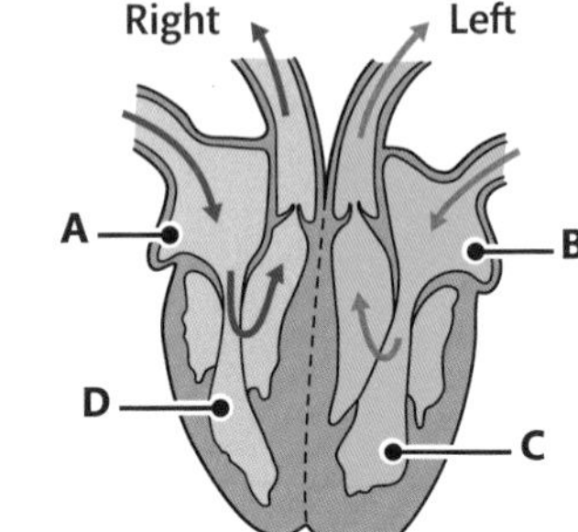

Figure 2

(iii) Name the part labelled **D**. .... **[1 mark]**

(b) Draw **one** line from each blood vessel to its function. **[3 marks]**

Blood vessel
aorta
pulmonary artery
pulmonary vein
vena cava

Function
carries deoxygenated blood away from the heart to the lungs
carries deoxygenated blood from the body to the heart
carries oxygenated blood away from the heart to the body
carries oxygenated blood from the lungs to the heart

Pulmonary is from Latin and means relating to the lungs.

(c) Explain why the left ventricle has a thicker wall than the right ventricle. **[2 marks]**

....

....

You need to say two things here – what a thicker wall does and why this is important.

 **Made a start**  **Feeling confident**  **Exam ready**

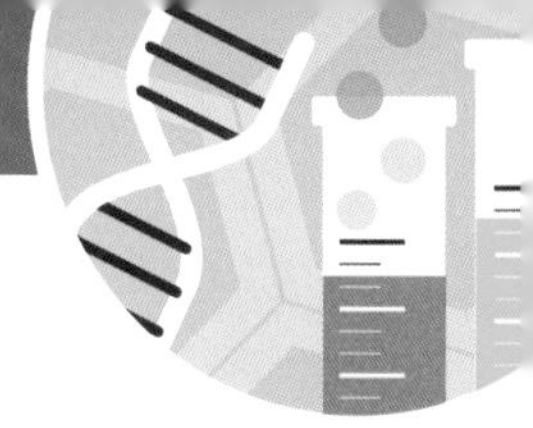

Health issues

Quick quiz

Tick the correct box to show whether each disease is communicable or non-communicable.

Disease	Lung cancer	Measles	Cardiovascular disease	HIV	Flu
Non-communicable					
Communicable					

Communicable and non-communicable diseases

Grade 2

1. Give the correct term for a state of physical and mental well-being. .... **[1 mark]**

2. Name **two** factors that can cause non-communicable disease. **[2 marks]**

1 diet ....

2 ....

Non-communicable diseases are usually caused by lifestyle factors.

3. Which of these is a pathogen? Tick **one** box. **[1 mark]**

bacteria ☐ chloroplasts ☐ flagella ☐

Measles

Grades 4–5

4. **Figure 1** shows the number of cases of measles in England and Wales between 1998 and 2008.

Exam focus
You will be expected to interpret data from graphs. Read the axis labels carefully to find out what the data are showing.

Source: *Health Protection Agency*

Figure 1

(a) Which conclusions can be drawn from the data shown?
Tick **two** boxes. **[2 marks]**

The number of cases of measles has decreased. ☐

The number of cases of measles is highest in 2008. ☐

The lowest number of cases of measles is in 2000. ☐

There were over 300 cases of measles in 2004. ☐

There is a large decrease in the number of cases of measles between 2003 and 2005. ☐

(b) In 1998, a doctor claimed that the vaccine for measles caused autism. This claim has now been shown to be false. Use this information to suggest reasons for the trend in the data shown in **Figure 1**. **[3 marks]**

....

....

....

Vaccines give immunity to some infectious diseases, for example, measles.

Autism is a disorder where people can struggle with social interactions.

 Made a start 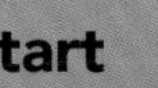 Feeling confident Exam ready

Coronary heart disease

2 Quick quiz

Circle the correct words in bold to complete the sentences about cardiovascular disease.

Cardiovascular disease involves the **bladder / lungs / heart**.

Coronary arteries supply the heart with **carbon dioxide / oxygen / urea**.

Statins / stents / valves prevent the blood from flowing backwards.

10 Heart disease

Grades 3–5

1. Complete **Table 1** to show the effects of different diseases of the heart. **[3 marks]**

Table 1

Type of heart disease	Effects
blocked coronary artery	
.... valves	harder for the heart to pump blood around the body
heart failure	the heart is unable to efficiently pump blood around the body

2. Describe how heart attacks are caused. **[4 marks]**

There is a build-up of fat in the ....

This causes them to become ....

The heart muscle does not get any ....

So the heart stops ....

10 Cardiovascular disease

Grades 2–5

3. Name **two** ways that blocked coronary arteries can be treated. **[2 marks]**

1 .... 2 ....

4. Evaluate the advantages **and** disadvantages of getting a heart transplant. **[4 marks]**

....

....

....

....

Think about the risks of surgery as well as the person's quality of life after surgery if the surgery is successful.

Exam focus

You will be expected to evaluate different treatments for cardiovascular disease and discuss the benefits and risks of each treatment.

For this question, you need to give the benefits and risks of having a heart transplant so make sure you give points from both sides. There are four marks available so make sure you make at least four separate points – ideally, two advantages and two disadvantages.

Made a start

Feeling confident

Exam ready

Effects of lifestyle

2 Quick quiz

Name **three** lifestyle factors that can lead to poor health.

1 .... 2 .... 3 ....

10 Obesity and type 2 diabetes

Grades 3–5

1. **Figure 1** shows the risk of developing type 2 diabetes of people with different BMIs.

(a) Describe what BMI is. **[2 marks]**

BMI stands for .... It is a measure of obesity.

(b) What conclusions can be drawn from the data shown in **Figure 1**? Tick **two** boxes. **[2 marks]**

- As BMI increases the risk of developing type 2 diabetes increases. ☐
- People with a BMI of <23 are most at risk of type 2 diabetes. ☐
- The data prove that high BMI causes type 2 diabetes. ☐
- The data show there is a correlation between high BMI and type 2 diabetes. ☑

Figure 1

(c) Suggest why the government promotes initiatives for people to adopt healthier lifestyles. **[3 marks]**

If people are healthier they are less likely to develop ....

So they will not need to use ....

This means it will cost the ....

A lot of money is spent by the government on the NHS for treatment of diseases. Many non-communicable diseases can be avoided with lifestyle changes.

10 Risk factors for non-communicable diseases

Grades 2–4

2. The table below shows some profiles of patients.

Patient A	Patient B	Patient C	Patient D
heavy drinker	smokes 20 cigarettes a day	smokes 5 cigarettes a day	heavy drinker
sedentary job	has a normal BMI	has a normal BMI	has an active lifestyle
has a high fat diet	has an office job	has an active lifestyle	has a normal BMI
is obese		has a high salt diet	has a healthy diet

(a) Which patient is most at risk of developing lung cancer? .... **[1 mark]**

(b) Which patient is most at risk of developing type 2 diabetes? .... **[1 mark]**

3. Explain why a pregnant woman should not drink or smoke. **[2 marks]**

....

....

Relate the risks of drinking and smoking to the health of the growing baby rather than the health of the woman.

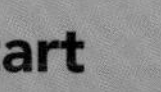

Made a start
Feeling confident

Exam ready

Cancer

Quick quiz

Are these statements about cancer true or false?

All cancers are inherited.	**True / False**
Benign tumours spread around the body through the blood supply.	**True / False**
Carcinogens are cancer-causing substances.	**True / False**
Lung cancer is a communicable disease.	**True / False**

Lifestyle risk factors

Grades 2–3 

1. Carcinogens are substances that are risk factors for some cancers.
Name **two** substances that are carcinogens. **[2 marks]**

1 radon .... 2 ....

Tumours

2. Table 1 shows some features of malignant and benign tumours.
Complete the table by ticking the boxes to show the correct features of each type of tumour. **[4 marks]**

Table 1

Feature	Type of tumour	
	Benign	**Malignant**
are growths of abnormal cells	✓	✓
are cancerous		
grow slowly		
produce secondary tumours		

Exam focus
You need to be able to describe the differences between benign and malignant tumours.

Malignant tumours are much more harmful than benign tumours.

Genetic risk factors

Grades 4–5 

3. Women with a mutation on the BRCA gene are more likely to develop breast cancer. **Figure 1** shows the difference in risk.

(a) Calculate the difference in risk of someone with the BRCA gene mutation and someone without the gene developing breast cancer. **[1 mark]**

....

	Risk of developing breast cancer in %
general population	(bar approx. 8)
people with BRCA gene mutation	(bar approx. 88)

Figure 1

Exam focus
You are expected to be able to translate information between graphical and numerical forms.

Exam focus
When asked to do a calculation from a graph make sure you read from the graph carefully.

(b) Suggest **two** reasons why people may want to get tested for the BRCA gene if they have a family history of breast cancer. **[3 marks]**

....

....

You inherit genes from your parents. Early detection of breast cancer means it can be treated more successfully.

Exam focus
The command word 'suggest' means that you might not know the correct answer but you will be expected to apply your knowledge from other parts of the syllabus and the information given in the question.

 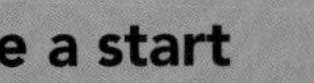  

Made a start | Feeling confident | Exam ready

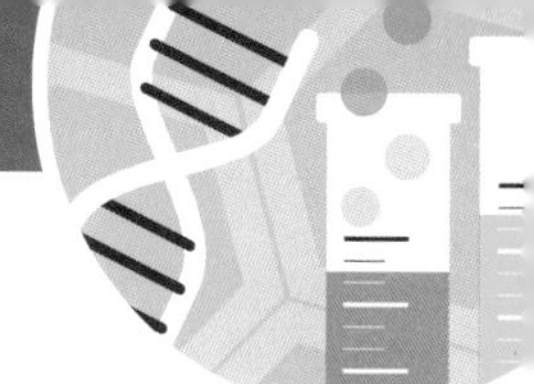

Communicable diseases

2 Quick quiz

Are these statements about infections true or false?

Communicable diseases are sometimes called infectious diseases.	**True / False**
Pathogens are plants that cause infectious diseases.	**True / False**
Communicable disease can be spread by touch.	**True / False**
Antibiotics kill viruses.	**True / False**

5 Pathogens — Grade 4

1. (a) Bacteria and viruses are two types of pathogen. Describe how viruses cause disease. **[2 marks]**

Viruses enter cells and ....

The cells are damaged when they ....

15 Spread of communicable disease — Grades 4–5

2. Communicable diseases can be spread by direct contact or indirect contact. Complete **Table 1** by ticking the boxes to show if each type of contact is direct or indirect. **[3 marks]**

Infectious diseases are spread from organism to organism. If they are spread by going through air, water or food then they are not spread directly from organism to organism.

Table 1

	Direct contact	Indirect contact
drinking contaminated water		
touching a diseased animal		
breathing in pathogens in air droplets		

3. Influenza is a common infectious viral disease that can be spread through the air and by touch. What are **two** ways that the spread of influenza can be stopped? Tick **two** boxes. **[2 marks]**

- cooking food thoroughly ☐
- using surgical masks ☐
- washing hands ☐
- sterilising water ☐
- using antibiotics ☐

Think about what type of pathogens antibiotics kill.

4. Figure 1 shows some doctors performing surgery.

Describe **three** precautions they have taken to prevent the spread of disease to the patient. **[3 marks]**

....

....

....

Figure 1

Think about ways that communicable diseases can be spread. What equipment is being used that will prevent airborne pathogens and pathogens that are passed by touch?

Exam focus

If the question refers to a diagram or a photograph, use the information in the image to help you answer the question.

 Made a start  Feeling confident  Exam ready

Viral diseases

2 Quick quiz

Circle the correct words in bold.

Measles is a viral disease that affects **humans / plants / bacteria**.

HIV can lead to **AIDS / measles / immunity**.

People with HIV can take **antibiotics / antiviral drugs**.

5 Measles — Grades 2–3

1. (a) **Table 1** shows some ways that measles is spread and some symptoms of measles. Complete the table by ticking the boxes. **[3 marks]**

Table 1

	Way measles is spread	Symptom
fever		✓
droplets in coughs and sneezes		
red skin rash		

Symptoms are the visible signs of a disease.

(b) Give a reason why most children are immune to measles. **[1 mark]**

At a young age, children are given ....

.... which provides immunity to measles.

Think about the ways the spread of infectious diseases can be prevented. How can we prevent lots of people getting a disease at once?

5 HIV — Grades 2–5

2. (a) Name the body system that HIV infects. .... **[1 mark]**

(b) How is HIV spread? Tick **two** boxes. **[2 marks]**

droplets in the air ☐
physical contact ☐
through uncooked food ☐
sexual contact ☐
sharing contaminated needles ☐

(c) Explain how HIV can lead to a person's death. **[2 marks]**

....

....

Think about the other diseases that HIV can lead to and which body system HIV affects.

5 TMV — Grades 3–5

3. (a) Give the full name of TMV. .... **[1 mark]**

(b) TMV causes discolouration of leaves. Suggest how this affects the organism's ability to produce food. **[2 marks]**

....

....

Think about what the main function of leaves is.

☐ Made a start  Feeling confident  Exam ready

Bacterial and fungal diseases

2 Quick quiz

Circle the diseases caused by bacteria.

gonorrhoea	salmonella	measles	rose black spot	tobacco mosaic

5 Bacterial diseases — Grade 5

1. Suggest why a government giving away free condoms can reduce the spread of gonorrhoea. **[3 marks]**

Gonorrhoea is a sexually ....

Condoms are a .... *of contraception.*

If condoms are free more people ....

Exam focus

The command word 'suggest' means that you will have to apply your knowledge. Think about what you know about how the spread of gonorrhoea can be controlled. How will providing condoms help?

5 Salmonella — Grades 2–4

2. Figure 1 shows the number of cases of food poisoning caused by Salmonella bacteria in England and Wales between 1992 and 2005.

(a) Which year had the most cases of salmonella? **[1 mark]**

....

(b) Describe the trend in the number of cases of salmonella between 2001 and 2005. **[1 mark]**

....

Figure 1

(c) Which **two** reasons may explain the trend seen between 2001 and 2005? Tick **two** boxes. **[2 marks]**

- new antibiotics were found ☐
- condoms were given away free ☐
- fewer people were eating undercooked meat ☐
- chickens were vaccinated ☐
- blood donations were screened ☐

Salmonella causes food poisoning and is spread by poor hygiene and contaminated food that is not thoroughly cooked.

3. The black spot fungus is a fungus that affects rose bushes.

(a) Explain how you can tell if a rose has been infected with black spot fungus. **[1 mark]**

....

This disease affects the leaves of the rose plant.

(b) Black spot fungus is spread by wind and water.

Suggest **two** ways that the spread of black spot fungus could be controlled. **[2 marks]**

1 ....

2 ....

This disease is caused by a fungus. How can the spread of fungal diseases be controlled?

Protist diseases

2 Quick quiz

What is the best definition for the term 'vector'? Tick **one** box.

A carrier of a disease ☐ A unicellular organism ☐

A pathogen ☐ A bacterium ☐

5 Malaria — Grades 2–3

1. Which is a symptom of malaria? Tick **one** box. **[1 mark]**

pain when urinating ☐ fever ☐ diarrhoea ☐ coughing ☐

A fever is a high temperature of 38°C or more.

2. Name the **two** main parts of the body affected by the malaria protist. **[2 marks]**

1 liver .... 2 ....

5 The spread of malaria — Grades 4–5

3. Figure 1 shows how malaria is transmitted.

(a) What is the organism that causes malaria? Tick **one** box. **[1 mark]**

human ☐ mosquito ☐ protist ☐

(b) Explain why using mosquito nets can stop the spread of malaria. **[2 marks]**

....

....

Think about the way that malaria is spread. How will mosquito nets stop this?

Exam focus
Use all the information provided to you in a question. Read extra material carefully, such as figures and graphs, as it will give you information needed to answer the question.

5 Data analysis — Grades 4–5

4. Figure 2 shows the number of deaths in Ethiopia from malaria.

(a) Give the year that has the most deaths. **[1 mark]**

....

(b) Calculate the difference in the number of deaths between 2005 and 2007. **[1 mark]**

....

(c) Suggest how an increased use of insecticide has caused a decrease in the number of deaths from malaria. **[2 marks]**

....

....

Number of deaths in Ethiopia from malaria

People: 0, 5,000,000, 10,000,000, 15,000,000, 20,000,000, 25,000,000

Year: 2003, 2004, 2005, 2006, 2007

Figure 2

Insecticides kill insects.

Think about how malaria is spread. Does one of the stages involve an insect?

Human defence systems

2 Quick quiz

Circle the physical defences of the body.

antigens	skin	antibiotics	mucus

5 Physical defences — Grades 3–4

1. Name **two** features that the nose has, which prevent pathogens entering the body. **[2 marks]**

1 mucus .... 2 ....

2. Describe how cilia in the trachea and bronchi, and mucus protect the body from pathogens. **[2 marks]**

Cilia moves ....

Mucus ....

5 Digestive defences — Grades 1–3

3. Figure 1 shows the digestive system.

(a) Name organ **X**. **[1 mark]**

....

(b) What is the substance that organ **X** produces that kills pathogens? Tick **one** box. **[1 mark]**

saliva	☐	hydrochloric acid	☐
scabs	☐	urine	☐

(c) Describe how the pathogens would get to organ **X**. **[1 mark]**

....

Figure 1

Think about what the digestive system does. How do things enter the digestive system?

10 The immune system — Grades 3–5

4. In **Table 1** draw **one** line from each way that white blood cells defend against disease to its description. **[2 marks]**

Way of defending against disease
phagocytes
antibodies
antitoxins

Description
proteins that target antigens and coat pathogens so they can be destroyed by white blood cells
proteins that neutralise poisons produced by pathogens
white blood cells that engulf pathogens

5. What is the correct definition of an antigen? Tick **one** box. **[1 mark]**

a protein on a pathogen that causes an immune response ☐

a drug that kills bacteria ☐

a unicellular organism that causes disease ☐

Exam focus

The words antigen, antibiotic, antitoxin and antibody all sound very similar. Make sure you know the difference between them so you do not get confused.

Vaccination

2 Quick quiz

Complete the following sentences using the words in the box.

specific	illness	communicable

Vaccinations have been used to prevent the spread of .... diseases such as polio and eradicate diseases such as smallpox.

A vaccination is .... to the pathogen that causes a particular disease.

Vaccinations are used to prevent .... in an individual.

5 How vaccination works

Grades 3–4

1. The statements in **Table 1** show how vaccination works. They are not in the correct order.

Write numbers 1–5 next to the statements to show the correct order. **[2 marks]**

Table 1

White blood cells produce antibodies and memory cells.	
Memory cells rapidly produce antibodies.	
The live pathogen is destroyed before you get ill.	
A dead / inactive pathogen is injected into the body.	1
A live pathogen infects the body.	

Think about how your body defends against disease. What do white blood cells do when they encounter a pathogen?

10 Data analysis

Grades 3–5

2. Figure 1 shows the number of cases of measles in the USA between 1950 and 1991.

(a) Give the year that the vaccine for measles was introduced. **[1 mark]**

....

Exam focus

Read data from the graph carefully. Your answers need to be accurate.

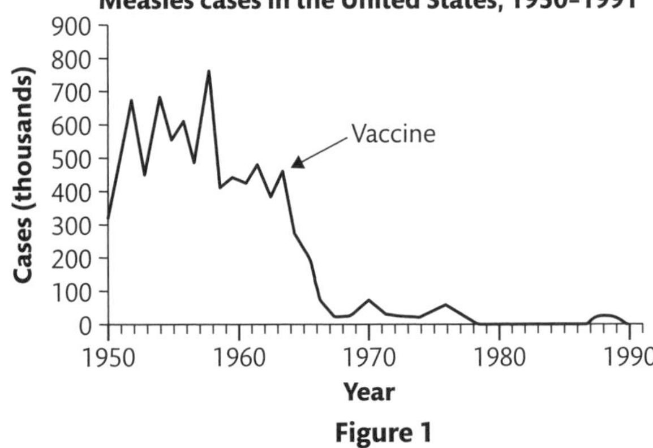

Figure 1

(b) Describe the trend in the number of cases of measles after the vaccine was introduced. **[1 mark]**

....

(c) There has been an increase in the number of cases of measles in the UK and the US recently. Suggest why. **[1 mark]**

....

(d) Explain why it is important for as many people in a population as possible to have the measles vaccination. **[2 marks]**

....

....

Think about the way that measles is spread.

 Made a start  Feeling confident  Exam ready

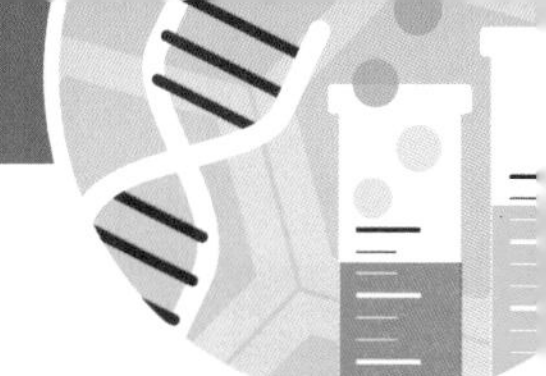

Antibiotics and painkillers

2 Quick quiz

Match each type of drug to what it does.

antibiotic	medicine that relieves pain
antiviral	drug that kills bacteria
painkiller	treats diseases caused by viruses

5 Drug sources — Grades 3–4

1. Traditionally, drugs were extracted from plants and microorganisms.

Complete each sentence. Use words from the box. **[2 marks]**

foxglove | heart conditions | mould

The drug digitalis was originally extracted from foxglove.

The drug digitalis is used to treat ....

The antibiotic penicillin was discovered by Alexander Fleming after studying a bacterial plate infected by a ....

2. Complete **Table 1** by ticking the boxes to show the correct features of antibiotics, antiviral drugs and painkillers. **[4 marks]**

Table 1

Feature	Antibiotics	Antiviral drugs	Painkillers
kills bacteria			
treats symptoms of disease			
affects pathogens			
is a type of medicine			

Some of the features might apply to more than one type of drug so you might need to tick more than one box for each feature.

5 Antibiotics and resistance — Grades 3–5

3. Figure 1 shows the number of deaths from infectious diseases per 100 000 people between 1900 and 1996 in the US.

(a) Use **Figure 1** to give **two** ways infectious diseases have been controlled. **[2 marks]**

1 ....

2 ....

Figure 1

(b) There has been an increase in the number of antibiotic-resistant bacteria. Why is this a concern? Tick **one** box. **[1 mark]**

Bacterial infections are harder to treat. ☐

HIV is spread more easily. ☐

The risk of coronary heart disease increases. ☐

More people develop cancers. ☐

Development of drugs

2 Quick quiz

New drugs are tested for toxicity, efficacy and dose. Draw lines to link each term with its definition.

Term
Toxicity
Efficacy
Dose

Definition
how well the drug works
how much drug to use safely at a time
how poisonous a drug is

5 Research and development — Grade 5

1. (a) How long does the research and development stage of developing a new drug take? Tick **one** box. **[1 mark]**

1–2 months ☐ 3–6 months ☐ 1–2 years ☐ 3–6 years ☐

(b) Describe what scientists do during the research and development stage. **[3 marks]**

Scientists find out what .... are needed.

....

....

During the research and development stage, scientists need to find out what drug to make and what substances they will need to make it.

10 Timescale of drug development — Grades 4–5

2. (a) The stages of drug development are shown below in the wrong order. Write numbers 1–4 in the boxes to show the correct order. **[3 marks]**

clinical trials	
review and approval	
research and development	
pre-clinical studies	

(b) Draw **one** line from each stage to what happens during that stage. **[3 marks]**

Stage
clinical trials
pre-clinical studies
research and development
review and approval

What happens
drugs are made or discovered
drugs are used on volunteers
drugs are used on patients
drug is tested on animals

(c) When a drug is first tested in the lab it is tested *in vitro*. Give the meaning of *in vitro*. **[1 mark]**

....

(d) Give a reason why only a small dose of the drug is given to healthy volunteers at first. **[1 mark]**

....

(e) Give a reason why drugs are still monitored even after they have been approved. **[1 mark]**

....

Not all effects develop straight away.

(f) Suggest **one** advantage and **one** disadvantage of testing in mammals before testing on humans. **[2 marks]**

advantage ....

disadvantage ....

Think about what type of organisms are going to have bodies most similar to ours.

Made a start

Feeling confident

Exam ready

Photosynthesis

2 Quick quiz

Complete the word equation for photosynthesis using words from the box.

oxygen	carbon dioxide	water

.... + ... → glucose + ...

10 Photosynthesis — Grades 3–5

1. Draw **one** line from each thing needed for photosynthesis to where it is found. **[3 marks]**

light energy	in chloroplasts
carbon dioxide	from the soil
water	from the Sun
chlorophyll	from the air

2. Complete **Table 1** to show the names of some substances and their chemical formulae. **[3 marks]**

Table 1

Name of substance	Chemical formula
carbon dioxide	CO_2
	$C_6H_{12}O_6$
water	
oxygen	

C is the symbol for carbon, O is the symbol for oxygen and H is the symbol for hydrogen.

10 Energy transfers in plants — Grades 4–5

3. Photosynthesis is an example of which type of reaction? Tick **one** box. **[1 mark]**

combustion ☐ endothermic ☐ exothermic ☐ physical ☐

4. Complete the sentence about energy transfer in plants in photosynthesis. Use words from the box. **[2 marks]**

chemical	heat	light	sound

.... energy is transferred to .... energy.

5. Explain why plants kept in the dark will eventually die. **[3 marks]**

....

....

....

Think about what things are needed for photosynthesis to happen and what products are made. Why are these products important to a plant?

 Made a start  Feeling confident Exam ready

Rate of photosynthesis

2 Quick quiz

Circle the **four** factors that can affect the rate of photosynthesis.

amount of chlorophyll   intensity of light   temperature

biomass   oxygen concentration   carbon dioxide concentration

5 Light intensity — Grades 3–4

1. Figure 1 shows how light intensity affects the rate of photosynthesis.

(a) Describe the results shown in **Figure 1**. **[2 marks]**

Initially, as light intensity increases the rate of photosynthesis ....

As light intensity increases further, the rate of photosynthesis ....

Think about what other factors affect the rate of photosynthesis.

Rate of photosynthesis / Light intensity

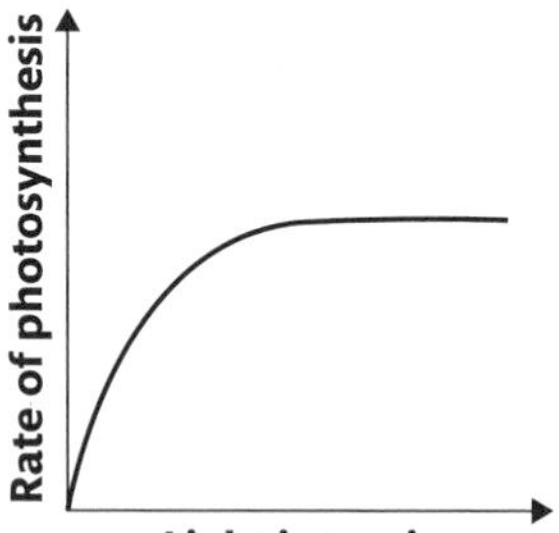

Figure 1

(b) The investigation was repeated with a decreased carbon dioxide concentration. Predict the effect this would have on the results. **[1 mark]**

The rate of photosynthesis would ....

10 Chlorophyll and photosynthesis — Grades 3–5

2. Figure 2 shows a variegated leaf. It has white patches. These parts do not contain any chlorophyll.

(a) Which area of the leaf will photosynthesise the most? Give a reason for your answer. **[1 mark]**

....

(b) A student tested the white part of the leaf for starch with iodine solution. The white part of the leaf did not contain any starch.

Figure 2

(i) What colour would the iodine solution be? Tick **one** box. **[1 mark]**

black ☐   blue ☐   purple ☐   amber ☐

(ii) Explain why the white part of the leaf did not contain starch. **[4 marks]**

....

....

....

5 Temperature — Grades 4–5

3. Figure 3 shows the relationship between temperature and rate of photosynthesis.

Describe what happens to the rate of photosynthesis as the temperature increases. **[2 marks]**

....

....

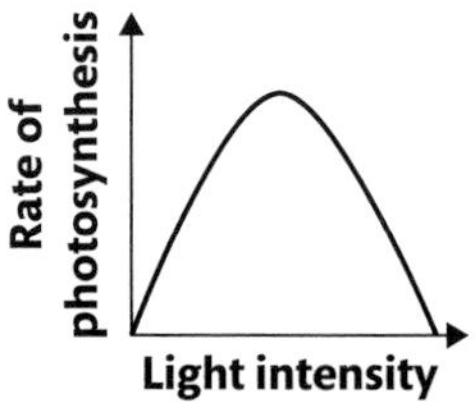

Rate of photosynthesis / Light intensity

Figure 3

Made a start   Feeling confident   Exam ready

Uses of photosynthesis

2 Quick quiz

Underline the correct process that each word equation shows.

carbon dioxide + water → glucose + oxygen **photosynthesis / respiration**

glucose + oxygen → carbon dioxide + water **photosynthesis / respiration**

10 Uses of glucose — Grades 3–4

1. The glucose made in photosynthesis is used for other processes and can be stored for later use.

(a) How can glucose be stored in a plant? Tick **two** boxes. **[2 marks]**

carbon dioxide ☐ chlorophyll ☐ light ☐

oil ✓ starch ☐

Glucose can also be stored as a carbohydrate. Which choice is a carbohydrate?

(b) Draw **one** line to link each substance with its function in the plant. **[2 marks]**

Substance	Function
cellulose	used to make proteins for growth and repair
glucose	strengthens cell walls
amino acids	used for respiration

Think about what proteins and glucose are used for in humans. They do the same thing in plants.

(c) Proteins are made up of amino acids. Complete the sentences to describe how plants make amino acids. Use words from the box. **[4 marks]**

air	glucose	root hair	leaf	nitrate	soil

Amino acids are made from .... and ....nitrate.... ions.

Nitrate ions are absorbed from the .... by the .... cells.

10 Respiration and photosynthesis — Grades 4–5

2. Figure 1 shows how the rates of photosynthesis and respiration in a plant change over 24 hours.

(a) Give the time the rate of photosynthesis is fastest. **[1 mark]**

....

(b) Explain why there is no photosynthesis at midnight. **[2 marks]**

....

Rate of process

photosynthesis

respiration

2am 4am 6am 8am 10am 12 midday 2pm 4pm 6pm 8pm 10pm 12 midnight

Time

Figure 1

(c) Which gas is being released by the plant at midnight? Give a reason for your answer. **[2 marks]**

....

....

Think about the products of respiration and photosynthesis. Which process is occurring at midnight?

Investigating photosynthesis

2 Quick quiz

Name **two** factors that can affect the rate of photosynthesis.

1 .... **2** ....

Light intensity and photosynthesis

Grades 3–4

1. Table 1 shows the method a student used to investigate how light intensity affects the rate of photosynthesis. Write numbers next to the statements to put them in the correct sequence. **[2 marks]**

Table 1

Record the number of bubbles released in one minute.	
Place the lamp at a set distance from the plant.	
Repeat the practical with the lamp at different distances.	
Set up the apparatus.	1

This is a required practical. Think back to the method you used in this investigation.

Variables

Grade 4

2. Complete **Table 2** to show the independent, dependent and control variables. Use words from the box. **[2 marks]**

number of bubbles produced   temperature   volume of water   distance of lamp from plant

Table 2

Independent variable	Dependent variable	Control variables

The independent variable is the variable that you change.

The dependent variable is the variable that you measure.

A control variable is a variable that you want to keep the same.

10 Recording results

Grade 5

3. A student investigated the effect of light intensity on the number of bubbles produced by pondweed. **Table 3** shows the results.

Table 3

Distance from lamp in cm	10	15	20	25	30
Number of bubbles produced per minute	60	40	25	15	8

Draw a graph of the results to show number of bubbles against distance from lamp. **[4 marks]**

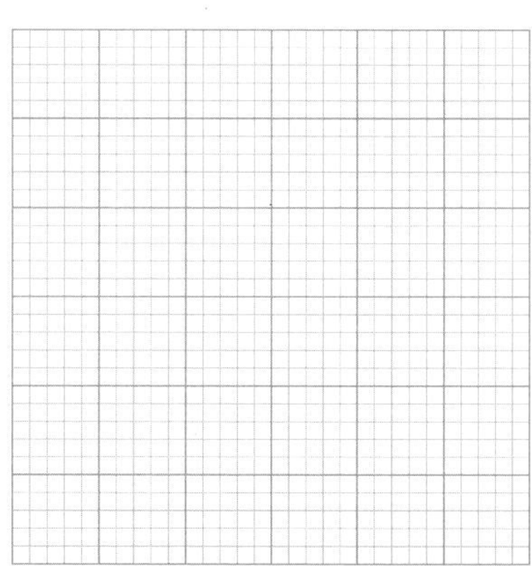

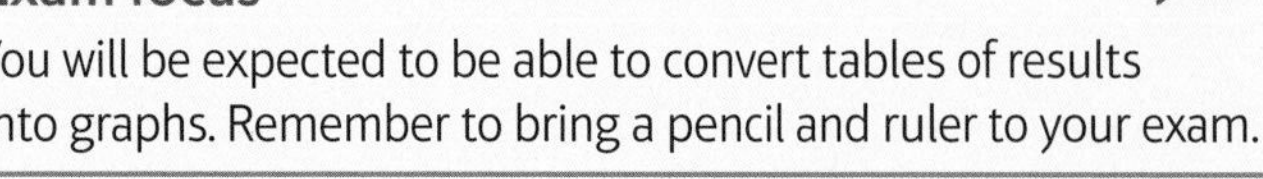

Exam focus

You will be expected to be able to convert tables of results into graphs. Remember to bring a pencil and ruler to your exam.

 Made a start 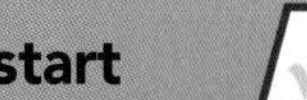  Feeling confident  Exam ready

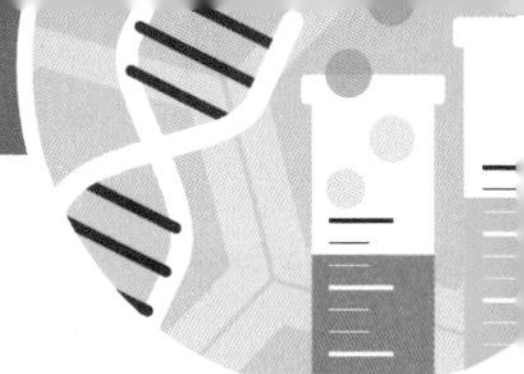

Aerobic and anaerobic respiration

2 Quick quiz

Are these statements true or false?

Respiration is an endothermic reaction. **True / False**

Anaerobic respiration needs oxygen. **True / False**

Respiration releases energy. **True / False**

Anaerobic respiration in plants and yeast is called fermentation. **True / False**

5 Aerobic and anaerobic respiration — Grade 3

1. (a) Give the word equation for aerobic respiration. **[2 marks]**

glucose + ... → .... + water

Aerobic means with oxygen.

Exam focus
For the exam, you will be expected to recall the word equations for aerobic and anaerobic respiration.

(b) Give the word equation for anaerobic respiration in muscle cells. **[2 marks]**

....

(c) Respiration releases energy. Give **two** ways energy is used in the body. **[2 marks]**

1 muscle contractions ....

2 ....

(d) Complete the sentence about respiration. **[1 mark]**

Anaerobic respiration transfers .... energy than aerobic respiration.

5 Anaerobic respiration — Grade 3

2. (a) Give another name for anaerobic respiration in plant and yeast cells. .... **[1 mark]**

(b) What are the **two** products of the anaerobic respiration in plant and yeast cells? Tick **two** boxes. **[2 marks]**

glucose	☐	carbon dioxide	☐	lactic acid	☐
oxygen	☐	ethanol	☐	water	☐

(c) Give **two** products that are made using the products of anaerobic respiration of plant and yeast cells. **[2 marks]**

1 ....

2 ....

These products are types of food or drink.

Response to exercise

2 Quick quiz

Are these statements true or false?

When you exercise you need more energy.	**True / False**
Aerobic respiration produces oxygen.	**True / False**
Heart rate decreases during exercise.	**True / False**
Breathing rate goes back to normal as soon as you stop exercising.	**True / False**

2 Breathing and exercise — Grade 3

1. Describe **two** ways your breathing changes during exercise. **[2 marks]**

The rate of breathing .... The depth of breathing

so the volume of each breath increases

10 Response to exercise — Grade 4

2. Figure 1 shows a spirometer which is used to measure the volume of breath during exercise.

Describe how you would use a spirometer to measure the effect of exercise. **[3 marks]**

....

....

....

Figure 1

Think about what a spirometer measures. When would you take these measurements?

5 Oxygen debt — Grade 4

3. Complete the sentences to describe what happens in the body during long periods of vigorous exercise. Use words from the box. **[4 marks]**

active transport	aerobic respiration	anaerobic respiration	carbon dioxide	oxygen	lactic acid

During vigorous exercise, energy cannot be supplied fast enough to the muscle cells by ....

....

The body starts to use ....

Anaerobic respiration produces .... The muscles will become fatigued and stop contracting efficiently.

After exercise, the person will still breathe deeply to repay the .... debt.

Body cells normally use aerobic respiration and will only use anaerobic respiration if there is not enough oxygen available.

Exam focus

Read through the sentences carefully before you decide which words go where. Start with the ones that you are sure about, then see which words are left.

Made a start   Feeling confident   Exam ready

Metabolism

2 Quick quiz

Underline the correct words in bold to complete the definition of the term 'metabolism'.

Metabolism is the sum of all of the **reactions / gases / cells** happening in a **cell / egg / nucleus** or organism in which **molecules / elements / atoms** are made or broken down.

5 Respiration — Grade 3

1. Complete **Table 1** to show the different ways glucose is broken down during respiration. Use words from the box. **[2 marks]**

Table 1

glucose → lactic acid	
glucose + oxygen → carbon dioxide + water	
glucose → ethanol + carbon dioxide	fermentation

aerobic respiration   anaerobic respiration   fermentation

Aerobic means with oxygen.

10 Making new molecules — Grade 4

2. In metabolism, glucose is converted into other substances. Draw **one** line to link each substance with its use. **[2 marks]**

Substance
cellulose
glycogen
starch

Use
storage in muscle cells
storage in plants
strengthen cell walls

3. (a) Lipids are formed during metabolism. They are fats and oils. Name **two** uses of lipids in animals. **[2 marks]**

1 .... 2 ....

(b) Lipids are made from fatty acids and glycerol molecules. Give the number of fatty acids and glycerol molecules in one lipid molecule. Use numbers from the box. **[2 marks]**

1   2   3   5   10

fatty acids .... glycerol ....

10 Amino acids and proteins — Grade 5

4. (a) Which ions does glucose combine with to form amino acids, which then form proteins? Tick **one** box. **[1 mark]**

calcium ☐   nitrate ☐

magnesium ☐   potassium ☐

(b) Name **two** proteins in animals. **[2 marks]**

1 .... 2 ....

(c) Describe how excess proteins are removed from the body. **[3 marks]**

....

....

What happens to the proteins and how do they leave the body? Which organ is involved?

The human nervous system

Quick quiz

Circle the **two** parts of the central nervous system (CNS).

brain	heart	skin	spinal cord	stomach

Coordinating a response — Grades 2–4

1. The central nervous system senses stimuli and coordinates a response. Light and touch are examples of stimuli.

(a) Define the term 'stimulus'. **[1 mark]**

A stimulus is a .... in the body or a change in the ....

(b) The parts involved in a response by the nervous system are shown below. They are not in the correct order. Write numbers 1–5 to show the correct sequence. **[2 marks]**

coordinator [ ] effector [ ] receptor [ ] response [5] stimulus [1]

Neurones — Grades 3–4

2. (a) **Figure 1** shows a type of neurone. What is this type of neurone? Tick **one** box. **[1 mark]**

motor neurone [ ]

sensory neurone [ ]

relay neurone [ ]

Figure 1

(b) Draw one line to link each type of neurone with its function. **[2 marks]**

Type of neurone
motor neurone
sensory neurone
synapse relay neurone

Function
carry impulses from receptors to the CNS
carry impulses from a sensory neurone to a motor neurone within the spinal cord
carry impulses from the CNS to effectors

(c) (i) Describe what a synapse is. .... **[1 mark]**

(ii) Explain how information passes across a synapse. **[2 marks]**

....

....

Think about what form the information takes and which process is used for the movement.

Reflex arc — Grade 5

3. (a) Name the part of the CNS that is **not** involved in a reflex arc. .... **[1 mark]**

(b) Explain why it is important that a reflex arc does not use this part of the CNS. **[2 marks]**

....

....

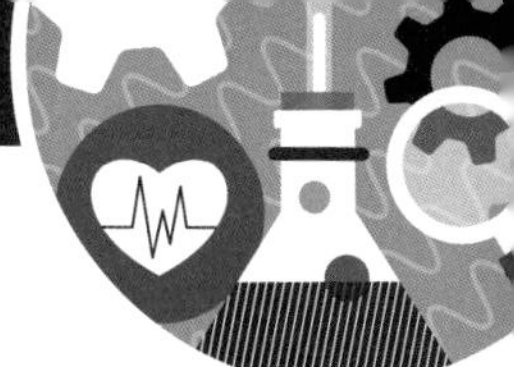

Reaction times

Quick quiz

Complete the definition of the term 'reaction time'.

Reaction time is the .... of time taken for a person to respond to a given ....

Reaction time investigation

Grades 3–5

1. Two students measured each other's reaction times using the ruler drop test shown in **Figure 1**.

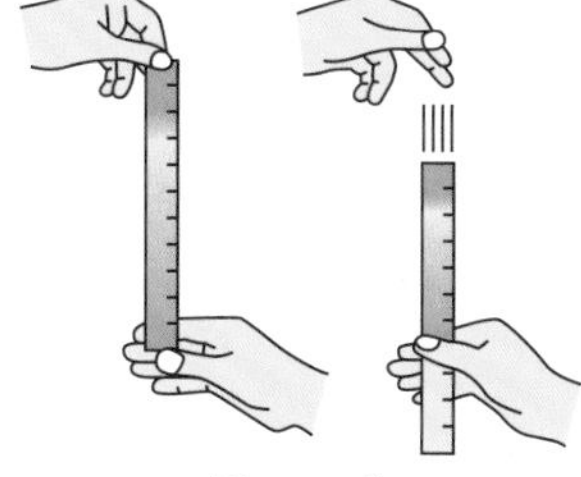

Figure 1

(a) Draw **one** line to link each variable in the investigation with its correct description. **[2 marks]**

independent variable
dependent variable
control variable

distance ruler dropped
the ruler used
the person catching the ruler

(b) Name **one** other variable that should be controlled in this investigation. **[1 mark]**

....

The results of the investigation for student 1 are shown in **Table 1**.

(c) Calculate the mean score. **[1 mark]**

$$\text{mean score} = \frac{\text{sum of scores}}{\text{number of times dropped}}$$

= ....

Exam focus

Always show your working in a calculation. You can gain marks for the correct use of an equation even if you get the calculation wrong.

Table 1

Student 1	Distance ruler dropped in cm
1	11.1
2	12.1
3	10.1
Mean score	

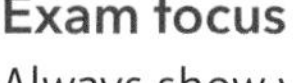

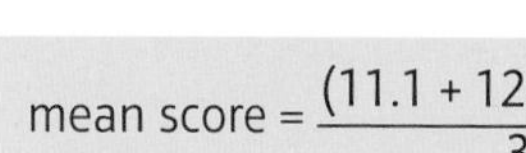

$$\text{mean score} = \frac{(11.1 + 12.1 + 10.1)}{3}$$

Factors that affect reaction times

Grade 5

2. A student wants to investigate how being distracted by a loud sound affects reaction time using the ruler drop test. Plan this investigation. **[4 marks]**

....

....

....

....

Think about the method you used during the required practical. This time you need to test the reaction times of the person while they are being distracted by a loud sound.

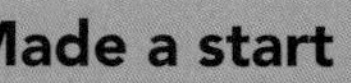

Made a start

Feeling confident

Exam ready

Homeostasis

2 Quick quiz

Which **three** things are controlled in the body as part of homeostasis?

....

5 Homeostasis — Grades 3–4

1. Draw **one** line to match each part of a homeostatic control system with its function. **[2 marks]**

Part
coordination centre
effector
receptor

Function
brings about a response
detects stimuli (changes in the environment or body)
receives and processes information from receptors

5 Controlling blood glucose — Grade 3

2. Complete the sentences about the control of blood glucose concentration. Use words from the box. **[4 marks]**

decreases	enzyme	glucose	hormone	increases	protein	stays the same

We get ....glucose.... from digesting carbohydrates in the food we eat. When we eat a meal, the blood glucose concentration .... When we fast, the blood glucose concentration ....

The concentration is controlled by the ....hormone.... insulin.

10 Controlling water levels and temperature — Grades 2–5

3. (a) Give **two** ways your body gains water. **[2 mark]**

1 .... 2 ....

(b) Which organ regulates the levels of water in our bodies? Tick **one** box. **[1 mark]**

heart ☐ kidney ☐ liver ☐

(c) Complete **Table 1** to show whether the volume of urine would **increase** or **decrease** in each situation. **[3 marks]**

Table 1

Situation	How volume of urine changes
drinking lots of water	
a very hot day with no extra drink	
lots of exercise with no extra drink	

(d) One of the ways our body loses water is as sweat. We sweat to cool down if it gets too hot. Explain why it is important the body does not get too hot. **[2 marks]**

....

....

Enzymes control many reactions in the body. What happens to enzymes when the temperature increases?

 Made a start  Feeling confident Exam ready

Human endocrine system

Quick quiz

Circle the correct words in bold.

Hormones are secreted by **glands / muscles / skin**.

Hormones are carried in the **air / blood / mucus**.

The effects of the hormone system are **slower than / faster than / the same as** the nervous system.

The effects of the hormone system last **longer than / shorter than / the same time as** the nervous system.

Endocrine glands

Grades 2–4

1. **Figure 1** shows some of the endocrine glands.

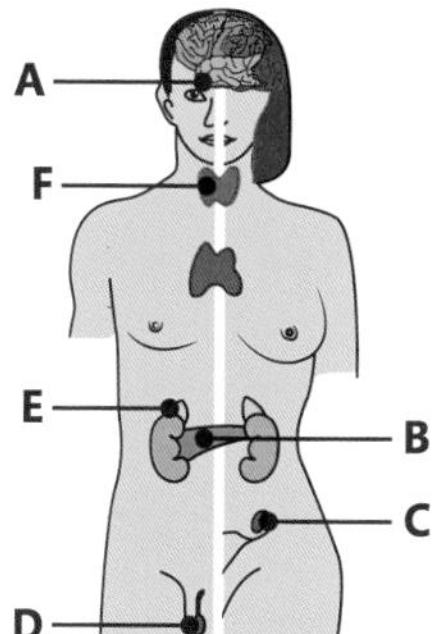

Figure 1

(a) Name the part labelled **F**. .... **[1 mark]**

(b) Give the letter that represents the testis. .... **[1 mark]**

(c) Give the letter that represents the part that releases hormones that control the menstrual cycle. .... **[1 mark]**

Only females have a menstrual cycle. Think about the parts on **Figure 1** that belong only to females.

Exam focus

Read instructions carefully. Some parts of this question ask you to write a name and some parts ask you to give a letter from the diagram. Make sure you are following the correct instructions.

Hormones and their glands

Grades 3–5

2. (a) Draw **one** line to link each gland with the hormone it produces. **[2 marks]**

Gland
adrenal
pancreas
thyroid

Hormone
thyroxine
adrenaline
insulin

(b) Give **two** functions of the hormone thyroxine. **[2 marks]**

1 .... 2 ....

(c) Describe why the pituitary gland is sometimes called the 'master gland'. **[3 marks]**

The pituitary gland secretes .... that stimulate ....

to secrete their own ....

Exam focus

For a full description you need to include what the pituitary gland secretes, what these secretions do, how they do it and when they do it.

 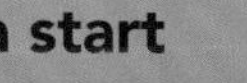 Made a start  Feeling confident 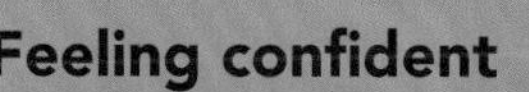  Exam ready

Control of blood glucose

2 Quick quiz

Which process does the body need glucose for?

breathing ☐ photosynthesis ☐ excretion ☐ respiration ☐

5 Control of blood glucose concentration — Grade 4

1. The sentences in **Table 1** describe the control of your blood glucose concentration after you eat a meal. They are not in the correct order. Write numbers 1–5 to show the correct sequence. **[2 marks]**

Table 1

Insulin causes the cells to take glucose from the blood.	
The pancreas releases insulin.	2
It also causes the liver and muscles to store glucose in the form of glycogen.	4
Blood glucose concentration increases.	
This causes the blood glucose concentration to decrease.	

5 Diabetes — Grade 4

2. Complete **Table 2** by ticking the boxes to show the correct features of type 1 and type 2 diabetes. **[2 marks]**

Table 2

Feature	Type 1 diabetes	Type 2 diabetes
controlled by insulin injections		
controlled by diet		
pancreas does not produce insulin		
body cells do not respond to insulin		

Exam focus
You will be expected to know the causes and control of type 1 and type 2 diabetes.

10 Type 2 diabetes and obesity — Grades 3–5

3. Figure 1 shows how different activities increase or decrease the risk of developing type 2 diabetes.

(a) Give the increase in diabetes risk of sitting at work for two hours a day. **[1 mark]**

....

(b) Explain why brisk walking for one hour a day decreases the risk of diabetes. Refer to glucose and obesity in your answer. **[3 marks]**

....

....

....

....

Figure 1

Think about the link between obesity and exercise. People who do regular exercise are less likely to be obese.

 Made a start 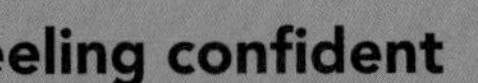 Feeling confident  Exam ready

Hormones in reproduction

2 Quick quiz

Complete the definition of the term 'puberty'.

Puberty is the time when the .... starts developing in ways that will allow

....

5 Hormones in reproduction — Grade 3

1. Complete **Table 1** to show the main reproductive hormones in men and women and where they are produced. **[2 marks]**

Table 1

	Name of hormone	Where it is produced
men	testosterone	
women		

5 Functions of hormones — Grade 4

2. Complete **Table 3** to show the function of each hormone. Use words from the box. **[3 marks]**

follicle-stimulating hormone (FSH)	oestrogen	luteinising hormone (LH)	progesterone

Hormone(s)	Function
	builds up and maintains the uterus lining
	causes an egg to mature
	secreted by the ovaries and causes only one egg to mature
	triggers ovulation

Exam focus
You need to know the roles of the different reproductive hormones.

10 The menstrual cycle — Grades 4–5

3. **Figure 1** shows the changes that occur to the thickness of the uterus lining during the menstrual cycle.

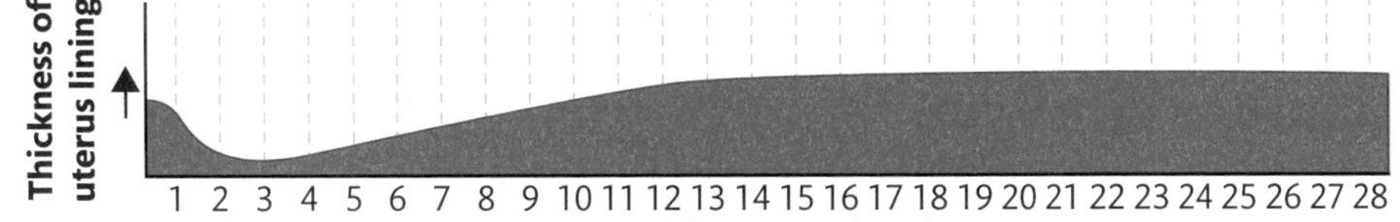

Figure 1

Menstruation is when the lining of the uterus breaks down and leaves the body.

(a) Give the days menstruation occurs. .... **[1 mark]**

(b) Give the day ovulation occurs. .... **[1 mark]**

(c) Describe what ovulation is. .... **[2 marks]**

....

....

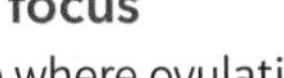

Exam focus
Include where ovulation occurs in your answer.

 Made a start  Feeling confident  Exam ready

Contraception

2 Quick quiz

What is contraception used for?

prevent brain damage ☐ | prevent lung cancer ☐

prevent pregnancy ☐ | prevent obesity ☐

5 Hormonal and non-hormonal contraception — Grade 3

1. Complete **Table 1** to show whether the types of contraception in the box are hormonal or non-hormonal. **[2 marks]**

condom | contraceptive pill | contraceptive patch | IUD | sterilisation | rhythm method

Table 1

Non-hormonal	Hormonal
rhythm method	contraceptive pill

Hormonal methods of contraception involve use of reproductive hormones to prevent an egg from being fertilised or from being implanted into the uterus.

5 How contraception works — Grade 4

2. Draw **one** line to link each type of contraception to how it works. **[3 marks]**

condom
IUD
spermicide
contraceptive pill

stops FSH being released
provides a physical barrier so sperm don't reach egg
prevents fertilised egg from implanting in the uterus
kills sperm

10 Evaluating contraception — Grades 4–5

3. Table 2 shows a summary of four different types of contraception and their effectiveness, how long they last and whether they protect against sexually transmitted diseases (STIs). Use the table to answer the questions.

Table 2

Type of contraception	Effectiveness	How long does it last?	Protects against STIs?
condom	98%	once only	yes
sterilisation	100%	permanent	no
IUD	99%	up to 5 years	no
contraceptive pill	99.7%	has to be taken daily	no

Exam focus
Read all the information in a table if you are given one in the exam.

(a) Give **one** advantage of using a condom rather than an IUD. **[1 mark]**

....

(b) A woman wants a long-term method of contraception but might want children in the future. Explain which method of contraception from **Table 2** would be the most suitable. Give a reason for your answer. **[2 marks]**

....

Made a start  Feeling confident Exam ready

Asexual and sexual reproduction

2 Quick quiz

Which type of reproduction is each statement describing?

Offspring are clones of the parent.	**Sexual / Asexual**
This type of reproduction produces genetic variation in the offspring.	**Sexual / Asexual**
This type of reproduction involves male and female gametes.	**Sexual / Asexual**
Offspring of this type of reproduction have only one parent.	**Sexual / Asexual**

10 Sexual reproduction — Grades 3–5

1. (a) Which **two** statements are correct for gametes? Tick **two** boxes. **[2 marks]**

They are body cells. ☐ They are sex cells. ☐ They are specialised cells. ☐

(b) Name the male and female gametes in humans. **[2 marks]**

male gamete .... female gamete ....

(c) Name the type of cell division that produces gametes. **[1 mark]**

....

There are two types of cell division – mitosis and meiosis.

(d) Explain **one** advantage of sexual reproduction. **[2 marks]**

Sexual reproduction produces offspring that are ....

This means they may be better adapted than ....

to the environment.

Think about a feature of sexual reproduction and how this might help some of the offspring survive better.

5 Types of reproduction — Grade 2

2. Draw **one** line to match each organism with its type of reproduction. **[2 marks]**

bacteria
cat
budding yeast cells
human
potato producing potato tubers

asexual reproduction
sexual reproduction

5 More about reproduction — Grade 4

3. Figure 1 shows one type of reproduction.

(a) Identify the type of reproduction shown in **Figure 1**. **[1 mark]**

....

Think about which type of reproduction needs only one parent.

Figure 1

(b) Which term describes the cells labelled **X** in **Figure 1**? Tick **one** box. **[1 mark]**

clones ☐ embryos ☐ zygotes ☐

Meiosis

Quick quiz

Are these statements true or false?

Meiosis happens in cells within reproductive organs.	**True / False**
Gametes are always produced by mitosis.	**True / False**
Fertilisation is when the male and female sex cells fuse together.	**True / False**
Meiosis produces cells that contain only one set of chromosomes.	**True / False**

The process of meiosis — Grades 3–5

1. Draw **one** line to link each key term with its definition. **[2 marks]**

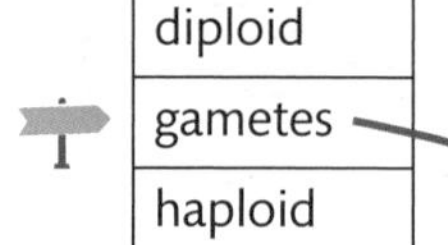

diploid		a cell containing a single set of unpaired chromosomes
gametes		a cell containing two sets of chromosomes
haploid		sex cells: sperm and egg

2. **Figure 1** shows the stages of meiosis.

The statements in **Table 1** describe the stages of meiosis. They are not in the correct order. Write numbers (1–5) next to the statements to show the correct sequence. **[2 marks]**

Table 1

Pairs of chromosomes divide.	
Parent chromosomes make copies of themselves.	
Cells divide into gametes.	
Similar chromosomes pair up.	2
Chromosomes exchange genetic material.	

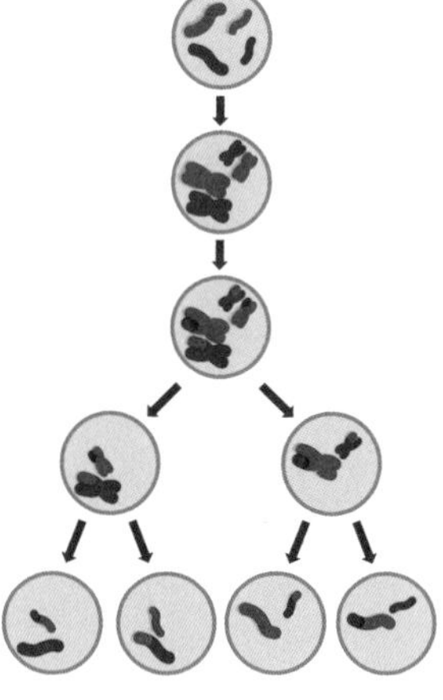

Figure 1

Exam focus

Look carefully at figures given to you in the exam. They will contain information that will help you to answer the question.

Remember there are two lots of cell division in meiosis.

Fertilisation — Grade 4

3. (a) There are 46 chromosomes in most human body cells. Use numbers from the box to answer the questions.

1	2	23	46	92

(i) How many chromosomes are in a skin cell? .... **[1 mark]**

(ii) How many chromosomes are in a sperm cell? .... **[1 mark]**

(iii) How many chromosomes are in an embryo? .... **[1 mark]**

(b) Describe what happens after gametes have joined together at fertilisation. **[3 marks]**

....

....

....

Describe what happens to the cell to make the zygote develop into an embryo. Think about what needs to happen to the cell?

 Made a start 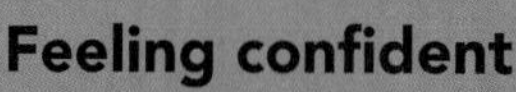 Feeling confident 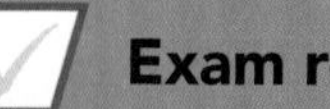 Exam ready

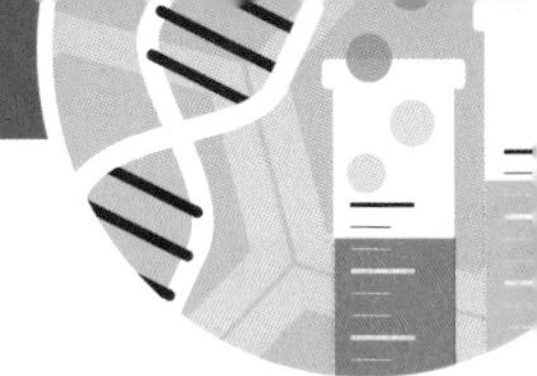

DNA and the genome

2 Quick quiz

Which is a definition of the term 'genome'?

the genetic material in an egg cell ☐

the genetic material in a sperm ☐

the total genetic material of an organism ☐

10 The structure of DNA — Grades 3–5

1. Write the following parts in order of size starting with the smallest. **[2 marks]**

cell	chromosome	nucleus	gene

The genetic material is found in the nucleus of a cell.

gene ....

2. Describe the structure of DNA. **[2 marks]**

DNA consists of .... strands twisted into a ....

....

3. DNA is a polymer. Define the term 'polymer'. **[1 mark]**

'poly' means many.

A polymer is a long chain made of ....

4. Complete the sentences to describe what a gene is. Use words from the box. **[4 marks]**

amino acids	carbohydrate	chromosome	DNA	gametes	protein

A gene is a small section of .... on a .... that codes for a particular sequence of amino acids to make a specific ....

10 The human genome — Grade 5

5. Figure 1 shows an animal cell.

Which part of the cell contains the genetic material? Tick **one** box. **[1 mark]**

A ☐

B ☐

C ☐

A
B
C

Figure 1

6. Describe **two** ways that mapping the whole human genome could be useful for the National Health Service (NHS). **[2 marks]**

....

....

Think about the types of diseases you could find out about if you looked at a person's genome.

One of the roles of the NHS is to treat and prevent diseases. Think about how knowing the genome could help this.

Genetic inheritance

2 Quick quiz

Circle the correct words in **bold**.

An allele is one version of a **gene / phenotype**.

A genotype is the alleles present for a **gene / phenotype**.

A **phenotype / gene** is the physical characteristic determined by the alleles.

5 Genetic terms — Grade 4

1. Draw **one** line to match each key term with its definition. **[3 marks]**

dominant	both alleles for a gene are identical
recessive	only one allele is needed for a characteristic to be expressed in the phenotype
homozygous	the alleles for a gene are different
heterozygous	two of these alleles are usually needed for the characteristic to be expressed in the phenotype

15 Genetic cross — Grade 5

2. Huntington disease is an inherited disease. The dominant allele, H, has a mutation that causes Huntington disease.

(a) Which is the genotype of an embryo that will **never** develop into a person with Huntington disease?
Tick **one** box. **[1 mark]**

Hh ☐ hh ☐ HH ☐

You have two copies of each gene. Dominant means that only one allele needs to be present for it to be shown in the phenotype. Recessive means that both alleles need to be present for it to be shown in the phenotype.

(b) **Figure 1** shows a Punnett square which shows the inheritance of Huntington disease.

(i) Which term can be used to describe the genotype of the parent **A**?
Tick **one** box. **[1 mark]**

heterozygous ☐ homozygous ☐ dominant ☐ recessive ☐

Exam focus
You need be able to extract and interpret information from Punnett squares.

Parent A

Parent B	H	h
h	Hh	hh
h	Hh	hh

Figure 1

(ii) What is the chance of the offspring in **Figure 1** inheriting Huntington disease? **[1 mark]**

....

(iii) Complete the Punnett square in **Figure 2** to show the probability of an embryo **not** having Huntington disease. **[2 marks]**

probability ....

Parent A

Parent B	H	h
H		
h		

Figure 2

Made a start ☐ Feeling confident ☐ Exam ready ☐

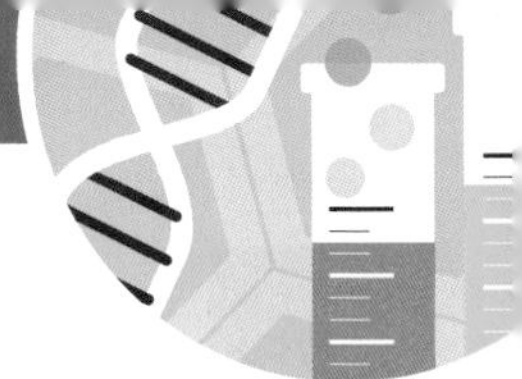

Inherited disorders

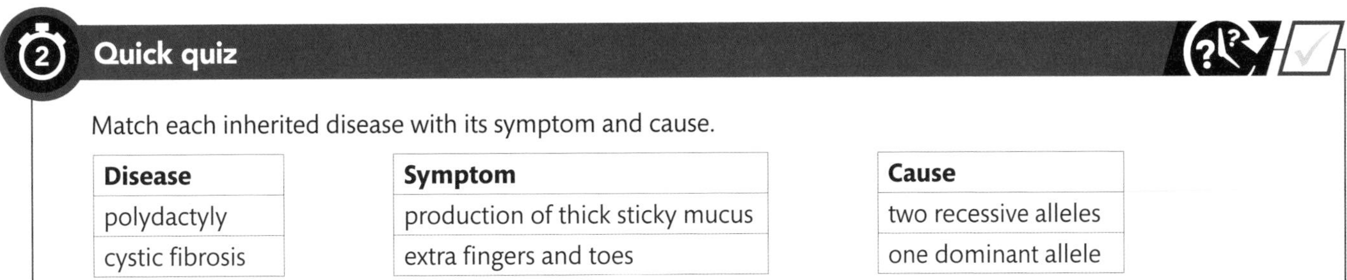

2 Quick quiz

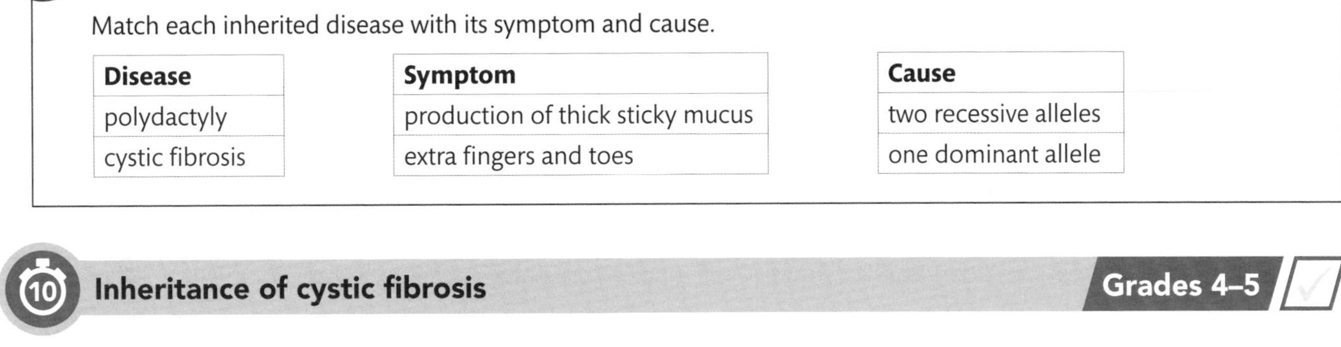

Match each inherited disease with its symptom and cause.

Disease
polydactyly
cystic fibrosis

Symptom
production of thick sticky mucus
extra fingers and toes

Cause
two recessive alleles
one dominant allele

10 Inheritance of cystic fibrosis — Grades 4–5

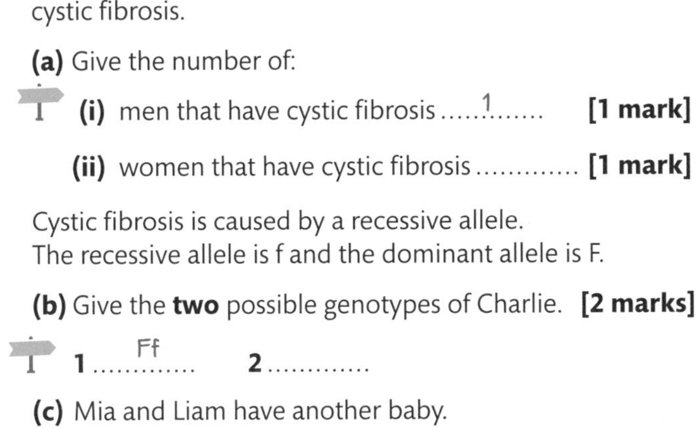

1. Figure 1 is a family tree showing the inheritance of cystic fibrosis.

(a) Give the number of:

(i) men that have cystic fibrosis .....1...... **[1 mark]**

(ii) women that have cystic fibrosis .... **[1 mark]**

Cystic fibrosis is caused by a recessive allele.
The recessive allele is f and the dominant allele is F.

(b) Give the **two** possible genotypes of Charlie. **[2 marks]**

1 ....Ff.... **2** ....

(c) Mia and Liam have another baby.

(i) Complete the Punnett square to show the baby's possible genotypes. **[2 marks]**

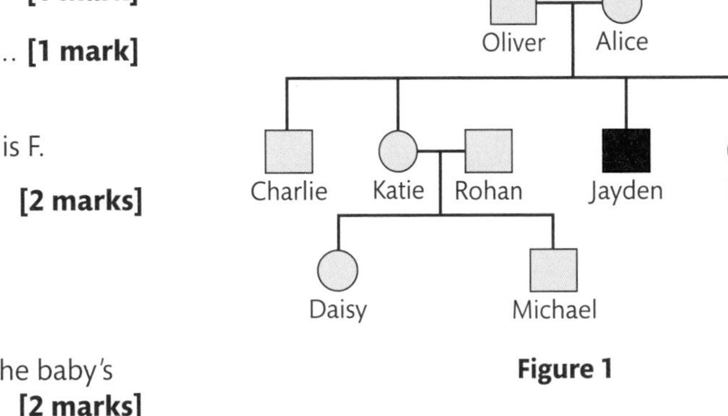

Figure 1

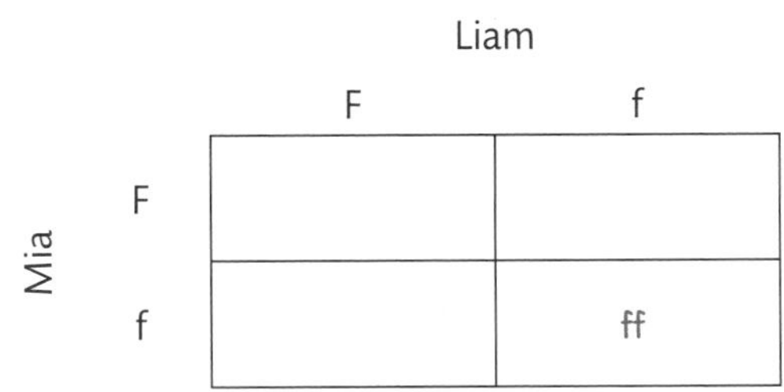

Mia \ Liam	F	f
F		
f		ff

Does Charlie have cystic fibrosis? Cystic fibrosis is caused by a recessive allele so you need two alleles to have the disease.

(ii) Give the percentage chance of the baby having cystic fibrosis. **[1 mark]**

....

10 Embryo screening — Grade 5

2. Describe the disadvantages of screening embryos for genetic disorders. **[3 marks]**

....

....

....

Remember to include economic, social and ethical issues. Economic issues are to do with money, social issues affect people living in a society and ethical issues are to do with whether something is right or wrong.

 Made a start  Feeling confident  Exam ready

Variation and mutation

2 Quick quiz

Variation within a species can be due to **two** factors. What are these factors?

....

10 Causes of variation — Grades 3–4

1. Complete **Table 1** to show whether the characteristics in the box are caused by genes or the environment. **[2 marks]**

blood group	cystic fibrosis	eye colour	language spoken	tattoos

Characteristics caused by genes	Characteristics caused by environment
blood group	language spoken

2. (a) Describe how a person's height can be due to both environmental and genetic factors. **[2 marks]**

A person may have inherited ....

However, environmental factors such as having a poor diet can lead to ....

(b) Suggest **one** other characteristic that can be affected by both genetic and environmental factors. **[1 mark]**

....

Exam focus

The command word 'suggest' means that although you may not know the answer you should be able to apply your knowledge of the causes of characteristics to suggest an answer.

5 Mutations — Grades 3–4

3. Define the term 'mutation'. **[1 mark]**

....

4. Which **two** statements about mutations are correct? Tick **two** boxes. **[2 marks]**

Mutations are only caused unnaturally. ☐

Mutations occur all the time. ☐

Mutations are always negative. ☐

Mutations will always lead to a new phenotype. ☐

Mutations may cause genetic variation. ☐

5. Give **one** advantage and **one** disadvantage of mutations. **[2 marks]**

advantage ....

disadvantage ....

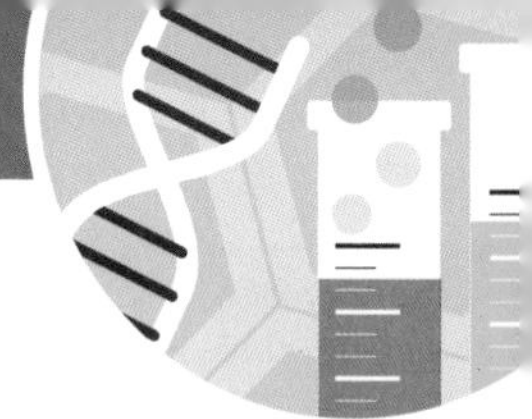

Sex determination

2 Quick quiz

Are these statements true or false?

Male gametes are called sperm.	**True / False**
Human body cells have 23 chromosomes.	**True / False**
Sex chromosomes are the 23rd pair.	**True / False**
Meiosis produces gametes.	**True / False**

10 Sex chromosomes — Grades 2–4

1. Complete the sentences about sex chromosomes. **[5 marks]**

In humans, the sex chromosomes in a female are ...XX.....

The sex chromosomes in a male are ....

Female gametes contain one .... chromosome.

Male gametes contain an .... or a .... chromosome.

> Gametes contain only one of each chromosome pair. Body cells contain two. They are haploid.

2. Give the type of cell division that produces male and female gametes in humans. .... **[1 mark]**

> Think about the type of cell division that produces haploid cells.

3. Name the male and female gametes in humans. **[2 marks]**

male ......sperm......... female ....

4. What is the percentage chance of inheriting a Y chromosome from a male gamete? Tick **one** box. **[1 mark]**

0% ☐ 25% ☐ 50% ☐ 75% ☐ 100% ☐

5 Inheritance of sex — Grade 4

5. (a) Complete the genetic cross diagram (**Figure 1**) to show the inheritance of sex. **[1 mark]**

		male gametes X	male gametes Y
female gametes	X		
	X		

Figure 1

> **Exam focus**
> Make sure you know how to complete genetic crosses.

(b) (i) Give the ratio of possible male to female offspring. .... **[1 mark]**

(ii) Give the percentage chance of the baby being a boy. .... **[1 mark]**

> **Exam focus**
> You should be able to express the possible genotypes of the offspring in terms of a ratio or a percentage.

Evolution

Quick quiz

Match each term to its correct definition.

evolution
natural selection
speciation

new species form; they can no longer interbreed to form fertile offspring
a change in the inherited characteristics of a population over time, leading to new species arising from ancestral species
organisms that are the best suited to their environment are more likely to survive and reproduce

Evolution

Grade 5

1. Give **two** pieces of evidence for the theory of evolution by natural selection. **[2 marks]**

1 fossil record ....

2 ....

2. **Figure 1** shows variation in peppered moths. After the industrial revolution, there was a lot more pollution, which covered the trees in towns and cities in soot and turned them a dark colour. Suggest how natural selection caused the numbers of the darker peppered moth to increase. **[4 marks]**

The lighter coloured moths were more visible to predators and ....

The dark coloured moths ....

The dark coloured moths bred, passing on ....

This increased the number of ....

Figure 1

Exam focus

You need to be able to interpret information on an organism's features from photographs.

Natural selection

Grade 5

3. **Figure 2** shows a porcupine.

(a) The statements in **Table 1** show stages in the evolution of porcupines. The statements are not in the correct order. Write numbers 1–5 to show the correct sequence. **[2 marks]**

Table 1

Passing on the alleles for long spikes.	
Porcupines with longer spikes had an advantage.	
There was variation in the length of porcupine spikes.	
They survived and bred.	
Eventually all the porcupines in the species had long spikes.	

Figure 2

(b) Suggest **one** reason why longer spikes are an advantage for the porcupine. **[1 mark]**

....

 Made a start  Feeling confident  Exam ready

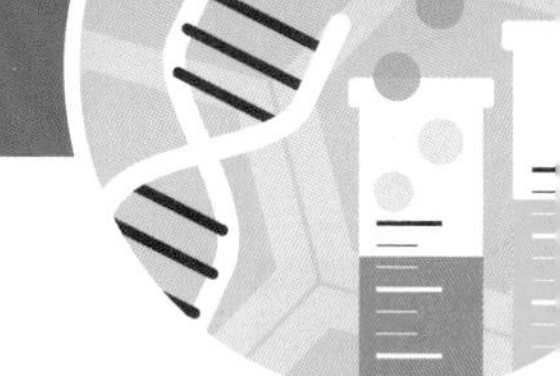

Selective breeding

2 Quick quiz

Label each organism with what it can be selectively bred for.

high milk yield

coloured markings on coat

sweet smell

10 The process of selective breeding

Grades 4–5

1. A horse breeder wants to breed horses for racing. Racehorses need to be fast to win races.

(a) Describe how the horse breeder would selectively breed horses for racing. **[3 marks]**

The horse breeder would choose .... and breed them. The horse breeder would observe the offspring, select .... and breed them again. The horse breeder would continue this over many ....

(b) Suggest **one** other feature that the horse breeder might want to selectively breed in racehorses. **[1 mark]**

....

2. Complete **Table 1** by ticking the boxes to show some of the features of selective breeding and natural selection. **[2 marks]**

Table 1

Feature	Selective breeding	Natural selection
organisms' features can change	✓	✓
environment chooses features		
reduces variety of alleles		

10 Advantages and disadvantages

Grade 5

3. (a) What is an advantage of breeding crop plants? Tick **one** box. **[1 mark]**

- creates varieties that are rare ☐
- increases the genetic variety of crop plants ☐
- produces more food for human consumption ☐

(b) Wheat is a crop plant that has been selectively bred. **Figure 1** shows a monoculture of wheat. A monoculture is a large area that contains the same type of plant. A new disease develops that affects wheat. Explain how this might affect food production. **[3 marks]**

....

....

....

....

....

Figure 1

Think about how similar the wheat plants will be to each other.

 Made a start  Feeling confident  Exam ready

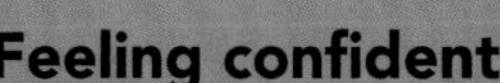

Genetic engineering

2 Quick quiz

Complete the definition of genetic engineering using words from the box.

different	diploid	gene	genome	protein	the same

Genetic engineering is a process used to insert a .... from one organism into the .... of a .... organism to give a desired characteristic.

5 The process of genetic engineeering — Grade 4

1. **Figure 1** shows a simplified diagram of genetic engineering. The statements in **Table 1** describe the process of genetic engineering. They are not in the right order. Write numbers 1–4 to put them in the correct sequence. **[2 marks]**

Table 1

The gene is inserted into a bacterial plasmid.	
The bacterial DNA is put into cells of the desired organism.	
The required gene is removed from the cell.	1
The organism develops showing the desired characteristic.	

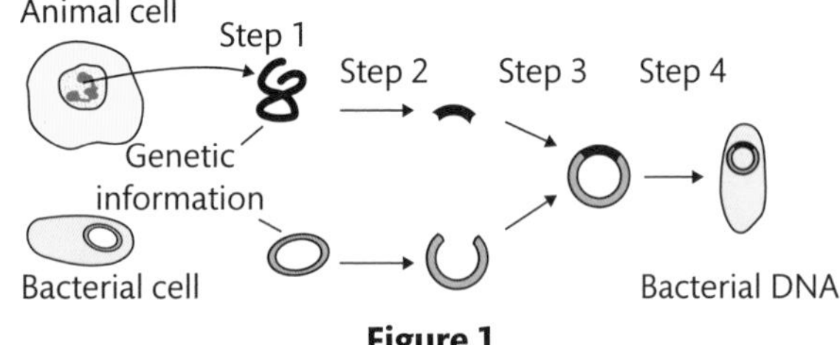

Figure 1

Use the figure to help you decide on the correct order.

5 Genetic engineering — Grades 4–5

2. Bacteria have been genetically engineered to produce useful products for humans. Give **one** product. **[1 mark]**

....

3. Complete **Table 2** by ticking the boxes to show some features of artificial selection and genetic engineering. **[3 marks]**

Table 2

Feature	Artificial selection	Genetic engineering
humans choose desired features		
involves inserting genes from other organisms		✓
interbreeding can occur		

Some features apply to both artificial selection and genetic engineering.

5 Benefits and risks — Grade 5

4. Give **two** benefits and **two** risks of genetic engineering. **[4 marks]**

Benefits ....

....

Risks ....

....

Think about how genetic modification can be used in medicine and agriculture, possible effects on the environment and on human health, and ethical and social issues.

Made a start

Feeling confident

Exam ready

Fossils

2 Quick quiz

Complete the definition of the term 'fossil'.

Fossils are the .... of organisms that lived .... of years ago and they are found in ....

10 Formation of fossils — Grades 2–4

1. (a) Name **one** place where fossils are found. Tick **one** box. **[1 mark]**

the atmosphere ☐ rocks ☐ floating in rivers ☐

(b) Describe **two** ways that fossils can be formed. **[2 marks]**

1 Hard parts of the organism that have not decayed, for example, ...

2 Traces of the organism are preserved, for example, ...

(c) What are **two** conditions needed for fossils to form? Tick **two** boxes. **[2 marks]**

oxygen	☐	alkaline environment	☐
toxic gases	☐	lack of moisture	✓
hot temperatures	☐		

10 Fossilisation and the fossil record — Grade 5

2. Figure 1 shows a fossil of an extinct giant elk that was preserved in a peat bog. Explain how the giant elk was preserved. **[4 marks]**

....

....

....

....

....

....

> Think about which parts of the giant elk have been preserved and the conditions needed for this type of preservation to occur.

Figure 1

3. Give **two** reasons why the fossil record is not complete. **[2 marks]**

1 ....

2 ....

Extinction

2 Quick quiz

Are these statements true or false?

Extinction is the permanent loss of species.	**True / False**
Extinction only occurs in animals.	**True / False**
Extinction only occurs due to the actions of humans.	**True / False**
Extinction occurs when there are no more individuals of that species alive.	**True / False**

10 Causes of extinction — Grades 2–4

1. (a) Draw **one** line to link each key factor with how it contributes to extinction. **[2 marks]**

Key factor
catastrophic event
mutations
speciation

How it contributes to extinction
a new species evolves and the old one becomes extinct
e.g. an asteroid collision can wipe out a community
a new species can evolve and be more successful than its competitor

(b) Describe how environmental change can cause extinction. **[3 marks]**

Destruction of an organism's .... can leave it without ....

.... or ....

(c) Give **four** other factors that contribute to extinction. **[4 marks]**

1 new diseases ....

2 ....

3 ....

4 ....

10 Human influences on extinction — Grade 5

2. Figure 1 shows a black rhinoceros. These animals are endangered and may soon become extinct. Suggest how humans have contributed to the reduction in numbers of the black rhino. **[4 marks]**

....

....

....

....

Figure 1

Think about what human activities affect animals directly and what activities affect the environment.

Exam focus

The command word 'suggest' means that you might not know the answer. Here, you need to apply your knowledge of how humans can cause extinctions.

 Made a start  Feeling confident  Exam ready

Resistant bacteria

Quick quiz

Complete the sentences about resistant bacteria by circling the correct words in **bold**.

Some bacteria are **pathogens / enzymes** and cause diseases.

Bacterial infections can be treated using **antibiotics / painkillers**.

Some bacteria have become resistant to treatment by **natural / artificial** selection.

Development of resistant bacteria

Grade 4

1. The statements in **Table 1** describe the development of resistance in bacteria. They are not in the correct order. Write numbers 1–5 to put them in the correct sequence. **[2 marks]**

Table 1

Bacteria that have the mutation survive longer and reproduce more.	
Bacteria reproduce very rapidly and soon all the bacteria are resistant to the antibiotic.	
Some bacteria have mutations that make them more resistant to an antibiotic.	1
Bacteria that do not have that mutation are killed when the antibiotic is used.	2
Resistant strains can then spread.	

The development of resistance in bacteria is caused by natural selection. Think about how the process of natural selection occurs.

MRSA and the development of resistance

Grade 5

2. Figure 1 shows the number of deaths caused by MRSA in England and Wales from 1994 to 2012.

(a) Give the year that MRSA bacteria caused the most deaths in females. **[1 mark]**

....

(b) Approximately how many deaths per million population in males were caused by MRSA bacteria in 2004? Tick **one** box. **[1 mark]**

2 ☐ 9 ☐ 17 ☐

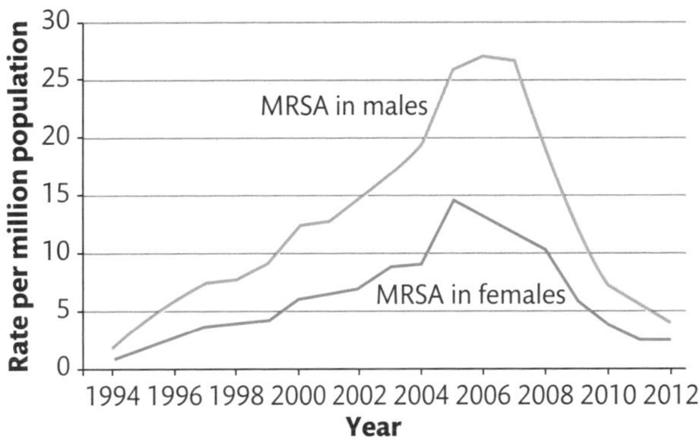

Figure 1

(c) Describe the main trends in the data for females shown in **Figure 1**. **[2 marks]**

The number of deaths caused by MRSA ....

After the year increases between ....

The main trends are the patterns you can see in the results. Use the axis labels to help you. Think about what happens to the number of deaths as the number of years increases.

Exam focus

When answering data analysis questions, make sure you read the axis labels and quote the correct units. Take care to be accurate when you are reading values from graphs.

(d) Give **two** ways that the development of antibiotic resistance in bacteria can be reduced. **[2 marks]**

1 Not taking antibiotics for viral infections ....

2 ....

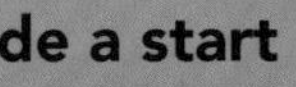

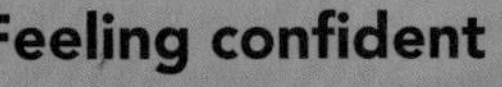

Made a start | Feeling confident | Exam ready

Classification

2 Quick quiz

Put the classification groups in the Linnaean classification system in order from largest to smallest.

class	family	genus	kingdom	order	phylum	species

....

largest ⟶ smallest

10 Classification systems — Grades 2–4

1. Animals and plants are two kingdoms. Name **two** other kingdoms. **[2 marks]**

1 .... 2 ....

2. Draw **one** line to link each of Woese's domains with the organisms in that domain. **[2 marks]**

Domain
archaea
bacteria
eukaryota

Organisms
protists, fungi, plants and animals
primitive bacteria that live in extreme environments
true bacteria

3. The binomial name of an organism includes the names of which **two** parts of the Linnaean classification system? Tick **two** boxes. **[2 marks]**

class ☐ family ☐ genus ☐ kingdom ☐

order ☐ phylum ☐ species ☐

10 Evolutionary trees — Grade 5

4.

The tree shows that the mammoths are extinct.

(a) Suggest what evidence was used to place steppe mammoths in the tree. **[1 mark]**

....

(b) Use **Figure 1** to identify the proboscideans that have complex teeth. **[1 mark]**

....

Look for the branches of the tree that link above that label.

(c) Use **Figure 1** to identify the proboscidean whose most recent shared ancestor is with Asian elephants. Give a reason for your answer. **[2 marks]**

.... because it is most

.... the Asian elephant.

☐ Made a start ☐ Feeling confident ☐ Exam ready

Communities

2 Quick quiz

Put these terms in order of size from smallest to largest.

community	ecosystem	organism	population

....

10 Features of an ecosystem — Grades 2–4

1. (a) Draw **one** line to link each term to its correct definition. **[3 marks]**

Term	Definition
community	all the organisms of one species in an ecosystem
ecosystem	all the populations of different species living in the same habitat
habitat	the environment where an organism lives
population	the interaction of a community of all the living organisms with the non-living parts of their environment

Exam focus
Make sure you know the difference between these terms and can use them appropriately.

(b) Name **two** things that plants compete for. **[2 marks]**

1 .... 2 ....

(c) Name **two** things that animals compete for. **[2 marks]**

1 .... 2 ....

10 Interdependence and competition — Grade 5

2. Figure 1 shows a diagram of a food web. Foxes eat rabbits.

(a) Name **one other** species, shown in **Figure 1**, that is eaten by the fox. **[1 mark]**

....

(b) Figure 1 shows competition between the rabbit and the roe deer. What are they are competing for? **[1 mark]**

....

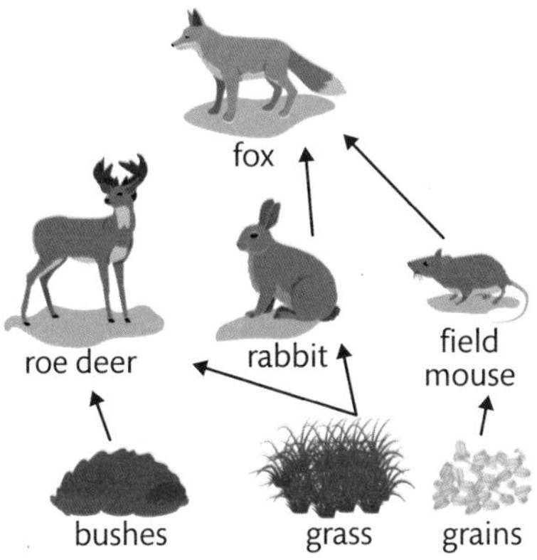

fox
roe deer
rabbit
field mouse
bushes
grass
grains

Figure 1

(c) (i) Explain what happens initially to the population of rabbits if the population of foxes decreases. **[2 marks]**

....

....

(ii) Explain what happens to the population of roe deer if the number of bushes increases. **[2 marks]**

....

....

You need to describe what happens to the numbers of roe deer and why it happens.

Abiotic factors

Quick quiz

Are these statements true or false?

Abiotic factors are living organisms. **True / False**

Abiotic factors only affect animals. **True / False**

Oxygen concentration is an example of an abiotic factor. **True / False**

Abiotic factors — Grade 3

1. Name **two** abiotic factors that affect plants. **[2 marks]**

1 .... **2** ....

Effect of pH — Grade 5

2. Figure 1 shows the range of pH values that some different species of animals can survive in.

(a) Name the organism that can live in the most acidic environment. **[1 mark]**

....

The lower the pH value the higher the acidity.

(b) Name the **two** organisms that can survive in the smallest pH range. **[2 marks]**

1 ....

2 ....

The species with the largest pH range has the biggest bar.

Acid Tolerance	pH 6.5	pH 6.0	pH 5.5	pH 5.0	pH 4.5	pH 4.0
Trout						
Bass						
Perch						
Frogs						
Salamanders						
Clams						
Crayfish						
Snails						
Mayfly						

Figure 1

(c) Give the pH range that the mayfly can survive in. .... **[1 mark]**

(d) Describe the relationship between pH and number of species able to survive. **[1 mark]**

As the pH value decreases the number of species ....

Exam focus

Look carefully at any diagrams given to you in the exam. Make sure you understand what the diagram is showing you. Quote any data accurately and use the labels and units given.

3. The concentration of dissolved oxygen affects the number of species living in a lake.
Suggest what happens to the number of species as the dissolved oxygen concentration decreases.
Give a reason for your answer. **[3 marks]**

....

....

....

Think about what animals need oxygen for.

 Made a start  Feeling confident  Exam ready

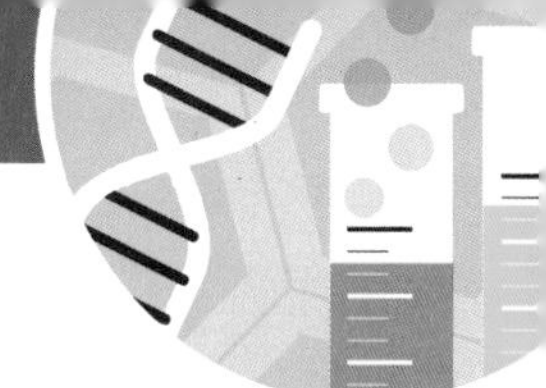

Biotic factors

Quick quiz

Are these factors abiotic or biotic?

temperature	**abiotic / biotic**
predators	**abiotic / biotic**
pH	**abiotic / biotic**
disease	**abiotic / biotic**
food availability	**abiotic / biotic**

Biotic factors

Grade 3

1. Complete **Table 1** by ticking the boxes to show whether different biotic factors would increase or decrease the population. **[2 marks]**

Table 1	**Increase the population?**	**Decrease the population?**
introduction of disease		
decrease in food availability		
decrease in competition for mates		
new predators		

Data analysis

Grade 5

2. Wolves are predators of elk. Wolves were re-introduced into a national park in the US in 1999. **Table 2** shows the numbers of wolves and elk in the park.

Table 2

Year	Number of wolves	Number of elk
1998	0	14 000
2000	177	13 400
2002	271	9200
2004	342	9500
2006	390	6600
2008	449	6300
2010	501	4600

Exam focus

The command word 'describe' does not require you to explain the results. This is a data analysis question and all the information you need is in the table.

(a) Describe the changes to the number of wolves between 1998 and 2010. **[2 marks]**

In 1998, the number of wolves was ....

Between 2000 and 2010, the number of wolves ....

Look at the information in the table and identify the general trends in the data.

(b) Explain the changes to the number of elk between 2000 and 2010. **[3 marks]**

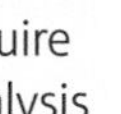

Wolf numbers increased so ....

Think about the reasons for the change in the number of elk.

(c) Give **one** other biotic factor that could reduce the number of elk. **[1 mark]**

....

Remember that biotic factors are living factors.

Adaptations

2 Quick quiz

Complete the sentence about adaptation.

An adaptation is a .... that helps an organism .... and reproduce in its habitat.

10 Adaptations — Grades 3–4

1. Draw **one** line to link each type of adaptation to its description. **[2 marks]**

Type of adaptation
behavioural
functional
structural

Description
physical features of the organism
ways the animal adjusts its behaviour
functions that an organism has to survive

2. Figure 1 shows a camel. Complete **Table 1** by ticking the boxes to show whether each adaptation of the camel is behavioural, functional or structural. **[3 marks]**

Table 1

Feature	Behavioural	Functional	Structural
long eyelashes to keep sand out			
spitting to deter predators			
shuts nostrils to keep sand out			

Exam focus
Make sure you know the difference between behavioural, structural and functional adaptations.

Figure 1

5 Adapting to the environment — Grade 5

3. Figure 2 shows a polar bear. Explain how the following features enable polar bears to survive in their environment.

(i) thick fur **[1 mark]**

helps to protect the bear from ....

(ii) large paws **[1 mark]**

give a large surface area so that the bear ....

(iii) sharp teeth **[1 mark]**

help the bear to ....

Figure 2

The polar bear is a predator that lives in a very cold environment. Think about what adaptations it would need.

5 Extreme environments — Grade 3

4. Extremophiles live in extreme environments. Which are **two** examples of extreme environments? Tick **two** boxes. **[2 marks]**

a forest ☐ a garden ☐ salt marsh ☐

hot springs ☐ a field ☐

Made a start ☐ Feeling confident  Exam ready ☐

Organisation of an ecosystem

Quick quiz

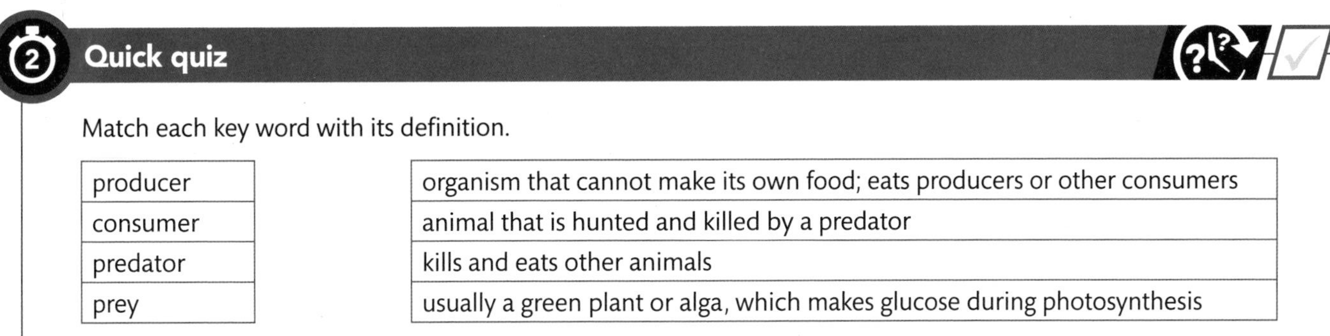

Match each key word with its definition.

Key word	Definition
producer	organism that cannot make its own food; eats producers or other consumers
consumer	animal that is hunted and killed by a predator
predator	kills and eats other animals
prey	usually a green plant or alga, which makes glucose during photosynthesis

Food chains

Grades 2–4 

1. Figure 1 shows a simple food chain.

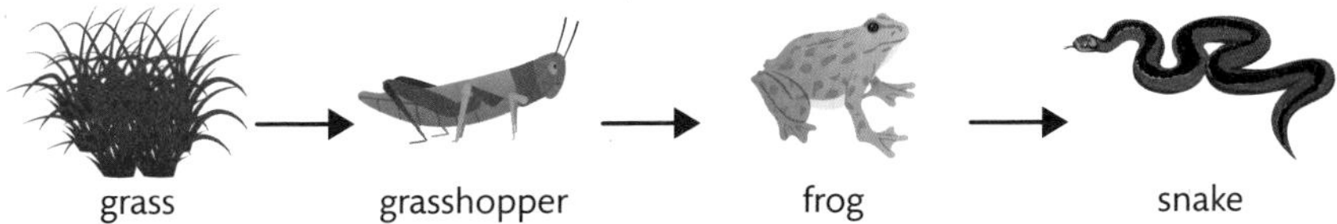

Figure 1

(a) Complete **Table 1** by ticking the boxes to show how the organisms in this food chain can be described. **[4 marks]**

Table 1

Organism	Producer	Predator	Prey	Primary consumer
grass				
grasshopper				
frog		✓	✓	
snake				

Some organisms can be described as more than one thing. For example, some organisms can be predators and secondary consumers.

(b) Explain why all food chains must start with a producer. **[3 marks]**

Producers use the process of .... to produce ....

which is .... by other organisms.

Use the term 'biomass' in your answer.

Producers are usually plants. Think about the process a plant carries out that an animal cannot.

Predator–prey cycles

Grades 4–5 

2. Figure 2 shows the changes in population of wolves and moose. Wolves are predators of moose.

(a) Look at **Figure 2**. Which statement is true? Tick **one** box. **[1 mark]**

The population of wolves does not change. ☐

There are always more moose than wolves. ☐

The population of wolves increases when the population of moose increases. ☐

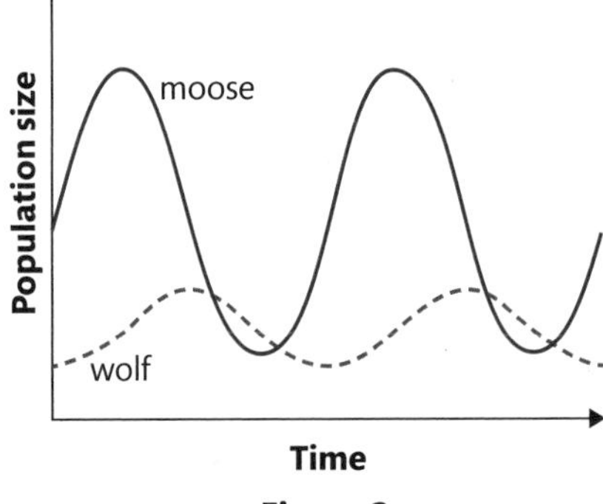

Figure 2

(b) Explain what happens to the population of moose when the population of wolves increases. **[2 marks]**

....

....

The command word 'explain' means you have to say what happens to the population and why this change happens.

Investigating population size

2 Quick quiz

What is a quadrat?

a circular frame used to sample the distribution of plants only ☐

a square frame used to sample the distribution of plants or animals ☐

a square frame used to sample the distribution of animals only ☐

5 Using quadrats

Grade 4

1. The sentences in **Table 1** describe how to estimate population size of snails in a garden. They are not in the correct order. Write numbers 1–5 next to the sentences to put them in the correct sequence. **[2 marks]**

Table 1

Repeat these steps several times and record the results.	
Multiply the average number per quadrat by the total number of quadrats that can fit into the garden.	
Place a quadrat on the ground at a random point.	1
Calculate the mean number of squares per quadrat.	
Count the number of snails in the quadrat.	

15 Estimating population size

Grade 5

2. A student measured the distribution of daisies in a quadrat (**Figure 1**). **Table 2** shows the results.

Table 2

Quadrat number	Number of daisies
1	21
2	4
3	12
4	7
5	3

Exam focus
Numerical information is given to you in the question. Make sure you know what each value is and what its units are.

Figure 1

The area of the field was 125 m^2. The quadrat had an area of 1 m^2. Estimate the number of daisies in the field. **[4 marks]**

1. 21 + 4 + ... = ...

2. $\frac{\text{total number of daisies}}{\text{number of quadrats}}$ = mean number of daisies per quadrat

$\frac{\dots\dots}{\dots\dots}$ = ...

3. $\frac{\text{total area of field}}{\text{area of one quadrat}}$ = number of quadrats in the field

$\frac{\dots\dots}{\dots\dots}$ = ...

4. mean number of daisies per quadrat × number of quadrats in the field = the number of daisies in the field

.... × .... = ...

Step 1: find the total number of daisies in all the quadrats.

Step 2: find the mean number of daisies per quadrat.

Step 3: find how many quadrats fit into the field.

Step 4: estimate how many daisies are in the field.

 Made a start 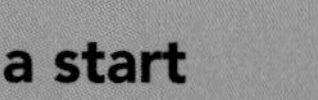  Feeling confident  Exam ready

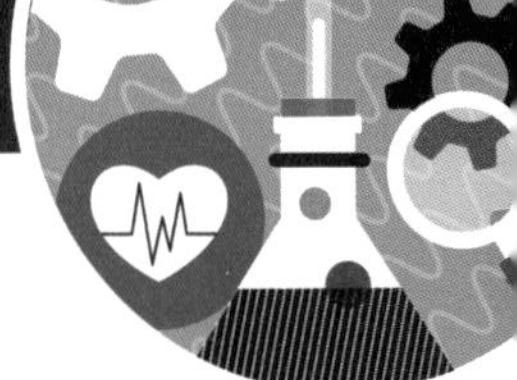

Using a transect

Quick quiz

Complete the sentences by circling the correct words in **bold**.

A transect is usually used to investigate a **gradual / sudden** change in the **distribution / size / shape** of species across a habitat.

Using a transect

Grade 5

1. **(a)** The steps below describe how to investigate the percentage cover of mosses from a footpath. Which step is incorrect? Tick **one** box. **[1 mark]**

Step 1: Lay a tape marked at set intervals from the footpath. ☐

Step 2: Place a quadrat next to 0 m and record percentage cover of moss. ☐

Step 3: Move the quadrat a random distance along the tape and repeat step 2. ☐

Step 4: Continue to repeat along the tape until the end is reached. ☐

(b) **Figure 1** shows a kite diagram of the results.

Describe the distribution of moss. **[3 marks]**

Moss was found between .... and

.... m

There was no moss found beyond ....

.... The most moss was found at .... m

....

The larger the shaded area on the diagram, the greater number of moss plants there were in the quadrat.

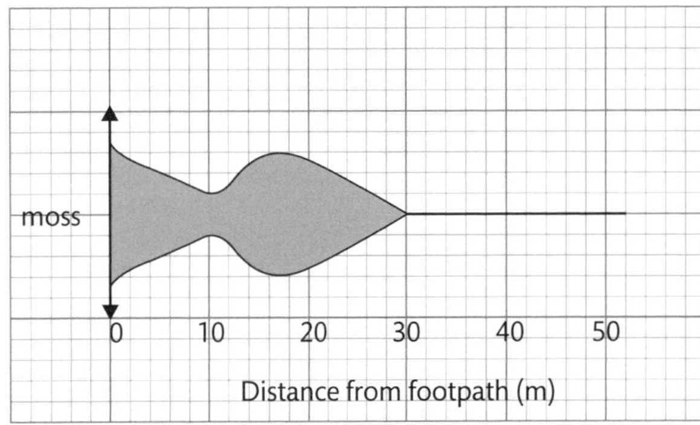

Figure 1

Investigating distribution

Grade 5

2. A transect was set from the base of a large tree. Students took quadrat measurements of the number of daisy plants every 2 m from the tree base. **Table 1** shows the results.

Table 1

Distance from tree base in m	0	2	4	6	8	10
Number of daisies in each quadrat	0	0	2	6	9	7

(a) Give the distance that had the most daisies. Include the unit. .... **[2 marks]**

(b) **Table 1** shows that the nearer to the tree, the fewer the daisies. One reason is that water affects the distribution of plants. Suggest and explain **one** other reason for fewer daisies between 0 m and 4 m. **[3 marks]**

....

....

Think about the abiotic factors that might affect the distribution of the daisies.

....

....

Cycling materials

Quick quiz

Does each process occur in the water cycle or the carbon cycle?

combustion	**water cycle / carbon cycle**
decomposition	**water cycle / carbon cycle**
evaporation	**water cycle / carbon cycle**

The water cycle

Grades 2–4

1. **Figure 1** shows part of the water cycle.

(a) Draw **one** line to match each letter in **Figure 1** with its process. **[2 marks]**

A		condensation
B		evaporation
C		precipitation

Think about the changes of state that are occurring in the water cycle.

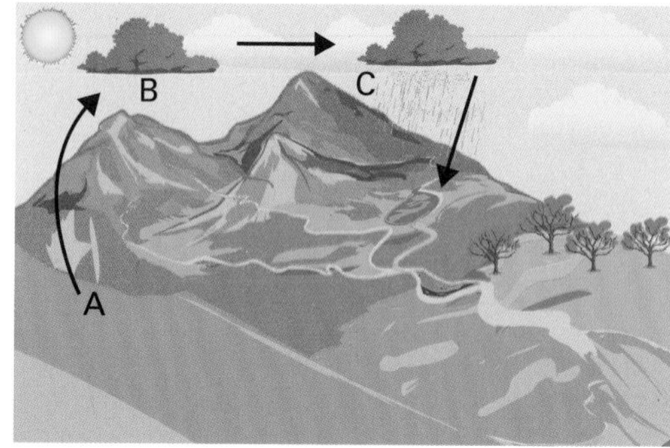

Figure 1

(b) Name **two** types of precipitation. **[2 marks]**

1 .... 2 ....

(c) Describe the movement of a water particle through a plant and then into the air. **[3 marks]**

The plant absorbs water from the ....

The water .... from the leaves of a plant into the ....

.... This is called ....

Exam focus

Make sure you know the correct scientific words for the processes in the water cycle and the carbon cycle.

The carbon cycle

Grade 4

2. (a) Answer each question by choosing words from the box.

photosynthesis	combustion	condensation	decomposition	evaporation	precipitation	respiration

(i) Name **one** process carried out by microorganisms. .... **[1 mark]**

(ii) Name **two** processes carried out by plants. **[2 marks]**

1 .... 2 ....

(iii) Name **two** processes that add carbon dioxide to the atmosphere. **[2 marks]**

1 .... 2 ....

(b) Deforestation is the destruction of forests and is increasing in some countries. Describe how deforestation affects the amount of carbon dioxide in the atmosphere. **[3 marks]**

....

....

....

Made a start

Feeling confident

Exam ready

Biodiversity

Quick quiz

What is the correct definition of the term 'biodiversity'?

Biodiversity is the number of organisms living in a habitat. ☐

Biodiversity is the variety of species within an ecosystem. ☐

Biodiversity is the number of animals in an ecosystem. ☐

Biodiversity is the number of plants in a habitat. ☐

Biodiversity — Grades 2–3

1. (a) Give **two** ways in which human activities are leading to a reduction in biodiversity. **[2 marks]**

1 .... 2 ....

(b) Complete **Table 1** by ticking the boxes to show whether the situations would increase or decrease biodiversity. **[2 marks]**

Table 1

Situation	Increase biodiversity	Decrease biodiversity
farmers planting hedgerows between fields		
farmers clearing forest to plant crops		
using a field to create a landfill site		
increase in plastic pollution in the ocean		

Comparing biodiversity — Grade 4

2. Table 2 shows the results from a quadrat survey of two different habitats.

Table 2

Species	Number of spiders in habitat A	Number of spiders in habitat B
A	0	2
B	3	3
C	8	0
D	1	0

(a) Give the number of species found in each habitat. **[1 mark]**

Habitat **A** .... Habitat **B** ....

(b) Which habitat has the most biodiversity. Give a reason for your answer. **[1 mark]**

....

Biodiversity and climate change — Grade 5

3. Figure 1 shows an Adélie penguin, which lives on the ice in Antarctica. The numbers of Adélie penguins and other species in Antarctica have been decreasing because of the effects of global warming. Suggest how biodiversity in Antarctica is affected by global warming. **[4 marks]**

As the temperature increases, the ice ....

Fish migrate so there is no ....

Areas for the penguins and other species to shelter ....

So the biodiversity ....

Figure 1

Waste management

2 Quick quiz

Write down three examples of waste substances.

1 .... 2 .... 3 ....

10 Pollution — Grades 2–4

1. Pollution can affect the water and the air.

(a) Name **two** sources of water pollution. **[2 marks]**

1 sewage .... 2 ....

(b) Name **two** types of air pollution. **[2 marks]**

1 smoke .... 2 ....

(c) Give **one** other area that pollution affects. .... **[1 mark]**

2. Describe how an increase in pollution can affect biodiversity. **[3 marks]**

Pollution .... habitats and .... animals and plants.

This leads to a .... in biodiversity.

Think about the direct effect pollution can have on organisms as well as the effect on the environment.

10 Recycling — Grades 4–5

3. Figure 1 shows a graph of the percentages of materials that are recycled in the UK.

(a) Which material is recycled the most? **[1 mark]**

....

(b) What percentage of paper is recycled? **[1 mark]**

....

(c) Explain why the amount of waste materials from households in the UK is increasing. **[2 marks]**

....

....

(d) Suggest why it is important to recycle waste materials. **[4 marks]**

....

....

....

....

Percentage recycled: 0, 10, 20, 30, 40, 50, 60, 70, 80, 90, 100

Type of recycled material: aluminium cans, paper, glass, plastic, cardboard

Figure 1

Exam focus
Look at the axes of the graph carefully so you know what the graph is showing you.

Where do materials end up if they are not recycled? Will this do to the environment and biodiversity?

What is happening to the population size of the UK and the standard of living?

 Made a start  Feeling confident  Exam ready

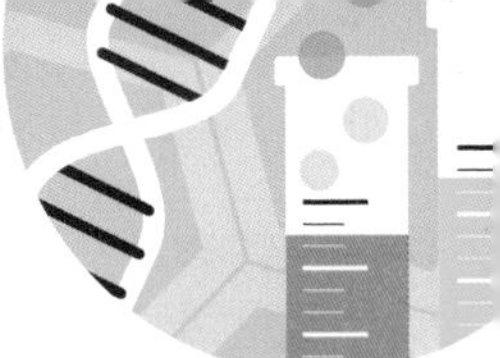

Land use

Quick quiz

Complete the sentences about land use by circling the correct words in **bold**.

The world's population is **increasing / decreasing**. We need to use **more / less** land for building and for **agriculture / conservation** to provide food. This produces more waste which causes **pollution / biodiversity**.

Peat bogs

Grade 4

1. Figure 1 shows a peat bog. Peat bogs are drained and the peat cut from the land.

(a) Peat was used for fuel. Explain another reason why peat bogs are destroyed by humans. **[2 marks]**

Peat bogs are destroyed so that peat can be used for ....

This is used for ....

Figure 1

(b) Describe how the destruction of peat bogs through being used for fuel and being left to decay can lead to global warming. **[4 marks]**

....

....

....

Think about the gas released when peat is burnt or decays.

Land use

Grades 4–5

2. Figure 2 shows a city. Building is an example of land use.

(a) Give **two** other examples of land use. **[2 marks]**

1 .... 2 ....

Think about where materials come from and what happens to the materials we don't need any more.

Figure 2

(b) Explain how an increase in human population may affect land use. **[6 marks]**

....

....

....

Think about how an increase in population would affect the amount of food we need to produce, the land we need for living and the amount of waste we produce.

....

....

....

....

Exam focus

Some of the marks in a six-mark question are for giving the answer in an ordered and logical way.

 Made a start  Feeling confident  Exam ready

Deforestation

2 Quick quiz

What is the best definition of the term 'deforestation'?

removal of a few trees on a small scale ☐

removal of trees on a large scale ☐

creation of protected nature reserves ☐

5 Deforestation — Grades 3–4

1. Give **three** reasons why large-scale deforestation may occur. **[3 marks]**

1 clearing land for housing .... 2 ....

3 ....

2. Which type of crop is mostly used to produce biofuel? Tick **one** box. **[1 mark]**

sugar-rich crops ☐ coffee ☐ rice ☐

15 Impacts of deforestation — Grades 4–5

3. Explain how deforestation can cause water pollution. **[3 marks]**

Tree roots anchor .... Lack of tree roots leads to ....

Silt enters .... which causes ....

4. **Figure 1** shows the total forest cover in South America between 1990 and 2010.

(a) Which year had the greatest total forest cover?
Tick **one** box. **[1 mark]**

1990 ☐ 2005 ☐ 2010 ☐

(b) Describe the trend shown in **Figure 1**. **[1 mark]**

....

(c) Explain the impact of deforestation on the animals living in these forests. **[3 marks]**

....

....

....

Forest cover in thousand km²: 9600, 9400, 9200, 9000, 8800, 8600, 8400, 8200
Year: 1990, 2005, 2010

Figure 1

Think about what will happen to the animals' habitat and food sources.

5. An area of forest is cleared for a cattle farm. Describe how this contributes to global warming. **[4 marks]**

....

....

....

....

Think about the process carried out by trees and how this affects the concentration of gases in the atmosphere.

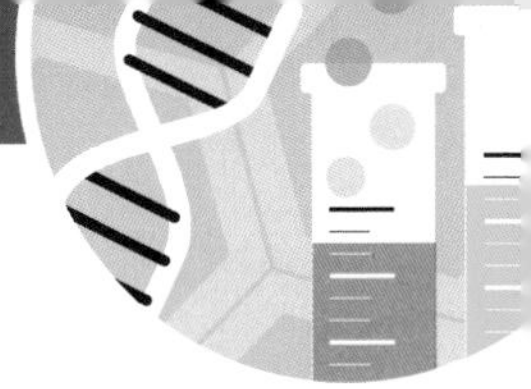

Global warming

2 Quick quiz

Which **two** gases in the atmosphere contribute to global warming?

carbon dioxide ☐ methane ☐

nitrogen ☐ oxygen ☐

10 Global warming and climate change

Grades 2–4

1. Define the term 'global warming'. **[1 mark]**

....

2. Changes in climate can cause earlier frosts than normal. How can an early frost affect plant reproduction? Tick **one** box. **[1 mark]**

Early frost increases the number of pests. ☐

Flowering plants can be damaged. ☐

Early frost causes drought so no water for the plants. ☐

3. Describe the effect of an increase in ocean temperature. **[4 marks]**

Increasing ocean temperature causes ice to .... and oceans to ....

Sea levels rise and this causes ....

Increasing ocean temperatures causes dissolved oxygen to ....

This causes organisms ....

Increasing ocean temperature affects sea level and the amount of dissolved oxygen.

10 Global warming and migration

Grades 4–5

4. Figure 1 shows the average distance that migratory birds moved north.

(a) Give the average distance that the birds moved north in 2000. Give the unit. **[2 marks]**

....

(b) Global warming can cause birds to migrate at different times to normal. Suggest and explain **one** problem that may be caused by early migration. **[2 marks]**

....

....

....

....

Average distance moved north in km: 80, 70, 60, 50, 40, 30, 20, 10, 0, −10, −20

Year: 1965, 1970, 1975, 1980, 1985, 1990, 1995, 2000, 2005, 2010, 2015

Figure 1

Maintaining biodiversity

2 Quick quiz

Are these statements true or false?

Deforestation increases biodiversity.	**True / False**
Breeding programmes can save species from extinction.	**True / False**
Recycling waste causes habitat loss.	**True / False**
Carbon dioxide is a gas that causes climate change.	**True / False**

10 Maintaining biodiversity — Grades 4–5

1. The governments in many countries have agreed to reduce the amount of carbon dioxide emissions their countries produce. Explain why governments want to reduce carbon dioxide emissions. **[2 marks]**

Carbon dioxide is .... and causes ....

.... and causes ....

2. A farmer wants to increase biodiversity on their farm.

State two ways the farmer could increase biodiversity. **[2 marks]**

Tick **two** boxes.

create larger fields ☐ grow only one type of crop ☐

plant hedgerows ☐ create field margins ☐ use pesticides ☐

Large monocultures reduce biodiversity. Monocultures are fields of one type of crop.

3. Describe how breeding programmes maintain biodiversity. **[3 marks]**

In breeding programmes, wild animals are bred in ....

This increases ....

The wild animals are then released ....

10 Conservation of gorillas — Grades 4–5

4. Table 1 shows the number of gorillas in a mountain area in Rwanda.

(a) Describe what happened to the number of gorillas between 1950 and 1980. **[1 mark]**

....

(b) Suggest possible reasons why the number of gorillas has been increasing since 1990. **[3 marks]**

....

....

....

Table 1

Year	Number of gorillas
1950	500
1960	500
1970	275
1980	250
1990	300
2000	350

Think about why the number of gorillas decreases. Think about what can be done to the environment to maintain gorilla numbers.

Exam focus

The command word 'suggest' means that you might not recall the answer to this question but you should be able to apply your knowledge to a new situation.

 Made a start  Feeling confident  Exam ready

Atoms, elements and compounds

2 Quick quiz

Match each word to its definition.

Word		Definition
atom		consists of two or more different elements chemically combined
element		the smallest part of an element that can exist
compound		made of only one type of atom

5 Elements and compounds — Grade 2

1. Use the periodic table (on page 274) to complete **Table 1**. **[2 marks]**

Table 1

Element name	Element symbol
	Na
bromine	
	Pb
iron	

2. Complete **Table 2** by placing a tick (✓) to identify each substance as an element or a compound. **[3 marks]**

Table 2

Substance	Element	Compound
oxygen	✓	
sodium chloride		
gold		
water		
aluminium		

10 Chemical equations and atoms — Grade 3

3. Magnesium reacts with oxygen to form magnesium oxide. Write the word equation for the reaction. **[1 mark]**

magnesium .... + ... → ....

4. The formula for methane is CH_4.

(a) Determine the number of different elements in a methane molecule. .... **[1 mark]**

Each symbol for an element begins with a capital letter.

(b) Determine the number of atoms in a methane molecule. .... **[1 mark]**

5 Reactions and compounds — Grade 3

5. What compound is produced when barium and chlorine react together? Tick **one** box. **[1 mark]**

chlorine baride ☐ barium chlorate ☐ chlorine barate ☐ barium chloride ☐

6. Hydrogen reacts with oxygen to form water, H_2O.

(a) Write the word equation for this reaction. **[1 mark]**

....

(b) Describe **two** features that the chemical formula H_2O shows about a water molecule. **[2 marks]**

....

....

Mixtures

Quick quiz

Match the component in the mixture to the best technique used to separate it out.

ethanol from a mixture of alcohols
water from coal slurry
salts from seawater
pure water from seawater
coloured substances from leaves, dissolved in ethanol

simple distillation
paper chromatography
filtration
fractional distillation
crystallisation

Crystallisation

Grade 4 

1. Define the term 'mixture'. **[1 mark]**

A mixture consists of two or more ....

2. Crystals can be obtained from solutions by crystallisation.

(a) Table 1 gives the steps for producing dry crystals by crystallisation. Write the numbers 1–5 to place the steps in the correct order, starting with 1. **[3 marks]**

Table 1

Step	Number
Heat the solution until about half of the water has evaporated.	
Allow the solution to cool down.	
Pour the solution into an evaporating basin.	1
Pat the crystals dry with a paper towel.	
Place the solution and basin on a tripod and gauze mat.	

(b) Suggest **one** safety precaution to take when carrying out crystallisation. **[1 mark]**

....

Separating mixtures

Grade 4 

3. A student collects a bucket of sand and seawater from the beach.

(a) Give a suitable method to separate the sand from the seawater. **[1 mark]**

....

(b) Explain how the method given in part **(a)** works. **[3 marks]**

....

....

....

(c) Describe how the student could produce pure water from seawater. **[2 marks]**

....

....

Made a start  Feeling confident Exam ready

The model of the atom

Quick quiz

Sort the events into the order in which they occurred, from earliest to latest, by numbering the boxes 1–4.

Chadwick proves that neutrons exist. ☐

Alpha particle scattering experiments lead to the nuclear model of the atom. ☐

Electrons are discovered. ☐

The plum pudding model of the atom is developed. ☐

Atomic models

Grade 4

1. Figure 1 shows two models for the structure of an atom.

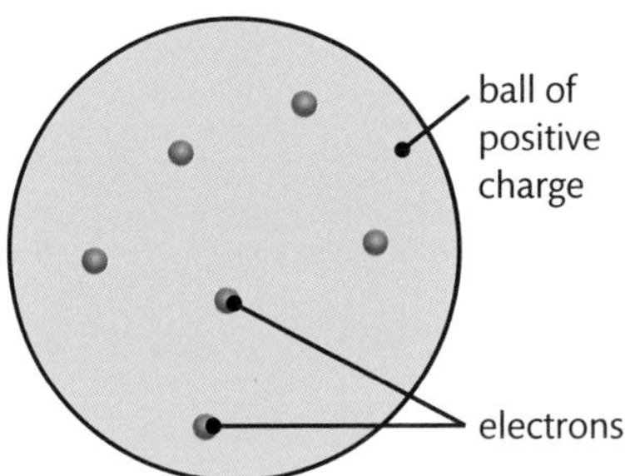

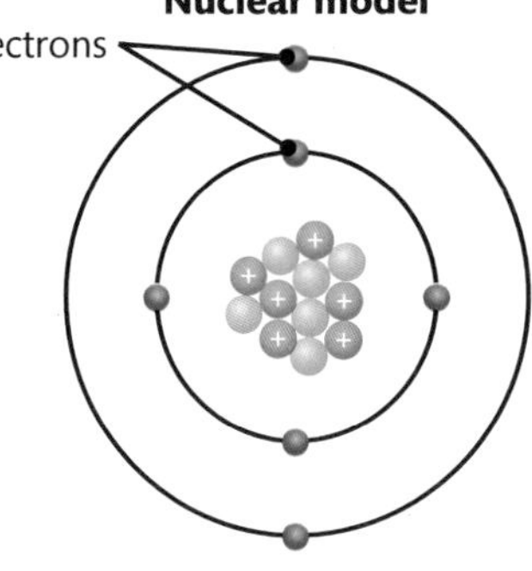

Figure 1

Table 1 shows different features. Complete the table by placing a tick (✓) in the box if the model has the feature. **[4 marks]**

Table 1

Feature	Plum pudding model	Nuclear model
Protons in a nucleus		✓
Contains electrons		
Contains positive charges		
Electrons at fixed distances		

Some rows will have two ticks in them.

2. (a) Name the scientist who suggested that electrons travel in circular orbits around the nucleus. **[1 mark]**

....

Give the scientist's full name or just their last name.

(b) Neutrons were discovered after the nuclear model had been accepted. Give the approximate number of years between these two events. **[1 mark]**

....

Evidence for the nuclear model

Grade 4

3. The plum pudding model was tested. Positively charged alpha particles were aimed at a thin sheet of gold foil. Draw **one** line from each observation to the correct conclusion. **[3 marks]**

Observation
Most alpha particles passed straight through.
Some alpha particles were defl ected.
A very small number of alpha particles were deflected backwards.

Conclusion
The nucleus has most of the atom's mass.
Most of the atom is empty space.
The nucleus is negatively charged.
The nucleus is positively charged.

Subatomic particles

2 Quick quiz

(a) What are the parts of the atom shown by labels **x**, **y** and **z**?

x = ...

y = ...

z = ...

(b) What is the part of the atom where **y** and **z** are located?

....

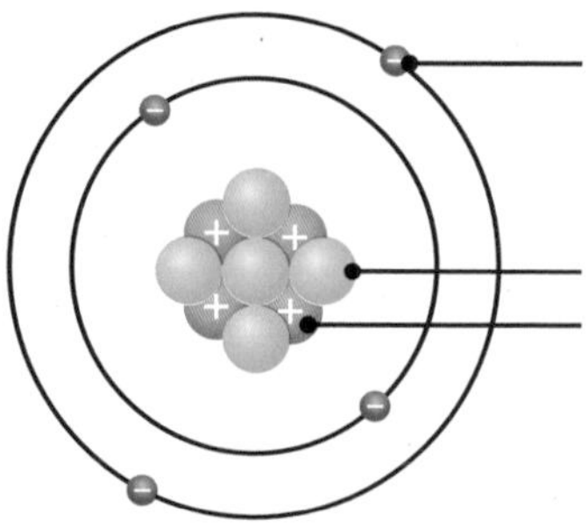

10 Subatomic particles — Grade 4

1. Complete **Table 1** to show the names of the three subatomic particles and their electrical charges. **[2 marks]**

Table 1

Name of subatomic particle	Electrical charge
proton	
	neutral

2. Name the subatomic particle that gives the element its atomic number. .... **[1 mark]**

3. Give a reason why atoms have no overall electrical charge. **[1 mark]**

They have equal numbers of .... and ....

4. Describe the location of electrons in an atom. **[2 marks]**

....

Think about the circles in diagrams of the atom. Name these circles and say where they are found.

10 Atomic structure — Grade 3

5. A carbon atom contains 6 protons and 6 neutrons. Give the atomic number of carbon. .... **[1 mark]**

6. A sodium atom contains 11 protons. Give the number of electrons in a sodium atom. .... **[1 mark]**

7. The radius of an atom is about 0.1 nm. What is the radius of an atom in m? Tick **one** box. **[1 mark]**

0.0001 m ☐

0.0000001 m ☐

0.0000000001 m ☐

0.0000000000001 m ☐

Made a start  Feeling confident  Exam ready

Size and mass of atoms

2 Quick quiz

Complete the table to show the relative mass of each subatomic particle.

Subatomic particle	Relative mass
proton	
neutron	
electron	

10 Atomic number and mass number — Grade 3

1. An atom of gold is represented by this symbol: $^{197}_{79}Au$

(a) Give the atomic number of this atom. .... **[1 mark]**

(b) Give the mass number of this atom. .... **[1 mark]**

(c) Calculate the number of neutrons in the nucleus of this atom. **[1 mark]**

number of neutrons = mass number – atomic number

2. Define the term 'mass number'. **[1 mark]**

Mass number is the sum of the protons and ....

3. The atomic number of magnesium is 12. The mass number of a magnesium atom is 25. Calculate the number of protons, neutrons and electrons in an atom of magnesium. **[3 marks]**

Protons .... Neutrons .... Electrons ....

4. There are 17 electrons in a chlorine atom. Calculate the number of electrons in a chloride ion, Cl^-. **[1 mark]**

Atoms gain electrons when they form negative ions.
Atoms lose electrons when they form positive ions.

10 Particle numbers — Grade 5

5. The atomic number of beryllium is 4. The mass number of a beryllium atom is 9. Calculate the number of protons and neutrons in an atom of beryllium. **[2 marks]**

Protons .... Neutrons ....

6. The atomic number of potassium is 19. The mass number of a potassium ion, K^+, is 39. Calculate the number of neutrons and electrons in a potassium ion. **[2 marks]**

Neutrons .... Electrons ....

 **Made a start** 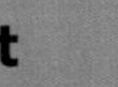 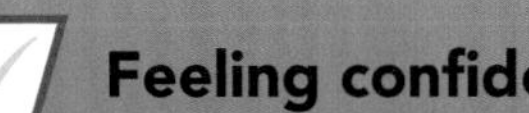 **Feeling confident**  **Exam ready**

Isotopes and relative atomic mass

2 Quick quiz

Which statements about isotopes of an element are correct?

They have the same mass number but a different atomic number. ☐

They have the same chemical properties. ☐

They have the same number of protons and neutrons, but a different number of electrons. ☐

They can have different percentage abundances. ☐

5 Isotopes — Grade 5

1. Which **two** atoms, A to D, in **Table 1** are isotopes of the same element? Tick **two** boxes. **[1 mark]**

Table 1

Atom	Number of protons	Number of electrons	Number of neutrons	
A	21	21	24	☐
B	10	10	10	☐
C	24	24	28	☐
D	10	10	12	☐

5 Calculating relative atomic mass — Grade 5

2. Table 2 shows the percentage abundances of two isotopes of copper.

Calculate the relative atomic mass of copper. Give your answer to 3 significant figures. **[3 marks]**

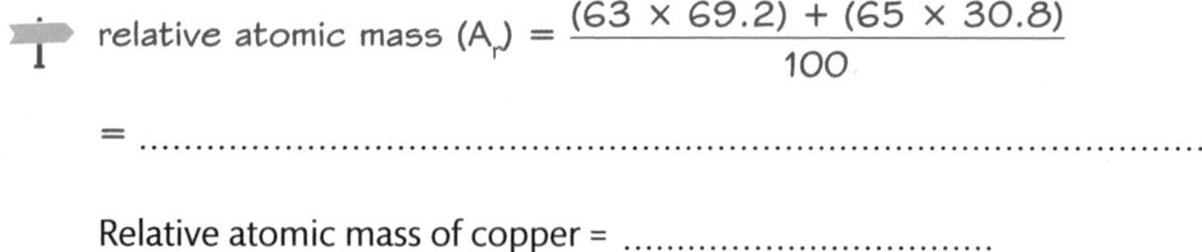

relative atomic mass (A_r) $= \frac{(63 \times 69.2) + (65 \times 30.8)}{100}$

= ....

Relative atomic mass of copper = ...

Table 2

Isotope	Percentage abundance
$^{63}_{29}Cu$	69.2%
$^{65}_{29}Cu$	30.8%

10 Isotopes and particles — Grade 5

3. One of the isotopes of helium is $^{3}_{2}He$.

(a) Give the number of each subatomic particle found in an atom of this isotope of helium. **[3 marks]**

....

(b) Suggest why the relative atomic mass of helium is shown as 4 on the periodic table. **[1 mark]**

....

Electronic structure

Quick quiz

Complete the table to show the maximum number of electrons that can occupy each electron shell.

Electron shell	Maximum number of electrons
first	
second	
third	

Electronic structure

Grade 5

1. (a) The electronic structure of a potassium atom is 2,8,8,1. Complete **Figure 1** to show this structure. **[1 mark]**

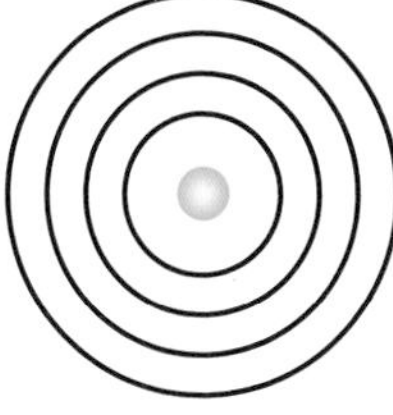

Figure 1

(b) Determine the number of electrons in an atom of potassium. Give a reason for your answer. **[2 marks]**

There are .... electrons, because this is equal to all the numbers in the electronic structure added together.

2. The electronic structure of helium is 2. The electronic structure of neon is 2,8.
Both elements are placed in Group 0. Describe what their electronic structures have in common. **[1 mark]**

....

Think about the number of electrons that each shell can hold.

3. Silicon atoms have 14 electrons.

(a) Silicon is placed in Group 4. Give the number of electrons in the outer shell of a silicon atom. .... **[1 mark]**

(b) Write the electronic structure of silicon. .... **[1 mark]**

Using electronic structure

Grade 5

4. Magnesium atoms have 12 electrons. The electronic structure for magnesium can be represented by **Figure 2**.

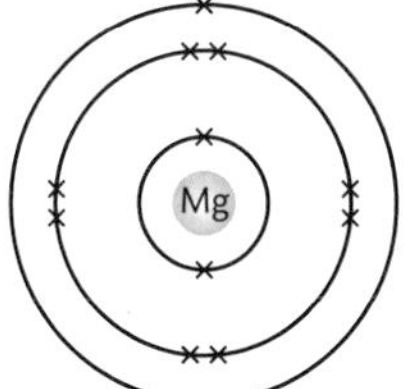

Figure 2

(a) Write the electronic structure of magnesium. **[1 mark]**

....

(b) Calcium atoms have 20 electrons. Draw a diagram to show the electronic structure for calcium. **[2 marks]**

The periodic table

2 Quick quiz

(a) Match the name to its group number.

alkali metals	Group 0
halogens	Group 1
noble gases	Group 7

(b) Which statements are correct?

Elements with similar properties occur at regular intervals in the periodic table. ☐

Hydrogen is often placed above helium in the periodic table. ☐

The position of an element in the periodic table lets you predict its possible reactions. ☐

5 Periodic table arrangement — Grades 3–4

1. The periodic table is a chart showing all the known elements.

(a) Name the vertical columns in the periodic table. **[1 mark]**

....

(b) Describe the order of the elements in the periodic table. **[2 marks]**

The elements are arranged in order of increasing ....

(c) Give a reason why the elements in a group have similar chemical properties. **[1 mark]**

....

Think about their electronic structures. What do they have in common?

5 Predicting reactions — Grade 4

2. Rubidium is an element in Group 1. Rubidium oxide dissolves in water to give an alkaline solution. Francium is also in Group 1. Predict whether francium oxide will form an acid or alkaline solution. Give a reason for your answer. **[2 marks]**

It will form an .... *solution because both elements are in Group 1. This means they have similar chemical* ....

10 Groups and periods — Grade 4

3. The electronic structure of an element is 2,4.

(a) Give its group number. **[1 mark]** ....

(b) Give its atomic number. **[1 mark]** ....

4. Element X is in Group 7. Its atoms have 17 electrons.

(a) Write the electronic structure of element X. **[1 mark]** ....

(b) Give the group number of an element with similar chemical properties to element X. **[1 mark]**

....

 Made a start  Feeling confident ☐ Exam ready

Developing the periodic table

Quick quiz

Are these statements about Mendeleev's work on the periodic table true or false?

He left gaps for undiscovered elements. **True / False**

He knew about isotopes of elements. **True / False**

He changed the order of some elements. **True / False**

He arranged the elements in order of increasing atomic number. **True / False**

Before Mendeleev

Grade 3

1. John Newlands developed an early version of the periodic table that contained groups of eight elements (**Figure 1**). He arranged the elements in order of increasing atomic weight.

H	Li	G	Bo	C	N	O
F	Na	Mg	Al	Si	P	S
Cl	K	Ca	Cr	Ti	Mn	Fe
Co, Ni	Cu	Zn	Y	In	As	Se
Br	Rb	Sr	Ce, La	Zr	Di, Mo	Ro, Ru
Pd	Ag	Cd	U	Sn	Sb	Te
I	Cs	Ba, V	Ta	W	Nb	Au
Pt, Ir	Os	Hg	Tl	Pb	Bi	Th

Figure 1

(a) Give the group in the modern periodic table that most closely resembles Newlands' right-hand column. **[1 mark]**

Which group in the modern periodic table begins with oxygen, O?

....

(b) Give **two** differences between the elements in this group and Newlands' column. **[2 marks]**

Polonium and some other elements are missing, but there are extra elements such as ....

....

Mendeleev's work

Grade 4

2. After Newlands published his table, Mendeleev developed a more successful periodic table.

(a) Describe how Mendeleev first ordered the elements in his table. **[1 mark]**

Newlands used the same way to order the elements.

....

(b) Give **two** ways in which Mendeleev's table overcame some of the problems of earlier tables. **[2 marks]**

Mendeleev changed the order of some elements, and he left ....

....

Explaining Mendeleev's table

Grade 4

3. (a) Give a reason why Mendeleev changed the order of some elements in his periodic table. **[1 mark]**

....

(b) Describe how Mendeleev was able to predict the existence of elements that were not discovered at that time. **[2 marks]**

....

....

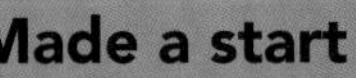

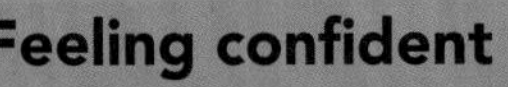

Made a start | Feeling confident | Exam ready

Metals and non-metals

Quick quiz

Where are metals and non-metals found in the periodic table? Place **two** ticks in each row of the table.

	On the left	On the right	Towards the top	Towards the bottom
metals				
non-metals				

Properties of metals and non-metals

Grade 3 

1. Metals and non-metals have different properties. Complete **Table 1** by placing a tick in each row to show whether the property belongs to metals or non-metals. **[3 marks]**

Table 1

Property	Metals	Non-metals
poor conductor of electricity		
good conductor of heat		
strong		
brittle when solid		
shiny		
 malleable when solid	✓	

Elements, ions and electrons

Grade 5 

2. Metals and non-metals form ions when they react together. Describe the difference between the ions formed by metals and the ions formed by non-metals. **[2 marks]**

> Decide whether negatively charged ions or positively charged ions are formed in each case.

 Metals lose electrons to form ....

Non-metals gain electrons to form ....

3. Elements with fewer than four electrons in their outer shell are metals. This is true for most of the elements in the first three rows of the periodic table.

(a) An element has the electronic structure 2,8,3. Determine whether this element is a metal or a non-metal. Give a reason for your answer. **[1 mark]**

....

(b) Helium has the electronic structure 2. Explain why this is unusual. **[2 marks]**

> Is helium a metal or a non-metal? What information about electronic structures are you given in the question?

....

....

Unusual non-metals

Grade 5 

4. Graphite is a form of carbon, a non-metal. It is brittle, conducts electricity and boils at about 4000 °C. Describe **two** ways in which graphite is unusual. **[2 marks]**

....

....

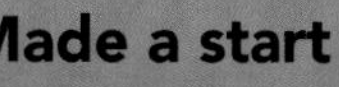 Made a start  Feeling confident 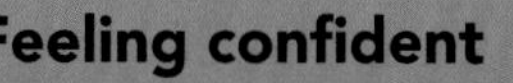  Exam ready

Group 0

2 Quick quiz

Which statement(s) are correct?

The number of atoms in each molecule increases as you go down Group 0. ☐

The size of the atoms increases as you go down Group 0. ☐

The relative atomic mass decreases as you go down Group 0. ☐

5 Trends in properties of Group 0 — Grades 3–4

1. Table 1 gives information about some of the noble gases.

Table 1

Noble gas	Relative atomic mass	Melting point in °C	Boiling point in °C
helium	4	−272	−269
neon	20	−248	−246
argon	40	−190	
krypton	84	−157	−153

Estimate the melting and boiling point for argon. Write your answers in **Table 1**. **[2 marks]**

10 Chemical properties of Group 0 — Grade 5

2. The electronic structures of neon and argon are 2,8 (neon) and 2,8,8 (argon).

(a) Describe what these two electronic structures have in common. **[2 marks]**

They both have eight electrons in their outer shells, so they both have ……………………

(b) The electronic structure of helium is 2. Give **one** way in which this differs from the electronic structures of neon and argon. **[1 mark]**

……………………………………………………………………………………

(c) Give **one** way in which the electronic structures of helium, neon and argon are similar. **[1 mark]**

……………………………………………………………………………………

5 Unreactive elements — Grade 5

3. The noble gases are unreactive and do not easily form molecules.

(a) Give a reason why the noble gases are unreactive. Answer in terms of their electronic structures. **[1 mark]**

……………………………………………………………………………………

(b) Molecules form when atoms share electrons. Explain why the noble gases do not easily form molecules. **[2 marks]**

……………………………………………………………………………………

……………………………………………………………………………………

Group 1

2 Quick quiz

(a) Are the Group 1 elements metals or non-metals? ....

(b) Name **two** Group 1 elements, other than lithium. ....

(c) What is the common name for Group 1? ....

10 Reactions of Group 1 elements — Grades 3–4

1. When the Group 1 elements react with water, an alkaline solution and a gas are produced.

(a) Which **two** statements about the reactions of lithium, sodium and potassium with water are correct?

Tick two boxes. **[2 marks]**

They all sink in the water. ☐

They all produce an orange flame. ☐

They all fizz in the water. ☐

They all explode at the end of the reaction. ☐

The water turns universal indicator purple after all the reactions. ☐

(b) Give a word equation to show the reaction of potassium and water. **[1 mark]**

potassium + water → potassium hydroxide + ...

2. Lithium reacts with oxygen to produce lithium oxide.

(a) Write a word equation for this reaction. **[1 mark]**

....

(b) Give the colour of the flame that is seen during the reaction. **[1 mark]**

....

Group 1 metals burn with coloured flames, such as lilac, red or yellow–orange.

5 Trends in reactivity — Grade 5

3. The electronic structures of lithium and sodium are 2,1 (lithium) and 2,8,1 (sodium).

(a) Describe what these two electronic structures have in common. **[1 mark]**

Their outer shells both ....

(b) Group 1 elements form ions when they react. Give the charge on the ions they form. **[1 mark]**

....

(c) Describe how the reactivity of the Group 1 elements changes in the group. **[2 marks]**

....

....

Work out whether the ions will be positive or negative, and how many charges they will have.

Group 7

2 Quick quiz

(a) Are the Group 7 elements metals or non-metals? ....

(b) Name **two** Group 7 elements, other than fluorine. ....

(c) What is the common name for Group 7? ....

10 Properties of Group 7 — Grade 3

1. Which **two** statements about the properties of Group 7 elements are correct? Tick **two** boxes. **[2 marks]**

They have low melting and boiling points. ☐

They form colourless vapours. ☐

They exist as molecules with pairs of atoms. ☐

They are good conductors of electricity. ☐

They are easily worked when solid. ☐

5 Trends in reactivity — Grade 5

2. The electronic structures of fluorine and chlorine are: 2,7 (fluorine) and 2,8,7 (chlorine).

(a) Describe what these two electronic structures have in common. **[1 mark]**

Their outer shells both ....

(b) Group 7 elements form ions when they react. Give the charge on the ions they form. **[1 mark]**

....

Work out whether the ions will be positive or negative, and how many charges they will have.

(c) Describe how the reactivity of the Group 7 elements changes down the group. **[1 mark]**

....

5 Displacement reactions — Grade 5

3. A student investigates the reactivity of three Group 7 elements (**X**, **Y** and **Z**). Each element is mixed with solutions of their salts. **Table 1** shows the results. A cross means that there is no visible reaction.

Table 1

Element	Potassium bromide	Potassium iodide	Potassium chloride
X	×	reaction	×
Y	×	×	×
Z	reaction	reaction	×

Use the results to determine the order of reactivity of the three elements (**X**, **Y** and **Z**), starting with the most reactive. **[2 marks]**

....

....

Chemical bonds

Quick quiz

Which statements are true?

Ionic bonding occurs between a metal and a non-metal element. ☐

Two types of metal are needed to form a metallic bond. ☐

Covalent bonding involves transfer of electrons. ☐

Metallic bonding and ionic bonding both involve delocalised electrons. ☐

Covalent bonds form in non-metals only. ☐

Types of bonding

Grade 4

1. (a) Describe what a covalent bond is. **[1 mark]**

A bond formed when two atoms share a pair of ....

(b) Water is a compound of hydrogen and oxygen. Explain how you know that it must contain covalent bonds. **[2 marks]**

Both hydrogen and oxygen are non-metals and so can only ....

2. Some elements react together to form compounds containing ionic bonds. Other elements form compounds that contain covalent bonds. Complete **Table 1** by placing a tick to show the type of bond in each compound. **[2 marks]**

Table 1

		Type of bond	
Compound	**Made from**	**Ionic**	**Covalent**
water	hydrogen + oxygen		✓
carbon dioxide	carbon + oxygen		
sodium chloride	sodium + chlorine	✓	
iron sulfide	iron + sulfur		
methane	carbon + hydrogen		
magnesium oxide	magnesium + oxygen		

Compounds made from a metal and a non-metal contain ionic bonds.

3. Complete the sentence about metallic bonding. Use words from the box. **[3 marks]**

attraction	electrons	an electrostatic	ions	a magnetic	repulsion

Metallic bonding is .... force of .... between atoms and delocalised ....

Ionic and metallic bonding

Grade 5

4. Sodium chloride contains ionic bonds. Describe ionic bonding. **[2 marks]**

....

....

5. Brass is an alloy of zinc and copper. Describe the bonding present in this alloy. **[2 marks]**

....

....

 Made a start  Feeling confident ☐ Exam ready

Ionic bonding

2 Quick quiz

Give the symbol for the ion that each element forms. (For example, lithium forms Li^+.)

magnesium .... oxygen .... sodium ....

aluminium .... fluorine .... calcium ....

5 Forming ions — Grade 4

1. Metals and non-metals form ions when they react together.

(a) Which statement about the formation of ions is correct? Tick **one** box. **[1 mark]**

Metals lose electrons to form negative ions. ☐

Metals gain electrons to form positive ions. ☐

Non-metals lose electrons to form positive ions. ☐

Non-metals gain electrons to form negative ions. ☐

(b) The charge on the ions produced by elements in Groups 1, 2, 6 and 7 are related to the group number. Complete **Table 1** to show the charges on the ions formed by elements in each group. **[4 marks]**

Table 1

Group number	1	2	6	7
Charge on ions formed	1+			

5 Ionic compounds — Grade 5

2. Lithium reacts with chlorine to form lithium chloride. Draw dot and cross diagrams to show the ions in lithium chloride. **[2 marks]**

[ ] [ ]

Lithium is in Group 1 and chlorine is in Group 7.

10 Forming an ionic compound — Grade 5

3. Magnesium reacts with oxygen to form magnesium oxide. Describe how magnesium ions and oxide ions form in this reaction. **[3 marks]**

Magnesium ions, Mg^{2+} ....

....

Oxide ions, O^{2-} ....

....

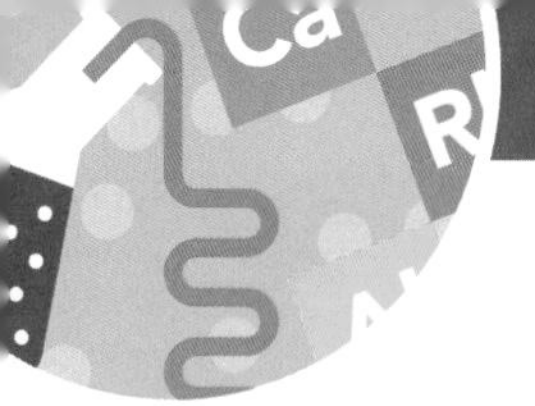

Ionic compounds

2 Quick quiz

Name **four** different ways of drawing the structure of ionic compounds.

....

....

15 Representing ionic compounds — Grade 5

1. Calcium sulfide is an ionic compound of calcium and sulfur. It has a similar structure to sodium chloride. **Figure 1** is a two-dimensional diagram that represents the structure of calcium sulfide.

(a) What type of structure does calcium sulfide have? Tick **one** box. **[1 mark]**

giant ☐

metallic ☐

molecular ☐

simple ☐

Figure 1

(b) Name what the labelled circles represent. **[1 mark]**

....

(c) Describe ionic bonding. **[2 marks]**

It is strong electrostatic forces of attraction between ....

(d) Determine the empirical formula of calcium sulfide. **[2 marks]**

....

....

Count the number of positively charged particles and the number of negatively charged particles in **Figure 1**. Find the simplest whole number ratio of these numbers.

2. Three-dimensional diagrams can be used to represent the structure of an ionic compound. Give **one** advantage and **one** disadvantage of using these diagrams. **[2 marks]**

Advantage ....

Disadvantage ....

5 Ball and stick vs dot and cross — Grade 5

3. Ionic compounds can be represented by ball and stick diagrams and by dot and cross diagrams.

(a) Give **one** limitation of a ball and stick diagram. **[1 mark]**

....

(b) Give **one** limitation of a dot and cross diagram. **[1 mark]**

....

☐ Made a start  ☐ Feeling confident  ☐ Exam ready

Covalent bonding

2 Quick quiz

Choose the correct options. There may be more than one correct answer.

(a) Chemical bonding involves:

electrons ☐
protons ☐
neutrons ☐

(b) Covalent bonds form in:

metals ☐
small molecules ☐
polymers ☐
giant covalent structures ☐

5 Forming covalent bonds — Grade 4

1. (a) What is a covalent bond? Tick **one** box. **[1 mark]**

a bond formed by swapping of electrons ☐
a bond formed between a metal and a non-metal ☐
a bond formed by a shared pair of atoms ☐
a bond formed by a shared pair of electrons ☐

(b) Identify the electron shell that is involved in covalent bonding. **[1 mark]**

....

Is it the inner shell, the outer shell, or some other shell?

(c) Hydrogen atoms can form one covalent bond. The number of bonds that other atoms can form is related to the group number. **Table 1** shows some examples.

Table 1

Group number	4	5	6	7
Example element	carbon	nitrogen	oxygen	chlorine
Number of covalent bonds	4	3	2	1

Describe the relationship between the group number and the number of covalent bonds. **[1 mark]**

The number of bonds equals eight minus ....

10 Representing covalent bonds — Grade 5

2. Draw a dot and cross diagram of the electron arrangement in a chlorine molecule. **[2 marks]**

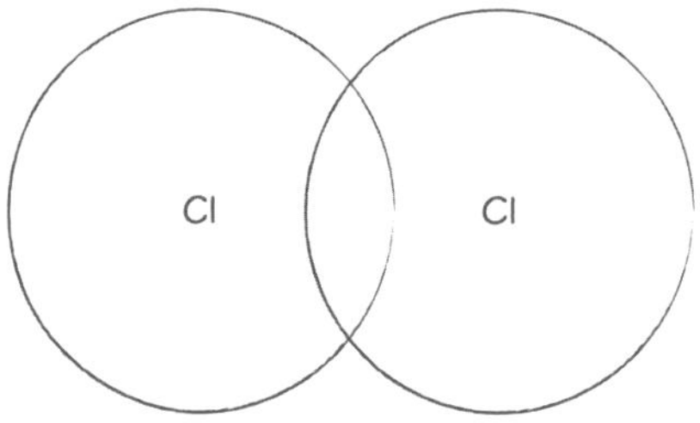

Cl Cl

Exam focus

Remember you only need to draw the outer shell of electrons for covalent bonding diagrams.

3. Draw a dot and cross diagram to show the bonding in a molecule of water, H_2O. **[2 marks]**

Metallic bonding

2 Quick quiz

(a) Label the diagram to show an electron and a metal ion.

(b) What charge do the electrons have? ....

15 Describing metallic bonding — Grade 4

1. Describe how the electrons are arranged in a metal. **[1 mark]**

Look at the diagram at the top of the page.

....

2. (a) Name the main type of force of attraction between the particles in metals. Tick **one** box. **[1 mark]**

- magnetic ☐
- electrostatic ☐
- gravitational ☐
- contact ☐

(b) Give the charge of a metal ion. **[1 mark]**

positive ....

3. Give **two** features of 'delocalised' electrons. Tick **two** boxes. **[2 marks]**

- They are not free to move in an atom. ☐
- They are free to move between atoms. ☐
- They are free to move in the outer shells of atoms. ☐
- They are in fixed positions in an atom. ☐

4. Suggest why metals have high boiling points. **[1 mark]**

Think about the strength of metallic bonding.

....

5 Metallic bonding — Grade 4

5. In a metal, positively charged nuclei are attracted to negatively charged particles. Name these negatively charged particles. **[1 mark]**

....

6. Describe the structure of a metal in the solid state. **[2 marks]**

Is the structure random or regular, giant or simple?

....

....

Made a start  Feeling confident Exam ready

States of matter

2 Quick quiz

(a) Name the **three** states of matter.

....

(b) What **two** state changes can happen at the melting point? Underline the correct words.

freezing boiling condensing melting

10 The particle model — Grade 3

1. Figure 1 shows particles of the same substance in three states of matter.

gas liquid solid

Figure 1

(a) Complete **Table 1** to show the closeness and arrangement of particles in each state of matter. Place a tick (✓) in each correct box. **[3 marks]**

Table 1

	Closeness		Arrangement	
	Close together	**Far apart**	**Regular**	**Random**
solid				
liquid	✓			
gas				

(b) Complete the sentences. Use words from the box. **[3 marks]**

gas	liquid	solid	slowly	quickly	two	all

Particles can only vibrate in fixed positions in a ....

In a gas, particles move .... in .... directions.

5 Change of state — Grade 4

2. Describe how the boiling point of a substance depends on the forces between its particles. **[2 marks]**

As the strength of the forces increase, the boiling point ....

3. The melting point of gallium is 30 °C and its boiling point is 2200 °C. Give the state of gallium at 100 °C. **[1 mark]**

....

2 State symbols — Grade 3

4. (a) Identify the states of matter represented by the state symbols below. **[3 marks]**

(s) .... (l) .... (g) ....

(b) Give the state symbol used in chemical equations to represent an aqueous solution. .... **[1 mark]**

Made a start Feeling confident Exam ready

Properties of ionic compounds

2 Quick quiz

Which of these are ionic compounds?

sodium chloride	☐	magnesium oxide	☐	diamond	☐
water	☐	aluminium	☐	copper sulfate	☐

5 Structure and bonding — Grade 4

1. (a) How are the ions arranged in an ionic compound? Tick **one** box. **[1 mark]**

in a giant structure with a regular pattern ☐

in a giant structure with a random pattern ☐

in a simple structure with a regular pattern ☐

in a simple structure with a random pattern ☐

(b) Complete the sentence about ionic bonding. Use words from the box. **[3 marks]**

atoms	electrons	electrostatic	ions	oppositely	same

Ionic bonding is the electrostatic force of attraction in all directions between .... charged

....

10 Conducting electricity — Grades 3–4

2. Ionic compounds are able to conduct electricity when dissolved in water or molten.

Give a reason why ionic compounds are able to conduct electricity in these conditions. **[1 mark]**

....

3. Sodium chloride conducts electricity when it is dissolved in water but not when it is solid. Describe an experiment to show this. You are given a battery, a beaker, wires and a lamp. You may draw a simple diagram to help your answer. **[4 marks]**

> **Exam focus**
> You may need to link topics together to answer a question. This one also relates to electrolysis of solutions.

....

....

....

....

....

....

Made a start  Feeling confident  Exam ready

Properties of small molecules

2 Quick quiz

Which of these substances consists of small molecules?

sodium chloride	☐	sodium	☐
water	☐	diamond	☐
chlorine	☐	methane	☐

15 Melting and boiling points

Grade 4

1. (a) Which statement in **Table 1** about the melting points and forces in substances that consist of small molecules is correct?
Tick **one** box. **[1 mark]**

Table 1

Melting points	Forces	
low	strong	☐
low	weak	☐
high	strong	☐
high	weak	☐

(b) Bromine is a substance that consists of small molecules. Which forces are overcome when bromine boils?
Tick **one** box. **[1 mark]**

covalent ☐

intermolecular ☐

ionic ☐

metallic ☐

2. Table 2 shows the relative formula mass and boiling point of some elements in Group 7.

Table 2

Name	Relative formula mass	Boiling point in °C
fluorine	38	−188
chlorine	71	−34
bromine	160	59
iodine	254	184

For a negative value, the larger the number the lower the value.

(a) Name the element in **Table 2** that has the lowest boiling point. **[1 mark]**

....

(b) Name the element in **Table 2** that has the strongest intermolecular forces. .... **[1 mark]**

(c) Describe how the relative formula mass affects the boiling point. **[2 marks]**

As the relative formula mass increases ....

....

5 Conducting electricity

Grade 4

3. Explain why substances that consist of small molecules do not conduct electricity. **[2 marks]**

....

....

Polymers

1 Quick quiz

Match the polymer to its monomer.

Monomer
ethene
tetrafluoroethene
chloroethene

Polymer
poly(chloroethene)
poly(ethene)
poly(tetrafluoroethene)

10 Recognising polymers — Grade 4

1. Figure 1 shows part of a polymer molecule.

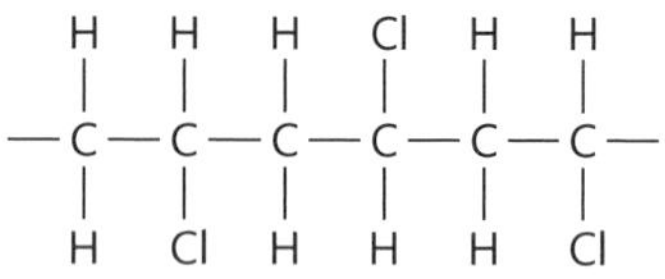

(a) Give a reason why **Figure 1** only shows part of the molecule. **[1 mark]**

....

(b) Name the type of bond between the atoms in **Figure 1**. **[1 mark]**

....

```
   H   H   H   Cl  H   H
   |   |   |   |   |   |
 — C — C — C — C — C — C —
   |   |   |   |   |   |
   H   Cl  H   H   H   Cl
```

Figure 1

(c) Polymers are solids at room temperature. Describe what this shows about the strength of the bonds between the polymer molecules. **[1 mark]**

....

Types of bond include ionic bonds, covalent bonds and metallic bonds.

2. Figure 2 shows part of the same polymer molecule shown in **Figure 1**, and the substance that the polymer is made from. The part in brackets is called the repeat unit.

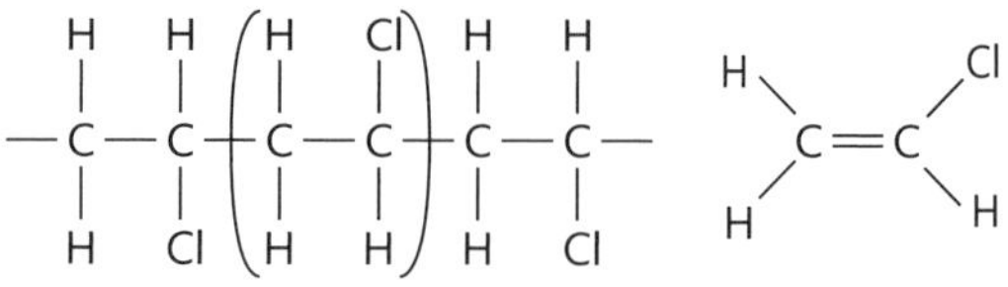

```
   H   H  (H   Cl)  H   H          H       Cl
   |   |   |   |    |   |           \     /
 — C — C — C — C —  C — C —          C = C
   |   |   |   |    |   |           /     \
   H   Cl (H   H)   H   Cl         H       H
```

Figure 2

(a) Give **two** similarities between the repeat unit and the substance the polymer is made from. **[2 marks]**

Both have three hydrogen atoms and one ....

(b) Give **one** difference between the repeat unit and the substance the polymer is made from. **[1 mark]**

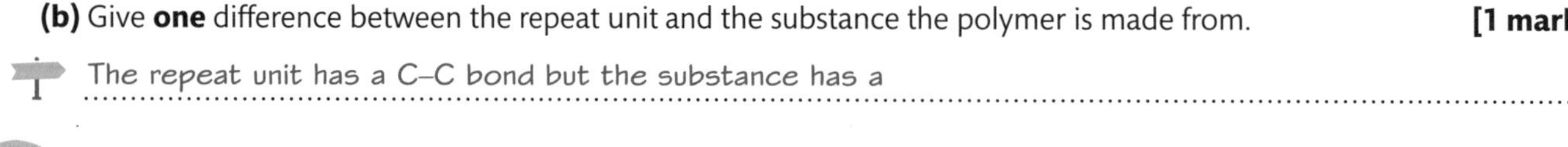

The repeat unit has a C–C bond but the substance has a ....

10 Identifying polymers — Grade 5

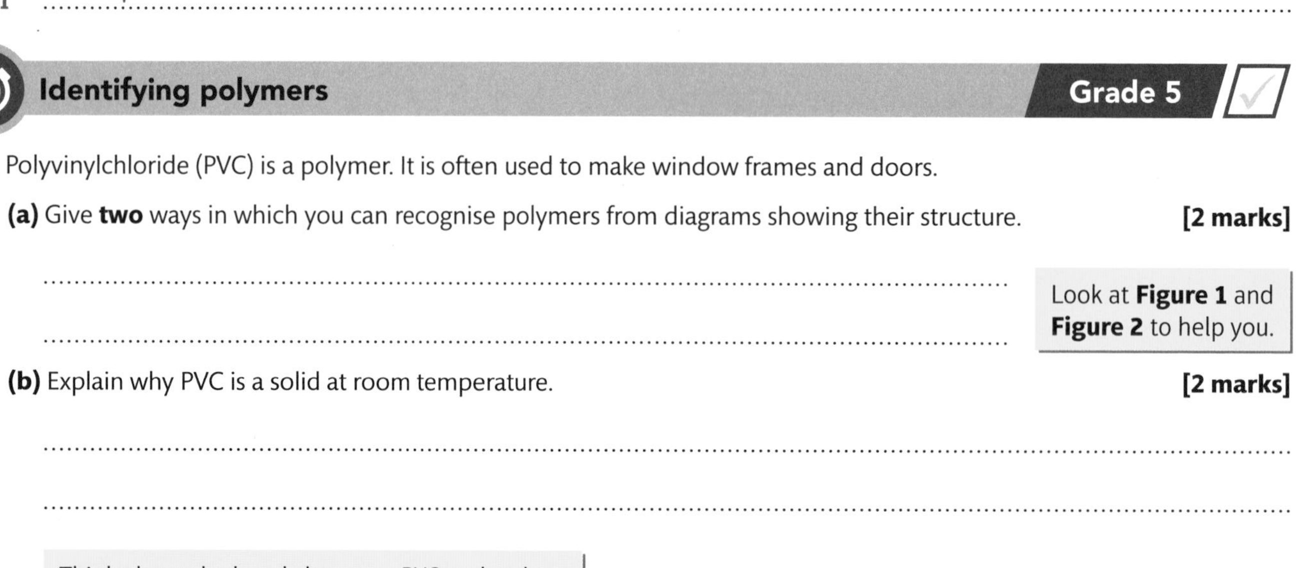

3. Polyvinylchloride (PVC) is a polymer. It is often used to make window frames and doors.

(a) Give **two** ways in which you can recognise polymers from diagrams showing their structure. **[2 marks]**

....

....

Look at **Figure 1** and **Figure 2** to help you.

(b) Explain why PVC is a solid at room temperature. **[2 marks]**

....

....

Think about the bonds between PVC molecules and whether these are easily broken.

 Made a start  Feeling confident  Exam ready

Giant covalent structures

Quick quiz

Label the diagrams to show whether these molecules have a giant covalent structure or are small molecules.

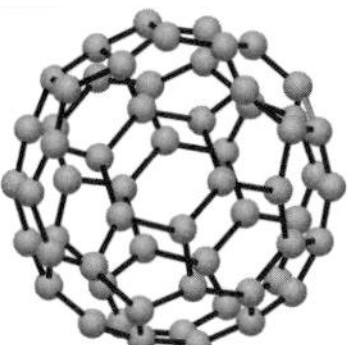

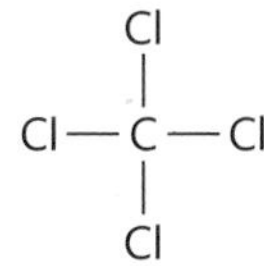

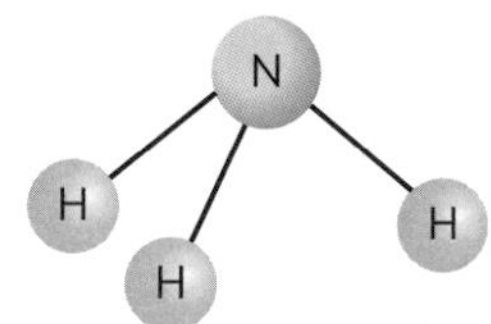

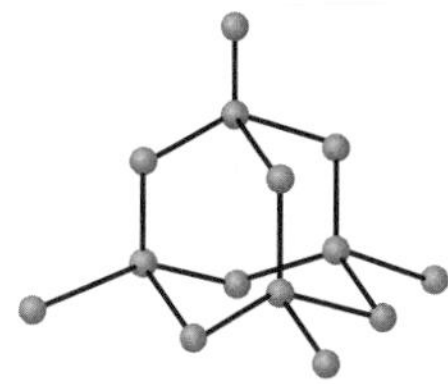

Silicon dioxide

Grade 4

1. Sand contains silica (silicon dioxide). Silica is a compound of two non-metals, silicon and oxygen.

> Types of bond include ionic bonds, covalent bonds and metallic bonds.

(a) Name the type of bond that forms between two non-metal elements. **[1 mark]**

....

(b) **Figure 1** shows part of the structure of silica.

How are the atoms arranged in silica? Tick **one** box. **[1 mark]**

- in a giant structure with a regular pattern ☐
- in a giant structure with a random pattern ☐
- in a simple structure with a regular pattern ☐
- in a simple structure with a random pattern ☐

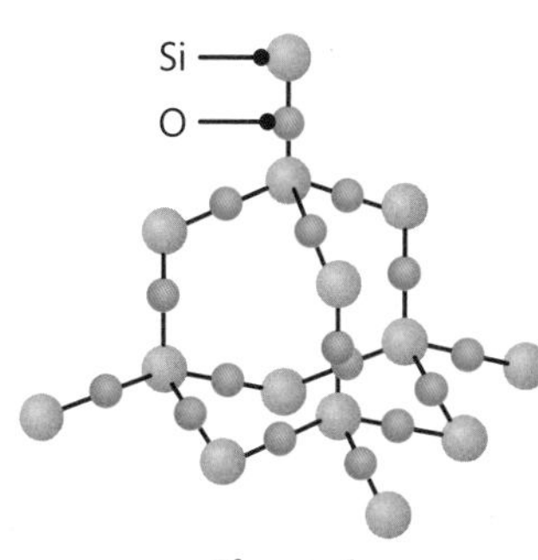

Figure 1

(c) Explain why silica does **not** conduct electricity. **[2 marks]**

To conduct electricity, a substance needs charged particles that can move about, but

....

Other giant covalent structures

Grade 5

2. Diamond is a form of carbon. **Figure 2** shows part of the structure of diamond. It is similar to the structure of silica.

(a) Describe the structure and bonding in diamond. **[3 marks]**

....

....

....

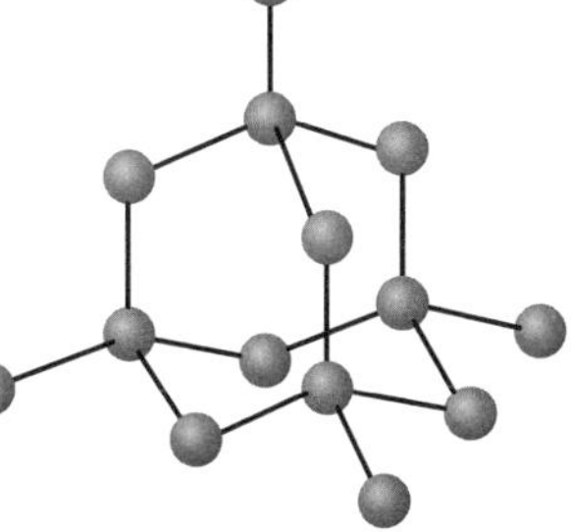

Figure 2

(b) Predict **two** physical properties that you would expect diamond to have, based on its structure and bonding. **[2 marks]**

....

....

Properties of metals and alloys

2 Quick quiz

What is an alloy?

- A compound of a metal and a non-metal ☐
- A mixture of at least one metal and another element ☐
- A mixture of non-metals ☐
- A compound of two metals ☐

10 Properties of alloys and metals — Grade 4

1. Which statement in **Table 1** about the melting point and bonding in metals is correct? Tick **one** box. **[1 mark]**

Table 1

Melting points	Bonding	
low	strong	☐
low	weak	☐
high	strong	☐
high	weak	☐

2. Figure 1 shows the arrangement of particles in a pure metal.

When a force is applied to a metal, it may bend without breaking.
Describe what happens to the metal atoms when a metal bends. **[2 marks]**

The layers of atoms ....

Figure 1

3. Figure 2 shows the arrangement of particles in an alloy.

(a) Describe what you notice about the sizes of the atoms in the alloy shown in **Figure 2**. **[1 mark]**

....

Figure 2

(b) Compare the arrangement of atoms in **Figure 1** with the arrangement of atoms in **Figure 2**. **[1 mark]**

What is different?

....

10 Alloys — Grade 5

4. Explain why alloys are harder than the pure metals they are made from. In your answer, refer to the size of the atoms and how this affects the layers in an alloy. **[2 marks]**

....

....

5. 5p and 10p coins in the UK used to be made from an alloy called cupro-nickel. Suggest why an alloy was used rather than a pure metal. **[1 mark]**

....

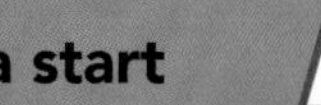 Made a start  Feeling confident  Exam ready

Metals as conductors

2 Quick quiz

Draw and label a diagram to show the arrangement of particles in a metal.

10 Metallic structure — Grade 4

1. Metals consist of atoms with delocalised electrons.

(a) Give the charge carried by an electron. **[1 mark]**

> Particles can be negative, neutral or positive.

....

(b) What does 'delocalised' mean? Tick **one** box. **[1 mark]**

Electrons are in fixed positions in an atom. ☐

Electrons are free to move in an atom. ☐

Electrons are free to move in an inner shell. ☐

Electrons are free to move between atoms. ☐

(c) Describe the arrangement of atoms in a metal in the solid state. **[2 marks]**

They are in a giant structure with a ....

....

5 Conducting thermal energy — Grade 4

2. (a) A solid is heated without melting it. Describe what happens to the particles in this solid. **[1 mark]**

> Remember that particles vibrate about a fixed position in solids.

....

(b) When a metal is heated, energy is transferred to the delocalised electrons. Describe what will happen to these delocalised electrons. **[1 mark]**

> Remember that delocalised electrons can move through the structure of a metal.

....

(c) Suggest what happens to some of the energy stored in moving electrons when they collide with atoms. **[1 mark]**

....

5 Conducting electricity — Grade 4

3. Explain why metals are good conductors of electricity. **[2 marks]**

....

....

 Made a start  Feeling confident Exam ready

Diamond

1 Quick quiz

Give **two** uses of diamond.

....

10 Structure and bonding in diamond — Grade 4

1. Diamond is a form of carbon. **Figure 1** shows part of the structure of diamond.

(a) How many bonds can a carbon atom form? Tick **one** box. **[1 mark]**

1 ☐ 2 ☐ 3 ☐ 4 ☐

(b) Name the type of bond present in diamond. **[1 mark]**

....

(c) Complete the sentence about diamond. Use words from the box. **[2 marks]**

giant	random	regular	small

The atoms in diamond have a .... structure with a .... arrangement.

Figure 1

Types of bond include ionic bonds, covalent bonds and metallic bonds.

5 Properties of diamond — Grade 4

2. Which statement in **Table 1** about the boiling point and bonding in diamond is correct? Tick **one** box. **[1 mark]**

Table 1

Boiling point	Bonding	
low	strong	☐
low	weak	☐
low	strong	☐
low	weak	☐

3. Diamond is very hard. Explain in terms of structure and bonding why diamond is very hard. **[2 marks]**

It has a giant structure where its atoms are joined together by ....

....

5 Conducting electricity — Grade 5

4. Explain whether diamond is able to conduct electricity. **[2 marks]**

....

....

Exam focus
Explain means you must give a reason for your answer.

☐ Made a start  Feeling confident  Exam ready

Graphite

1 Quick quiz

Give **two** uses of graphite.

....

10 Structure and bonding in graphite — Grade 4

1. Graphite is a form of carbon. **Figure 1** shows part of the structure of graphite.

(a) How many bonds does a carbon atom form in graphite? Tick **one** box. **[1 mark]**

1 ☐ 2 ☐ 3 ☐ 4 ☐

(b) Name the type of bond present between atoms in a layer of graphite. **[1 mark]**

....

Types of bond include ionic bonds, covalent bonds and metallic bonds.

(c) Describe the shape of the rings made by atoms in a layer of graphite. **[1 mark]**

....

Figure 1

2. Graphite contains delocalised electrons.

(a) Complete the sentence about delocalised electrons. Use words from the box. **[2 marks]**

between	free	inside	unable

Delocalised electrons are ......free...... to move .... atoms.

(b) Identify how many electrons from each carbon atom become delocalised in graphite. **[1 mark]**

....

(c) Name **one** other type of substance that contains delocalised electrons. **[1 mark]**

....

5 Properties of graphite — Grade 5

3. Graphite is slippery and can be used in pencils to make markings on paper.
Explain why graphite is slippery. **[3 marks]**

It has weak forces between ....

....

5 Conducting electricity — Grade 5

4. Explain whether graphite is able to conduct electricity. Give reasons for your answer. **[2 marks]**

....

....

 Made a start  Feeling confident 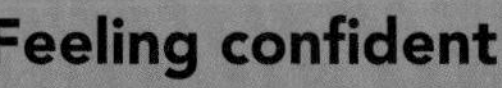  Exam ready

Graphene and fullerenes

2 Quick quiz

True or false?

Graphene is a single layer of graphite. **True / False**

The carbon atoms in graphene form four covalent bonds. **True / False**

Fullerenes can form rings with different numbers of carbon atoms. **True / False**

Graphene cannot conduct electricity. **True / False**

10 Graphene and graphite — Grade 5

1. **Figure 1** shows a section of a sheet of graphene.

   (a) Give the number of covalent bonds formed between each carbon atom. **[1 mark]**

   ....

   (b) Give **two** ways in which the properties of graphene and graphite are similar. **[2 marks]**

   Both have high melting and boiling points so are solid at room temperature. Both ....

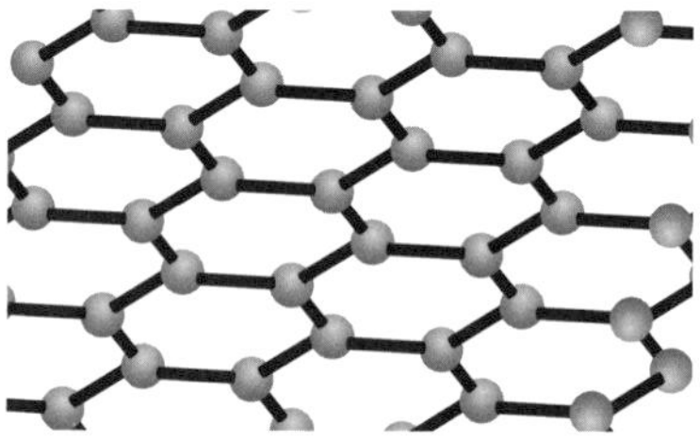

Figure 1

2. Explain in terms of structure and bonding why graphene is strong. **[3 marks]**

....

....

Remember to mention both the structure **and** the bonding in your answer.

5 Fullerenes — Grade 5

3. Carbon nanotubes are cylindrical fullerenes (**Figure 2**).

   Which statement describes some of their properties? Tick **one** box. **[1 mark]**

   - high tensile strength, very low length to diameter ratios ☐
   - high tensile strength, very high length to diameter ratios ☐
   - low tensile strength, very high length to diameter ratios ☐
   - low tensile strength, very low length to diameter ratios ☐

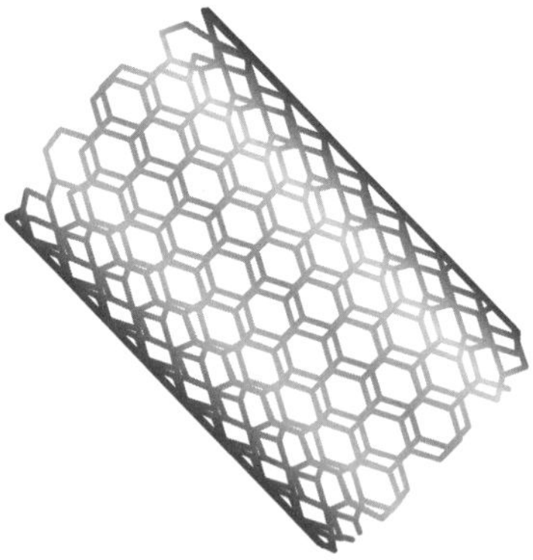

Figure 2

4. Name **two** uses for fullerenes. **[2 marks]**

   nanotechnology and ....

5 Conducting electricity — Grade 5

5. Explain whether carbon nanotubes are able to conduct electricity. Give reasons for your answer. **[2 marks]**

....

....

Made a start  Feeling confident ☐ Exam ready ☐

Conservation of mass

2 Quick quiz

Sodium hydroxide reacts with hydrochloric acid to form sodium chloride and water.

Write a word equation for this reaction and underline the names of the products.

....

5 Conservation of mass — Grades 3–4

1. Describe what happens to the atoms involved in a chemical reaction. **[1 mark]**

....

> Think about what happens to the total number of atoms in a chemical reaction.

2. The law of conservation of mass applies to chemical reactions in a closed system.

(a) Describe the relationship between the mass of products and the mass of reactants. **[1 mark]**

The mass of products is ....

(b) 3 g of dry ice completely sublimes into carbon dioxide gas in a closed vessel. What mass of carbon dioxide is formed? Tick one box.

0 g ☐ 3 g ☐ 6 g ☐

> Dry ice is carbon dioxide in the solid state.

10 Using conservation of mass — Grade 5

3. 24 g of magnesium reacts completely with 16 g of oxygen in a closed system:

magnesium + oxygen → magnesium oxide

Calculate the mass of the magnesium oxide produced in the reaction. **[1 mark]**

Mass of magnesium oxide = ... g

4. Calcium carbonate decomposes to form two products when heated in a closed system:

calcium carbonate → calcium oxide + carbon dioxide

50 g of calcium carbonate forms 28 g of calcium oxide. Calculate the mass of the carbon dioxide produced in the reaction. **[1 mark]**

Mass of carbon dioxide = ... g

10 Conservation of mass calculations — Grade 5

5. Silver nitrate reacts with sodium bromide to form two products:

silver nitrate + sodium bromide → sodium nitrate + silver bromide

1.70 g of silver nitrate reacts completely with 1.03 g of sodium bromide in a closed system.

(a) Calculate the total mass of the reactants. **[1 mark]**

(b) In the reaction, 0.85 g of sodium nitrate is produced. Calculate the mass of silver bromide formed. Use your answer to part **(a)**. **[1 mark]**

Relative formula mass

Quick quiz

True or false?

The symbol for relative formula mass is M_r. **True / False**

Relative formula mass is found by adding the atomic numbers of the elements together. **True / False**

Relative formula masses are always whole numbers. **True / False**

Element calculations

Grade 5

Use these relative atomic masses (A_r) in your calculations:

H = 1; N = 14; O = 16; Na = 23; S = 32; Cl = 35.5; Ca = 40; Cu = 63.5

You can also find relative atomic masses in the periodic table.

1. Calculate the relative formula mass of the following elements.

(a) Hydrogen, H_2 **[1 mark]**

$2 \times 1 =$

(b) Nitrogen, N_2 **[1 mark]**

(c) Oxygen, O_2 **[1 mark]**

(d) Chlorine, Cl_2 **[1 mark]**

Compound calculations

Grade 5

2. Calculate the relative formula mass of the following compounds.

(a) HCl **[1 mark]**

$(2 \times 1) + 16 =$

(b) H_2O **[1 mark]**

(c) NH_3 **[1 mark]**

(d) $CuCl_2$ **[1 mark]**

(e) NaOH **[1 mark]**

(f) $CuSO_4$ **[1 mark]**

1 × Cu; 1 × S; 4 × O

3. Calculate the relative formula mass of the following compounds.

(a) $Ca(OH)_2$ **[1 mark]**

1 × Ca; 2 × O; 2 × H

(b) $Cu(OH)_2$ **[1 mark]**

(c) $Ca(NO_3)_2$ **[1 mark]**

If there are brackets, you need to multiply the contents of the brackets by the number that follows, e.g. $(NO_3)_2$ means 2 × NO_3 (two units of NO_3). This is 2 × N and 6 × O.

 Made a start  Feeling confident Exam ready

Balancing equations

2 Quick quiz

Tick each correctly balanced equation.

$Na + Cl_2 \rightarrow NaCl$ ☐ $2Ca + O_2 \rightarrow 2CaO$ ☐

$N_2 + 2H_2 \rightarrow 2NH_3$ ☐ $CH_4 + 2O_2 \rightarrow CO_2 + 2H_2O$ ☐

5 A balanced equation — Grade 4

1. Magnesium reacts with oxygen to form magnesium oxide. **Figure 1** shows the particles involved and the formula of each substance.

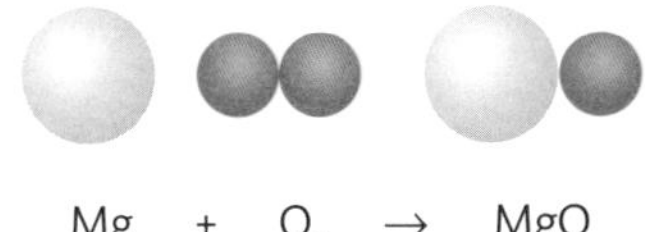

$Mg + O_2 \rightarrow MgO$

Figure 1

(a) Complete **Table 1** to show the number of atoms in each substance. **[2 marks]**

Table 1

	Magnesium	Oxygen	Magnesium oxide
magnesium atoms		0	
oxygen atoms		2	

(b) Explain, in terms of atoms, why the following equation is **not** balanced. **[1 mark]**

$Mg + O_2 \rightarrow 2MgO$

....

Count the number of atoms of each element on the left-hand side, and on the right-hand side.

(c) Balance the equation. ....$Mg + O_2 \rightarrow 2MgO$ **[1 mark]**

10 Balancing symbol equations — Grade 5

2. Balance the following equations.

(a) $BaO + 2HCl \rightarrow BaCl_2 + H_2O$ **[1 mark]**

(b) ....$Na + Br_2 \rightarrow$ ....$NaBr$ **[1 mark]**

(c) $N_2 +$ ....$H_2 \rightarrow$ ....NH_3 **[1 mark]**

(d) ....$Al +$ ....$O_2 \rightarrow 2Al_2O_3$ **[1 mark]**

(e) ....$NaOH + H_2SO_4 \rightarrow Na_2SO_4 +$ ....H_2O **[1 mark]**

(f) $Li_2CO_3 +$ .....$HNO_3 \rightarrow$ .....$LiNO_3 + H_2O + CO_2$ **[1 mark]**

10 More symbol equations — Grade 5

3. Balance the following equations.

(a) ....$Na + TiCl_4 \rightarrow$ ....$NaCl + Ti$ **[1 mark]**

(b) ....$SO_2 + O_2 \rightarrow$ ....SO_3 **[1 mark]**

(c) $Fe_2O_3 +$ ....$CO \rightarrow$ ....$Fe +$ ....CO_2 **[1 mark]**

 Made a start  Feeling confident  Exam ready

Mass changes

2 Quick quiz

Give the law of conservation of mass.

....

....

15 Non-enclosed systems — Grades 3–5

1. Reactions can take place in closed systems. They can also take place in non-enclosed systems (also called open systems). Complete **Table 1** by placing **one** tick in each row to show whether the system described is closed, or non-enclosed. **[4 marks]**

Table 1

Description of system	Closed	Non-enclosed
two solutions reacting in a beaker to form an insoluble solid	✓	
an evaporating basin containing a boiling liquid		
a reaction mixture in a stoppered flask		
a solid being heated in an open boiling tube		

2. Silver oxide, Ag_2O, decomposes when heated: silver oxide → silver + oxygen

(a) 6.22 g of silver oxide is heated, producing 5.79 g of silver. Calculate the expected mass of oxygen produced in the reaction. **[1 mark]**

6.22 g – 5.79 g = ...   Expected mass of oxygen = ... g

(b) Give a reason why the actual mass of oxygen collected may be less than the expected mass. **[1 mark]**

....

3. A pack of iron nails is left uncovered in a shed. The iron reacts with oxygen and water to form rust.

(a) Describe what happens to the mass of the pack of nails. **[1 mark]**

....

(b) Give a reason why this happens. **[1 mark]**

....

5 Mass changes — Grade 5

4. A teacher heats a strip of copper in a boiling tube containing iodine vapour. A layer of copper iodide forms on the surface of the copper.

(a) Write a word equation for the reaction. **[1 mark]**

....

(b) Explain what happens to the mass of the strip. **[2 marks]**

....

....

Chemical measurements

2 Quick quiz

Calculate the mean of these measurements: 1.0 g 1.2 g 1.3 g 1.1 g 1.4 g

.... = ... g

10 Mean, range and uncertainty

Grade 5

1. Draw **one** line from each term to its definition. **[2 marks]**

Term
mean
accuracy
range
anomalous results

Definition
a measure of how close a value is to its true value
the difference between the highest and lowest values
results that do not fit the pattern
the total of the values divided by the number of values

2. A student measures the volume of gas produced in a reaction. The experiment is repeated three times. **Table 1** shows the results.

Table 1

Trial	1	2	3
Volume of gas produced in cm^3	87	93	84

(a) Calculate the mean volume of gas produced by the three trials. **[1 mark]**

mean $= \frac{87 + 93 + 84}{3} =$ ....

Mean volume of gas = ... cm^3

(b) Calculate the range of the three trials. **[1 mark]**

range = highest value − lowest value = ...

Range = ... cm^3

(c) Calculate the uncertainty of the results. **[1 mark]**

uncertainty $= \frac{\text{range}}{2} =$ ....

Uncertainty of the mean = ... cm^3 ± .... cm^3

5 Types of error

Grade 5

3. Errors may be systematic errors or random errors. Complete **Table 2** by placing **one** tick in each row to show which feature applies to each type of error. **[4 marks]**

Table 2

Feature	Systematic error	Random error
error is reproducible		
can be reduced by taking the mean of several results		
gives values above and below the true value		
the inaccurate reading is the same each time		

Concentrations of solutions

2 Quick quiz

(a) Match each keyword to its description.

Keyword
solute
solvent
solution

Description
liquid that a substance can dissolve in
mixture of a liquid and a dissolved substance
substance that is dissolved in a liquid

(b) What is the equation for calculating concentration of solutions?

concentration in g/dm^3 = ...

10 Concentration calculations

Grade 3

1. The volume of a solution is 250 cm^3. Give this volume in dm^3. **[1 mark]**

volume in dm^3 $= \frac{\text{volume in cm}^3}{1000} = \frac{250}{100} =$ .... dm^3

Remember that 1000 cm^3 = 1 dm^3.

2. 3.7 g of salt is dissolved in water to make 100 cm^3 of solution.

(a) Give the volume of this solution in dm^3. .... **[1 mark]**

(b) Calculate the concentration of this solution. **[1 mark]**

concentration in g/dm^3 $= \frac{\text{mass in g}}{\text{volume in dm}^3} =$ ....

Concentration of solution = ... g/dm^3

3. A solution has a concentration of 40 g/dm^3. Calculate the mass of solute dissolved in 0.5 dm^3 of this solution. **[2 marks]**

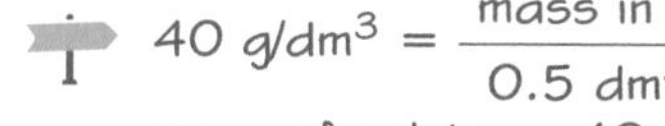

40 g/dm^3 $= \frac{\text{mass in g}}{0.5\ \text{dm}^3} =$ ....

mass of solute = 40 × ....

Rearrange the equation.

Mass of solute = ... g

10 Concentration and mass calculations

Grade 4

4. A student dissolves 2 g of sugar in 50 cm^3 of water. Calculate the concentration of the solution made. **[3 marks]**

Concentration of solution = ... g/dm^3

5. Calculate the mass of salt needed to make 125 cm^3 of a 4 g/dm^3 salt solution. **[3 marks]**

Mass of salt = ... g

 Made a start  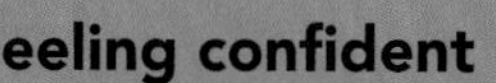 Feeling confident  Exam ready

Metal oxides

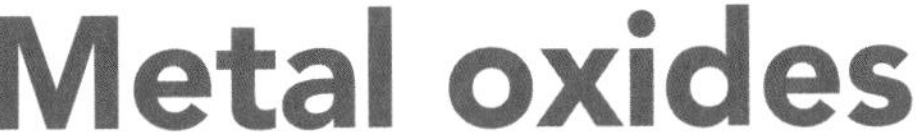

2 Quick quiz

(a) Describe where metals are found in the periodic table.

....

(b) Is oxygen a metal or a non-metal? ....

5 Naming oxides — Grade 3

1. Name the oxides produced in the following reactions:

(a) calcium reacting with oxygen — calcium oxide .... **[1 mark]**

(b) iron wool burning in air .... **[1 mark]**

(c) magnesium burning in air .... **[1 mark]**

2. Name these compounds:

(a) PbO_2 — lead oxide .... **[1 mark]** **(b)** Na_2O .... **[1 mark]**

(c) ZnO .... **[1 mark]** **(d)** Al_2O_3 .... **[1 mark]**

5 Oxidation reactions — Grades 4–5

3. (a) Write a word equation for the reaction between aluminium and oxygen. **[1 mark]**

....

(b) Give a reason why this reaction is described as an 'oxidation reaction'. **[1 mark]**

In the reaction, aluminium gains ....

5 Identifying oxidation and reduction — Grade 5

4. When heated, copper oxide reacts with hydrogen: $CuO + H_2 \rightarrow Cu + H_2O$

Identify the substance that is reduced and the substance that is oxidised. Give reasons for your answer. **[2 marks]**

Copper oxide is reduced because it loses ....

Hydrogen is oxidised because it ....

5 Oxidation and reduction — Grade 5

5. When heated, iron oxide reacts with carbon:

iron oxide + carbon → iron + carbon dioxide

Identify the substance that is reduced and the substance that is oxidised. Give reasons for your answer. **[2 marks]**

....

....

 **Made a start**  **Feeling confident**  **Exam ready**

The reactivity series

2 Quick quiz

Fill in the missing metals in each reactivity series using the words in the box.

magnesium	sodium	iron

potassium .... lithium

calcium .... zinc

zinc .... copper

10 Ordering metals — Grades 4–5

1. A student studies the reactions of three metals (**X**, **Y** and **Z**) with a dilute acid. **Table 1** shows the results.

Table 1

Metal	Reaction with a dilute acid
X	Slow bubbling
Y	No reaction
Z	Vigorous bubbling

(a) Identify the most reactive metal in **Table 1**. Give a reason for your answer. **[2 marks]**

Metal Z because ....

(b) Place the three metals in order of **decreasing** reactivity. **[1 mark]**

....

(c) Identify the metal in **Table 1** that will most easily lose electrons to form positive ions. **[1 mark]**

....

The reactivity of metals is related to how readily they lose electrons.

10 Metal reactions — Grade 5

2. A student investigates the reactions of three metals (**X**, **Y** and **Z**) with solutions of their salts. **Table 2** shows the results ('NC' means 'no visible change').

Table 2

Metal	X nitrate solution	Y nitrate solution	Z nitrate solution
X	NC	NC	NC
Y	black coating on metal	NC	brown coating on metal
Z	brown coating on metal	NC	NC

(a) Determine the order of reactivity of the metals. **[1 mark]**

....

(b) Explain your answer to part **(a)**. **[3 marks]**

....

....

....

Made a start  Feeling confident  Exam ready

Extraction of metals and reduction

2 Quick quiz

Place these metals in order of **decreasing** reactivity. Write 1 for the most reactive and 4 for the least reactive.

aluminium	copper	iron	gold

5 Ores — Grade 2

1. (a) Describe what is meant by an 'ore'. **[2 marks]**

A naturally occurring rock that contains ....

....

(b) Some metals are found in the Earth as the metal itself. Name **one** of these metals. **[1 mark]**

These metals are unreactive metals.

....

5 The reactivity series — Grade 4

2. Some metals can be extracted by heating their ores with carbon. This works if the metal is less reactive than carbon. **Table 1** shows a reactivity series with carbon included.

Table 1

Most reactive				**Least reactive**
potassium	magnesium	carbon	zinc	copper

Name **one** metal that can be extracted from its ore by heating with carbon. **[1 mark]**

....

5 Extracting iron — Grades 4–5

3. Iron ore contains iron oxide. Iron is extracted by heating iron ore with carbon. Carbon dioxide is also produced in the reaction.

(a) Write a word equation for the reaction. **[1 mark]**

.... + carbon → iron + ...

(b) Give a reason why iron can be extracted from its ore by heating with carbon. **[1 mark]**

....

(c) Identify the substance that is oxidised and the substance that is reduced. Give reasons for your answer. **[2 marks]**

Oxidised: ....

Oxidation is gain of oxygen.

Reduced: ....

Reactions of acids with metals

2 Quick quiz

(a) Put these three metals into order of decreasing reactivity.

Write 1 for the most reactive, 3 for the least reactive and 2 for the metal in between.

Metal	Reactivity
iron	
magnesium	
zinc	

(b) Which gas is produced when a metal reacts with an acid? ....

5 Reactants and products — Grade 2

1. Complete **Table 1** to show the name of the salt made by each metal and acid. **[6 marks]**

Table 1

Metal	Hydrochloric acid	Sulfuric acid
magnesium		
zinc		zinc sulfate
iron	iron chloride	

10 Writing equations — Grade 4

2. Write a word equation for the reaction between iron and hydrochloric acid. **[2 marks]**

.................................+.................................... ⟶ ....+ hydrogen

3. Write a word equation for the reaction between a metal and an acid to produce zinc sulfate. **[2 marks]**

....

4. Calcium reacts with dilute sulfuric acid, H_2SO_4. Calcium sulfate, $CaSO_4$, and hydrogen are produced.

Write a balanced symbol equation for this reaction. **[2 marks]**

Ca + ... ⟶ .... + H_2

10 Metals, acids and salts — Grade 4

5. Name the acid needed to react with magnesium to make magnesium sulfate. .... **[1 mark]**

6. Name the salt made when zinc reacts with dilute hydrochloric acid. .... **[1 mark]**

7. Write a word equation for the reaction between iron and sulfuric acid. **[2 marks]**

....

8. Explain why bubbling is seen when magnesium reacts with hydrochloric acid. **[2 marks]**

....

....

Made a start  Feeling confident  Exam ready

Salt production

2 Quick quiz

Match the acid to the type of salt it can produce.

hydrochloric acid	sulfate
nitric acid	chloride
sulfuric acid	nitrate

5 Salts from acids — Grade 3

1. Acids react with bases, alkalis and metal carbonates. Complete **Table 1**. **[3 marks]**

Table 1

Reaction	Product		
	Salt	**Water**	**Carbon dioxide**
acid + metal hydroxide	✓	✓	
acid + metal oxide			
acid + metal carbonate			

5 Predicting salts — Grade 4

2. Predict the name of the salt formed in the following reactions.

(a) sodium hydroxide + hydrochloric acid .... **[1 mark]**

(b) copper oxide + sulfuric acid .... **[1 mark]**

(c) zinc carbonate + nitric acid .... **[1 mark]**

5 Salt formulae — Grade 4

3. Table 2 shows the formulae of some common ions. Determine the chemical formula of each of the following salts.

(a) sodium chloride .... **[1 mark]**

(b) magnesium nitrate $Mg(NO_3)_2$ .... **[1 mark]**

(c) copper sulfate .... **[1 mark]**

(d) copper chloride .... **[1 mark]**

Table 2

Positive ions		Negative ions	
sodium	Na^+	chloride	Cl^-
magnesium	Mg^{2+}	nitrate	NO_3^-
copper	Cu^{2+}	sulfate	SO_4^{2-}

5 Making salts — Grade 4

4. Write word equations for the reactions between the following substances.

(a) Zinc oxide and hydrochloric acid **[2 marks]**

....

(b) Calcium carbonate and nitric acid **[2 marks]**

....

 Made a start  Feeling confident  Exam ready

Soluble salts

2 Quick quiz

True or false?

Soluble substances can dissolve in water. **True / False**

All salts are soluble. **True / False**

Sodium hydroxide is a soluble base. **True / False**

5 Making salts — Grade 2

1. Complete the sentences about making a soluble salt. Use words from the box. **[2 marks]**

crystallising	dissolving	distilling	filtering

The solid insoluble substance is added to the acid until no more reaction takes place.

The excess solid is removed by filtering. The solid salt is produced from the solution by heating then ....

10 Choosing reactants — Grade 5

2. Soluble salts can be made by reacting an acid with an insoluble substance. Some insoluble substances cannot be used.

(a) Suggest a reason why potassium cannot be used to make potassium chloride. **[1 mark]**

Think about the reactivity series of metals.

....

(b) Suggest a reason why silver cannot be used to make silver nitrate. **[1 mark]**

....

3. A student makes magnesium sulfate solution using magnesium ribbon.

(a) Predict **two** observations that the student would see. **[2 marks]**

The magnesium ribbon would become smaller or disappear, and ....

(b) Suggest how the student could remove any unreacted magnesium from the reaction mixture. **[1 mark]**

....

5 Making soluble salts — Grade 4

4. Zinc chloride is a soluble salt. It can be produced by mixing dilute hydrochloric acid with an insoluble solid, such as zinc hydroxide.

(a) Name **three** other solids that could be used. **[3 marks]**

1 ....

2 ....

3 ....

(b) Write a word equation for the reaction between hydrochloric acid and **one** of the substances you named in part **(a)**. **[1 mark]**

....

 Made a start  Feeling confident Exam ready

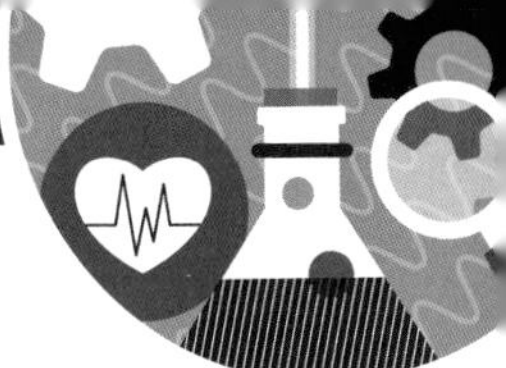

Making salts

Quick quiz

The diagram shows apparatus for making salts. Label the pieces of apparatus with the words in the box.

tripod	filter funnel	beaker	evaporating basin	Bunsen burner

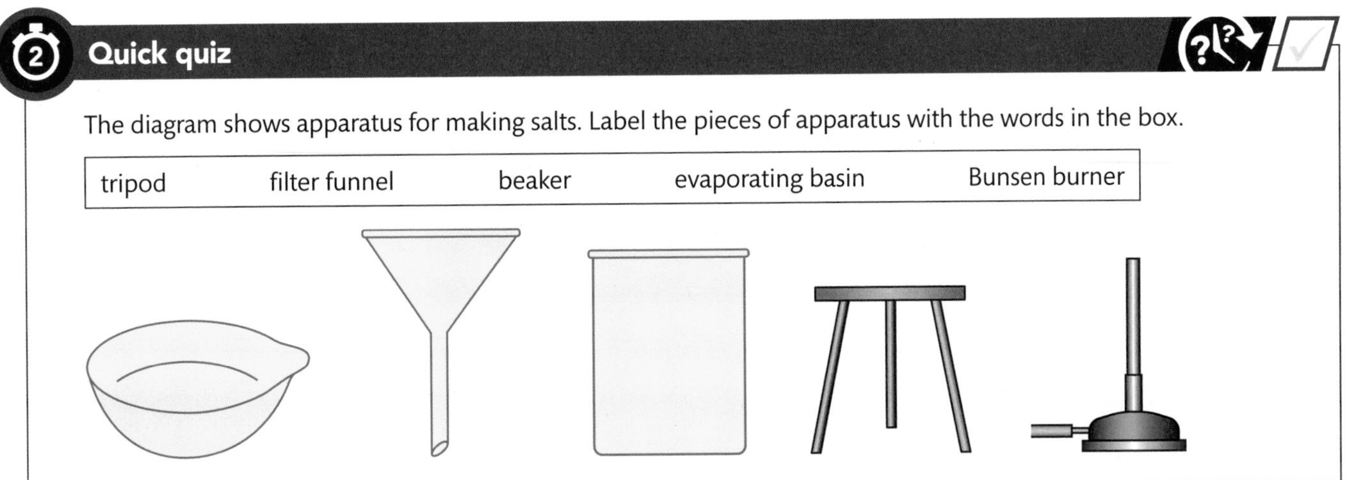

Making a salt

Grade 3 

1. Pure, dry copper chloride crystals can be made using dilute hydrochloric acid and copper carbonate. Copper carbonate is insoluble in water.

Table 1 gives the steps for the method in the wrong order. Complete the table by writing numbers 1 to 7 in the correct boxes, where 1 is the first step. **[5 marks]**

Table 1

Description of step	Step number
Add copper carbonate to the acid until no more reacts.	
Filter the mixture to remove the excess copper carbonate.	
Leave the filtrate to cool so that crystals form.	
Add dilute hydrochloric acid to a beaker.	1
Warm the acid gently in the beaker.	
Pat the crystals dry with filter paper.	
Heat the filtrate gently in an evaporating basin.	

Experimental methods

Grade 4 

2. Design a method to make pure, dry crystals of zinc nitrate from dilute nitric acid and insoluble zinc oxide. Use apparatus from the box. **[5 marks]**

beaker	Bunsen burner	conical flask	evaporating basin	filter funnel
filter paper	gauze mat	stirring rod	tripod	

You only need to describe essential steps in your answer.

....

....

....

....

....

....

The pH scale and neutralisation

2 Quick quiz

Label the pH scale to show the acidic, alkaline and neutral regions.

0 1 2 3 4 5 6 7 8 9 10 11 12 13 14

10 pH scale — Grade 3

1. Describe what the pH scale is a measure of. **[1 mark]**

It is a measure of the acidity ....

2. A student uses a pH meter to measure the pH values of different solutions. **Table 1** shows the results.

Table 1

Solution	baking soda	vinegar	shampoo	battery acid	tomato juice	pure water
pH	8.3	2.6	7.5	1.0	4.5	7.0

(a) Identify the acidic solutions. **[3 marks]**

battery acid, ...

(b) Identify the alkaline solutions. **[2 marks]**

....

5 Neutralisation — Grade 4

3. Aqueous solutions of acids and alkalis always contain certain ions.

(a) Complete **Table 2** to show the names and formulae of these ions. **[4 marks]**

Table 2

	Acidic solutions	**Alkaline solutions**
Name of ion	hydrogen	
Formula of ion		OH^-

(b) Complete the equation to show how these ions react together during a neutralisation reaction. **[1 mark]**

.... + $OH^- \longrightarrow$ ....

5 Estimating pH of solutions — Grade 3

4. Describe how to use universal indicator paper to measure the approximate pH of a solution. **[3 marks]**

....

....

....

Made a start Feeling confident Exam ready

Electrolysis

2 Quick quiz

(a) Match each keyword to its description.

electrode	using electricity to decompose a compound
electrolysis	a solid electrical conductor
electrolyte	a liquid or solution that can conduct electricity

(b) What are the charged particles in an electrolyte called? ....

5 The components of electrolysis — Grade 3

1. Give the names of these two electrodes:

(a) negative electrode .... **[1 mark]** **(b)** positive electrode .... **[1 mark]**

2. What happens to the ions in an ionic compound when it is melted? **[1 mark]**

They become free to ....

Think about the movement of the particles in a liquid.

3. For electrolysis to work, there must be an electricity supply, two electrodes and an electrolyte.

(a) Name **one** non-metal that can be used as an electrode. .... **[1 mark]**

(b) Give **two** ways that sodium chloride can become an electrolyte. **[2 marks]**

1 Dissolve it in water ....

2 ....

5 The process of electrolysis — Grade 4

4. Complete the sentences. Use words from the box. **[4 marks]**

atoms	compounds	elements	ions	negative	positive

During electrolysis, ...positive...... ions move to the negative electrode.

Negative ions move to the .... electrode. .... are discharged at the electrodes,

producing ....

10 An electrolysis experiment — Grade 4

5. Copper sulfate solution is an electrolyte. Describe a simple electrolysis experiment to show that copper ions are positively charged. **[4 marks]**

....

....

....

....

Your answer could include a diagram.

Electrolysis to extract metals

Quick quiz

Place these metals in order of **decreasing** reactivity.
Write **1** for the most reactive and **4** for the least reactive.

iron	copper	potassium	zinc

Electrolysis

Grade 4

1. Some metals can be extracted by heating their ores with carbon. However, electrolysis must be used if the metal is more reactive than carbon. **Table 1** shows a reactivity series with carbon included.

Table 1

Most reactive				**Least reactive**
sodium	magnesium	carbon	iron	gold

Name **one** metal that must be extracted from its ore using electrolysis. **[1 mark]**

....

2. The ions in an electrolyte must be free to move for electrolysis to happen. Give the **two** ways an ionic compound can act as an electrolyte. **[2 marks]**

When it is dissolved in water and when it is ....

3. Aluminium is extracted by the electrolysis of a molten mixture of aluminium oxide and cryolite.

Table 2 shows the melting points of aluminium oxide and cryolite.

(a) Suggest a reason why aluminium oxide is dissolved in molten cryolite rather than using water. **[1 mark]**

....

(b) Explain why the use of cryolite reduces the use of energy in extracting aluminium. **[2 marks]**

Table 2

Compound	**Melting point in °C**
aluminium oxide	2072
cryolite	1012

Cryolite melts at a lower temperature than aluminium oxide, so ....

....

Extracting aluminium

Grade 4

4. Aluminium is extracted by the electrolysis of a molten mixture of aluminium oxide and cryolite. A lot of energy is needed to melt the compounds for electrolysis.

(a) Give **one** other reason why extracting aluminium using electrolysis is very expensive. **[1 mark]**

....

(b) Predict the product discharged at the anode during the extraction of aluminium. **[1 mark]**

....

(c) The anodes are made from carbon. Explain why the anodes must be replaced regularly. **[2 marks]**

....

 Made a start  Feeling confident Exam ready

Electrolysis of aqueous solutions

2 Quick quiz

(a) Name the positive electrode. ....

(b) Name the negative electrode. ....

(c) What is an electrolyte? ....

5 At the negative electrode — Grade 4

1. Table 1 shows a reactivity series of some metals, with hydrogen included.

Predict the products formed at the negative electrode during the electrolysis of the following aqueous solutions.

Hydrogen is produced if the metal is more reactive than hydrogen.

(a) Sodium chloride hydrogen .... **[1 mark]**

(b) Copper sulfate .... **[1 mark]**

(c) Magnesium bromide .... **[1 mark]**

(d) Silver nitrate .... **[1 mark]**

Table 1

potassium	Most reactive ↑
sodium	
magnesium	
zinc	
hydrogen	
copper	
silver	Least reactive

5 At the positive electrode — Grade 4

2. Predict the products formed at the positive electrode during the electrolysis of the following aqueous solutions.

Oxygen is produced unless the solution contains halide ions.

(a) Sodium chloride chlorine .... **[1 mark]**

(b) Copper sulfate .... **[1 mark]**

(c) Magnesium bromide .... **[1 mark]**

(d) Silver nitrate .... **[1 mark]**

5 Ions in solutions — Grade 4

3. (a) A small proportion of water molecules, H_2O, break down to produce two types of ion. Identify these **two** ions. **[2 marks]**

hydroxide ions, OH^-, and ....

(b) Identify the ions that produce oxygen during the electrolysis of aqueous solutions. **[1 mark]**

....

4. Predict the product formed at each electrode during the electrolysis of:

(a) Sodium hydroxide solution .... **[1 mark]**

(b) Potassium iodide solution .... **[1 mark]**

Electrolysis of copper(II) chloride

2 Quick quiz

Tick **two** boxes to show the rules for predicting the products of electrolysis.

Hydrogen is produced at the cathode if the metal is more reactive than hydrogen. ☐

Hydrogen is produced at the cathode if the metal is less reactive than hydrogen. ☐

Oxygen is produced at the anode unless the solution contains halide ions. ☐

Chlorine is produced at the anode unless the solution contains hydroxide ions. ☐

5 Electrolysis cells — Grade 4

1. Figure 1 shows how the electrolysis of copper(II) chloride solution may be carried out.
Label the diagram. Use words from the box. **[2 marks]**

anode	cathode	copper(II) chloride solution	electrolyte

anode — cathode

Figure 1

5 Electrolysis of copper(II) chloride solution — Grade 4

2. Figure 1 shows how the electrolysis of copper(II) chloride solution can be carried out.

(a) Predict the substance produced at the cathode. **[1 mark]**

....

The cathode is the negative electrode and the anode is the positive electrode.

(b) Predict the substance produced at the anode. **[1 mark]**

....

(c) Explain why inert electrodes are used in this investigation. **[2 marks]**

....

....

'Inert' means unreactive.

10 Electrode reactions — Grade 4

3. A student investigates the electrolysis of three aqueous solutions: sodium chloride, copper sulfate and sodium sulfate. Complete **Table 1** to show the products formed at the electrodes. **[3 marks]**

Table 1

Aqueous solution	Product at cathode	Product at anode
sodium chloride		
copper sulfate		
sodium sulfate		

 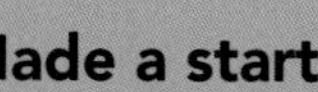 Made a start  Feeling confident  Exam ready

Exothermic and endothermic reactions

Quick quiz

Link the statements by drawing lines to form **two** correct sentences.

In endothermic reactions	energy is transferred to the surroundings,	which get warmer.
In exothermic reactions	energy is transferred from the surroundings,	which get colder.

Example reactions

Grade 4

1. **Table 1** shows some different types of reaction. Complete the table by placing a tick in each row to show whether the reaction is exothermic or endothermic. **[3 marks]**

Table 1

Type of reaction	Exothermic	Endothermic
combustion		
electrolysis		✓
neutralisation		
oxidation		
thermal decomposition		

2. Sherbet is a type of fizzy powdered sweet. It contains citric acid and sodium hydrogen carbonate. These react together when the sherbet gets wet, making the mouth feel cold. Determine whether the reaction in sherbet is exothermic or endothermic. Give a reason for your answer. **[1 mark]**

....

Temperature change and data analysis

Grade 5

3. A student adds identical masses of four different powdered metals (**A**, **B**, **C** and **D**) to the same volume of dilute acid. **Table 2** shows the results.

Table 2

Metal	A	B	C	D
Starting temperature in °C	21	21	22	22
Maximum temperature in °C	38	26	59	34
Temperature change in °C		5	37	

(a) Complete **Table 2** to show the temperature change for metals **A** and **D**. **[2 marks]**

(b) Determine the order of reactivity of the metals, starting with the most reactive. **[1 mark]**

....

(c) Give a reason for your answer. **[1 mark]**

....

Temperature changes

Quick quiz

Exothermic or endothermic changes? Circle the correct answers.

oxidation	**Exothermic** / **Endothermic**	metal displacement	**Exothermic** / **Endothermic**
combustion	**Exothermic** / **Endothermic**	photosynthesis	**Exothermic** / **Endothermic**
electrolysis	**Exothermic** / **Endothermic**	thermal decomposition	**Exothermic** / **Endothermic**

Neutralisation data analysis

Grades 4–5

1. Neutralisation reactions are exothermic. A student investigates temperature changes in neutralisation reactions using the apparatus shown in **Figure 1**.

(a) The student tries to reduce the transfer of energy to the surroundings. Give **three** ways in which the apparatus reduces heat losses from the reaction mixture. **[3 marks]**

1 There is an air gap between the polystyrene cup and the beaker.

2 ....

3 ....

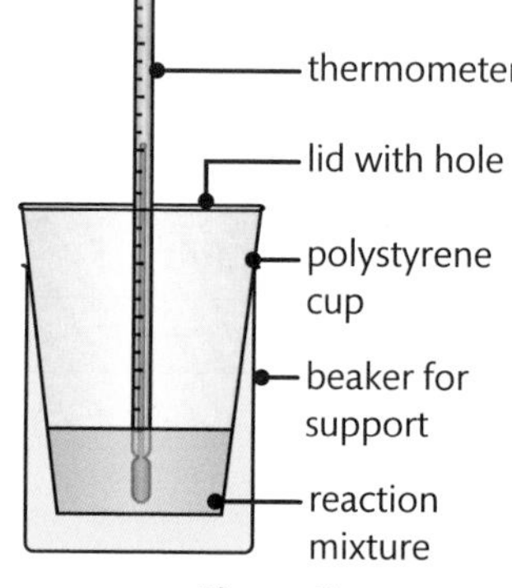

Figure 1

(b) The student adds 50 cm^3 of hydrochloric acid to 50 cm^3 of sodium hydroxide solution. The concentration of the sodium hydroxide solution is different each time. **Table 1** shows the results.

Table 1

Concentration of sodium hydroxide in g/dm³	0.5	1.0	1.5	2.0
Maximum temperature increase in °C	2.0	3.8	5.4	6.8

(i) Identify **two** control variables in this experiment. **[2 marks]**

1 .... 2 ....

(ii) Describe what the results show. **[3 marks]**

....

....

Remember to say in your answer whether the reaction is exothermic or endothermic.

Experimental methods

Grade 4

2. Powdered zinc reacts with dilute hydrochloric acid. Design an experiment to show that this reaction is exothermic. You are given the apparatus in the box. **[5 marks]**

beaker	polystyrene cup	thermometer	measuring cylinder

You only need to describe essential steps in your answer.

....

....

....

....

 Made a start  Feeling confident  Exam ready

Reaction profiles

2 Quick quiz

This reaction profile shows an exothermic reaction. Label it to show reactants, products, activation energy and the overall energy change.

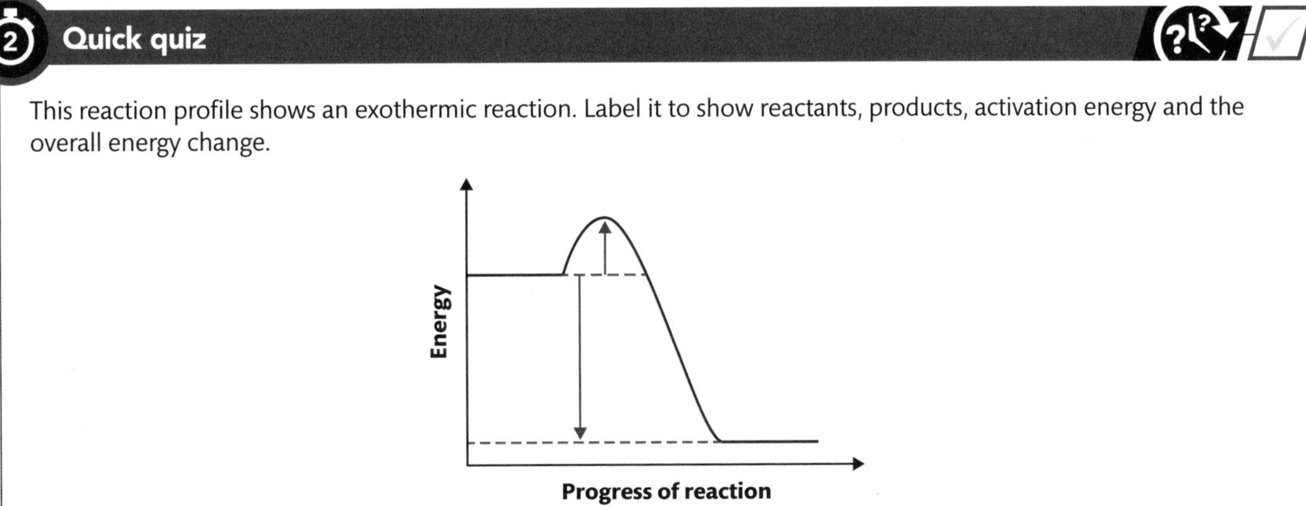

10 Energy level diagrams — Grade 5

1. The reaction profile in **Figure 1** shows an exothermic reaction.

(a) Give a reason why the diagram shows that the reaction is exothermic. **[1 mark]**

The products have less energy than ....

(b) Identify what is shown by **X**. **[1 mark]**

X is the overall energy ....

(c) Define the term 'activation energy'. **[1 mark]**

The energy needed for ....

Energy
2000 kJ
X
Progress of reaction

Figure 1

10 Endothermic reaction profile — Grade 5

2. Draw and label a reaction profile for an endothermic reaction, using the labels in the box. **[3 marks]**

reactants	product	activation energy	energy change	progress of reaction	energy

Exam focus

The number of marks indicates how much information is required.

For drawing and correctly labelling the following you will be given one mark for each:

- both axes
- a correct profile line with the relative energies of the reactants and products, and the overall energy change
- the activation energy.

Calculating rate of reaction

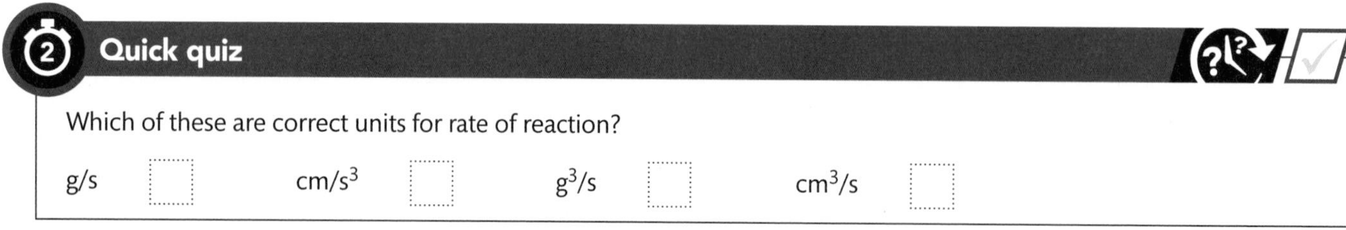

2 Quick quiz

Which of these are correct units for rate of reaction?

g/s ☐ cm/s^3 ☐ g^3/s ☐ cm^3/s ☐

5 Calculating rate — Grade 3

1. A student investigates the reaction between magnesium and dilute hydrochloric acid. 0.12 g of magnesium is put into a beaker of acid. It takes 50 s for the magnesium ribbon to completely disappear.

Calculate the mean rate of this reaction. Give the units for rate in your answer. **[2 marks]**

mean rate of reaction $= \frac{\text{quantity of reactant used}}{\text{time taken}} = \frac{0.12\,g}{50\,s} =$ .... g/s

10 Calculating rate — Grade 4

2. **Figure 1** shows the volume of gas released during a reaction.

(a) Describe how you can tell that the reaction finished at 60 s. **[1 mark]**

....

....

Look at what the line on the graph does after 60 s.

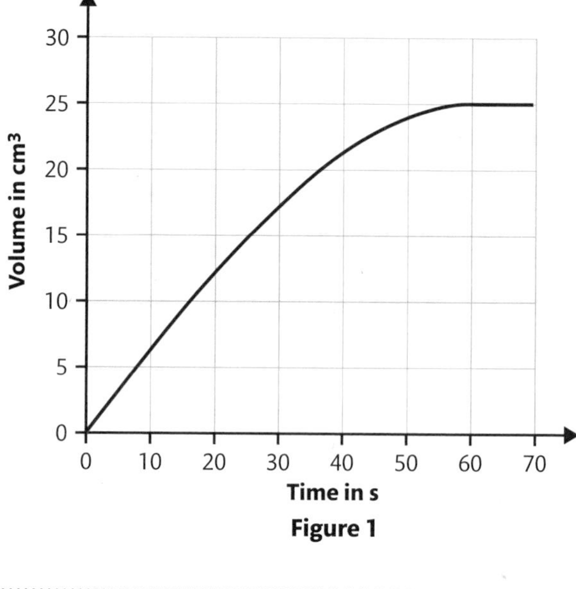

Figure 1

(b) Draw a tangent to the line at 10 s. **[1 mark]**

(c) The slope of the line changes as the reaction goes on. Explain what this means. **[2 marks]**

The slope decreases, for example, from 10 s to the end of the reaction. This means that the rate ....

....

....

5 Catalysts and rate — Grades 4–5

3. **(a)** Calculate the mean rate of the reaction shown in **Figure 1**. Give the units for rate in your answer. **[2 marks]**

(b) Draw a tangent to the line at 40 s. **[1 mark]**

(c) Draw a curve on **Figure 1** to represent the same reaction but with a catalyst added. **[2 marks]**

The total time of the reaction is from 0 s to when it ends at 60 s.

Maths skills

A tangent is a straight line that just touches one point on a curve. Make sure that the line follows the general direction of the curve at that point.

 Made a start  Feeling confident  Exam ready

Factors affecting rate of reaction

2 Quick quiz

Give **three** methods to measure the rate of a reaction in an experiment.

1 ....

2 ....

3 ....

5 Changing the rate — Grade 3

1. Tick **one** box in each row of **Table 1** to show how each factor affects reaction rate. **[3 marks]**

Table 1

Change in factor	Increases rate	Decreases rate
increase in temperature	✓	
increase in concentration of a reactant in solution		
decrease in the pressure of reacting gases		

5 Temperature and rate — Grade 4

2. Give **two** reasons why the rate of reaction increases as the temperature increases. **[2 marks]**

Particles collide more often and with more ....

3. Give a reason why a catalyst increases the rate of a reaction. **[1 mark]**

It reduces the ....

10 Surface area and rate — Grade 4

4. A student investigates the reaction between acid and marble chips. The mass lost after 60 s is measured for different-sized chips. The results of the investigation are shown in **Table 2**.

(a) Explain what the results show about the rate of this reaction. **[2 marks]**

....

....

(b) Identify the factor that changes as the size of the marble chips is changed. **[1 mark]**

....

(c) Give **two** other ways to change the rate of this reaction. **[2 marks]**

1 ....

2 ....

Table 2

Size of chips	Mass lost in g
small	2.1
medium-sized	1.3
large	0.5

Rate of reaction

Quick quiz

Catalysts affect the rate of reaction. Give **four** other factors that affect the rate of reaction.

....

....

Measuring volume of gas — Grade 4

1. Magnesium ribbon reacts with dilute hydrochloric acid. Hydrogen gas is one of the products. A student investigates the effect of changing the concentration of the acid on the rate of this reaction. **Figure 1** shows the apparatus used.

Figure 1

(a) Suggest **one** change to the apparatus that would let the student measure the volume of gas. **[1 mark]**

....

Gas jars do not have any graduations on them.

(b) Give **three** factors that the student should control in this investigation. **[3 marks]**

1 the mass of magnesium

2 ....

3 ....

What factors must the student keep the same?

(c) Predict what will happen when the concentration of the acid is increased. **[1 mark]**

....

Measuring colour change — Grade 4

2. Sodium thiosulfate solution reacts with dilute hydrochloric acid to produce a cloudy precipitate of sulfur. A student investigates the effect of changing the concentration of sodium thiosulfate on the rate of this reaction. The time taken for the sulfur to hide a cross under the flask is measured. **Table 1** shows the results.

Table 1

Concentration of sodium thiosulfate in g/dm^3	2.5	5	7.5	10
Time taken for the cross to be hidden in s	100	73	52	25

(a) Describe the effect of changing the concentration on the time taken for the cross to be hidden. **[2 marks]**

....

....

(b) Describe the effect of increasing the concentration on the rate of reaction. Use your answer to part **(a)** to help you. **[1 mark]**

....

Made a start

Feeling confident
Exam ready

Catalysts

2 Quick quiz

(a) What are catalysts in biological systems called?

....

(b) Circle the correct answer in the sentence.

Different reactions need **the same catalyst** / **different catalysts**.

5 Identifying catalysts — Grade 3

1. A student adds manganese dioxide powder to hydrogen peroxide solution. The mixture starts to bubble rapidly. The word equation for the reaction is:

hydrogen peroxide → water + oxygen

(a) Define the term 'catalyst'. **[2 marks]**

A substance that changes the rate of a chemical reaction but ....

(b) Give a reason why the word equation shows that manganese dioxide is a catalyst for this reaction. **[1 mark]**

....

Think about the substances that the student mixes together.

(c) Give **one** observation in the reaction that shows that a catalyst was added. **[1 mark]**

....

15 Reaction profiles and catalysts — Grade 5

2. (a) Complete the reaction profile (**Figure 1**) to show an exothermic reaction, using the labels in the box. **[2 marks]**

reactants	product	activation energy	energy change

Exam focus
In this type of question, remember to include the relative energies of the reactants and products, activation energy and overall energy change.

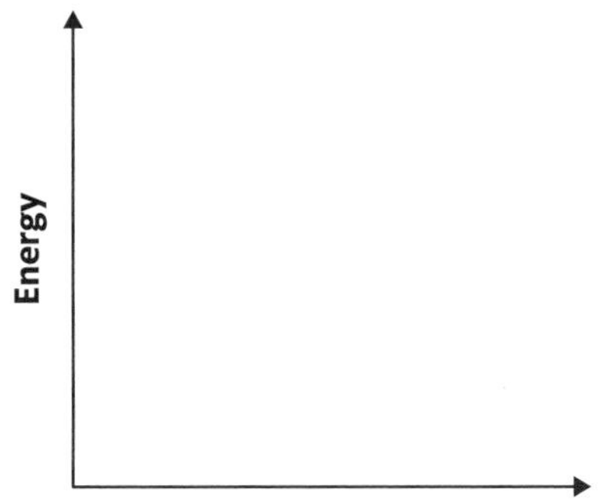

Energy

Progress of reaction

Figure 1

(b) Describe how the reaction profile would look different for the same reaction with a catalyst added. **[1 mark]**

....

(c) Draw the curve for the catalysed reaction on the reaction profile in **Figure 1**. **[1 mark]**

(d) Explain why a catalyst makes the reaction happen faster. **[2 marks]**

....

....

Made a start  Feeling confident  Exam ready

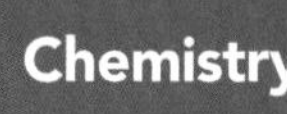

Reversible reactions

2 Quick quiz

A reaction is shown as: A + B ⇌ C + D

How do you know this is a reversible reaction, rather than a reaction that goes to completion?

....

5 Reversible reactions — Grade 5

1. Cobalt chloride paper can be used to test for water:

- It is blue when it is dry.
- It is pink when it is damp.

This is a reversible chemical change.

(a) Predict what will happen if damp cobalt chloride paper is dried in an oven. **[2 marks]**

....

Both colours are needed for a full answer.

(b) Complete the equation to describe what happens to the cobalt chloride paper. **[3 marks]**

blue cobalt salt + ... pink cobalt salt

Remember to write in the missing substance(s) and the correct symbol.

2. Give **three** changes in conditions that can alter the direction of a reversible reaction. **[3 marks]**

1 change in pressure

2 ....

3 ....

10 More reversible reactions — Grade 5

3. Ammonium chloride is a white solid. When it is heated it breaks down to form two gases:

ammonium chloride ⇌ ammonia + hydrogen chloride

Give the change in conditions needed for ammonia and hydrogen chloride to change back into ammonium chloride. **[1 mark]**

....

4. A reaction reaches equilibrium in a sealed container. Compare the rates of the forward and reverse reactions at equilibrium. **[1 mark]**

....

Made a start  Feeling confident  Exam ready

Energy changes in reversible reactions

2 Quick quiz

Link the statements by drawing lines to form **two** correct sentences.

In endothermic reactions,	energy is released	and the reaction mixture warms up.
In exothermic reactions,	energy is taken in	and the reaction mixture cools down.

15 Reversible reactions and energy — Grades 4–5

1. (a) Describe what happens to the temperature of the surroundings when an exothermic reaction takes place. **[1 mark]**

....

(b) Explain, in terms of energy transfer, what happens in an exothermic reaction. **[2 marks]**

Energy is transferred .... *the reaction mixture* .... *the surroundings.*

2. This reversible reaction is one of the steps in making sulfuric acid:

sulfur dioxide + oxygen ⇌ sulfur trioxide

(a) Write a word equation for the forward reaction. **[1 mark]**

....

The forward reaction goes from left to right.

(b) The forward reaction is exothermic. Determine whether the reverse reaction is exothermic or endothermic. Give a reason for your answer. **[2 marks]**

....

....

(c) Compare the amount of energy transferred in each direction. **[1 mark]**

....

Is the amount of energy the same or different?

5 More reversible reactions — Grades 4–5

3. (a) Carbon monoxide reacts with hydrogen to form methanol. The reaction is reversible. Write a word equation for this reaction. **[2 marks]**

....

(b) 2800 J is given out to the surroundings when 1 g of methanol is made. Give the amount of energy needed to break down 1 g of methanol. **[1 mark]**

....

Crude oil, hydrocarbons and alkanes

1 Quick quiz

Use words from the box to complete the sentences.

biomass	finite	millions	mixture

Crude oil is a .... resource found in rocks.

It is the remains of .... buried in mud many .... of years ago.

Crude oil is a .... of substances.

10 Crude oil — Grades 2–3

1. Most of the substances found in crude oil are hydrocarbons. Define the term 'hydrocarbon'. **[2 marks]**

A compound of ....

2. Crude oil will run out one day if we keep using it. Name the type of resource that crude oil is. **[1 mark]**

....

3. Most of the hydrocarbons in crude oil are alkanes.

(a) Complete **Table 1** to give the names of the first four alkanes. **[4 marks]**

Table 1

Number of carbon atoms	Name of alkane
1	*methane*
2	
3	
4	

(b) **Figure 1** shows the structure of one of these substances.

Give the molecular formula of the alkane **in Figure 1**. **[1 mark]**

....

```
    H   H   H   H
    |   |   |   |
H — C — C — C — C — H
    |   |   |   |
    H   H   H   H
```

Figure 1

5 General formula of alkanes — Grade 4

4. (a) What is the general formula for alkanes? Tick **one** box. **[1 mark]**

C_nH_n ☐ C_nH_{2n} ☐ C_nH_{n+2} ☐ C_nH_{2n+2} ☐

Look at **Figure 1** if you need to work out the relationship between C atoms and H atoms.

(b) Calculate the number of hydrogen atoms in an alkane containing one carbon atom. **[1 mark]**

....

5 Structure of alkanes — Grade 4

5. The molecular formula of an alkane is C_3H_8.

(a) Name this alkane. .... **[1 mark]**

(b) Draw the structure of this alkane, showing all the atoms and chemical bonds. **[1 mark]**

 Made a start  Feeling confident  Exam ready

Fractional distillation

2 Quick quiz

The petrochemical industry uses crude oil to make useful substances, such as lubricants.

Name **three** other types of useful substance produced by the petrochemical industry.

....

5 Fractions from crude oil

Grades 3–5

1. (a) Figure 1 shows a fractionating column used to separate crude oil into useful mixtures called fractions. Label **Figure 1** to show where each of the missing fractions are collected. Use the words in the box. **[2 marks]**

diesel oil	heavy fuel oil	petrol

Figure 1

(b) LPG stands for liquefied petroleum gases. Define the term 'liquefied'. **[1 mark]**

....

(c) Name **three** fuels, other than LPG, obtained from the column in **Figure 1**. **[3 marks]**

1 petrol .... 2 .... 3 ....

2. Crude oil is separated into useful mixtures by fractional distillation.

(a) Give the hottest level of the fractionating column. .... **[1 mark]**

(b) Describe what happens to the substances in crude oil when they enter the fractionating column. **[1 mark]**

....

This is a change in state.

(c) The different substances in crude oil travel up inside the fractionating column. Describe what happens when they cool down. **[1 mark]**

This is also a change in state.

....

4 Properties of fractions

Grade 5

3. The boiling points of three fractions are given in **Table 1**.

(a) Give **one** way in which the molecules in a fraction are similar to each other. **[1 mark]**

....

(b) Give **two** ways in which **Table 1** shows that fractions are mixtures. **[2 marks]**

Table 1

Fraction	Number of carbon atoms in molecule	Boiling point in °C
petrol	4–12	30–200
kerosene	11–15	150–300
diesel oil	14–20	200–350

1 ....

2 ....

Hydrocarbons

2 Quick quiz

Circle which formulae in the box are hydrocarbons.

C_3H_8	$C_5H_{11}OH$	$C_{12}H_{24}$	$C_{100}H_{202}$	$CH_3CH_2CH_3$	$CH_3CHCHCH_2Br$	CH_2CHCH_3

10 Combustion of hydrocarbons — Grades 3–5

1. Methane is a hydrocarbon fuel.

(a) Balance the equation for the complete combustion of methane. **[1 mark]**

$CH_4 + \ldots\ldots O_2 \rightarrow CO_2 + 2H_2O$

(b) Name the **two** products formed in this reaction. **[2 marks]**

1 .... 2 ....

(c) Determine whether the carbon and hydrogen in methane are oxidised or reduced in the reaction. Give a reason for your answer. **[2 marks]**

....

....

Look at what happens to the C and H from CH_4.

(d) The combustion of methane releases energy. Identify the type of reaction. **[1 mark]**

....

5 Properties of hydrocarbons — Grade 4

2. The fractions from crude oil have different properties. These include viscosity and flammability.

(a) Give the meaning of the following terms:

(i) high viscosity thick rather than runny **[1 mark]**

(ii) high flammability .... **[1 mark]**

(b) Describe what happens to the viscosity and flammability as the size of the molecule increases.

Viscosity .... Flammability .... **[2 marks]**

5 More about hydrocarbons — Grade 5

3. Describe how the boiling points of alkanes change as the molecule size increases. **[1 mark]**

....

4. Camping gas contains propane, C_3H_8. Write a balanced equation for the complete combustion of propane in oxygen, O_2. The products are CO_2 and H_2O only. **[2 marks]**

....

....

 Made a start  Feeling confident Exam ready

Cracking and alkenes

1 Quick quiz

Name the **two** types of cracking. ....

10 Cracking reactions — Grades 3–4

1. Which statement correctly describes what happens during cracking? Tick **one** box. **[1 mark]**

Small hydrocarbons are joined together to form larger more useful molecules. ☐

Small hydrocarbons are joined together to form larger less useful molecules. ☐

Large hydrocarbons are broken down to form smaller less useful molecules. ☐

Large hydrocarbons are broken down to form smaller more useful molecules. ☐

2. Complete the sentences about why cracking is needed. Use words from the box. **[4 marks]**

cracking	ending	high	large	low	small	starting

There is a ....high..... demand for fuels that contain .... molecules. Some of the products of .... are useful as these fuels. They are also useful as .... materials for making other substances such as polymers.

3. Complete the equations to show the cracking of hydrocarbons.

Make sure the number of C and H atoms are the same on both sides of the arrow.

(a) $C_8H_{18} \rightarrow C_4H_{10} + C_4H$................ **[1 mark]**

(b) $C_{10}H_{22} \rightarrow C_8H_{18} +$ .... **[1 mark]**

(c) .... $\rightarrow C_3H_8 + C_2H_4$ **[1 mark]**

(d) $C_4H_{10} \rightarrow$ .... $+ C_3H_6$ **[1 mark]**

5 Alkanes and alkenes — Grade 3

4. Some of the products of cracking are alkanes and some are alkenes. Bromine water is an orange solution of bromine dissolved in water.

(a) Describe what you see when an alkane is mixed with bromine water. **[1 mark]**

....

(b) Describe what you see when an alkene is mixed with bromine water. **[1 mark]**

....

Exam focus
When describing an observation of colour, 'clear' is not a colour – it just means that you can see through it.

 Made a start  Feeling confident  Exam ready

Pure substances

2 Quick quiz

Which diagrams represent a pure substance?

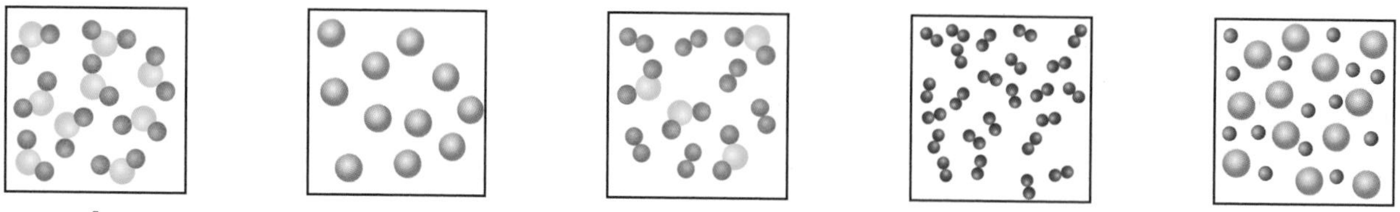

A B C D E

5 Pure substances and mixtures — Grade 3

1. Which of the following substances are **always** impure? Tick **two** boxes. **[2 marks]**

iron ☐ orange squash ☐ sugar ☐ milk ☐

2. Explain why oxygen and carbon dioxide are pure substances, but air is not. **[2 marks]**

Oxygen is a single element and carbon dioxide is a single compound, but ....

....

10 Identifying mixtures — Grade 3

3. Table 1 shows properties of pure water and seawater.

Seawater is a mixture of water and dissolved salts. Describe the effect of dissolving salts on

(a) the melting point of water **[1 mark]**

....

(b) the boiling point of water **[1 mark]**

....

Table 1

	Pure water	Seawater
Melting point in °C	0	−2
Boiling point in °C	100.0	100.5

4. Octane is a substance found in petrol. Octane boils at 125 °C. Petrol boils between 30 °C and 200 °C.

Describe how you can tell that petrol contains a mixture of substances and is not pure octane. **[2 marks]**

A pure substance melts and boils at a specific temperature, but petrol ....

....

5 Pure substances — Grade 4

5. (a) Give **two** properties of a substance that can be used to distinguish pure from impure substances. **[2 marks]**

1 .... **2** ....

(b) 'Pure orange juice' is produced from the juice of oranges with nothing added. Give a reason why chemists would not consider orange juice to be a pure substance. **[1 mark]**

....

....

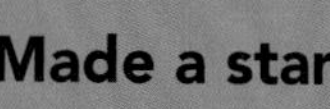
 Made a start
Feeling confident
 Exam ready

Formulations

2 Quick quiz

Use words from the box to complete the sentences about mixtures.

combined	compounds	two	three	unchanged

A mixture contains at least .... elements or .... These substances are not chemically ...., so their chemical properties are ....

10 Mixtures and formulations

Grades 3–4

1. Complete **Table 1** to show the correct features of a formulation. Tick the correct boxes. **[3 marks]**

Table 1

Feature	Tick if correct
Each component has a particular purpose.	
It has components in random amounts.	
It is a natural substance.	
It is a complex mixture.	
It is designed to be useful.	

2. Which of the following substances are formulations? Tick **three** boxes. **[3 marks]**

alloys	☐	fertiliser	✓	medicine	☐
mud	☐	oil and water	☐	seawater	☐

3. Baby milk powder is a formulation. It contains cow's milk and other ingredients. Suggest why other substances are added to cow's milk to produce baby milk powder. **[2 marks]**

....

....

A human baby has different needs from a calf.

10 Identifying formulations

Grade 5

4. **Table 2** shows the ingredients of a washing-up liquid. These include surfactants, which remove oil and grease from dirty dishes. Sodium chloride increases the thickness of the washing-up liquid.

(a) Describe how you can tell that washing-up liquid is a formulation. **[2 marks]**

....

....

Table 2

Ingredient	% by mass
water	55%
surfactants	35%
sodium chloride	8%
perfume	2%
colour	2%

(b) Suggest **two** reasons why perfume and colour are ingredients in the washing-up liquid. **[2 marks]**

1 ....

2 ....

(c) Suggest what would happen if washing-up liquid did not contain surfactants. **[1 mark]**

....

Chromatography

Quick quiz

True or false?

Under the same conditions, the R_f value of a particular substance is always the same. **True / False**

The paper used in chromatography is called the mobile phase. **True / False**

The smaller the R_f value, the more soluble the ink in the solvent. **True / False**

Chromatograms — Grade 3

1. Figure 1 shows a chromatogram of different inks. Black ink is a mixture of blue, red and yellow substances. Complete **Figure 1** to show what the chromatogram of black ink will look like. **[2 marks]**

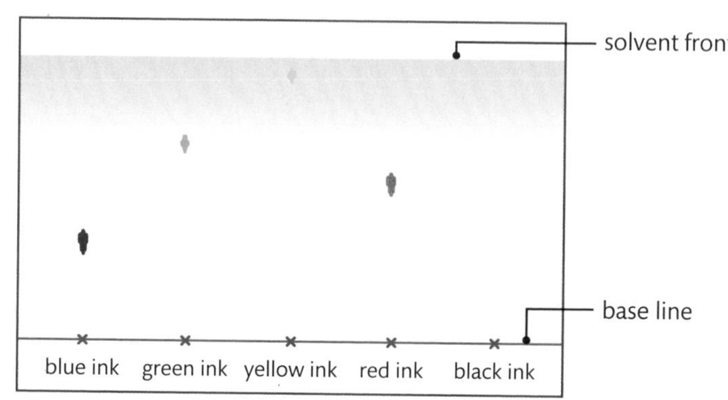

Figure 1

Calculating R_f values — Grade 4

2. A student carried out chromatography on food colouring. The solvent front travelled 7.3 cm and the yellow food colouring travelled 3.7 cm. Calculate the R_f value for the food colouring. Give your answer to two significant figures. **[2 marks]**

$$R_f = \frac{\text{distance moved by substance}}{\text{distance moved by solvent}} = \frac{3.7}{7.3} = \text{.......................}$$

R_f = ...

R_f values have no units. This is because both values used are distances and so their units cancel out. The R_f value is a ratio.

Maths skills

You need to know how to give answers to a stated number of significant figures (usually 1, 2 or 3 significant figures). To work out the number of significant figures, start at the first non-zero number, then count the number of figures you need to the right (including zeros). If the number after that is 5 or more, round up. If it is 4 or less, do not round up.

Paper chromatography — Grade 5

3. Explain how paper chromatography separates mixtures. **[5 marks]**

Remember that all types of chromatography rely upon two different phases.

....

....

....

....

....

Made a start — Feeling confident — Exam ready

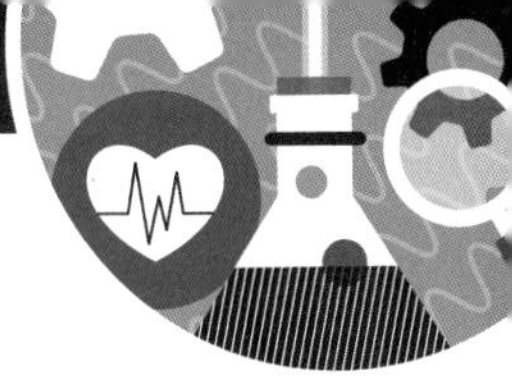

Paper chromatography

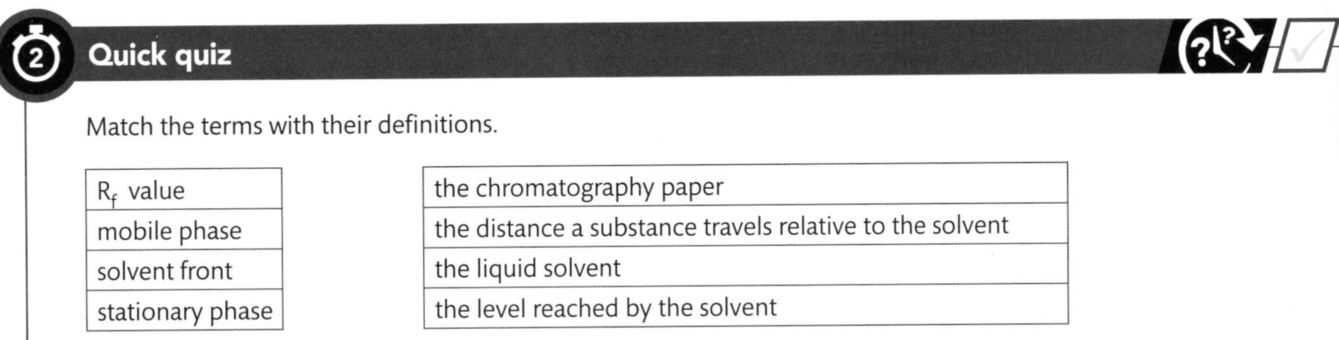

Quick quiz

Match the terms with their definitions.

Term
R_f value
mobile phase
solvent front
stationary phase

Definition
the chromatography paper
the distance a substance travels relative to the solvent
the liquid solvent
the level reached by the solvent

Preparing and using chromatograms — Grade 3

1. A student carries out a chromatography experiment. **Table 1** shows the steps used but they are in the wrong order. Write numbers 1 to 6 in the boxes to place the steps in the correct order. **[5 marks]**

Table 1

Step	Step number
Allow the solvent to rise through the paper.	
Add a small sample spot on the base line.	
Remove the paper and let it dry.	
Pour some solvent into a beaker.	1
Place the paper in the solvent.	
Draw a base line using a pencil and ruler.	

2. **Figure 1** shows a chromatogram of paint samples from an original 18th-century picture and from a possible modern forgery.

(a) Describe **one** way in which the results from the paint samples are similar. **[1 mark]**

....

(b) Describe **two** ways in which the results from the paint samples are different. **[2 marks]**

....

....

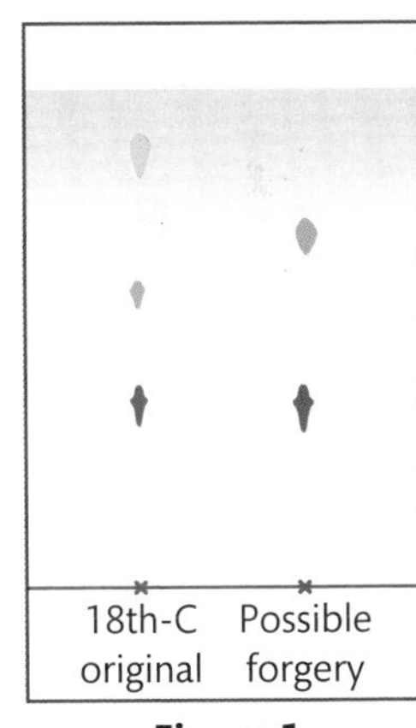

Figure 1

Analysis of chromatograms — Grade 4

3. **Figure 2** shows a chromatogram of a sample of pure cocaine and a sample of powder found in a police raid. Explain why the chromatogram shows that the sample of powder is impure cocaine. **[2 marks]**

....

....

cocaine sample

Figure 2

Testing for gases

2 Quick quiz

What are **four** gases produced in common reactions that can be tested for in the laboratory?

....

15 Gas tests — Grade 4

1. Describe a simple laboratory test for each of the following gases.

(a) chlorine **[2 marks]**

Place damp litmus paper near the mouth of a test tube of the gas. If chlorine is present, ...

....

(b) hydrogen **[2 marks]**

....

....

2. Hydrogen peroxide solution decomposes to form water and a gas. Describe a test to show that the gas produced is oxygen. **[2 marks]**

Say what you would do, and what you would expect to observe.

....

....

3. A student heats calcium carbonate using the apparatus shown in **Figure 1**.

(a) Name the gas identified using limewater. **[1 mark]**

....

(b) Describe **two** observations the student would see in the boiling tube of limewater. **[2 marks]**

....

....

Figure 1

5 Identifying gases — Grade 4

4. A student carries out an electrolysis experiment. The gas produced at the positive electrode is chlorine or oxygen. Describe how the student could test for both gases. **[4 marks]**

....

....

....

....

Made a start  Feeling confident Exam ready

Gases in the atmosphere

2 Quick quiz

(a) Name a relatively unreactive atmospheric gas that is not a noble gas. ....

(b) What gas in the atmosphere is needed for respiration? ....

(c) What gas in the atmosphere contributes to global warming? ....

10 Different gases — Grade 3

1. The air contains different gases.

(a) Draw **one** line from each name to its correct formula. **[4 marks]**

Name of gas
argon
oxygen
carbon dioxide
nitrogen
water

Formula of gas
O_2
N_2
CO_2
H_2O
Ar

(b) Some of the gases in part **(a)** are elements and some are compounds.

(i) Name **two** elements in the air. **[2 marks]**

1 .... 2 ....

(ii) Name **two** compounds in the air. **[2 marks]**

1 .... 2 ....

10 Percentages of gases — Grade 3

2. Approximately four-fifths of the atmosphere is nitrogen.

(a) Give the approximate percentage of nitrogen in the atmosphere. **[1 mark]**

....

(b) Give the approximate proportion of oxygen in the atmosphere. **[1 mark]**

....

(c) Name **one** gas in the atmosphere that accounts for less than 1% of the air. **[1 mark]**

....

3. (a) Name the **two** gases that make up almost all of the atmosphere. **[2 marks]**

....

(b) Approximately how long has the Earth's atmosphere remained mostly the same? Tick **one** box. **[1 mark]**

200 years ☐ 200 thousand years ☐ 200 million years ☐ 200 billion years ☐

 Made a start  Feeling confident ☐ Exam ready

Earth's early atmosphere

2 Quick quiz

Fill in the table to show whether the approximate percentage of each gas in the Earth's atmosphere has **increased** or **decreased** over time.

Gas	Approx. % in early atmosphere	Approx. % in atmosphere today	Change
nitrogen	3.5	80	
oxygen	0.5	20	
carbon dioxide	95	0.04	

15 Changes in Earth's atmosphere

Grades 3–5

1. Which of the following is the reason why evidence for the early atmosphere is limited? Tick **one** box. **[1 mark]**

- Scientists cannot analyse gases in the atmosphere. ☐
- Scientists have no interest in the early atmosphere. ☐
- The Earth formed over four billion years ago. ☐
- The Earth's atmosphere has changed very little. ☐

2. Where do scientists suggest the Earth's early atmosphere came from? Tick **one** box. **[1 mark]**

- photosynthesis by plants and algae ☐
- the Earth's inner core ☐
- the oceans when they boiled ☐
- volcanic activity ☐

3. Describe how the oceans formed. **[2 marks]**

As the Earth cooled, ...

....

4. The Earth's early atmosphere contained small proportions of compounds that contained hydrogen atoms. These included CH_4 and NH_3. Name these two gases. **[2 marks]**

CH_4 .... NH_3 ....

Each name consists of a single word.

5. Nitrogen gradually built up in the atmosphere over millions of years. Suggest a reason why it did not form compounds with other elements. **[1 mark]**

....

5 Changes over time

Grade 4

6. Table 1 shows the composition of the atmosphere of Mars today.

Table 1

Gas	nitrogen	oxygen	carbon dioxide	other gases
% in atmosphere	2.7	0.13	95.3	1.87

Describe **three** differences between the atmospheres of Mars and Earth today. **[3 marks]**

....

....

....

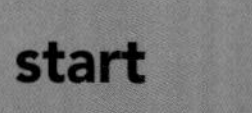

Made a start | Feeling confident

Exam ready

Oxygen and carbon dioxide levels

2 Quick quiz

(a) About how old is the Earth? ....

(b) About how long ago did algae first produce oxygen on Earth? ....

15 Photosynthesis — Grade 3

1. When algae and plants evolved, they absorbed carbon dioxide and released oxygen into the atmosphere. The balanced equation for photosynthesis is:

$6CO_2 + 6H_2O \rightarrow C_6H_{12}O_6 + 6O_2$

(a) Write a word equation for photosynthesis. **[2 marks]**

Look at the balancing numbers in the symbol equation.

.... → glucose + ...

(b) Compare the number of molecules of carbon dioxide absorbed with the number of molecules of oxygen released. **[1 mark]**

....

2. Explain why carbon dioxide levels changed when algae and plants evolved. **[2 marks]**

Carbon dioxide is absorbed when ....

....

5 Changes in carbon dioxide levels — Grade 4

3. Limestone is a sedimentary rock. The formation of limestone, and fossil fuels such as crude oil, also reduced carbon dioxide levels.

(a) Limestone is mostly a compound with the formula $CaCO_3$. Name this compound. **[1 mark]**

....

(b) Natural gas is a fossil fuel. It is mostly methane, CH_4.
Name the element that methane has in common with limestone. **[1 mark]**

Look at the formulae of the two compounds.

....

4. Coal is a fossil fuel. It is made from the ancient remains of plants. When the plants died, they were buried and turned to coal over millions of years.

(a) Name the process that produces glucose using carbon dioxide. **[1 mark]**

....

(b) Explain how the process named in part **(a)** affects carbon dioxide levels. **[2 marks]**

....

....

(c) Suggest a reason why the formation of coal reduced carbon dioxide levels. **[1 mark]**

....

Greenhouse gases

2 Quick quiz

Visible light reaches the Earth from the Sun. Name **two** other types of solar radiation.

....

10 Greenhouse gases — Grade 3

1. Table 1 shows the names and formulae of gases found in the atmosphere.

Table 1

Name of gas	Formula	Number of atoms	Number of elements
carbon dioxide	CO_2	3	2
nitrogen	N_2		
oxygen	O_2		
water vapour	H_2O		

(a) Complete **Table 1** to show the number of atoms and elements in a molecule of each substance. **[4 marks]**

(b) A gas can act as a greenhouse gas if its molecules contain two or more different elements.

(i) Name **one** gas in **Table 1** that can act as a greenhouse gas. **[1 mark]**

....

(ii) Name **one** gas in **Table 1** that does not act as a greenhouse gas. **[1 mark]**

....

(iii) Suggest why methane, CH_4, can act as a greenhouse gas. **[1 mark]**

....

How many elements are there in a methane molecule?

10 The greenhouse effect — Grade 4

2. Complete the sentences about the greenhouse effect. Use words from the box. **[5 marks]**

absorb	atmosphere	emit	infrared	Sun	surface	ultraviolet

Solar energy such as visible light and ....ultraviolet.... light reaches the Earth's surface from the ....

The Earth's .... warms up as it absorbs solar energy.

The warm surface emits .... radiation.

Greenhouse gases absorb and re-emit this radiation, warming the Earth's ....

 Made a start  Feeling confident Exam ready

Human contribution to greenhouse gases

2 Quick quiz

Name **two** human activities that increase the amounts of greenhouse gases in the atmosphere.

....

10 Natural gas — Grade 3

1. Natural gas is mostly methane, CH_4.

Fuels react with oxygen when they burn.

(a) Write a word equation for the complete combustion of methane. **[2 marks]**

.... + ... → carbon dioxide + ...

(b) Human activities release natural gas into the atmosphere. For example, natural gas can leak from pipes and storage tanks.

(i) Give a reason why these leaks increase the amount of greenhouse gases in the atmosphere. **[1 mark]**

....

(ii) Explain why **using** natural gas also increases the amount of greenhouse gases. **[2 marks]**

....

....

5 Population growth — Grade 3

2. The human population is increasing. This causes more demand for resources.

(a) Give **two** types of farming that cause the release of methane. **[2 marks]**

rice farming and ....

(b) Give **one** reason why transport releases carbon dioxide. **[1 mark]**

Think about how most vehicles are powered.

....

5 Predicting climate change — Grade 4

3. The concentration of carbon dioxide in the atmosphere was 302 parts per million in 1918. It was 412 parts per million, one hundred years later, in 2018.

(a) Calculate the increase in the concentration of carbon dioxide between 1918 and 2018. **[1 mark]**

(b) Calculate the mean change in concentration per year. Use your answer to part **(a)**. **[2 marks]**

Global climate change

2 Quick quiz

True or false?

Carbon dioxide is a greenhouse gas. **True / False**

Levels of carbon dioxide in the atmosphere are increasing. **True / False**

Average global temperature is increasing. **True / False**

5 Weather and climate — Grade 2

1. Complete the sentences about weather and climate. Use words from the box. **[5 marks]**

hours	long	short	snow	weather	years

Weather is the conditions of the atmosphere over a ...short... time, such as a few .... or weeks. Climate is the .... in a place, averaged over a .... time such as several .... or decades.

2. Which of the following correctly describes global warming and climate change? Tick **one** box. **[1 mark]**

Climate change and global warming are the same. ☐

Climate change is a cause of global warming. ☐

Global warming causes the greenhouse effect. ☐

Global warming is a cause of climate change. ☐

15 Effects of climate change — Grade 5

3. Table 1 shows information about 1 kg of water at different temperatures.

(a) Describe the effect of increasing temperature on the volume of water. **[1 mark]**

....

Table 1

Temperature in °C	4	20	40	60
Volume in dm^3	1	1.002	1.008	1.017
Mass of dissolved oxygen in mg	13	9.1	6.4	4.8

(b) Suggest an effect on sea levels as the temperature of seawater increases. **[1 mark]**

....

(c) Explain why increasing temperatures over land covered by ice may cause increasing sea levels. **[2 marks]**

Increasing temperatures will cause ice to melt. The water will ....

....

(d) Describe the effect of increasing temperature on the mass of dissolved oxygen in water. **[1 mark]**

....

(e) Suggest a reason why increasing seawater temperatures may affect fish. **[2 marks]**

....

....

Remember that fish and other animals need oxygen for respiration.

4. Climate change may cause increasing temperatures and reduced rainfall in some places. Give **two** possible effects this may have on farming in those places. **[2 marks]**

....

....

☐ Made a start ☐ Feeling confident  ☐ Exam ready

The carbon footprint

2 Quick quiz

Which of the gases in the table contain carbon? Which of them are greenhouse gases? Place a tick in each correct box.

Gas	Contains carbon?	Greenhouse gas?
carbon dioxide		
methane		
nitrogen		
water vapour		

5 Carbon footprint — Grade 3

1. (a) Which of the following correctly defines the carbon footprint of a product? Tick **one** box. **[1 mark]**

the total amount of carbon dioxide emitted over its full life cycle ☐

the total amount of carbon dioxide emitted over part of its life cycle ☐

the total amount of carbon dioxide and other greenhouse gases emitted over its full life cycle ☐

the total amount of carbon dioxide and other greenhouse gases emitted over part of its life cycle ☐

(b) Carbon footprint applies to products. Give **two** other things it applies to. **[2 marks]**

1 services .... 2 ....

15 Reducing the carbon footprint — Grade 4

2. The carbon footprint can be reduced by reducing emissions of greenhouse gases that contain carbon. Name **two** gases that should be reduced.

Think about your answers to the Quick Quiz.

1 .... 2 ....

3. Table 1 shows the major sources of carbon emissions in the UK.

Table 1

Source	Percentage of emissions
construction	5
energy	21
food	13
services	23
transport	24
others	

(a) Calculate the percentage of carbon emitted by 'others'. **[1 mark]**

others = 100 – 5 – 21 – 13 – 23 – 24 = ...

(b) (i) Identify the greatest source of carbon emissions in the UK. **[1 mark]**

....

(ii) Suggest **one** way to reduce emissions from this source. **[1 mark]**

....

4. (a) Describe **two** ways in which a family could reduce its carbon footprint. **[2 marks]**

....

....

(b) Suggest **one** reason why the family's actual reduction in carbon emissions might be limited. **[1 mark]**

....

Made a start | Feeling confident | Exam ready

Atmospheric pollutants

1 Quick quiz

Match the pollutant to its impact.

particulates
nitrogen oxides
carbon monoxide
toxic gas

respiratory problems
global dimming

15 Producing pollutants — Grades 3–4

1. Complete combustion happens when a fuel burns in a good supply of oxygen.

(a) Complete the word equation for the complete combustion of a hydrocarbon fuel. **[2 marks]**

hydrocarbon + oxygen → .... + water

(b) Incomplete combustion happens in a limited supply of air.

(i) Name the gas produced during incomplete combustion that is **not** produced during complete combustion. **[1 mark]**

.... It is an oxide of carbon.

(ii) Name a solid product formed during incomplete combustion of a hydrocarbon fuel. **[1 mark]**

.... This is black in colour.

2. Fuels such as coal, oil and natural gas may contain some sulfur. The sulfur is present as a natural impurity. Write a word equation for the reaction between sulfur and oxygen. **[2 marks]**

....

3. Air is mainly a mixture of nitrogen and oxygen. These two gases react together in hot engines and furnaces to produce oxides of nitrogen.

(a) Write a word equation for the reaction that produces oxides of nitrogen. **[1 mark]**

....

(b) Oxides of nitrogen can cause respiratory problems. Give **one** other environmental problem caused by oxides of nitrogen. **[1 mark]**

....

5 Pollution problems — Grade 3

4. Why is carbon monoxide not easily detected? Tick **one** box. **[1 mark]**

It is colourful and has a smell. ☐

It is colourful and does not have a smell. ☐

It is colourless and has a smell. ☐

It is colourless and does not have a smell. ☐

5. Name **two** atmospheric pollutants responsible for acid rain. **[2 marks]**

....

....

....

 Made a start  Feeling confident  Exam ready

Earth's resources

1 Quick quiz

Circle the things that the Earth's resources provide humans with.

building materials clothing food shelter transport warmth

10 Types of resource — Grade 3

1. Draw **one** line from each type of resource to its definition. **[3 marks]**

Type of resource
finite resource
non-renewable resource
renewable resource

Definition
It can be replaced after it has been used.
It is being used up faster than it can be replaced.
It is not being made any more, or is being made very slowly.

2. Farmers now mostly fertilise their crops using ammonium nitrate. This is manufactured using ammonia from the Haber process.

(a) Explain whether ammonium nitrate is natural or synthetic. Give a reason for your answer. **[2 marks]**

....

....

A synthetic material is made using chemical reactions.

(b) Suggest a natural fertiliser that farmers could use. .... **[1 mark]**

(c) Give a reason for your answer to part **(b)**. **[1 mark]**

....

5 Sustainable development — Grade 3

3. Complete the sentence about sustainable development. Use words from the box. **[3 marks]**

future	harming	helping	needs	now	past

Sustainable development means meeting the ..needs.. of people today, without .... the ability of people in the .... to meet their needs.

4. Many clothes are made from synthetic materials such as nylon. Give **one** natural resource that could be used to make clothes. .... **[1 mark]**

5 Copper — Grade 3

5. Copper is extracted from copper ore using chemical reactions. The world uses about 20 million tonnes of copper a year. There are about 700 million tonnes of copper left in the Earth's crust.

Estimate the number of years of copper left in the world. Show your working. **[2 marks]**

 Made a start  Feeling confident  Exam ready

Potable water

2 Quick quiz

(a) Give **three** sources of fresh water.

....

(b) Give **one** source of salty water.

....

5 Potable water — Grade 3

1. (a) Give the meaning of 'potable water'. **[1 mark]**

It is water that is safe to ....

(b) Give **one** reason why potable water is not pure water. **[1 mark]**

Think about what mixtures are.

....

10 Treating water — Grade 3

2. Fresh water is treated to make it safe to drink. **Figure 1** shows the three main stages in this treatment. Label the diagram. Use words from the box. **[3 marks]**

distillation	filtration	osmosis	sedimentation	sterilisation

Figure 1

3. Fresh water treatment involves killing microbes in the water. Name three sterilising agents used. **[3 marks]**

1 ultraviolet light .... **2** .... **3** ....

4. Salty water contains too much dissolved salt to make it safe to drink.

Salty water is sometimes described as being 'saline'.

(a) Name the process of removing salt from salty water. .... **[1 mark]**

(b) Reverse osmosis can be used to produce potable water from salty water. Name the essential piece of equipment needed for reverse osmosis. .... **[1 mark]**

....

(c) Name one other process used to produce potable water from salty water. **[1 mark]**

....

Made a start Feeling confident Exam ready

Purifying water

2 Quick quiz

Match each keyword to its definition.

purification
condensation
evaporation
pH

a measure of how acidic or alkaline a solution is
water changing from the liquid state to the gas state
removing contaminants
water changing from the gas state to the liquid state

5 Purifying water — Grade 3

1. A student purifies a sample of muddy water.

(a) Give a reason why the student filters the water. **[1 mark]**

....

(b) The student then distils the water. Describe how to carry out distillation of water. **[3 marks]**

Heat the water in a flask so that it boils.

....

15 Testing water — Grades 3–4

2. Two water samples were heated on watch glasses until all the water had boiled away. Describe what you would expect to see on the watch glass for

(a) pure water .... **[1 mark]**

(b) water containing dissolved salts.. **[1 mark]**

3. Table 1 shows the pH of three samples of water, **A**, **B** and **C**.

(a) Give the pH of pure water. **[1 mark]**

....

(b) Identify the purest sample of water in the table. Give a reason for your answer. **[2 marks]**

....

(c) Give a reason why the sample you identified will **not** be pure water. **[1 mark]**

It will contain

....

Table 1

Sample	pH
A	6.0
B	7.5
C	7.1

4. Table 2 shows the boiling points of three samples of water.

(a) Give the boiling point of pure water. **[1 mark]**

....

(b) Identify the purest sample of water. Give a reason for your answer. **[2 marks]**

....

Table 2

Sample	Boiling point in °C
X	100.2
Y	100.6
Z	100.4

Waste water treatment

2 Quick quiz

Name **three** sources of waste water.

....

15 Treating waste water — Grades 3–4

1. Complete **Table 1** to show the **main** contaminants found in each type of waste water. Tick all correct boxes. **[6 marks]**

Table 1

	Main contaminant		
Type of waste water	**Organic matter**	**Harmful microbes**	**Harmful chemicals**
sewage	✓	✓	
agricultural waste			
industrial waste			

A contaminant is something that makes a substance impure.

2. Draw **one** line from each treatment stage to the reason for doing it. **[3 marks]**

Treatment stage
aerobic biological treatment
anaerobic digestion
sedimentation
screening

Reason for doing it
lets solids settle out to produce sludge and effluent
removes rubbish and grit
breaks down effluent, releasing carbon dioxide
breaks down sludge, releasing methane

3. Two of the stages in waste water treatment release gases. Methane is one of these gases.

(a) Suggest **one** use for methane. **[1 mark]**

....

Methane is the main gas found in natural gas.

(b) Methane and carbon dioxide are greenhouse gases. Name **one** environmental problem caused by these gases. **[1 mark]**

....

5 Producing drinking water — Grade 4

4. It is possible to produce drinking water (potable water) from waste water.

(a) Give **two** contaminants that must be removed from waste water to make it safe to drink. **[2 marks]**

....

(b) Suggest a reason why it may be easier to produce drinking water from clean seawater, rather than from waste water or fresh water. **[1 mark]**

....

It may help to look back at page 148 about potable water.

Made a start  Feeling confident  Exam ready

Life cycle assessment

2 Quick quiz

Give **three** factors that are considered in a life cycle assessment (LCA) of a product.

....

5 Stages in an LCA — Grade 2

1. (a) Table 1 shows the four main stages in the life cycle assessment (LCA) of a product. They are not in the correct order. Write the numbers 1 to 4 to place them in the correct order, starting with 1. **[3 marks]**

Table 1

Description of stage	Order of stage
disposal of the product at the end of its useful life	
extracting and processing of raw materials	1
use of the product during its useful lifetime	
manufacturing and packaging the product	

(b) Give **two** things that are taken into account at every stage in an LCA. **[2 marks]**

1 distributing the product .... 2 ....

5 Stages in an LCA — Grade 3

2. Give **one** reason why companies carry out LCAs before they begin manufacture of a new product. **[1 mark]**

to assess the ....

3. It is difficult to quantify (to give numbers or values to) the effects of a pollutant in an LCA. It is relatively easy to quantify other factors, such as mass of waste produced. Give **three** other factors that are relatively easy to quantify. **[3 marks]**

1 the mass of natural resources used .... 2 .... 3 ....

10 Analysing LCA data — Grade 4

4. Table 2 compares the LCAs for the manufacture of two types of drinking cups.

(a) Identify the type of cup that uses the most energy in its manufacture. **[1 mark]**

....

(b) Suggest which type of cup would be least harmful to the environment. Give **two** reasons for your answer. Use information from **Table 2**. **[2 marks]**

....

....

Table 2

	Type of cup	
	Plastic	Paper
Energy used in J	12 000	21 000
Mass of CO_2 produced in g	270	603
Volume of fresh water used in dm^3	367	7245

(c) Plastic cups are made from crude oil, a non-renewable resource. Paper cups are made from wood, a renewable resource. Describe how this information may change the conclusion of an LCA based only on the information in **Table 2**. **[2 marks]**

....

....

Reducing the use of resources

Quick quiz

Give **three** ways in which we can reduce the use of resources.

....

Products from limited raw materials — Grade 2

1. Table 1 shows some products. Complete the table by placing a tick if the product is made from a limited raw material. **[3 marks]**

Table 1

Product	Made from a limited raw material
cotton	
glass	
metal	✓
plastic	
wood	

Recycling metals — Grade 3

2. Metals can be recycled.

(a) Give **two** ways in which metals can be recycled. **[2 marks]**

1 reforming into different products

2 ....

(b) Aluminium and steel are commonly recycled. Household waste usually contains a mixture of products made from these metals. Describe **one** way to separate steel objects from aluminium objects. **[2 marks]**

One of these metals is magnetic.

....

....

(c) Iron ore contains iron oxide. Iron is extracted by heating the iron ore with carbon in a blast furnace. Suggest **one** reason why scrap steel may be added to molten iron from a blast furnace. **[1 mark]**

....

Recycling glass — Grade 3

3. Glass is made from sand and some other substances. Glass is used to make bottles. Used milk bottles may be collected. They can be washed and reused, or recycled.

(a) Give the **three** main steps needed to recycle a glass bottle. **[3 marks]**

1 .... 2 .... 3 ....

(b) Give **one** way, other than recycling, to reduce the use of raw materials for glass. **[1 mark]**

....

(c) Suggest **one** reason why some products are recycled rather than reused. **[1 mark]**

....

Energy transfers in a system

2 Quick quiz

Complete the following descriptions to show the energy transfers that take place.

An object that is thrown up into the air: kinetic energy transfers to g..............................

p.............................. energy

A car moving along a race track when the brakes are applied to slow it down: k..............................

energy transfers to heating of the brakes.

Water in an electric kettle as its temperature rises: e.............................. energy

transfers to h.............................. of the water.

5 Conservation of energy — Grade 3

1. Define the term 'conservation of energy'. **[1 mark]**

Energy can be .... usefully, ... or

dissipated, but cannot be .... or ....

Remember to mention energy transfers and whether energy can be created or destroyed.

10 Energy stores — Grade 4

2. A toy crane powered by batteries is used to lift an object above the ground.

(a) Name the energy store that provides energy to move the toy crane. **[1 mark]**

.... energy

Where does the power come from?

(b) Which energy stores of the object increase as it is lifted from the ground? Tick **two** boxes. **[2 marks]**

gravitational potential energy ☐

electrical energy ☐

elastic potential energy ☐

kinetic energy ☐

nuclear energy ☐

Choose one of the energy stores listed in part **(b)**.

(c) When the crane stops, the object does not go higher. Give the energy store in which **all** the usefully transferred energy is stored. **[1 mark]**

....

5 Energy transfer — Grade 5

3. What is the energy transfer when a stretched spring is released to make a metal ball move in a pinball game? Tick **one** box. **[1 mark]**

kinetic energy to thermal energy ☐

elastic potential energy to kinetic energy ☐

elastic potential energy to thermal energy ☐

kinetic energy to elastic potential energy ☐

Gravitational potential energy

2 Quick quiz

Complete the equation by selecting words from the box.

force	field	weight	mass	kinetic	potential	position	height

gravitational .... energy

= .... × gravitational .... strength × .... above ground

5 Calculating energy — Grade 5

1. A 65 kg person climbs 1090 m to the top of a mountain. Use the following equation to calculate how much energy their gravitational potential energy store gains. Give your answer to three significant figures.

Gravitational field strength = 9.8 N/kg.

gravitational potential energy = mass × gravitational field strength × height **[3 marks]**

$E_p = mgh$

$= 65 \times$ .... × .... = ...

gravitational potential energy gain = ... J

5 Gravitational potential energy — Grade 5

2. Figure 1 shows a funicular railway that travels up the side of a steep hill. The mass of a carriage when it is fully loaded with passengers is 2600 kg. Gravitational field strength = 9.8 N/kg.

(a) Use the following equation to calculate the change in gravitational potential energy as the carriage travels up the hill, so it reaches a height of 40 m.

gravitational potential energy = mass × gravitational field strength × height

[2 marks]

gravitational potential energy = ... J

Figure 1

(b) Suggest how the change in gravitational potential energy would be different if the carriage stopped halfway up the hill. **[1 mark]**

....

5 Energy of a skydiver — Grade 5

3. A skydiver with a mass of 65 kg jumps from an aircraft 4000 m above the ground. Gravitational field strength = 9.8 N/kg

(a) Use the following equation to calculate the skydiver's gravitational potential energy just before jumping.

gravitational potential energy = mass × gravitational field strength × height **[2 marks]**

gravitational potential energy = ... J

(b) Energy is transferred between stores as the skydiver accelerates towards the ground. Write the energy transfer. **[1 mark]**

.... ⟶ ....

Kinetic energy

Quick quiz

True or false?

A moving object always has a kinetic energy store. **True / False**

A stationary object has a kinetic energy store. **True / False**

If a vehicle is travelling at a constant speed in a straight line, its kinetic energy store does not change. **True / False**

If a vehicle is accelerating, its kinetic energy store does not change. **True / False**

Kinetic energy — Grade 4

1. Complete the sentence. Tick **one** box. **[1 mark]**

The amount of energy in an object's kinetic energy store is

directly proportional to its speed ☐

inversely proportional to its speed ☐

directly proportional to its $(\text{speed})^2$ ☐

inversely proportional to its $(\text{speed})^2$ ☐

Remember the equation for kinetic energy.

'Directly proportional' means that one variable increases as another variable increases. 'Inversely proportional' means that one variable decreases as another increases.

Calculating kinetic energy — Grade 5

2. A bus with a mass of 10 000 kg is travelling at a speed of 10 m/s.

(a) Use the following equation to calculate the kinetic energy of the bus.

kinetic energy = 0.5 × mass × $(\text{speed})^2$ **[2 marks]**

kinetic energy = 0.5 × .... × (..............................)^2 = ...

kinetic energy = ...J

(b) The bus comes to a stop. Give the work done by the brakes on the bus to stop it moving. **[1 mark]**

work done = ...J

When work is done on the bus to get it moving, the bus is given kinetic energy. The same amount of work is needed to stop the bus moving.

Kinetic energy transfers — Grade 5

3. A bullet is shot at a target from a rifle. The bullet's mass is 4.0 g. The bullet travels at 1000 m/s.

(a) Use the following equation to calculate the kinetic energy of the moving bullet.

kinetic energy = 0.5 × mass × $(\text{speed})^2$ **[3 marks]**

Remember to convert the mass into kg.

kinetic energy = ...J

(b) Suggest what happens to the kinetic energy of the bullet when it is stopped by the target. **[1 mark]**

....

....

 Made a start  Feeling confident  Exam ready

Energy in a spring

2 Quick quiz

Match each quantity in the equation $E_e = \frac{1}{2} \times k \times e^2$ with its symbol and correct unit.

Quantity
spring constant
extension
elastic potential energy

Symbol
E_e
k
e

Unit
N/m
m
J

5 Stretching springs — Grade 3

1. Figure 1 shows a spring before and after it is stretched. Work is done on the spring to stretch it. Which energy store is this energy transferred to? Tick **one** box. **[1 mark]**

gravitational potential energy ☐

elastic potential energy ☐

kinetic energy ☐

chemical energy ☐

after stretching

Figure 1

5 Calculating the spring constant — Grade 5

2. A spring stores 20 J of elastic potential energy when it is stretched by 0.1 m. Use the following equation to calculate the spring constant.

elastic potential energy = 0.5 × spring constant × (extension)^2 **[3 marks]**

.... = 0.5 × spring constant × (.............................)^2

spring constant = 2 × $\frac{\text{....................}}{(\text{....................})^2}$ = ...

spring constant = ... N/m

You need to rearrange the equation so that the spring constant is the subject.

Moving the 0.5 to the other side of the equation turns it into a multiplication by 2.

5 Elastic potential energy — Grade 5

3. The equation for the energy stored in a stretched spring is: elastic potential energy = 0.5 × spring constant × (extension)^2

A spring is stretched by 5 cm to store elastic potential energy. The spring is then allowed to return to its original length. The same spring is then stretched by 10 cm. Compare the elastic potential energy stored by the spring when it is stretched by 5 cm and 10 cm. Tick **one** box. **[1 mark]**

Spring stretched by 10 cm has 4 times more energy stored as spring stretched by 5 cm. ☐

Spring stretched by 10 cm has 2 times more energy stored as spring stretched by 5 cm. ☐

Spring stretched by 10 cm has 0.5 times more energy stored as spring stretched by 5 cm. ☐

Spring stretched by 10 cm has 0.25 times more energy stored as spring stretched by 5 cm. ☐

The spring constant and the 0.5 in the equation are the same for both springs. So you can ignore them when comparing the two springs.

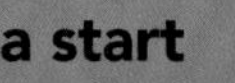 Made a start  Feeling confident  Exam ready

Using energy equations

2 Quick quiz

Match each energy transfer to its description.

Description
ball dropping from a height of 5 m
battery-powered model car moving
spring that is stretched then released

Energy transfer
elastic potential to kinetic
gravitational potential to kinetic
chemical to kinetic

10 Calculating energy — Grade 5

1. Figure 1 shows a compressed spring firing a ball into the air.

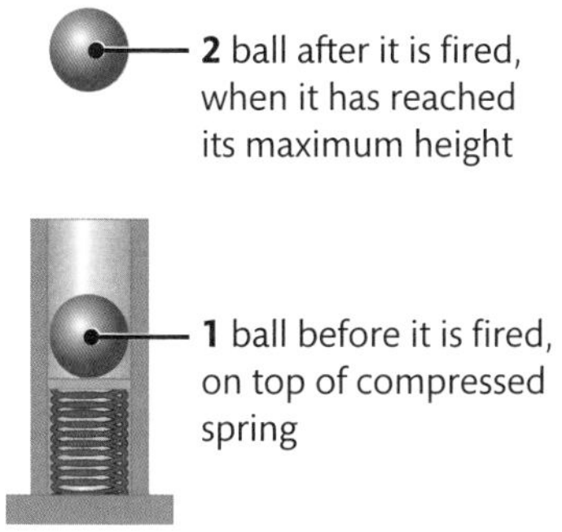

(a) The spring has a spring constant of 200 N/m. It is compressed by 0.25 m. Use the following equation to calculate the elastic potential energy stored by the spring.

elastic potential energy = 0.5 × spring constant × $(\text{extension})^2$ **[2 marks]**

elastic potential energy = 0.5 × .... × (..........................)^2

= ....

elastic potential energy stored = ... J

2 ball after it is fired, when it has reached its maximum height

1 ball before it is fired, on top of compressed spring

Figure 1

(b) Complete the energy transfer at the time of release for the ball. **[1 mark]**

elastic potential energy → ....

What is the energy store of movement?

(c) The ball rises vertically into the air. It slows down until it reaches a maximum height and has zero speed.

(i) Give the new energy store into which the energy of movement is transferred. **[1 mark]**

....

Which energy store involves a measurement of height?

(ii) Write down the equation that links energy, gravitational field strength, height and mass. **[1 mark]**

energy = mass × .... ×

10 Energy transfers — Grade 5

2. Figure 2 shows a waterslide ride at a theme park.

(a) Give the position of the carriage when it has maximum gravitational potential energy. **[1 mark]**

....

Figure 2

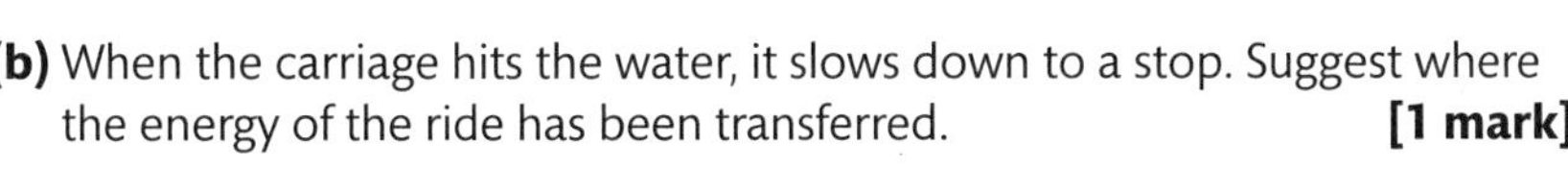

(b) When the carriage hits the water, it slows down to a stop. Suggest where the energy of the ride has been transferred. **[1 mark]**

....

Power

2 Quick quiz

Which equations are correctly arranged?

power = work done × time ☐

power = $\frac{\text{work done}}{\text{time}}$ ☐

time = $\frac{\text{work done}}{\text{power}}$ ☐

time = power × work done ☐

5 Calculating power — Grade 5

1. An electric fridge has a total energy input of 198 000 J per hour. Use the following equation to calculate its power.

power = $\frac{\text{energy transferred}}{\text{time}}$ **[3 marks]**

1 hour = 1 × 3600 = 3600 seconds

Power = $\frac{\text{.............................}}{\text{.............................}}$ = ...

For power, we need time in seconds so multiply the time in hours by 3600 to get the time in seconds.

power = ... W

5 Calculating energy from power — Grade 5

2. A kettle has a power of 2.5 kW. It takes 120 seconds to boil 1 kg of water in the kettle. Use the following equation to calculate the energy transferred to the water.

power = $\frac{\text{energy transferred}}{\text{time}}$ **[4 marks]**

2.5 kW = ... W

.... = $\frac{\text{...}}{120\,\text{s}}$

energy transferred = ... × 120 = ...

Make sure the quantities you use are in the correct units for the equation.

energy transferred = ... J

10 Power and energy — Grade 5

3. **Figure 1** shows a man climbing a set of steps. The man has a mass of 80 kg. The height of the steps is 7.5 m. Gravitational field strength = 9.8 N/kg.

(a) Use the following equation to calculate the change in gravitational potential energy of the man as he climbs from the bottom to the top of the steps.

gravitational potential energy = mass × gravitational field strength × height **[2 marks]**

Change in gravitational potential energy = ... J

Figure 1

(b) It takes 15 seconds for the man to climb the steps. Use the following equation to calculate the man's power.
Assume all the energy output by the man is transferred to useful energy.

power = $\frac{\text{energy transferred}}{\text{time}}$ **[2 marks]**

power = ... W

 Made a start 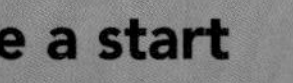  Feeling confident ☐ Exam ready

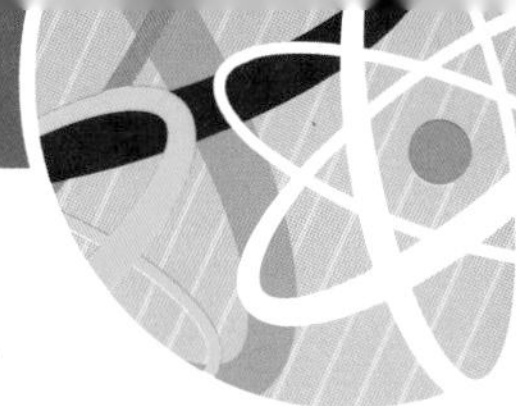

Efficiency

Quick quiz

Which statements about efficiency are correct?

Efficiency is measured in joules. ☐

The closer to 1 (or 100%), the more efficient the device. ☐

The lower the number for efficiency, the more efficient the device. ☐

A very efficient device will have an efficiency greater than 100%. ☐

If a device is 40% efficient, 40% of the energy is usefully transferred and 60% is wasted. ☐

If a device is 40% efficient, 60% of the energy is usefully transferred and 40% is wasted. ☐

Using efficiency data — Grade 5

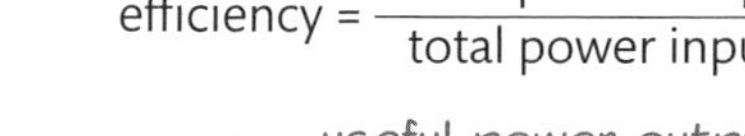

1. Table 1 shows information about lamp **A** and lamp **B**.

Table 1

Lamp	Power input in W	Useful power output in W
A	60	15
B	30	15

(a) Use the following equation to calculate the efficiency of each lamp. **[2 marks]**

$$\text{efficiency} = \frac{\text{useful power output}}{\text{total power input}}$$

Lamp A: $\frac{\text{useful power output}}{\text{total power input}} = \frac{\dots\dots}{\dots\dots} = \dots\dots$

Lamp B: $\frac{\text{useful power output}}{\text{total power input}} = \frac{\dots\dots}{\dots\dots} = \dots\dots$

(b) Give the efficiency of each lamp as a percentage. **[1 mark]**

Lamp A .... Lamp B ....

(c) Identify the most efficient lamp. Lamp .... **[1 mark]**

Convert a decimal or fraction into a percentage value by multiplying by 100.

Efficiency calculations — Grade 5

2. A 2000 W hairdryer provides useful power of 1500 W. All other power is wasted (the energy is dissipated to the surroundings).

(a) Calculate the power lost to the surroundings. **[1 mark]**

power lost = ... W

total power input
= useful power output + power lost to the surroundings

(b) Use the following equation to calculate the efficiency of the hairdryer. **[2 marks]**

$$\text{efficiency} = \frac{\text{useful power output}}{\text{total power input}}$$

efficiency = ...

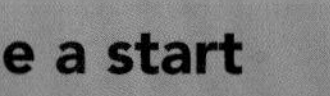

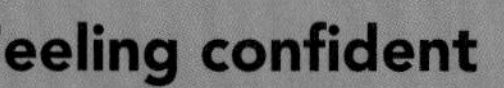

Exam ready

Renewable energy resources

2 Quick quiz

Match each energy resource to its description.

Resource
sunlight
geothermal
wind
tides

Description
air movement forces turbines to rotate, generating electricity
daily movement of the ocean is used to generate electricity
light energy is used to generate electricity using solar panels
heat energy from rocks underground is used to generate electricity

5 Wind power — Grade 3

1. **Figure 1** shows some wind turbines.

Give **two** advantages and **two** disadvantages of using wind power to generate electricity. **[4 marks]**

Advantages 1 Can be placed in isolated locations ....

2 ....

Disadvantages 1 Some people think they are an eyesore ....

2 ....

Figure 1

10 Tidal power and hydroelectricity — Grade 3

2. **Figure 2** shows **(a)** a tidal barrage and **(b)** a hydroelectric dam. Give **one** advantage and **one** disadvantage of using each one to generate electricity. **[4 marks]**

Tidal barrage:

advantage ....

disadvantage ....

Hydroelectric dam:

advantage ....

disadvantage ....

(a) (b)

Figure 2

5 Solar power — Grade 5

3. A medium-sized town in the UK wants to provide electricity to its houses and high-rise tower blocks using solar power only. What are **two** reasons why this is not realistic? Tick **two** boxes. **[2 marks]**

Solar panels are cheap to install but have very expensive running costs. ☐

Solar panels are expensive to install although they have low running costs. ☐

Solar panels do not produce renewable energy. ☐

Solar panels do not produce constant electricity; other sources of power or very expensive storage batteries are needed. ☐

Solar panels have many moving parts so are unreliable. ☐

Solar panels increase carbon dioxide and pollutant emissions. ☐

Non-renewable energy resources

Quick quiz

Name **three** fossil fuels.

....

Resources used for transport — Grade 5

1. Figure 1 shows a 'hybrid' car. This type of car has a fossil fuel powered engine. It can switch to battery power to reduce pollution. It uses any excess engine power to charge up the battery.

(a) What energy resources does this car use? Tick **one** box. **[1 mark]**

- renewable only ☐
- renewable and non-renewable ☐
- non-renewable only ☐
- neither renewable nor non-renewable ☐

Figure 1

(b) Table 1 gives some typical data about hybrid and electric cars. Suggest **two** reasons why hybrid cars are currently more popular in the UK than fully electric cars. **[2 marks]**

Table 1

Data	Hybrid car	Fully electric car
range in km (maximum distance it can travel before refuelling/recharging)	about 500	about 350
number of fuel stations or charging stations in the UK	about 8500	about 6000
number of passengers	4 or 5	4 or 5
cost to run per 100 km	£7.00	£3.70

Hybrid cars can travel .... than electric cars without having to stop for fuel or to recharge.

There are more .... for hybrid cars than there are ....

....

Which sets of data are better for hybrid cars than electric cars?

Comparing energy sources — Grade 5

2. Coal is an example of a non-renewable energy resource.

(a) Define the term 'non-renewable energy resource'. **[1 mark]**

....

(b) Describe **two** ways in which using coal to generate electricity affects the environment. **[2 marks]**

1 ....

2 ....

3. Figure 2 shows a nuclear power station.

Explain whether nuclear fuel is a renewable or a non-renewable energy resource. Justify your answer. **[2 marks]**

Figure 2

....

....

Made a start ☐ Feeling confident ☐ Exam ready ☐

Circuit diagrams

2 Quick quiz

Write the letter of the circuit symbol for each component.

cell		LED	
variable resistor		ammeter	
lamp		thermistor	

A, B, C, D, E, F

10 Series and parallel circuits — Grade 3

1. (a) Draw a circuit diagram to show three lamps connected in series with a power supply. **[2 marks]**

When components are connected in series, they form one single circuit loop.

(b) Draw a circuit diagram to show three lamps connected in parallel with a power supply. **[2 marks]**

In a parallel circuit, each component forms its own circuit loop with the power supply.

(c) Give the circuit, series or parallel, in which the lamps would be brighter. **[1 mark]**

The lamps in the .... circuit would be brighter.

10 Circuits and LEDs — Grade 4

2. A student wanted to measure the current through a lamp and the potential difference across it. Draw the circuit the student should use. **[3 marks]**

The circuit is the same for measuring the current and potential difference of any component.

3. A light-emitting diode (LED) is a device that allows current to pass through in one direction and then emits light.

(a) Draw a circuit diagram of a cell in series with a switch and an LED. The LED should light up when the switch is closed. **[1 mark]**

(b) Suggest a device that uses an LED. **[1 mark]**

....

Made a start  Feeling confident  Exam ready

Current, resistance and potential difference

Quick quiz

Match each key word with its definition.

Key word	Definition
current	opposes the flow of charge, caused by electrons colliding with metal ions inside wires; measured in ohms (Ω)
potential difference	the flow of charge; measured in amps (A)
resistance	the energy given to a charge as it flows; measured in volts (V)

Linking current, pd and resistance

Grade 5 

1. Each resistor in the circuit in **Figure 1** has a resistance of 10 Ω. The battery has a potential difference of 6 V.

(a) Explain what the reading on the voltmeter will be. **[2 marks]**

The reading will be .... V because ....

....

> There are three resistors connected in series, each with the same resistance.
> The voltmeter is measuring the potential difference across only one of these resistors.

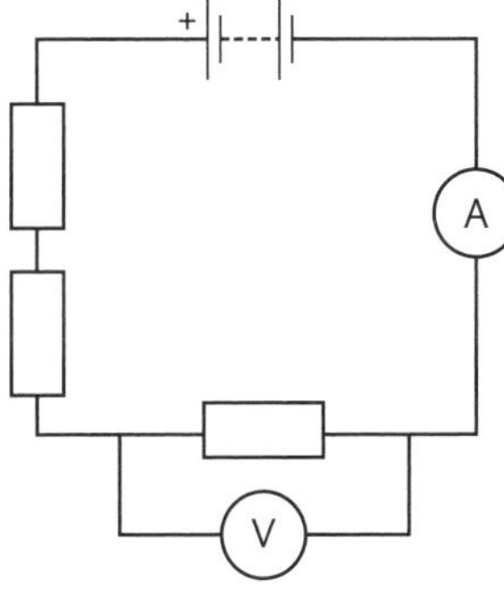

Figure 1

(b) Use the following equation to calculate the current in the circuit.

potential difference = current × resistance **[3 marks]**

6 = current × (3 × ....)

current = $\frac{6}{(3 \times \text{.................................})}$

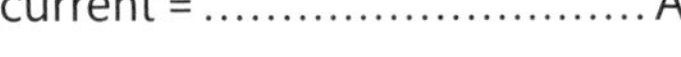

= ....

current = ... A

> You need to take all three resistors into account.

(c) The potential difference supplied by the battery is halved. Explain what effect this will have on the current in the circuit. **[2 marks]**

....

> Remember that voltage is proportional to current.

Resistance of a lamp

Grade 5 

2. Figure 2 shows a car headlight. A lamp is fitted in series with a battery. The potential difference from the battery is 12 V and the current is 5 A. **[3 marks]**

Use the following equation to calculate the resistance of the lamp.

potential difference = current × resistance

Figure 2

resistance of the lamp = ... Ω

 Made a start  Feeling confident  Exam ready

Electrical charge

2 Quick quiz

Fill in the gaps using the words in the box.

cell	electrons	move	negative	positive	repelled	wire

Current is produced when a .... causes the .... in a .... to .... The electrons have a .... charge. They are attracted to the .... terminal on the battery and .... by the negative terminal.

5 Charge calculations — Grade 4

1. A current of 10 A flows in an appliance. It is switched on for 30 minutes.

(a) Use the following equation to calculate the charge flow in the appliance.

charge flow = current × time **[3 marks]**

30 minutes = 30 × 60 = 1800 seconds

charge flow = current × time = ... × .... s = ...

charge flow = ... C

Always check that you have converted all quantities to the standard units needed for the equation. 1 minute = 60 seconds.

(b) The appliance is connected to the mains supply with a potential difference of 230 V. Use the following equation to calculate the energy transferred in 30 minutes.

energy transferred = charge flow × potential difference **[2 marks]**

energy transferred = ... × .... = ...

energy transferred = ... J

Use your answer to part **(a)** for charge.

2 Electrical circuits — Grade 3

2. Complete the following statement about electrical circuits. **[2 marks]**

For electrical charge to flow through a circuit, the circuit must be ....

and include a source of ....

5 Current and charge — Grade 4

3. **Figure 1** shows an ammeter connected between a lamp and a battery in a series circuit. The reading on the ammeter is 0.75 A.

(a) Give the reading on the ammeter if it is placed between the lamp and the closed switch in this circuit. **[1 mark]**

....

(b) Use the following equation to calculate the charge flow if the switch is closed for 120 seconds.

charge flow = current × time **[2 marks]**

A

Figure 1

charge = ... C

Made a start | Feeling confident | Exam ready

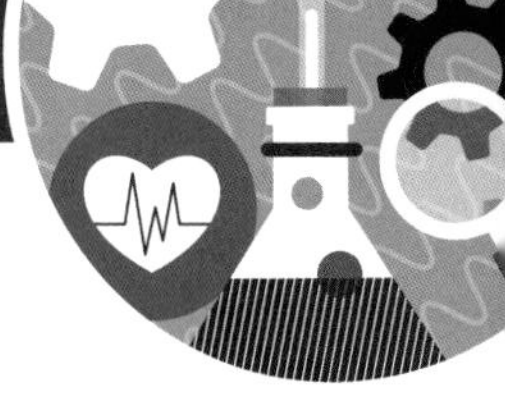

Resistance

2 Quick quiz

Choose the best definition of resistance.

- the flow of electrical current through a wire ☐
- the energy given to the charge as it flows ☐
- it opposes the flow of electrical current in a circuit ☐
- a measure of how many electrons are flowing in a circuit ☐

10 Reducing errors — Grade 3

1. A student investigated the effect of the length of a wire on its resistance using the circuit shown in **Figure 1**.

(a) The student cleaned the ends of the wire with wire wool before carrying out the experiment.

Explain why the student did this. **[1 mark]**

The wire needed to be cleaned to ....

(b) Give a reason why it is important that the wire should not get too hot. **[1 mark]**

....

(c) Give **two** ways to prevent the wire getting too hot in the experiment. **[2 marks]**

1 ....

2 ....

Figure 1

Think about what causes the wire to heat up and the amount of time the current is present.

10 Thermistor investigation — Grade 5

2. A thermistor is used in some electrical circuits instead of a resistor.

(a) Explain how a thermistor is different from a standard resistor. **[1 mark]**

....

....

(b) Describe how to carry out an experiment to find the effect of temperature on the resistance of a thermistor. Include the variables you would measure. Give the expected conclusion. **[6 marks]**

....

....

....

....

....

....

....

Exam focus

Remember to write your answers to extended response questions in a structured and logical way.

Continue your answer on your own paper if you need more space.

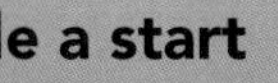

Resistors

Quick quiz

Match the shape of the I–V graph to its component.

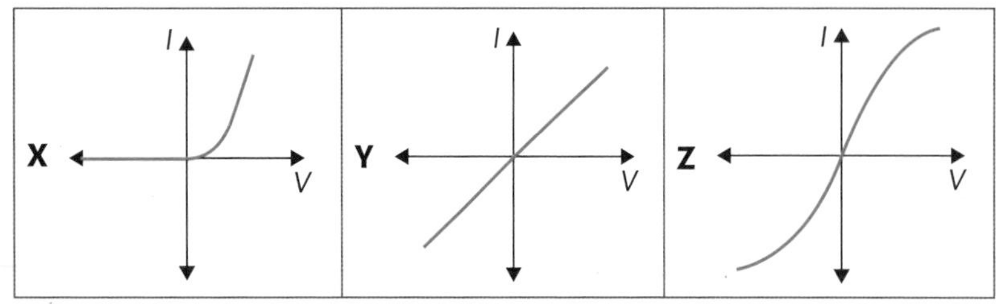

ohmic conductor	filament lamp	diode

Conductors

Grade 5

1. (a) Define what is meant by an 'ohmic conductor'. **[1 mark]**

For an ohmic conductor, the current is .... to the potential difference at a constant temperature.

(b) The gradient of a current–potential difference (I–V) graph indicates the resistance, R. The gradient of an I–V graph is steeper for component **X** than component **Y**. Explain what this tells us about the resistances of **X** and **Y**. **[2 marks]**

The .... the gradient, the .... the resistance. So the resistance of X is .... the resistance of Y.

The gradient of an I–V graph is equal to $\frac{1}{R}$.

(c) A conductor has a curved I–V graph. Explain what this tells us about the conductor. **[2 marks]**

The conductor is ....

The resistance is .... to the potential difference.

(d) Describe how a diode is different from a standard resistor or conductor. **[1 mark]**

....

Filament lamps

Grades 3–4

2. The resistance of a filament lamp is not constant.

(a) Use the axes (**Figure 1**) to sketch a current–potential difference (I–V) graph for a filament lamp. **[3 marks]**

(b) State how the resistance in a filament lamp changes as the current increases. **[1 mark]**

....

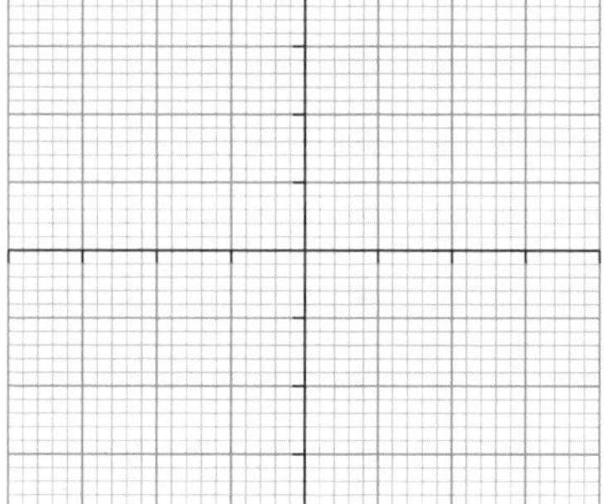

Figure 1

 Made a start  Feeling confident  Exam ready

Series and parallel circuits

Quick quiz

Which circuit does each statement apply to? (In the parallel circuits, each loop has only one component.)

The current is the same through all components.	**Series / Parallel**
The current is the sum of the currents through each component.	**Series / Parallel**
The potential difference is the same across each component.	**Series / Parallel**
The potential difference is split across the components.	**Series / Parallel**
The total resistance is the sum of all the resistances.	**Series / Parallel**

Resistors in series and parallel

Grade 3

1. Two resistors have resistances of 10W and 3 Ω.

(a) Give the total resistance when the resistors are connected in series. **[2 marks]**

total resistance = ... + ... = ...

total resistance = ... Ω

The total resistance in a series circuit is the sum of the individual resistances.

(b) Complete the sentence to describe the total resistance when the resistors are connected in parallel. Use words from the box. **[1 mark]**

the same as	greater than	less than

When the resistors are connected in parallel, the total resistance is .... when they are connected in series.

Series and parallel circuits

Grade 3

2. Figure 1 shows two different ways to set up a simple circuit using two lamps and a switch.

(a) When the switch is closed in each circuit, in which circuit (**A** or **B**) will the lamps shine most brightly? **[1 mark]**

....

A

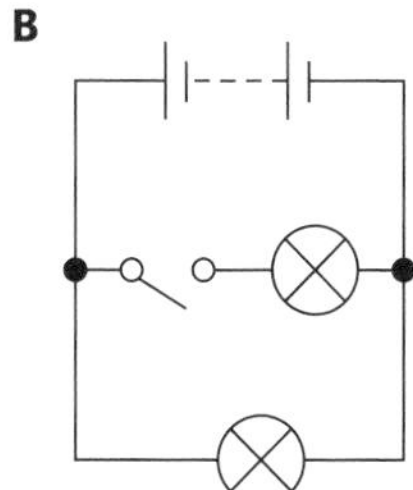

Figure 1

(b) Describe what will happen in circuit **B** when the switch is:

(i) open .... **[1 mark]**

(ii) closed .... **[1 mark]**

(c) Suggest how to change circuit **B** so that each lamp can be switched on or off separately. **[2 marks]**

....

....

Look carefully at which circuit loops are closed in each case.

You need to add a circuit component.

I–V characteristics

Quick quiz

Number the instructions to show the correct order of how to create an *I*–*V* graph for a given component. One has been done for you.

Plot potential difference on the *x*-axis and current on the *y*-axis.	
Measure the current passing through the component for a particular potential difference.	
Change the potential difference across the component using a variable resistor. and repeat the measurements.	
Set up a circuit with an ammeter to measure the current through the component and a voltmeter to measure the potential difference across it.	1
Change the direction of the current and potential difference by swapping the connections on the power supply.	

Diodes

Grade 5

1. A student investigates how the current in a diode changes with potential difference.

(a) Draw a circuit that could be used to investigate how the current in a diode changes with potential difference. **[3 marks]**

This will be a simple test circuit with a diode. Something is needed to measure current and something to measure potential difference.

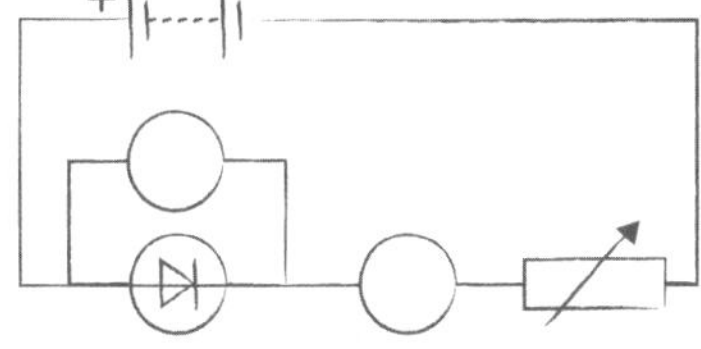

(b) Sketch the current–potential difference (*I*–*V*) graph the student should expect to obtain using the axes (**Figure 1**). **[2 marks]**

The resistance of a diode depends on the direction of the current.

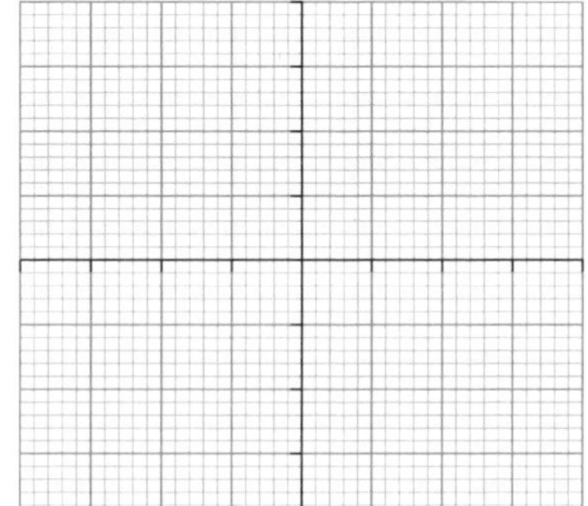

Figure 1

Resistance from an *I*–*V* graph

Grade 5

2. A student investigated the relationship between the current and potential difference of a piece of wire with the temperature kept constant.

(a) What shape of the current–potential difference (*I*–*V*) graph should the student expect to obtain? **[1 mark]**

Tick **one** box below **Figure 2**.

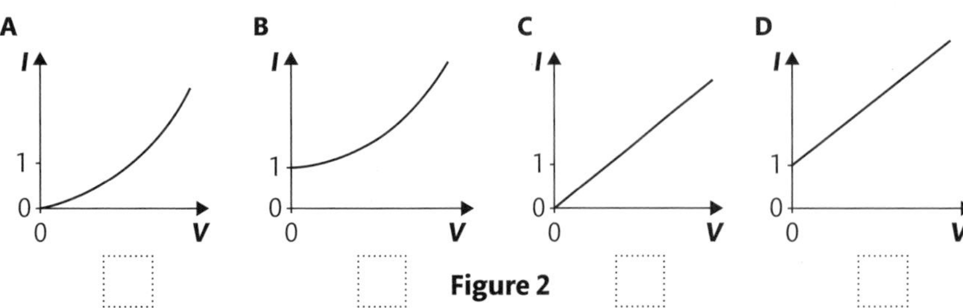

Figure 2

(b) Explain how the *I*–*V* graph shows that the wire is an ohmic conductor. **[2 marks]**

....

....

Mains electricity

2 Quick quiz

True or false?

Mains electricity is direct current.	**True / False**
There are three colour-coded wires in appliance plugs.	**True / False**
The frequency of mains electricity in the UK is 50 Hz.	**True / False**
The neutral wire in a three-core cable has a blue cover.	**True / False**
The live wire is at 0 V.	**True / False**

10 Electrical appliances and cables — Grade 3

1. (a) Explain why touching the live wire of an appliance is dangerous. **[2 marks]**

Touching the live wire is dangerous because you complete a ....

between .... *and* ....

Exam focus
Check how many marks each question is worth. For 2 marks you must make two distinct points.

(b) All metal-cased appliances should be earthed. Describe what it means when an appliance is earthed. **[1 mark]**

....

2. An appliance plug contains a three-core cable. What is the function of the live wire in a three-core cable? Tick **one** box. **[1 mark]**

- It is kept at 0 V. ☐
- It connects the outer case to the ground. ☐
- It carries a current if there is a fault. ☐
- It carries the (ac) voltage. ☐

5 Electricity supplies — Grade 3

3. (a) A kettle uses mains electricity while a torch uses a battery. Give the difference between these two supplies of electricity. **[2 marks]**

....

....

(b) Give the frequency of the domestic mains electricity supply in the UK. .... **[1 mark]**

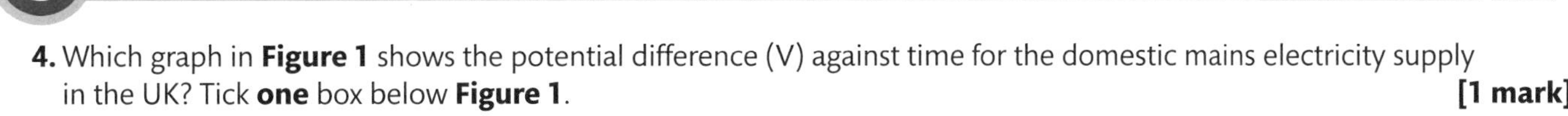

5 Mains supply — Grade 5

4. Which graph in **Figure 1** shows the potential difference (V) against time for the domestic mains electricity supply in the UK? Tick **one** box below **Figure 1**. **[1 mark]**

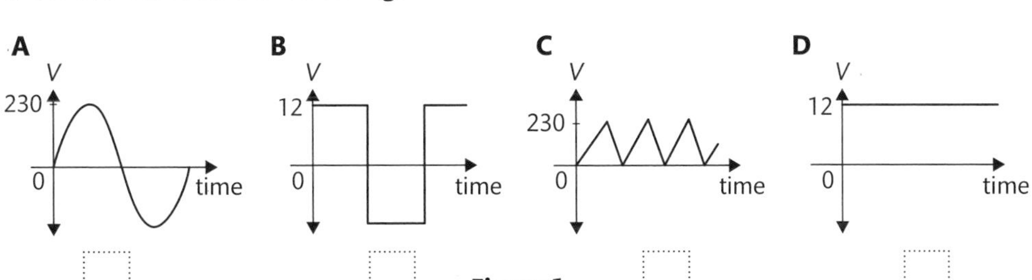

Figure 1

Graph **D** shows the potential difference against time for a battery

 **Made a start**  **Feeling confident**   **Exam ready**

Energy transfers in appliances

Quick quiz

Write **useful** or **wasted** next to each description of an energy transfer.

A torch transfers energy from its chemical store to the thermal store of its surroundings as light.

....

A drill transfers energy to the thermal store in the environment when it is used. ....

A laptop computer transfers energy from its chemical store to the thermal store in the environment when it is on. ....

Energy transfers

Grade 4

1. Figure 1 shows a partially completed diagram of the energy transfers that take place in a washing machine. Complete the diagram by labelling the energy stores. **[4 marks]**

> Wasted energy is most commonly transferred to thermal stores in the environment, or kinetic stores of particles (as sound).

2. A hairdryer uses mains electricity. Give the:

(i) useful energy outputs **[1 mark]**

....

(ii) wasted energy output. **[1 mark]**

....

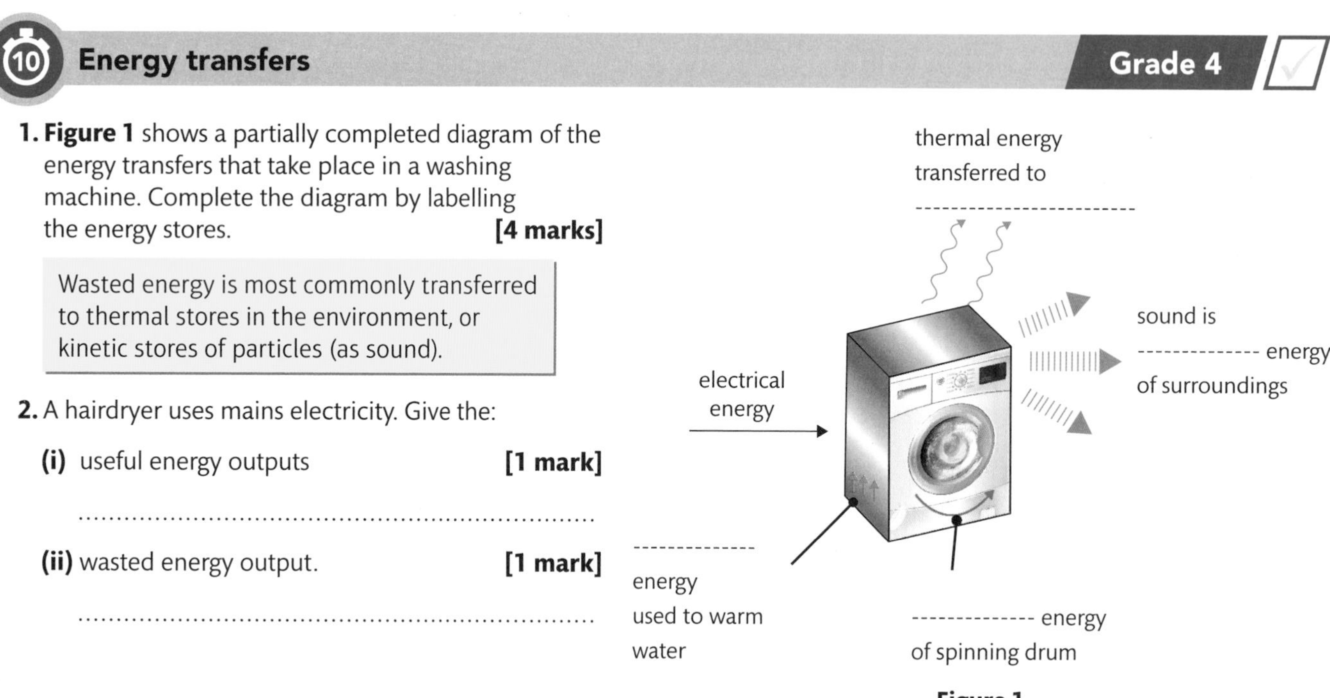

Figure 1

Energy transfers in a television

Grade 4

3. Figure 2 shows a television.

(a) Energy is transferred by electricity when the television is turned on. Give the energy stores that energy is transferred to. **[3 marks]**

....

(b) Identify which energy transfers in **(a)** are wasted and which are useful. **[2 marks]**

....

Figure 2

(c) Electricity from the mains supply carries 2000J of energy to the television. 1500J of this energy is usefully transferred to other stores. Calculate how much energy is wasted. **[1 mark]**

(d) Describe what happens to the wasted energy transferred. **[1 mark]**

....

Made a start  Feeling confident  Exam ready

Electrical power

2 Quick quiz

Match each quantity to its unit.

power	energy	time	current	potential difference	resistance
seconds (s)	volts (V)	joules (J)	amps (A)	ohms (Ω)	watts (W)

10 Power — Grade 3

1. (a) Define 'power'. **[2 marks]**

Power is the .... at which .... is transferred.

Write the definition in words rather than writing one of the equations for power.

(b) Use your definition in part **(a)** to write the general equation for power. **[2 marks]**

$$\text{power} = \frac{\ldots\ldots\ldots\ldots}{\ldots\ldots\ldots\ldots}$$

Here, 'general' means the equation that includes energy and time, not the version for electrical power.

(c) Which of the following equations are correct for electrical power? Tick **two** boxes. **[2 marks]**

$P = V \times I^2$ ☐ $P = V^2 \times I$ ☐ $P = I^2 \times R$ ☐

$P = I \times R$ ☐ $P = V \times I$ ☐

You need to remember what each symbol means for all the power equations.

10 Calculating power — Grade 5

2. An electric kettle transfers 200 000 J of energy when it boils water for 3 minutes.

(a) Write the equation that links energy transferred, power and time. **[1 mark]**

....

(b) Calculate the power of the kettle. **[3 marks]**

$$\text{power} = \frac{\text{energy transferred}}{\text{time}}$$

Rearrange the equation to make power the subject.

3 minutes = 3 × 60 = ...

Exam focus
Always check that the quantities in the question are in the standard units needed for the equation.

power = ... W

3. A microwave has a power rating of 800 W (**Figure 1**). It is connected to a mains supply with a potential difference of 230 V. Use the following equation to calculate the current in the microwave. Give your answer to two significant figures.

power = potential difference × current **[3 marks]**

Figure 1

current = ... A

Rearrange the equation to make current the subject.

Transformers and the National Grid

Quick quiz

True or false?

A transformer only works with direct current.	**True / False**
Step-up transformers increase potential difference.	**True / False**
Step-down transformers increase potential difference.	**True / False**
power = potential difference/current	**True / False**

Transformers — Grade 4

1. In a transformer, the input potential difference is 230 V and the output potential difference is 10 V.

Explain whether this is a step-up or a step-down transformer. **[2 marks]**

The input is .... V and the output is .... V, so the potential difference goes ....

.... This means it is a .... transformer.

Input greater than output = step-down; output greater than input = step-up

The National Grid — Grade 5

2. **Figure 1** shows the National Grid.

transmission cables
consumer
power station
step-up transformer
step-down transformer

Figure 1

(a) A power station outputs electrical power at a potential difference of approximately 25 kV. What is the main function of the step-up transformer between the power station and the transmission cables? Tick **one** box. **[1 mark]**

- increases the power transmitted by the cables ☐
- increases the electrical current transmitted in the cables ☐
- increases the potential difference at which the electrical power is transmitted ☐
- increases the resistance of the cables that transmit the electrical power ☐

(b) What is the main benefit of using a step-up transformer in this way? Tick **one** box. **[1 mark]**

- makes the transmission of electrical power safer ☐
- increases the efficiency of appliances in the home ☐
- means that the cables can transmit direct current rather than alternating current ☐
- reduces the energy wasted in the transmission cables ☐

Density

2 Quick quiz

Match each quantity to its correct unit.

mass	volume	density

m^3	kg/m^3	kg

10 Calculating density — Grade 5

1. An aluminium block has a volume of $750\,cm^3$ and a mass of 2025 g.

(a) Use the following equation to calculate the density of the block in g/cm^3. **[2 marks]**

$$\text{density} = \frac{\text{mass}}{\text{volume}}$$

density = ... / ....

density = ... g/cm^3

(b) Steel has a density of $7.8\,g/cm^3$. Use your answer to part **(a)** to compare the densities of aluminium and steel. **[1 mark]**

....

(c) Aluminium and steel are both strong. Suggest why passenger aircraft, regardless of size, are mostly made from aluminium and not steel. **[1 mark]**

....

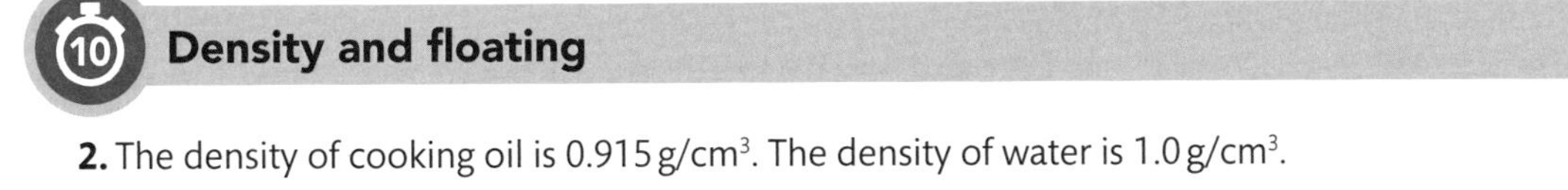

10 Density and floating — Grade 5

2. The density of cooking oil is $0.915\,g/cm^3$. The density of water is $1.0\,g/cm^3$.

(a) Explain what you would observe if cooking oil was mixed with water. **[2 marks]**

....

....

(b) $10\,cm^3$ of cooking oil was added to a pan. Use the following equation to calculate the mass of cooking oil that was added to the pan. **[3 marks]**

$$\text{density} = \frac{\text{mass}}{\text{volume}}$$

mass = ... g

2 Floating cork — Grade 5

3. Figure 1 shows a cork floating on water. Give a reason why the cork floats on the water. **[1 mark]**

....

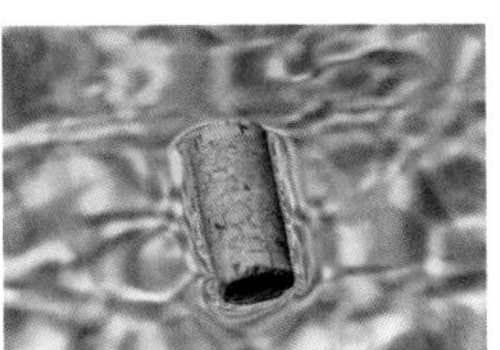

Figure 1

 Made a start  Feeling confident  Exam ready

Density of materials

2 Quick quiz

Number the steps to describe how to work out the density of an irregularly shaped solid.
The first and last steps have been done for you.

Find the mass of the object.	1
This is the volume of the irregular shape.	
Fill a displacement can to the spout.	
Place the object in the can.	
Use density = mass/volume to determine the density.	6
Collect the water that runs out into a measuring cylinder.	

10 Finding volume — Grade 5

1. (a) Describe the simplest method for measuring the volume of a large cuboid. **[3 marks]**

Use a .... to measure the length, ... and height of the cuboid.

Use the formula length .... to calculate the volume.

(b) What **two** pieces of equipment could be used to measure accurately the dimensions of a very small cuboid? Tick **two** boxes. **[2 marks]**

Vernier callipers ☐ 30 cm ruler ☐ set square ☐ micrometer ☐

(c) A student suggests the following method for measuring the volume of an irregular rock.

1 Partly fill a displacement can with water.

2 Submerge the rock in the water.

3 Collect the displaced volume of water in a measuring cylinder.

Identify the error in this method and describe how to correct it. **[2 marks]**

In step 1, the student says to ' .... ' a displacement can.

This will cause an error in the measurement of ....

The student should ....

10 Finding density — Grade 4

2. Figure 1 shows a bottle of shampoo. A student wants to find the density of the bottle of shampoo.

(a) Name **two** pieces of equipment needed to measure the volume of the bottle of shampoo. **[2 marks]**

1 .... 2 ....

Figure 1

(b) Name **one** other quantity that must be measured to calculate the density of the bottle of shampoo. **[1 mark]**

....

(c) Suggest **one** measuring device that can be used to measure the quantity you identified in part **(b)**. **[1 mark]**

....

(d) Write the equation used to calculate the density of the bottle of shampoo. **[1 mark]**

....

State changes

2 Quick quiz

Fill in the gaps using the words in the box.

kinetic	boiling	melting	mass

The temperature a substance condenses at is called the .... point. The temperature a substance freezes at is called the .... point. The density and volume of a substance can change during a change of state but the .... stays the same. As a substance is heated, the particles gain .... energy.

15 Changing state — Grade 5

1. A sample of liquid ethanol at room temperature is heated steadily. The temperature of the ethanol is measured at regular intervals. **Figure 1** shows a graph of temperature against time (a heating graph) for this experiment.

temperature in °C (20–100); time in minutes (0–9); sections A, B, C

Figure 1

(a) Describe the particles of ethanol in section **A** of **Figure 1**. Include how the particles are arranged and how they are moving. **[2 marks]**

The ethanol is a liquid so the particles are touching. They move ....

.... as more energy is

taken in. ....

Think about how the particles are moving and the effect of increasing the energy as the ethanol is heated.

(b) Use **Figure 1** to determine the boiling point of ethanol. Tick **one** box. **[1 mark]**

25 °C ☐ 78 °C ☐ 92 °C ☐ 100 °C ☐

(c) What is the best description of the particles of ethanol in section **B** of **Figure 1**? Tick **one** box. **[1 mark]**

The particles of ethanol are touching. ☐

The particles of ethanol bond to each other and the ethanol forms a solid. ☐

The particles of ethanol break apart to form molecules of water and carbon dioxide. ☐

The particles of ethanol separate from each other to move more freely. ☐

A change of state occurs where a heating graph forms a horizontal line.

5 Cooling graph — Grade 5

2. The melting point of stearic acid is about 70 °C. Some liquid stearic acid at 180 °C cools to 20 °C in 15 minutes. The temperature is recorded as the liquid cools.

Sketch the shape of the cooling graph on the grid. **[3 marks]**

Label each axis of your graph.

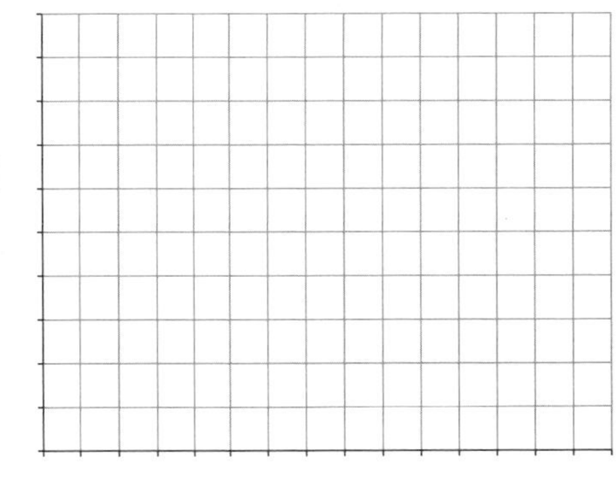

Specific heat capacity

2 Quick quiz

The symbol equation for specific heat capacity is $\Delta E = mc\Delta\theta$. Name each quantity.

ΔE change in .... m ....

c specific .... $\Delta\theta$ .... in temperature

2 Defining specific heat capacity — Grade 3

1. Define the term 'specific heat capacity'. **[2 marks]**

The specific .... capacity of a substance is the amount .... required to

raise the .... of 1 kg of the substance by ....

10 Calculating energy transfer — Grade 5

2. An electric kettle heats 1500 g of water from 20 °C to 100 °C. The specific heat capacity of water is 4200 J/kg °C.

(a) Calculate the change in temperature. **[1 mark]**

change in temperature = ... − .... = ... °C

> Subtract the starting value from the final value.

(b) Use the following equation to calculate the energy transferred from the kettle to the water.

change in thermal energy = mass × specific heat capacity × temperature change **[3 marks]**

1500g = ...

change in thermal energy = ... × 4200 × ....

= ....

change in thermal energy = ... J

> **Exam focus**
> Remember to check that units are correct before using the quantities in the equation.

10 Measuring energy transfers — Grade 5

3. Figure 1 shows the equipment used to determine the specific heat capacity of an aluminium block.

(a) Describe what the insulation is for. **[1 mark]**

....

(b) The mass of the aluminium block is 1 kg. The specific heat capacity of aluminium is 900 J/kg °C.
The temperature of the block at the start of the experiment was 20 °C. It increased to 32 °C.

Use the following equation to calculate the energy transferred by the heater to the block's thermal store.

Figure 1

change in thermal energy = mass × specific heat capacity × temperature change **[3 marks]**

change in thermal energy = ... J

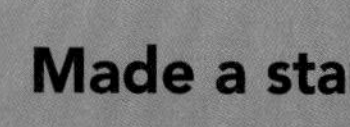 Made a start  Feeling confident  Exam ready

Specific heat capacity

Quick quiz

Cross out the incorrect words to give correct statements about specific heat capacity.

The **higher / lower** the specific heat capacity, the more energy it takes to warm up the same mass of the substance.

A liquid with a **high / low** specific heat capacity would be the most suitable for use in radiators.

A metal with a **high / low** specific heat capacity would be the most suitable to make cooking pans from.

Specific heat capacity by electrical heating

Grade 5

1. Describe a method to determine the specific heat capacity of a 1 kg aluminium block. Use the following equipment: electric heater, thermometer, 1 kg aluminium block. **[6 marks]**

Measure the start temperature of the aluminium block using the ....

Measure the highest temperature reached after ....

Calculate the energy input using the equation ....

Calculate the specific heat capacity using the equation ....

change in thermal energy = mass × specific heat capacity × temperature change

rearranged to give specific heat capacity = $\frac{\ldots\ldots\ldots\ldots}{(\ldots\ldots\ldots \times \ldots\ldots\ldots)}$

Exam focus

When asked a question about a required practical, try to remember the method that you followed.

Specific heat capacity data

Grade 5

2. The specific heat capacities of substance **X** and substance **Y** are shown in **Table 1**. 2 kg of substance **Y** is heated. The starting temperature is measured using the thermometer.

Table 1

Substance	Specific heat capacity in J/kg °C
X	300
Y	2200

(a) Give the thermometer reading for the starting temperature shown in **Figure 1**. **[1 mark]**

Starting temperature = ... °C

(b) Substance **Y** is heated to 22.5 °C. Calculate the change in temperature. **[1 mark]**

Change in temperature = ... °C

(c) Use the following equation to calculate how much energy is transferred.

change in thermal energy = mass × specific heat capacity × temperature change **[2 marks]**

change in thermal energy = ... J

Figure 1

 Made a start  Feeling confident Exam ready

Specific latent heat

2 Quick quiz

True or false?

The specific latent heat of fusion is the energy required to change 1 kg of a liquid into 1 kg of a gas at the same temperature. **True / False**

The units of specific latent heat are J/kg. **True / False**

The specific latent heat of vaporisation is the energy required to condense, boil or evaporate 1 kg of a substance. **True / False**

specific latent heat = energy for a change of state/mass **True / False**

10 Specific latent heat of fusion — Grade 4

1. A block of ice is heated to its melting point. The temperature of the ice is measured throughout the experiment. The amount of energy transferred to the ice is also measured.

(a) As it is heated, the temperature of the ice increases until it stops changing. Use the particle model to explain what happens to the ice after the temperature stops changing. **[2 marks]**

The particles in the solid ice are starting to ....

so that the ice .... to form a ....

(b) The block of ice has mass 5.2 kg. The specific latent heat of fusion of ice is 336 000 J/kg. Use the following equation to calculate the energy required to completely melt the ice.

energy for a change of state = mass × specific latent heat **[2 marks]**

energy for a change of state = ... × ....

energy for a change of state = ... J

10 Calculating specific latent heat — Grade 5

2. Figure 1 shows some ice cubes in a glass of lemonade.

The specific latent heat of fusion of water is 336 000 J/kg.

(a) 30 g of iced water is added to the lemonade. Use the following equation to calculate how much heat energy from the lemonade will be used to melt the ice.

energy for a change of state = mass × specific latent heat **[3 marks]**

energy = ... J

Remember to check the units used for mass and convert to kg.

Figure 1

(b) When measuring specific latent heat, it is important to measure the temperature of the substance at regular intervals. Suggest a reason why this is important. Tick **one** box. **[1 mark]**

to check the temperature is increasing slowly ☐

to check the temperature stays constant ☐

to check the temperature is falling slowly ☐

 Made a start  Feeling confident Exam ready

Particle motion in gases

Quick quiz

Which **two** statements explain why gases expand on heating?

When a gas is heated, the particles gain kinetic energy. ☐

When a gas is heated, the amount of kinetic energy of the particles decreases. ☐

A decrease in kinetic energy means the particles move less and so take up more space. ☐

An increase in kinetic energy causes the particles to move more and spread apart. ☐

Gas in containers — Grade 5

1. A student put an inflated balloon filled with air at room temperature in a freezer for 2 hours.

(a) What would the student observe when they inspected the balloon after 2 hours? Tick **one** box. **[1 mark]**

The balloon would have reduced in size. ☐

The balloon would be the same size as before. ☐

The balloon would have increased in size. ☐

The balloon would have burst. ☐

Does the volume of a gas increase or decrease when it is cooled?

(b) Explain your answer to part **(a)** using ideas about energy and pressure. **[2 marks]**

Particles in cooler gases have less kinetic energy so they move ....

.... This means the particles exert a ....

causing the balloon to become ....

Make sure you write about both energy and pressure.

Gas pressure — Grade 4

2. Figure 1 shows a container of propane gas. Propane gas is used as a fuel for camping stoves.

(a) Describe, using the particle model, what happens when a gas is heated. **[2 marks]**

....

....

(b) Propane containers are made of strong metal. Suggest a reason for this.
Tick **one** box. **[1 mark]**

to keep the propane cold ☐

to cope with the high pressure of the gas ☐

to reduce the weight of the container ☐

to stop the propane reacting with the container ☐

Gases exert a pressure on the walls of their container.

Figure 1

 Made a start  Feeling confident ☐ Exam ready

The structure of an atom

2 Quick quiz

A carbon-12 atom contains 6 protons, 6 neutrons and 6 electrons. Label the structure of a carbon-12 atom.

nucleus contains 6 [ ] and [ ] neutrons — 1 [ ]

5 Protons, neutrons and electrons — Grades 3–5

1. Atoms contain protons, neutrons and electrons. Complete **Table 1** to show the location of each subatomic particle in the atom and its relative charge. **[3 marks]**

Table 1

Particle	Location in the atom	Relative electric charge (+, – or 0)
proton		+
neutron		
electron	*outside the nucleus*	

2. The approximate size of an atom is 1×10^{-10} m. The nucleus of an atom is about 10 000 times smaller than the atom. Use this information to determine the approximate size of the nucleus. Tick **one** box. **[1 mark]**

1×10^{-6} m [ ] 1×10^{-10} m [ ] 1×10^{-14} m [ ] 1×10^{-18} m [ ]

10 000 times smaller $= 1 \times 10^{-4}$ times

3. Protons and neutrons are both types of subatomic particles. Compare a neutron and a proton. **[3 marks]**

....

....

....

10 Electrons and energy — Grade 4

4. Electrons fill energy levels around the nucleus of an atom.

(a) Describe what happens to an electron in an atom when it absorbs electromagnetic radiation. Tick **one** box. **[1 mark]**

The electron stays in the same energy level. [ ]   The electron moves to a higher energy level. [ ]

The electron moves to a lower energy level. [ ]   The electron is absorbed by the nucleus. [ ]

(b) Electrons in an atom absorb electromagnetic radiation. This affects their energy levels. Give **two** properties of the electrons that stay the same when they absorb electromagnetic radiation. **[2 marks]**

1 ....

2 ....

 Made a start  Feeling confident  Exam ready

Mass number, atomic number and isotopes

2 Quick quiz

True or false?

In an atom, the number of protons = the number of electrons.	**True / False**
The mass number of an atom is the total number of protons and electrons.	**True / False**
The atomic number tells you how many electrons an atom has.	**True / False**
mass number – atomic number = number of neutrons	**True / False**
The number of neutrons is always the same as the number of electrons.	**True / False**

5 Isotopes — Grade 4

1. Carbon-12 and carbon-14 are different forms of the element carbon. They are isotopes.

(a) Define the term 'isotopes'. **[2 marks]**

Isotopes are atoms with the same number of ....

but a different ....

Think about the numbers of subatomic particles.

(b) Give **one** difference between the isotopes carbon-12 and carbon-14. **[1 mark]**

Carbon-12 has ....

but carbon-14 has ....

15 Atomic structure — Grade 4

2. Table 1 shows the properties of three different atoms, **A**, **B** and **C**.

(a) Complete **Table 1** to show the atomic number and mass number of Atom **B** and Atom **C**. **[2 marks]**

(b) Give the **two** atoms which are isotopes of the same element. Justify your answer. **[2 marks]**

Atom .... Atom ....

....

....

Table 1

Property	Atom A	Atom B	Atom C
number of protons	5	4	5
number of neutrons	5	5	6
atomic number	5		
mass number	10		

3. The atomic symbol for calcium is $^{40}_{20}Ca$.

(a) Give the number of protons, neutrons and electrons in a calcium atom. **[3 marks]**

protons .... neutrons .... electrons ....

The calcium atom loses two electrons to become charged.

(b) What is a charged atom called? .... **[1 mark]**

(c) Give the number of electrons remaining on the charged calcium atom. .... **[1 mark]**

(d) Give the charge of the charged calcium atom. .... **[2 marks]**

Development of the atomic model

2 Quick quiz

In the plum pudding model, the mass of an atom is distributed throughout the atom.
Where is most of the mass of the atom in the nuclear model?

....

5 Developing the atomic model — Grade 4

1. The statements in **Table 1** describe developments in the accepted model of the atom.

Number each statement from 1 to 5 to place it in the correct historical order. **[3 marks]**

Table 1

James Chadwick discovered that neutrons existed inside the nucleus of an atom.	
The plum pudding model was suggested by scientists who thought that the atom was a positively charged 'pudding' with negatively charged electrons ('plums') stuck inside it.	
Niels Bohr suggested that electrons travel in orbits around the nucleus.	4
Rutherford's scattering experiment suggested that atoms were mostly empty space with a tiny, massive nucleus in the centre.	
The Ancient Greeks thought that atoms were tiny spheres that could not be divided.	

Each development became possible because, over time, scientists were able to see further into atoms at smaller and smaller scales.

5 Plum pudding and nuclear models — Grade 5

2. (a) Describe where the positive and negative charges were thought to be inside the plum pudding model of an atom. **[2 marks]**

The plum pudding model suggested that the atom is a ball of ....

with .... embedded in it. ....

Remember that electrons are negatively charged.

(b) Describe where positive and negative charges are found in the nuclear model of the atom. **[2 marks]**

The positive charge is found ....

The negative charge is found ....

5 The gold foil experiment — Grade 5

3. The scattering experiment with gold foil showed that the plum pudding model was not correct.

(a) Name the type of particles that were fired in a beam at gold foil during the scattering experiment. Tick **one** box. **[1 mark]**

alpha particles ☐ beta particles ☐ gamma particles ☐ photons ☐

(b) Describe what happened to most of the particles fired at the gold foil. **[1 mark]**

....

(c) Explain what this showed about the inside of an atom. **[1 mark]**

....

Made a start  Feeling confident  Exam ready

Radioactive decay and nuclear radiation

2 Quick quiz

Complete the sentences using the words in the box.

when	random	which

Radioactive decay is a .... process. This means that it is impossible to tell .... atoms will decay or .... each atom will decay.

5 Properties of nuclear radiation — Grade 3

1. Complete **Table 1** to show the properties of the **three** types of nuclear radiation: alpha, beta and gamma. **[3 marks]**

Table 1

Radiation	Description	Ionising power	Penetrating power	Range in air
alpha	2 proton and 2 neutrons (helium nucleus)	high	skin / paper	less than 5 centimetres
beta		low		
gamma				more than 1 kilometre

5 Uses of radiation — Grade 5

2. Beta radiation is used in paper mills to monitor the thickness of paper. **Figure 1** shows how this is done. Complete the sentences. Use words from the box. **[3 marks]**

metal	paper	less	more
be stopped by	pass through		

Beta radiation can pass through .... sheets.

If the sheets get too thick, ... beta radiation will pass through.

Alpha radiation cannot be used because it will ....

.... the paper.

Figure 1

5 Cancer and radiation — Grade 4

3. Cancer cells inside the body can be destroyed by radiation from a source placed outside the body. Which type of radiation is able to pass through skin and organs? Tick **one** box. **[1 mark]**

alpha radiation ☐ beta radiation ☐ gamma radiation ☐

 Made a start  Feeling confident 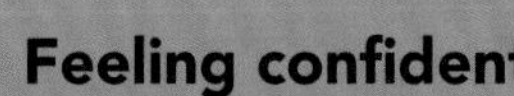  Exam ready

Half-lives

2 Quick quiz

Fill in the gaps using words from the box.

time	atoms	half-life	rate	half

The .... of a radioactive source is the .... it takes for the count .... to fall to .... its initial value. It is also the .... taken for half of the radioactive .... in a sample to decay.

5 Radioactive decay — Grade 3

1. Complete the sentence to say why the exact time at which atoms in a radioactive sample will decay cannot be predicted. **[1 mark]**

Radioactive decay is ....

10 Using half-life — Grade 5

2. A sample of caesium-137 has a half-life of 30 years and an initial activity of 1600 Bq. **Table 1** shows how the activity changes after 30 years.

(a) Complete **Table 1** to show the activity after 60, 90 and 120 years. **[3 marks]**

Table 1

Time in years	0	30		90	
Activity in Bq	1600	800			100

For each half-life, divide the activity by 2.

(b) The activity of another sample of caesium-137 is found to be 280 Bq. Estimate the age of the sample. Tick **one** box. **[1 mark]**

25 years ☐ 50 years ☐ 75 years ☐ 100 years ☐

The age will not be an exact multiple of half-lives, so you need to decide which two half-lives in Table 1 the activity reading lies between.

10 Using graphs to determine half-life — Grade 5

3. Give the **two** graphs in **Figure 1** that show radioactive decay. **[2 marks]**

.... and

....

A: activity / time
B: activity / time
C: activity / time
D: count rate / time
E: count rate / time

Figure 1

Made a start | Feeling confident |  Exam ready

Nuclear equations

Quick quiz

Match the radiation to its particle, atomic number and mass number.

Radiation
alpha (α)
beta (β)

Particle
fast-moving electron
helium nucleus

Atomic number
–1
2

Mass number
4
0

Alpha and beta decay

Grade 4

1. Nuclear equations use symbols such as $^{14}_{6}C$.

(a) State what the numbers 14 and 6 each represent. **[2 marks]**

The number 14 represents the .... number of carbon-14.

The number 6 represents the .... number of carbon-14.

(b) The following equation shows the radioactive decay of carbon-14. Complete the equation so that it is balanced. **[2 marks]**

$$^{14}_{6}C \rightarrow ^{14}_{7}N + ^{\square}_{\square}e$$

Fill in the two missing numbers so that the top and bottom numbers on both sides of the equation add up to the same totals.

(c) State the type of radioactive decay that this equation shows. **[1 mark]**

....

What type of subatomic particle does the 'e' represent?

Radioactive decay

Grade 5

2. (a) Which row in **Table 1** shows what happens to the atomic number and the mass number of a nucleus when it undergoes alpha decay? Tick **one** box. **[1 mark]**

Table 1

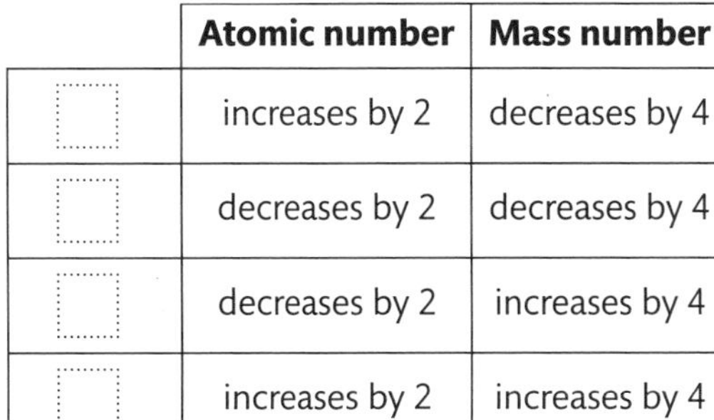

	Atomic number	Mass number
☐	increases by 2	decreases by 4
☐	decreases by 2	decreases by 4
☐	decreases by 2	increases by 4
☐	increases by 2	increases by 4

(b) The following equation shows the alpha decay of an isotope of radon. Complete the equation so that it is balanced. **[3 marks]**

$$^{198}_{86}R \rightarrow ^{\square}_{\square}Po + ^{\square}_{\square}He$$

3. The equation shows the radioactive decay of phosphorus-32.

$$^{32}_{15}P \rightarrow ^{32}_{16}S + ^{0}_{-1}e$$

Identify the type of radioactive decay that takes place. **[1 mark]**

....

Decide what type of radiation is emitted: alpha, beta or gamma.

Radioactive contamination

2 Quick quiz

Match each term to its definition.

Term
radioactive decay
radioactive contamination
irradiation

Definition
the unwanted presence of materials containing radioactive atoms.
the process of exposing an object to radiation, but the object does not itself become radioactive.
a random process in which unstable atomic nuclei give out radiation.

5 Irradiation and contamination — Grade 3

1. Complete the sentences. Use words from the box. **[2 marks]**

contamination radiation irradiation

In 1986, an explosion at the Chernobyl nuclear power station caused radioactive dust and gases to be scattered over a large area. This is an example of radioactive ....

In hospitals, some medical instruments are exposed to gamma radiation to kill any harmful microorganisms. This is an example of ....

5 Irradiation — Grade 5

2. (a) Some types of cancer can be irradiated with gamma radiation. Explain why the doctor stands in another room behind concrete walls when the patient is treated. **[2 marks]**

Gamma radiation can penetrate skin and cause ....

Standing in another room means that the doctor ....

Think about the penetrating power of radiation and the safety of the people involved.

(b) Suggest why the patient is only irradiated for a few minutes at a time. **[2 marks]**

The amount of radiation a patient receives depends on the .... they are exposed to the source. A longer .... means a .... dose.

Think about what affects the size of a dose of radiation.

5 Radiation research — Grade 4

3. Scientists publish research on the effects of radiation on humans and the environment. Other scientists then check the findings.

(a) What is this process called? Tick **one** box. **[1 mark]**

peer review ☐ competition ☐

writing a hypothesis ☐ drawing a conclusion ☐

(b) Give **two** ways in which scientists working with radioactive sources can avoid contamination or reduce its effects. **[2 marks]**

....

....

 Made a start  Feeling confident Exam ready

Scalar and vector quantities

2 Quick quiz

For each quantity, circle the correct word to show whether the quantity is scalar or vector.

distance	**Scalar / Vector**	displacement	**Scalar / Vector**
weight	**Scalar / Vector**	mass	**Scalar / Vector**
time	**Scalar / Vector**	force	**Scalar / Vector**
speed	**Scalar / Vector**	temperature	**Scalar / Vector**

5 Scalars and vectors — Grade 2

1. Describe the difference between speed and velocity. Tick **one** box. **[1 mark]**

Speed and velocity tell us the same thing. ☐

Velocity tells us the speed of an object and its direction of movement. ☐

Speed tells us the velocity of an object and its direction of movement. ☐

Velocity only tells us the speed of an object, not its direction. ☐

2. A train travels north along a straight track at a speed of 40 m/s. Give the velocity of the train. **[1 mark]**

Velocity = ... m/s in the .... direction

5 Adding vectors — Grade 3

3. Figure 1 shows two people pushing a car to move it. One person is exerting a force of 300 N and the other is exerting a force of 150 N. Both people are pushing the car in the same direction.

150 N

Figure 1

(a) The arrow in **Figure 1** represents the 150 N force. Draw an arrow next to it to represent the 300 N force. **[1 mark]**

(b) Calculate the resultant force on the car. **[1 mark]**

resultant force is .... + ... = ... N

resultant force = ... N

Both forces are acting in the same direction so the resultant force is the sum of the forces.

5 Subtracting vectors — Grade 4

4. A car is being tested on a race track. The engine produces a forwards force of 4000 N. A force of friction produces a backwards force of 2500 N on the car.

(a) Calculate the resultant force on the car. **[1 mark]**

resultant force = ... N

(b) Give the direction of the resultant force. **[1 mark]**

....

The direction will be forwards or backwards.

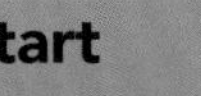

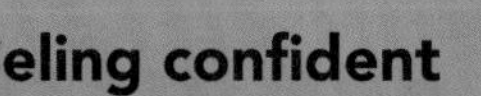

Made a start | Feeling confident | Exam ready

Forces

2 Quick quiz

Sort the forces in the box into contact and non-contact forces.

weight	tension	magnetic force
friction	electrostatic force	air resistance

Contact force	Non-contact force

5 Labelling forces — Grade 3

1. Figure 1 shows a box being pushed along a flat table. Two forces are labelled for you.

(a) Draw **two** more labelled arrows on the diagram to show the other forces acting on the box. **[2 marks]**

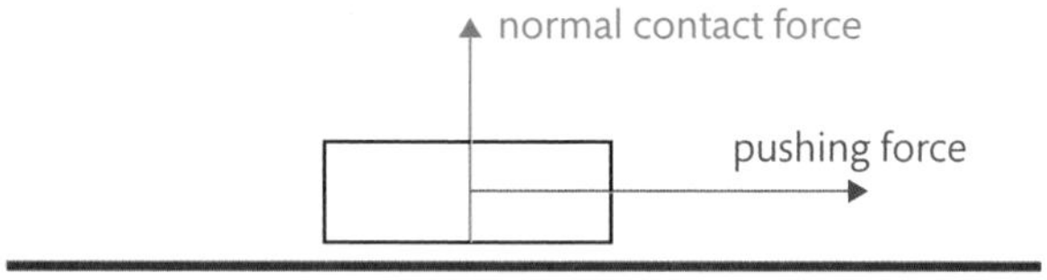

normal contact force

pushing force

Figure 1

> The two labelled forces are contact forces. There is one more contact force and one non-contact force acting on the box.

(b) Identify the **three** contact forces. **[2 marks]**

1 normal contact force .... **2** pushing force .... **3** ....

5 Drawing and balancing forces — Grade 4

2. Figure 2 shows an albatross in flight. Albatrosses can fly for many kilometres without needing to flap their wings.

Figure 2

(a) Draw an arrow on **Figure 2** to show the weight of the albatross. **[1 mark]**

> The weight is a force that acts downwards.

The albatross flies at a constant height above the ocean. The lift force balances the weight.

> Two balanced forces are the same size but act in opposite directions.

(b) Draw an arrow to show the lift force. **[2 marks]**

(c) Identify whether weight and lift are contact or non-contact forces. **[1 mark]**

Weight .... Lift ....

> The lift force is caused by the action of particles in the air as the bird moves through the air.

5 Drawing and balancing forces — Grade 4

3. Figure 3 shows two bar magnets. The bar magnets repel one another.

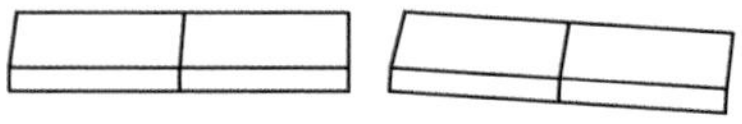

Figure 3

(a) Label the poles on each magnet to show that they repel. **[1 mark]**

(b) Describe how the diagram shows that the magnetic force between the magnets is an example of a non-contact force. **[1 mark]**

....

Made a start — Feeling confident — Exam ready

Gravity

2 Quick quiz

Match each quantity with its meaning and unit.

mass	the force acting on an object due to gravity	N/kg
weight	the strength of gravity at any one point	kg
gravitational field strength	the amount of matter in an object	N

5 Weight Grade 4

1. A rock has a weight of 25 N on Earth.

(a) Which force causes the rock to have weight? Tick **one** box. **[1 mark]**

electrostatic force ☐ magnetic force ☐

gravitational force ☐ normal contact force ☐

(b) Explain why a newtonmeter can be used to measure the weight of objects on different planets but a mass balance cannot. **[2 marks]**

A mass balance only measures the mass, which .... on different planets.

A newtonmeter measures .... which .... on different planets.

Think about which quantities change on different planets, and which quantities do not change.

5 Weight on Earth and the Moon Grade 3

2. (a) When astronauts landed on the Moon, they measured the weight of objects. They found that the objects weighed less on the Moon than on Earth. Explain their findings. **[2 marks]**

The weight of an object depends on the .... field strength of the planet or moon the object is near. The .... field strength on the Moon is .... than on Earth.

(b) The gravitational field strength on the Moon is 1.6 N/kg. Use the following equation to calculate the weight of an 8.0 kg object on the Moon.

weight = mass × gravitational field strength **[2 marks]**

weight = ... N

5 Mass and weight Grade 5

3. Figure 1 shows a cardboard shape. A student hangs the cardboard shape by two different corners and draws vertical lines as shown.

The student marks the point where the lines intersect.

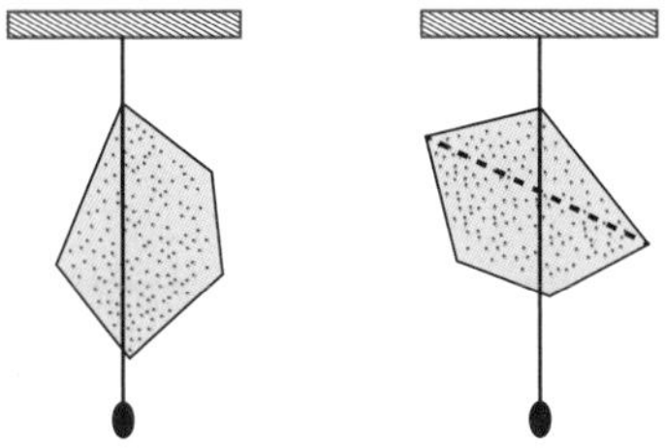

(a) The student is trying to find the single point where the weight of the shape can be considered to act.

Give what this point is known as. **[1 mark]**

....

Figure 1

(b) Describe **one** way in which the student could improve the accuracy of this experiment. **[1 mark]**

....

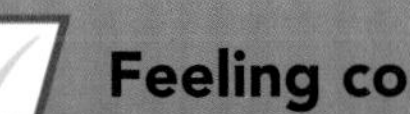

Resultant forces

Quick quiz

Order these statements to explain how a skydiver reaches terminal velocity.

As speed increases, drag increases. This cancels part of the weight. The resultant force, which causes acceleration, is a lot smaller. The speed is still increasing, but at a reduced acceleration.	
When weight and drag are equal, the resultant force and acceleration are zero. The skydiver has reached maximum speed. This is terminal velocity.	
As the skydiver jumps, they have no air resistance or drag. The resultant force is just due to the weight of the skydiver and closed parachute. They accelerate at 9.8 m/s^2.	

Calculating resultant forces

Grade 5

1. Two teams take part in a tug of war (**Figure 1**). One team pulls on a rope to the right. The other team pulls to the left.

Figure 1

(a) Calculate the resultant force. **[2 marks]**

resultant force = force 1 − force 2 = ... − ....

force = ... N to the ....

Always state the direction of a resultant force.

(b) Determine the size and direction of the extra force needed to make the two teams balanced.

extra force = N to the ....

Exam focus
'Determine' means use given data or information to obtain an answer.

Terminal velocity

Grade 5

2. A skydiver jumps out of a plane. She accelerates at 9.8 m/s^2 just as she leaves the plane. After about 10 seconds in flight, she reaches her terminal velocity.

(a) Define the term 'terminal velocity'. **[1 mark]**

....

(b) Describe any effect on the weight of the skydiver and the force due to air resistance as her velocity increases. **[2 marks]**

Weight .... The force due to air resistance ....

Think about when you cycle or run. If you go faster, how does the 'push' of air resistance against you change?

 Made a start  Feeling confident Exam ready

Work done and energy transfer

2 Quick quiz

True or false?

Work done is measured in N. **True / False**

Work is done when the force acts in the same direction as the displacement. **True / False**

Force is measured in joules. **True / False**

work done = $\frac{\text{force}}{\text{distance}}$ **True / False**

5 Work done — Grade 3

1. Complete the statement to define 'work done'. Use words from the box. **[1 mark]**

distance	energy	force

Work done = ... transferred when a .... moves an object through a ....

5 Energy transfers — Grade 4

2. A crane lifts a container up above the ground. Which energy store has been increased? Tick **one** box. **[1 mark]**

elastic potential energy store ☐ gravitational potential energy store ☐

kinetic energy store ☐ thermal energy store ☐

When work is done on an object, energy is transferred to an energy store. If a car is accelerated by a force, energy is transferred to the car's kinetic energy store. The crane does work by lifting the weight of the container.

5 Calculating work done — Grade 5

3. The braking force of a car is 2500 N.

(a) At a speed of 30 km/h the brakes stop the car in a distance of 12 m. Use the following equation to calculate the work done by the brakes to stop the car. **[2 marks]**

work done = force × distance

work done = ... N × .... m

work done = ... J

(b) When the same car stops from a speed of 50 km/h, the work done by the brakes is 60 000 J. Calculate the braking distance. **[3 marks]**

60 000 J = 2500 N × braking distance

braking distance = $\frac{\text{......................................}}{\text{......................................}}$

You need to rearrange the equation for work done.

braking distance = ... m

Exam focus
Check that your answer makes sense. In this case, as the car travels faster you should expect the braking distance to have increased.

 Made a start  Feeling confident 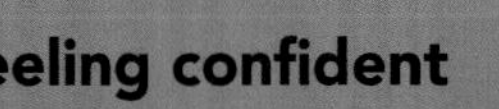  Exam ready

Forces and elasticity

Quick quiz

True or false?

Elastic deformation means that an object returns to its original shape when an applied force is removed. **True / False**

A spring stores energy when it is stretched. **True / False**

The extension of an elastic object is inversely proportional to the force applied to it. **True / False**

The units for the spring constant are N/m. **True / False**

force = spring constant × extension **True / False**

Elastic deformation

Grade 3

1. A mass is added to the end of a rubber band and it extends by 4 cm. Describe how you could test to confirm that the rubber band had deformed elastically. **[1 mark]**

If the mass is .... from the end of the rubber band,

the band should .... its original shape.

Remember the definition for elastic deformation.

Energy in a spring

Grade 5

2. Use the following equation to calculate the elastic potential energy stored in a spring when it is stretched by 10 cm. Spring constant = 100 N/m.

elastic potential energy = 0.5 × spring constant × (extension)^2 **[3 marks]**

10 cm = 0.1 m

Elastic potential energy = ... × .... × 0.1^2

= ....

elastic potential energy = ... J

Finding the spring constant

Grade 5

3. A rubber band extends by 0.1 m when a mass of weight 2.0 N is added to the end of it. The rubber band stretches elastically.

(a) Write the equation that links spring constant to force and extension. **[1 mark]**

force = spring constant × extension

(b) Calculate the spring constant of the rubber band. **[3 marks]**

2.0 = spring constant × 0.1

spring constant = $\frac{\text{..............}}{\text{..............}}$ = ...

You need to rearrange the equation.

spring constant = ... N/m

Made a start / Feeling confident  Exam ready

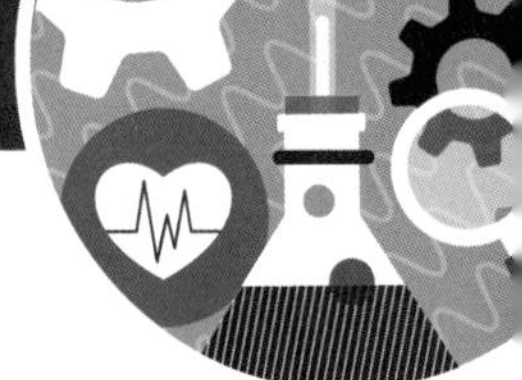

Force and extension

Quick quiz

True or false?

The extension of a spring is the final length subtracted from the initial length. **True / False**

The extension of a spring is the initial length subtracted from the final length. **True / False**

The greater the spring constant of a spring, the less easily stretched the spring. **True / False**

The smaller the spring constant of a spring, the less easily stretched the spring. **True / False**

Investigating the extension of a spring

Grade 4

1. A student predicted that the extension of the spring is directly proportional to the force on it. Explain how a graph could be used to show this. **[2 marks]**

Plot a graph of force against .... that should produce a ....

through the origin. Force should .... in proportion to extension.

Determining the spring constant

Grade 5

2. A student carried out an experiment to determine the spring constant of a spring. He added 100 g masses to the end of a spring and measured the extension of the spring. **Table 1** shows the results.

Table 1

Force added in N	0	1	2	3	4	5	6
Extension in cm	0	4	8	10	16	20	24

Figure 1 shows a graph of the results.

(a) Identify on **Figure 1**, the anomalous reading. **[1 mark]**

(b) Use **Figure 1** to suggest a correct value of extension for the anomalous reading. **[1 mark]**

.... cm

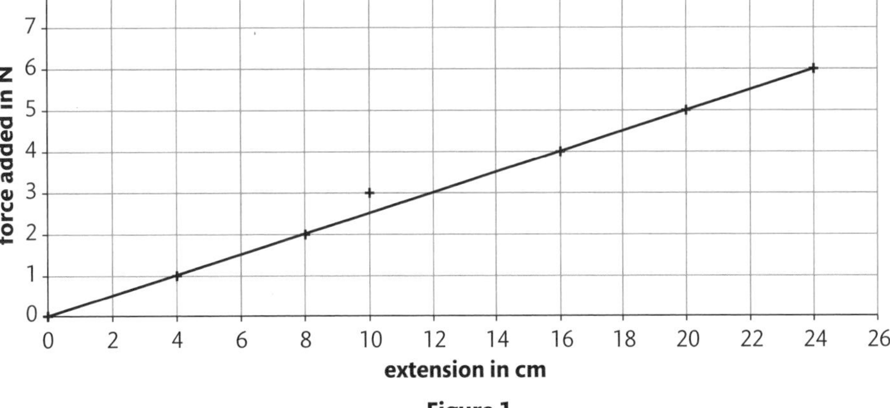

Figure 1

(c) The spring constant can be found by calculating the gradient of the graph. Determine the spring constant of the spring. Tick **one** box. **[1 mark]**

0.25 N/m ☐ 4.0 N/m ☐ 25 N/m ☐

Watch out for the units.

(d) Describe **two** ways that the student could improve the reliability of his method. **[2 marks]**

....

....

Distance and displacement

2 Quick quiz

True or false?

Distance is a scalar quantity. **True / False**

Displacement has no direction. **True / False**

Distance has a magnitude and a direction. **True / False**

Displacement is a vector quantity. **True / False**

5 Distance and displacement — Grade 3

1. Julie's work is 20 km away from her home along a straight road. She drives to work in the morning and home again in the evening.

(a) Give the total distance Julie travels during the day. **[1 mark]**

Julie travels 20 km to work and then another 20 km to return

distance = ... + ... = ...

total distance travelled = ... km

(b) Give Julie's displacement at the end of the day. **[1 mark]**

Julie returns to the place she started the day at, so her displacement is .... km

5 Final displacement — Grade 5

2. A car travels 3.5 km due north and then 5.0 km due east. Draw a scale diagram to calculate the magnitude and direction of the car's final displacement from its starting position. **[3 marks]**

magnitude of displacement = ... km

direction = ...° to ....

You will need a pencil, ruler and protractor. The first part of the journey has been completed for you.

Figure 1

Exam focus

Always choose a suitable scale to ensure your diagram is accurate. Check that your answer makes sense – displacement should never be greater than distance.

10 Direction of displacement — Grade 4

3. A car starts at point **A** and travels 300 m north to point **B**. It then turns and travels 250 m east, before arriving at point **C**.

(a) Sketch a scale diagram to show the movement of the car. **[1 mark]**

(b) Calculate the total distance travelled by the car. **[1 mark]**

total distance = ... m

(c) Which statement describes the direction of the displacement? Tick **one** box. **[1 mark]**

Displacement is at 0° (due north). ☐

Displacement is at 90° (due east). ☐

Displacement is between 0° and 90° (between north and east). ☐

Made a start  Feeling confident Exam ready

Speed and velocity

2 Quick quiz

Fill in the gaps using the words in the box.

direction	distance	speed	time

Velocity is the .... of an object travelling in a particular ....

Speed is a measure of the .... an object moves in a specific amount of ....

10 Speed — Grade 3

1. Write down the equation that links distance, speed and time. **[1 mark]**

....

10 Speed and velocity calculations — Grade 5

2. A person travelled in a straight line 3.6 km north. They travelled at a speed of 6.0 m/s.

(a) Use the following equation to calculate the time taken for the journey. **[3 marks]**

distance = speed × time

$3.6 \times 1000\,\text{m} = 6.0\,\text{m/s} \times \text{time}$

time = ... / ....

time taken = ... s

(b) Justify whether the person was walking, running or cycling. **[2 marks]**

Remember to convert the units to m.

The person was .... because a speed of .... m/s is closest to the approximate speed of that activity over that distance.

Approximate speeds: walking = 1.5 m/s, running = 3 m/s, cycling = 5 m/s

10 Speed and displacement — Grade 5

3. A bus travels 50 km in 1.5 hours between Hamforth and Stonebridge.

(a) Calculate the average speed of the bus in km/h. **[2 marks]**

There is no need to convert units as you are asked to give the answer in km/h.

Average speed = ... km/h

(b) Stonebridge is due west of Hamforth. In a straight line, the villages are 20 km apart. Give the displacement of Stonebridge from Hamforth. **[1 mark]**

.... km in a direction ....

(c) Suggest why the distance travelled by the bus is different to the displacement of Stonebridge from Hamworth. **[2 marks]**

....

....

Distance–time relationships

2 Quick quiz

Match the description of the distance–time graph to the motion of the object.

the gradient of the line increases
the gradient of the line decreases
the gradient of the line is zero
the gradient of the line is constant

the object is stationary
the object is accelerating
the object travels at a constant speed
the object is decelerating

Using distance–time graphs — Grade 5

1. Figure 1 shows the journey of a cyclist.

(a) Describe the part of the journey marked **A** to **B**. **[2 marks]**

The cyclist travels .... km in .... hours at a ....

constant ....

(b) Calculate the speed of the cyclist in km/h on the part of the journey marked **A** to **B**. **[2 marks]**

speed = $\frac{\text{distance}}{\text{time}}$

= $\frac{\dots\dots\dots\dots}{\dots\dots\dots\dots}$

The speed of the cyclist is .... km/h.

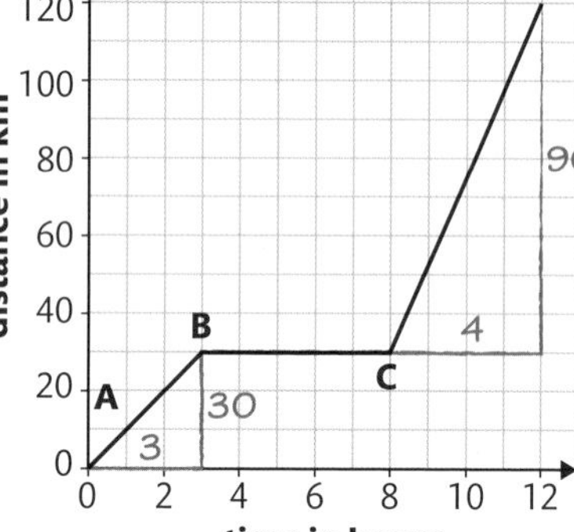

Figure 1

(c) Compare the cyclist's speed in the part of the journey marked **C** to **D** with the part of the journey marked **A** to **B**. Tick **one** box. **[1 mark]**

The cyclist travels slower in part **C** to **D** than in part **A** to **B**. ☐

The cyclist travels at the same speed in parts **C** to **D** and **A** to **B**. ☐

The cyclist travels faster in part **C** to **D** than in part **A** to **B**. ☐

When asked to compare two speeds, you do not have to work out all the speeds. You need to decide which line on the graph is steeper, and what that means.

Distance–time graphs — Grade 5

2. Figure 2 shows the distance–time graph for the first minute of a bus journey.

(a) Give the total distance travelled by the bus in the first minute of the journey. **[1 mark]**

....

(b) Describe the motion of the bus in the first 20 seconds of the journey. **[1 mark]**

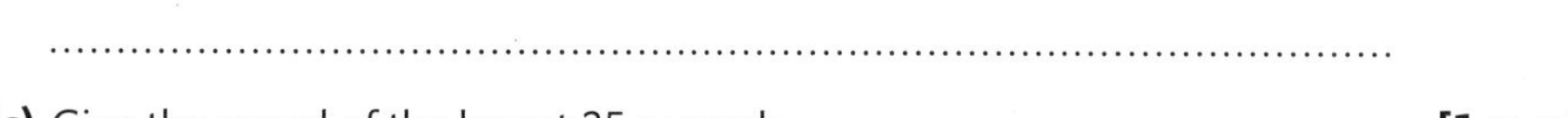

(c) Give the speed of the bus at 25 seconds. .... **[1 mark]**

(d) Describe the motion of the bus between 30 and 60 seconds. **[1 mark]**

....

distance in metres: 0, 50, 100, 150, 200, 250
time in seconds: 0, 10, 20, 30, 40, 50, 60

Figure 2

 Made a start  Feeling confident  Exam ready

Uniform acceleration

Quick quiz

Match the symbol, quantity and unit.

Symbol	Quantity	Unit
s	time	m/s²
u	acceleration	m/s
v	initial velocity	m
a	distance	s
t	final velocity	m/s

Using equations of motion

Grade 5

1. A leopard is resting and then accelerates in a straight line to chase a deer. It takes 6 seconds to accelerate to a velocity of 18 m/s.

Check the information in the question. What is the leopard doing before it accelerates?

(a) Give the initial velocity of the leopard. .... m/s **[1 mark]**

(b) Use the following equation to calculate the acceleration of the leopard.

$$\text{acceleration} = \frac{\text{change in velocity}}{\text{time taken}}$$

[2 marks]

Remember that change in velocity = final velocity – initial velocity

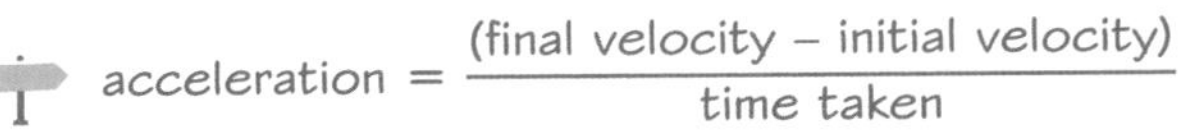

$$\text{acceleration} = \frac{\text{(final velocity} - \text{initial velocity)}}{\text{time taken}}$$

$$= \frac{\dots\dots\dots}{\dots\dots\dots}$$

acceleration = ... m/s²

Acceleration

Grade 5

2. A Formula 1 racing car accelerates from stationary in a straight line for 9 seconds. After 9 seconds, it has a velocity of 90 m/s.

(a) Use the following equation to calculate the car's acceleration.

$$\text{acceleration} = \frac{\text{change in velocity}}{\text{time taken}}$$

[2 marks]

acceleration = ... m/s²

(b) The Formula 1 car brakes at a velocity of 90 m/s. It decelerates at 36 m/s² and comes to a stop. Calculate the time the car takes to come to a stop. **[3 marks]**

You need to rearrange the equation first.

time taken = ... s

Initial and final velocity

Grade 5

3. A high-speed train accelerates steadily at 0.8 m/s² for 3 km from an initial velocity of 10 m/s. Use the following equation to calculate its final velocity.

$(\text{final velocity})^2 - (\text{initial velocity})^2 = 2 \times \text{acceleration} \times \text{distance}$ **[4 marks]**

final velocity = ... m/s

 Made a start  Feeling confident  Exam ready

Velocity–time graphs

Quick quiz

Match each feature of a velocity–time graph to the information it gives you.

gradient of a downward sloping line	constant speed
gradient of an upward sloping line	acceleration
a horizontal line	deceleration

Graphs of motion

Grade 3

1. Distance–time graphs and velocity–time graphs give different information about the motion of an object. Give what can be found from:

(i) the gradient of a distance–time graph **[1 mark]**

gradient $= \frac{\text{distance}}{\text{time}}$ so tells us the ....

(ii) the gradient of a velocity–time graph. **[1 mark]**

gradient $= \frac{\text{speed}}{\text{time}}$ so tells us the ....

Interpreting velocity–time graphs

Grade 5

2. Figure 1 shows the velocity–time graph of a cyclist.

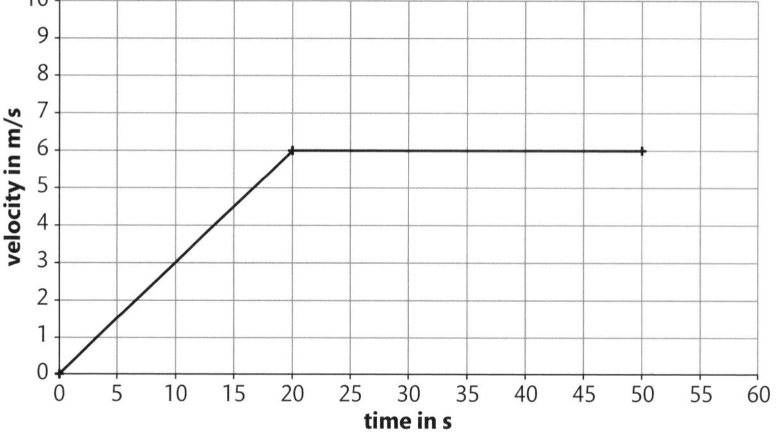

Figure 1

(a) Give the feature of the graph that shows that the cyclist is stationary at the start of the journey. **[1 mark]**

The graph starts at the ...., where velocity is .... when the time is ....

....

Look at the starting values on the graph.

(b) Describe the journey shown on the graph. **[3 marks]**

For the first .... seconds of the journey, the cyclist .... from rest to a velocity of .... m/s. The cyclist continues travelling at this velocity for a further .... seconds.

Remember to state the velocity and time for each section of the graph, and how the velocity is changing. If there is any acceleration, describe it.

(c) Over the next 10 seconds, the cyclist decelerates to a stop. Draw a line on **Figure 1** to show this part of the journey. **[2 marks]**

Remember what type of slope the graph will have when the cyclist decelerates.

 Made a start  Feeling confident Exam ready

Newton's laws of motion

2 Quick quiz

Match each law to the correct statement.

Law	Statement
Newton's first law	The acceleration of an object is proportional to the resultant force and inversely proportional to the mass of the object.
Newton's second law	When two objects interact, they exert an equal and opposite force on each other.
Newton's third law	An object will continue to move in the same direction at the same speed unless acted upon by a resultant force.

5 Newton's second law — Grade 4

1. (a) Give the equation for force that comes from Newton's second law. Tick **one** box. **[1 mark]**

force = mass × acceleration ☐

force = mass/acceleration ☐

force = acceleration/mass ☐

force = $(\text{acceleration})^2$/mass ☐

Newton's second law states that resultant force is proportional to acceleration.

(b) Explain why more massive trucks need bigger engines than less massive trucks to produce the same acceleration. **[2 marks]**

If mass is increased, a .... force is needed to produce the .... acceleration.

In Newton's second law equation, if you keep the acceleration the same and increase the mass, what does this do to the force needed?

5 Newton's third law — Grade 3

2. Complete the sentence about Newton's third law. Use words from the box. **[2 marks]**

at right angles	different sizes	equal	opposite	parallel

Newton's third law states that pairs of forces must be .... and ....

5 Newton's first law — Grade 4

3. (a) When an object is stationary, the resultant force is zero. Use Newton's first law to describe the other situation in which the resultant force on the object is zero. **[2 marks]**

....

....

(b) A car is parked at the top of a slope. It rolls down the slope when the brakes are released.

Give the factor that causes the car to accelerate. **[1 mark]**

....

 Made a start  Feeling confident  Exam ready

Newton's second law

Quick quiz

A car is accelerating. Are these statements true or false?

The resultant force needed to accelerate the car is proportional to its mass.	**True / False**
force = mass × acceleration	**True / False**
acceleration = force/mass	**True / False**
The resultant force needed to accelerate the car is inversely proportional to its acceleration.	**True / False**

Force and acceleration

Grade 5

1. Figure 1 shows a car. The forces on the car have been labelled.

Figure 1

(a) Calculate the resultant force on the car. **[2 marks]**

resultant force = forwards forces – backwards forces

= .... – ....

resultant force = ... N

(b) The mass of the car is 1500 kg. Use the following equation to calculate the acceleration of the car.

force = mass × acceleration **[3 marks]**

.... = 1500 kg × acceleration

acceleration = $\frac{\text{..............................}}{1500}$ = ...

acceleration = ... m/s^2

Add all the forwards forces and subtract all the backwards forces.

You need to rearrange the equation.

Remember that the force you need is the resultant force.

Applying the second law

Grade 5

2. Figure 2 shows a boy on a skateboard.

Figure 2

(a) The boy and the skateboard accelerate at 2 m/s^2. The total mass of the boy and the skateboard is 75 kg. Use the following equation to calculate the resultant force. Assume there is no air resistance.

force = mass × acceleration **[2 marks]**

resultant force = ... N

(b) Determine the force the boy needs to use to accelerate at 2 m/s^2 when there is an air resistance of 30 N. **[2 marks]**

forwards force needed = ... N

Remember that resultant force = forwards force(s) – backwards force(s). You need to rearrange this equation so forwards force is the subject.

 Made a start 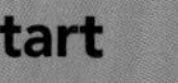  Feeling confident  Exam ready

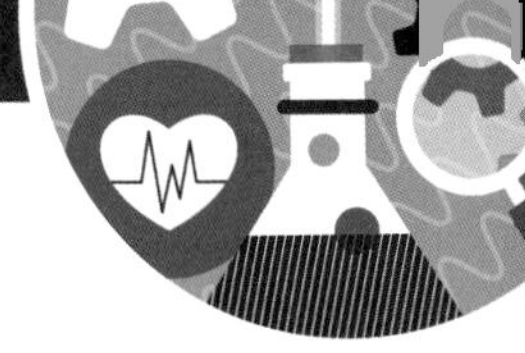

Investigating acceleration

1 Quick quiz

Match each quantity to its unit.

speed	m/s^2
mass	N
acceleration	m/s
force	kg

15 The effect of force and mass on acceleration — Grade 5

1. A student carried out an investigation into the effect of force on the acceleration of an object using the equipment shown in **Figure 1**.

The student changed the force by adding more masses to the holder at the end of the bench. The light gate measured the acceleration.

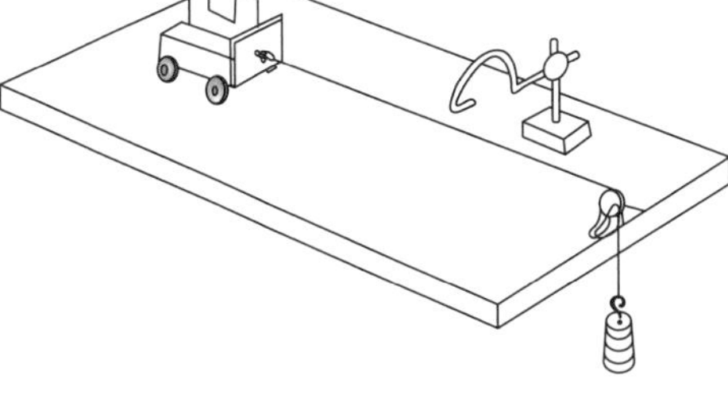

Figure 1

(a) Name the independent variable. **[1 mark]**

....

> The independent variable is the one that is changed deliberately in the experiment.

(b) Name the dependent variable. **[1 mark]**

....

> The dependent variable is the one that is measured in the experiment.

(c) Predict and explain what the student observes about the acceleration using Newton's second law of motion. **[3 marks]**

Newton's second law states that force = ... × ....

So if the force is increased and the .... stays the same,

the acceleration must ....

> Remember that the student is changing the force on the object, but is not changing the mass of the object. Think about the equation that results from Newton's second law of motion.

5 Investigating force — Grade 5

2. A student investigates the relationship between the mass of an object and its acceleration. The following equipment is available: light gate, trolleys of different masses, string, pulley, mass holder and masses. The mass of the object is the independent variable and the acceleration is the dependent variable. Give **one** factor that must be kept constant to ensure the investigation is valid. **[1 mark]**

....

> Think about the equation that results from Newton's second law of motion. Which variable is left after mass and acceleration are accounted for?

 Made a start  Feeling confident  Exam ready

Stopping distance

2 Quick quiz

True or false?

Being tired affects your braking distance. **True / False**

Your stopping distance is the distance travelled while the driver is reacting. **True / False**

Your thinking distance increases when your reaction time is longer. **True / False**

Icy roads increase your thinking distance. **True / False**

10 Calculating stopping distance — Grade 4

1. (a) Write down the equation linking distance, speed and time. **[1 mark]**

....

(b) A car travels at a speed of 30 mph (13.4 m/s). The driver has a reaction time of 1.3 s.
Calculate how far, in **metres**, the car will travel in this time. **[2 marks]**

distance travelled = speed × time

distance travelled = ... × ....

= ....

Exam focus

You need to able to recall and use the equation for distance travelled.

distance = ... m

(c) The car's braking distance at 30 mph is 14 m. Use the following equation to calculate the stopping distance.

stopping distance = thinking distance + braking distance **[2 marks]**

stopping distance = ... + ...

Use your answer to **(b)**.

stopping distance = ... m

10 Changing stopping distances — Grade 5

2. Table 1 shows the braking distances for a normal family car at different speeds.

Table 1

Speed in miles per hour	Braking distance in metres
20	6
30	14
40	24
50	
60	55

(a) Estimate the braking distance in metres when the car is travelling at 50 miles per hour. **[1 mark]**

braking distance = ... m

(b) Give **two** factors that affect thinking distance. **[2 marks]**

1 ....

2 ....

Made a start  Feeling confident  Exam ready

Braking distance

2 Quick quiz

Match each distance to its description.

thinking distance
braking distance
stopping distance

the distance it takes a car to stop after brakes are applied
the total distance it takes for a car to stop
the distance a car travels between something happening and the driver reacting to it

5 Factors affecting braking distance — Grade 4

1. (a) Give **two** factors that would increase the braking distance of a car. **[2 marks]**

1 worn brakes .... 2 ....

Braking distance depends on the condition of the car or the road conditions over which it is travelling.

(b) Describe what happens to the kinetic energy of a car when the brakes are applied. **[3 marks]**

....

....

....

There are three marks available so you need to make three points.

5 Braking distance and energy — Grade 4

2. A braking force of 10 000 N is applied when a van driver sees a hazard and applies the brakes. It takes 40 m to stop the vehicle.

(a) Use the following equation to calculate the work done by the brakes.

work done = force × distance **[2 marks]**

work done = ... J

(b) There is a risk that the brakes might overheat. Explain how this is linked to the work done you calculated in part **(a)**. **[2 marks]**

....

....

Think about energy transfers.

5 Thinking and braking distance — Grade 4

3. Normal values of thinking and braking distances assume that drivers are alert and healthy, and that vehicles are in good condition. A person driving a car is alert and healthy but the brakes and tyres on their car are worn. Complete **Table 1** by ticking the boxes to show how this will affect thinking distance and braking distance. **[2 marks]**

Table 1

Distance	Decreases?	Stays the same?	Increases?
thinking distance			
braking distance			

 Made a start  Feeling confident  Exam ready

Types of waves

2 Quick quiz

Match each statement to the type of wave it describes.

Statement
The vibrations are parallel to the direction the wave is travelling.
The vibrations are perpendicular to the direction the wave is travelling.
Ripples on water are an example of this type of wave.
Sound waves are an example of this type of wave.

longitudinal wave
transverse wave

5 Types of wave — Grade 3

1. Figure 1 shows the pattern of movement of particles in air caused by the vibration of a loudspeaker.

(a) Which type of wave does this diagram show?
Tick **one** box. **[1 mark]**

longitudinal sound wave ☐

transverse sound wave ☐

longitudinal light wave ☐

transverse light wave ☐

'Longitudinal' means 'along the direction of travel'. 'Transverse' means 'across the direction of travel'.

A B

Figure 1

(b) Name the features of the wave labelled **A** and **B**. **A** compression .... **B** .... **[2 marks]**

5 Comparing waves — Grade 4

2. Table 1 shows different types of waves and their properties.

(a) Complete the first two rows of **Table 1** for water waves and sound waves by ticking the boxes to show whether the waves are longitudinal or transverse. **[2 marks]**

Table 1

Type of wave	Longitudinal	Transverse	Speed of travel in m/s
water wave			2
sound wave			330
C		✓	300 000 000

(b) Suggest what type of wave **C** could be. Tick **one** box. **[1 mark]**

wave on a piece of string ☐ light wave ☐

surface wave from earthquake ☐ ultrasound wave ☐

5 Water waves — Grade 5

3. Water particles on the surface of the sea move up and down as a wave travels past.

Water waves do not transport water particles. Suggest what a water wave **does** transfer. **[1 mark]**

....

 Made a start  Feeling confident ☐ Exam ready

Properties of waves

Quick quiz

Match each key word with its definition.

amplitude	the number of waves passing a point each second
frequency	the distance from a point on a wave to an identical point on an adjacent wave
wavelength	the maximum displacement of a point on a wave away from its undisturbed position

Frequency and period

Grade 4

1. The period of a wave is the time it takes for one whole wave to travel past a point.

(a) How is the frequency of a wave related to its period? Tick **one** box. **[1 mark]**

frequency = $\frac{1}{(\text{period})^2}$ ☐ frequency = $\frac{1}{\text{period}}$ ☐ frequency = period ☐ frequency = $(\text{period})^2$ ☐

(b) Give the name of the units of frequency. .... **[1 mark]**

(c) Use the following equation to calculate the frequency of a wave with a period of 0.02 s. Give the unit.

period = $\frac{1}{\text{frequency}}$ **[3 marks]**

frequency = $\frac{1}{\text{period}}$ = $\frac{\dots\dots}{\dots\dots}$ = ...

frequency = ...

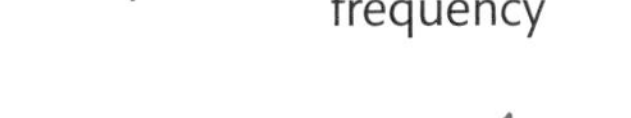

Wave features

Grade 3

2. Figure 1 shows a diagram of a transverse wave. Give the wave features, **B** and **C**, on **Figure 1**. **[2 marks]**

B .... **C** ....

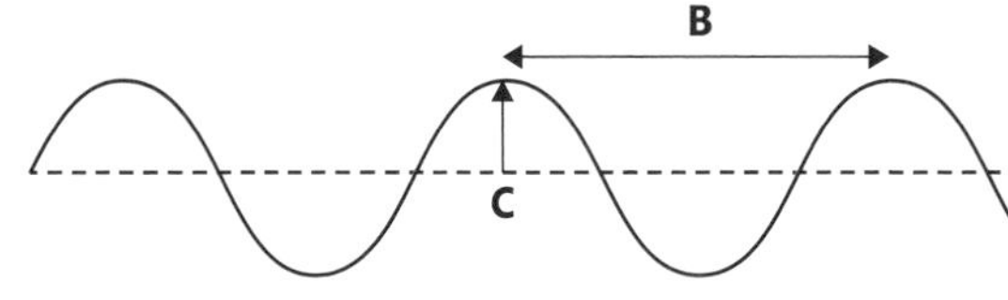

Figure 1

Wave speed

Grade 5

3. A stone is thrown into a pond. The stone causes waves in the water. The water waves have a frequency of 5.0 Hz. The ripples are 0.10 m apart.

(a) Write down the equation that links frequency, wavelength and wave speed. **[1 mark]**

....

(b) Calculate the speed of the water waves. **[3 marks]**

> The quantities are given to 2 significant figures, so you should give your answer to 2 significant figures.

wave speed = ... m/s

Investigating waves

2 Quick quiz

Number the steps to show the correct method for determining the wavelength of waves in a ripple tank. Two steps have been numbered for you.

Step	
Measure the distance the wave travelled.	
Calculate the wavelength of the wave using wave speed = frequency × wavelength.	
Time how long it takes for one wave to travel from the paddle to the edge of the ripple tank.	1
Calculate the wave speed using speed = distance/time.	
Time 10 rotations of the motor and divide by 10 to get the time period of the wave.	4
Calculate the frequency of the wave using frequency = 1/period.	

15 Waves on a string — Grade 4–5

1. The apparatus in **Figure 1** can be used to investigate the speed of a wave on a string. The frequency of the wave depends on the frequency set on the wave generator.

One wavelength contains one crest and one trough.

(a) Which value does the length **L** represent? Tick **one** box. **[1 mark]**

the wavelength ☐

half the wavelength ☐

twice the wavelength ☐

four times the wavelength ☐

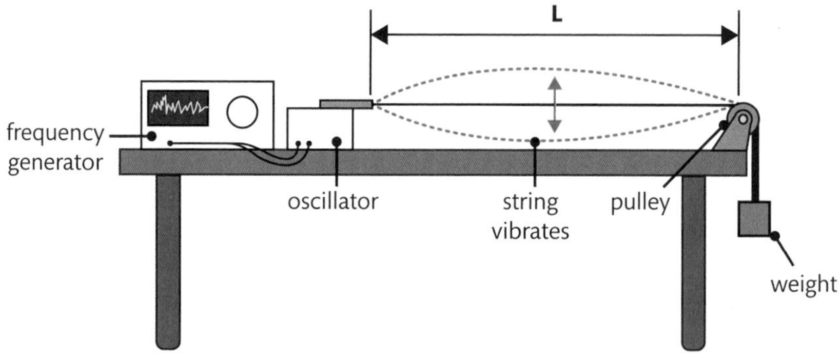

Figure 1

(b) Describe how to calculate the speed of the wave on the string. **[3 marks]**

Find the wavelength by ....

Use the frequency from the generator. Calculate the speed using the equation ....

....

(c) A student investigates the effect of length on the speed of waves on a string using the apparatus in **Figure 1**. The length of the string is changed by moving the oscillator. Suggest **two** factors the student must keep the same in order to make the experiment a fair test. **[2 marks]**

1 ....

2 ....

Remember that a fair test is one in which only one variable is changed; all others are kept the same.

5 Experimental technique — Grade 5

2. A student measures the frequency of waves on the sea. They count how many waves go past a point in 30 seconds. They then divide this number by 30. Explain why they count the waves over 30 seconds. **[2 marks]**

....

....

 Made a start  Feeling confident ☐ Exam ready

Types of electromagnetic waves

2 Quick quiz

Are these waves electromagnatic waves (**EM**) or not (**not**)?

light	**EM / not**	infrared	**EM / not**	water waves	**EM / not**
sound	**EM / not**	X-rays	**EM / not**	waves on a string	**EM / not**
radio	**EM / not**	microwaves	**EM / not**	ultrasound	**EM / not**

5 Light and ultraviolet radiation — Grade 4

1. (a) Give **two** properties of light waves. **[2 marks]**

1 .... 2 ....

(b) Ultraviolet radiation and visible light are both in the electromagnetic spectrum. Give **one** similarity and **one** difference between ultraviolet radiation and visible light. **[2 marks]**

....

....

....

Use the wave equation *wave speed* = *frequency* × *wavelength* to help you decide which quantities are different.

5 The electromagnetic spectrum — Grade 4

2. Table 1 shows the electromagnetic spectrum.

Table 1

Lowest frequency → Highest frequency

Radio waves	**A**	**B**	Visible light	**C**	**D**	Gamma rays

Complete the electromagnetic spectrum by identifying the waves represented by the letters **A** to **D**.
Write **one** letter from **A** to **D** in each box below. **[4 marks]**

[ ] X-rays [ ] infrared waves [A] microwaves [ ] ultraviolet waves

5 Gamma radiation — Grade 5

3. A medical handbook says that 'gamma rays are ionising radiation that can cause harm'.

(a) Name the part of an atom that produces gamma rays. .... **[1 mark]**

(b) Explain the term 'ionising radiation'. **[2 marks]**

....

....

(c) Suggest **one** type of harm that gamma rays can cause in a person. .... **[1 mark]**

Properties of electromagnetic waves

Quick quiz

Match the words to the descriptions.

refraction		Light is produced by an object.
reflection		Light changes direction at a boundary between two different materials.
emission		Light is taken in by an object.
absorption		Light bounces back from a surface.

Refraction — Grade 3

1. Figure 1 shows a wave being refracted. Label **Figure 1** using the words below. Write the letter of each label against the correct word. **[3 marks]**

angle of incidence ☐ angle of refraction ☐

refracted ray ☐ normal ☐

incident ray ☐

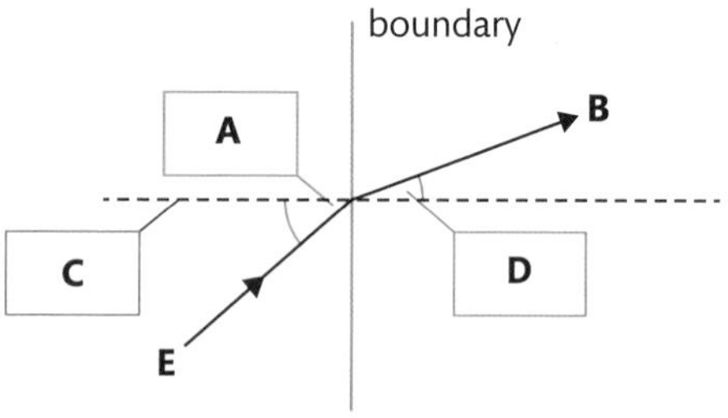

Figure 1

Ray diagrams — Grade 5

2. When a ray of light enters a glass block, it is refracted towards the normal. **Figure 2** shows a ray of light leaving a glass block, going into air. Draw the refracted ray on **Figure 2** after it leaves the block and label the angle of refraction. **[3 marks]**

Remember that the ray is leaving the glass; make sure you draw the ray at the correct angle compared to the angle of incidence.

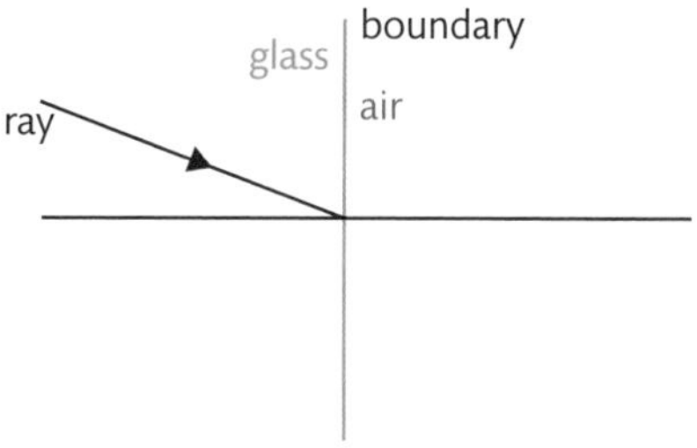

Figure 2

Wave properties — Grade 5

3. Figure 3 shows what is seen when a straight drinking straw is placed in a glass of water.

(a) Name the process that makes the straw appear to be bent. Tick **one** box. **[1 mark]**

absorption ☐ reflection ☐

emission ☐ refraction ☐

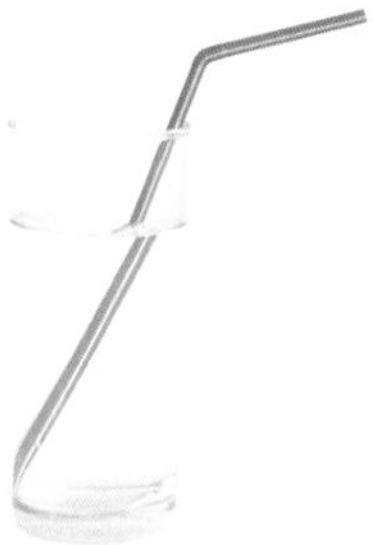

(b) Explain what is happening to light at the boundary between water and air. **[2 marks]**

....

....

Figure 3

 Made a start 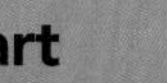  Feeling confident  Exam ready

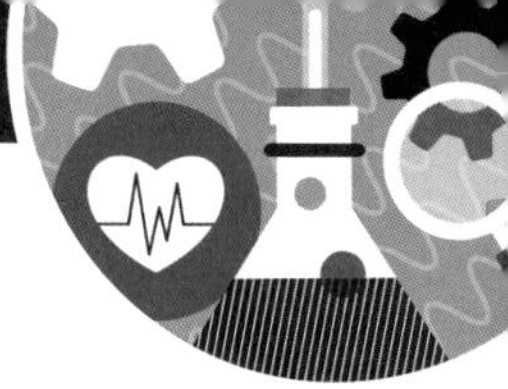

Infrared radiation

Quick quiz

Fill in the gaps using the words in the box.

electromagnetic	hot	thermal

Infrared waves, also called .... radiation, are ....
waves emitted by .... objects.

Absorption of infrared radiation — Grade 5

1. **Figure 1** shows apparatus that can be used to investigate the absorption of infrared radiation by different surfaces.

Figure 1

(a) Complete the sentences about variables. Use words from the box. **[2 marks]**

control	dependent	independent

The variable you change to investigate its effect is called the
...independent... variable.

The variable you measure is called the .... variable.

Any other variables that you must keep constant are .... variables.

(b) Give the variable that is changed in this investigation. **[1 mark]**

....

(c) Give **two** variables that must be kept constant in this investigation. **[2 marks]**

1 .... **2** ....

These variables must be kept constant to make sure the test is fair.

Emission of infrared radiation — Grade 5

2. **Figure 2** shows a Leslie cube. This is filled with hot water and used to investigate the amount of infrared radiation emitted by different surfaces.

(a) Predict which surface will emit the **most** radiation. Tick **one** box. **[1 mark]**

- matt black ☐
- matt white ☐
- shiny black ☐
- shiny silver ☐

Figure 2

(b) Predict which surface will emit the **least** radiation. **[1 mark]**

....

Applications of EM waves

2 Quick quiz

Match each type of wave to one of its applications.

light waves
X-rays
ultraviolet
gamma rays

medical imaging
skin tanning
viewing objects through microscopes
sterilising food

5 Microwaves — Grade 3

1. Figure 1 shows potatoes being cooked with microwaves. Complete the sentences using the words from the box. **[2 marks]**

energy	information

The potatoes in a microwave oven cook because the microwaves transfer

.... to the potatoes.

Microwaves are also used for satellite television, where they transfer ....

Figure 1

5 Communications — Grade 3

2. Radio waves are used for communication.

(a) Complete the sentence. **[1 mark]**

Radio waves can be used for communicating information because waves can transfer ....

(b) Give **two** types of communications that use radio waves. **[2 marks]**

1 radio ....

2 ....

5 X-rays — Grade 3

3. Figure 2 shows an image of a patient's broken arm made using X-rays. The light areas show where the X-rays were absorbed and the dark areas show where the X-rays passed through.

(a) X-rays are used for this type of imaging because they are absorbed by some materials and pass through others. Complete the table by ticking the boxes to show whether X-rays are absorbed or pass through skin and bone. **[2 marks]**

Material	X-rays are absorbed?	X-rays pass through?
skin		
bone		

Figure 2

(b) Give **two** dangers of X-rays. **[2 marks]**

1 ....

2 ....

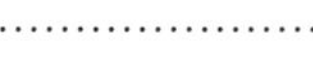

 Made a start  Feeling confident Exam ready

Magnetic fields

2 Quick quiz

Draw the magnetic field lines around the bar magnet.

N S

10 Bar magnets — Grade 4

1. Figure 1 shows three bar magnets with holes in the middle. They are free to rotate around the plastic rod.

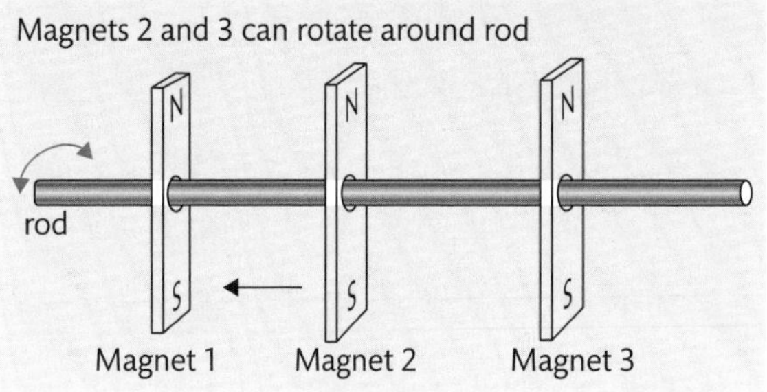

(a) Magnet 1 is held still with its north pole pointing upwards. Magnet 2 is free to rotate around the rod. Magnet 2 is moved towards magnet 1. Explain why magnet 2 rotates so that the south pole points upwards. **[2 marks]**

The north pole of magnet 1 repels the north pole of ....

magnet 2, and .... the .... pole of magnet 2.

Magnet 2 will rotate until the attracting poles are ....

....

Magnets 2 and 3 can rotate around rod

rod

N S N S N S

Magnet 1 Magnet 2 Magnet 3

Figure 1

Use your knowledge of how magnetic poles attract and repel.

(b) Magnet 3 is brought closer to magnet 2 with its south pole pointing upwards. Explain whether there will be a force pushing magnet 3 towards or away from magnet 2. **[2 marks]**

....

....

5 Magnetic poles — Grade 3

2. Describe how to find out which is the south pole of an unlabelled magnet. **[2 marks]**

....

....

5 Mapping field lines — Grade 5

3. (a) Describe how you can use a magnetic compass to map the field lines of a bar magnet. **[4 marks]**

....

....

....

(b) Describe how the field lines on the diagram show the relative strength of the magnetic field around the magnet. **[1 mark]**

....

 Made a start  Feeling confident  Exam ready

Electromagnetism

2 Quick quiz

Is each statement an advantage (**A**) or disadvantage (**D**) of an electromagnet?

Electromagnets use electricity and so cost money to run.	**A / D**
The strength of electromagnets can be altered by controlling the current.	**A / D**
Electromagnets can be switched on and off.	**A / D**
Electromagnets can get hot.	**A / D**

5 Solenoids — Grade 3

1. Define the term 'solenoid'. **[2 marks]**

A coil of wire ....

5 Magnetic field around a wire — Grade 4

2. (a) Figure 1 shows a wire carrying a current. Draw the magnetic field on **Figure 1**. **[2 marks]**

(b) Give **two** things that affect the field strength around the wire.

1 ....

2 ....

current

Figure 1

10 Investigating electromagnets — Grade 5

3. A student investigates the magnetic field strength of solenoids. **Figure 2** shows two solenoids made from the same material. Solenoid **A** contains twice as many turns as solenoid **B**.

Solenoid A

Solenoid B

Figure 2

(a) Apart from the number of turns, give **two** other things that affect the magnetic field strength of a solenoid. **[2 marks]**

1 ....

2 ....

(b) The student connects each solenoid in turn into a circuit to test how the number of turns affects its magnetic field strength. Suggest which variable the student must control. **[1 mark]**

....

(c) Predict which solenoid will have the strongest magnetic field. Give a reason for your prediction. **[1 mark]**

....

 Made a start  Feeling confident  Exam ready

Practice paper: Biology

Time: 1 hour 15 minutes

You must have: ruler, calculator.

The total number of marks for this paper is 70.

Answer all questions.

01 **Figure 1** shows a diagram of a plant cell.

The part labelled **X** represents a ribosome.

01.1 Describe the function of ribosomes. **[1 mark]**

01.2 Give **two** components of both animal and plant cells. **[2 marks]**

Tick **two** boxes.

cell membrane ☐

cell wall ☐

chloroplast ☐

mitochondria ☐

permanent vacuole ☐

X

Figure 1

01.3 The length of a plant cell is 50 μm.

Give this in mm. **[2 marks]**

Substances enter and exit cells by diffusion.

Figure 2 shows the concentrations of carbon dioxide inside and outside the cell.

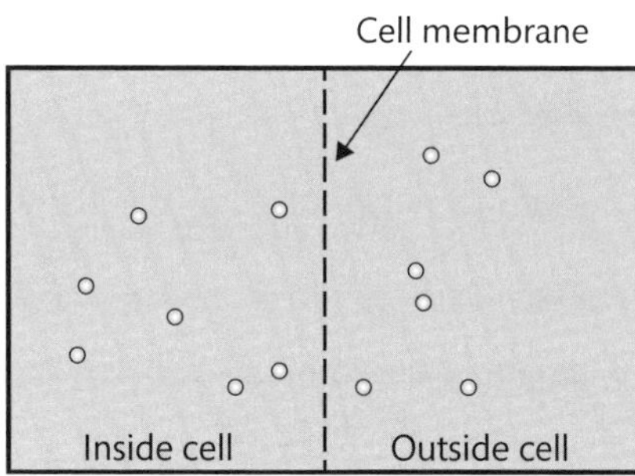

Figure 2

01.4 Draw an arrow on **Figure 2** to show the net direction of movement of carbon dioxide. **[1 mark]**

01.5 Name **one** other factor that affects the rate of diffusion. **[1 mark]**

02 **Figure 3** shows a food chain.

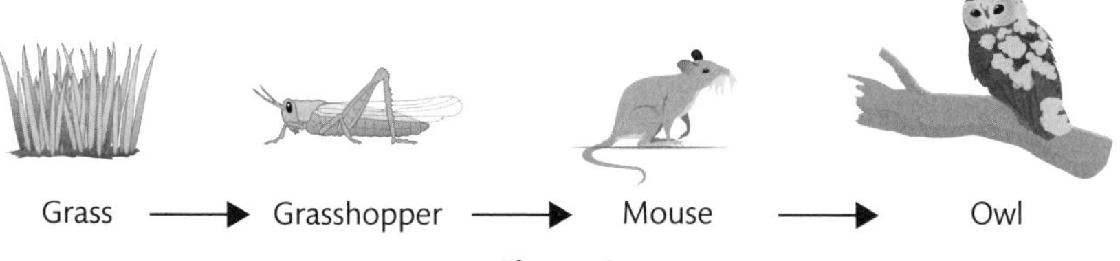

Figure 3

02.1 Complete **Table 1** by ticking the boxes to show which terms can be used to identify each organism. **[4 marks]**

Table 1

Organism	Producer	Secondary consumer	Prey
grass			
grasshopper			
mouse			
owl			

02.2 A new predator was introduced that ate mice.

Explain the effect this would have on the number of owls. **[2 marks]**

02.3 Name **two** factors that can cause animals to become extinct apart from predation. **[2 marks]**

03 This question is about contraception.

03.1 Name **one** male secondary sexual characteristic and **one** female secondary sexual characteristic. **[2 marks]**

03.2 Give **two** examples of hormonal contraception. **[2 marks]**

Tick **two** boxes.

- condom ☐
- contraceptive pill ☐
- implant ☐
- IUD ☐
- spermicide ☐

04 A student wanted to estimate the number of buttercups in the school field.

04.1 Describe a method that could be used. **[5 marks]**

04.2 Name **one** abiotic and **one** biotic factor that might affect the distribution of buttercups. **[2 marks]**

05 Students measured reaction times.

Student A dropped a ruler and student B tried to catch the ruler as quickly as possible. The distance it took for student B to catch the ruler was recorded.

The result was 8 cm. The experiment was repeated and the result was 10 cm. The students calculated the mean.

05.1 Suggest **one** way that the students could improve this investigation. **[1 mark]**

05.2 The students then wanted to test how sugar affects reaction time.

Explain how this could be tested. **[3 marks]**

06 This question is about blood and circulation.

06.1 Draw **one** line to link each component of blood with its function. **[3 marks]**

Component of blood
plasma
platelets
red blood cells
white blood cells

Function
help blood clotting
help protect the body from disease
transport oxygen
transport heat and other substances

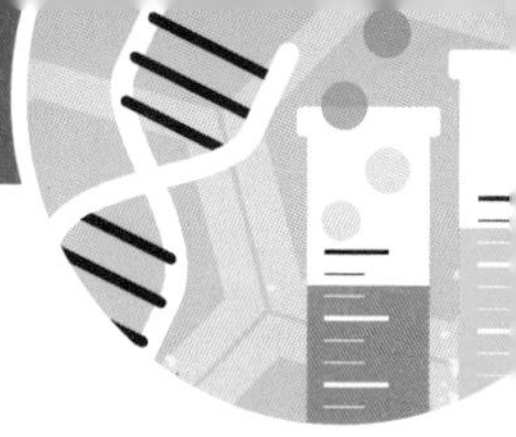

06.2 Describe and evaluate different treatments for coronary heart disease (CHD). **[6 marks]**

07 A student tested different food samples for different nutrients.

The results are shown in **Table 2**.

Table 2

Food sample	Colour with biuret reagent	Colour with Benedict's solution	Colour with iodine solution
A	purple	red	orange
B	blue	green	black
C	purple	blue	black

07.1 Give the food samples that contains protein. **[1 mark]**

07.2 Give the food sample that contains only a small amount of sugar. **[1 mark]**

07.3 Give how many of the food samples contain starch. **[1 mark]**

07.4 Describe how you would test for fat / lipid. Give the positive result. **[3 marks]**

A student measured the time it takes for amylase to break down starch at three different pH values.

Table 3 shows the results.

Table 3

pH	Time taken for starch to be broken down in seconds			
	Test 1	Test 2	Test 3	Mean time (to nearest whole number)
4	512	497	502	504
6	110	113	103	109
8	276	277	286	

07.5 Calculate the mean time taken for starch to be broken down at pH 8 and complete the table. Give this value to the nearest whole number. Show your working. **[2 marks]**

07.6 Which pH gives the highest rate of amylase activity? **[1 mark]**

Tick **one** box.

pH 4 ☐
pH 6 ☐
pH 8 ☐

08 A student investigated the rate of photosynthesis in an aquatic plant.

The apparatus is shown in **Figure 4.**

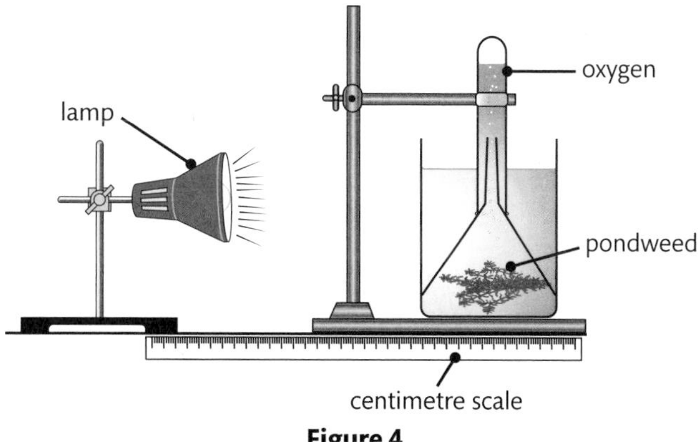

Figure 4

The student counted the number of bubbles released by the plant in one minute.

The student moved the lamp 10 cm closer to the plant and counted the number of bubbles in one minute again.

This was repeated for a distance of one metre.

08.1 Give the independent variable in this investigation. **[1 mark]**

08.2 Give **one** variable that should be controlled in this investigation. **[1 mark]**

08.3 Name the gas produced in this investigation. **[1 mark]**

Tick **one** box.

carbon dioxide ☐

oxygen ☐

nitrogen ☐

water vapour ☐

08.4 Predict what will happen when the lamp gets closer to the plant. **[1 mark]**

08.5 Give **one** use of the glucose produced during photosynthesis. **[1 mark]**

09 Polydactyly is an inherited condition that causes extra fingers or toes to grow.

The allele for polydactyly, **P**, is dominant.

The allele for no polydactyly, **p**, is recessive.

Figure 5 shows the hand of a person with polydactyly.

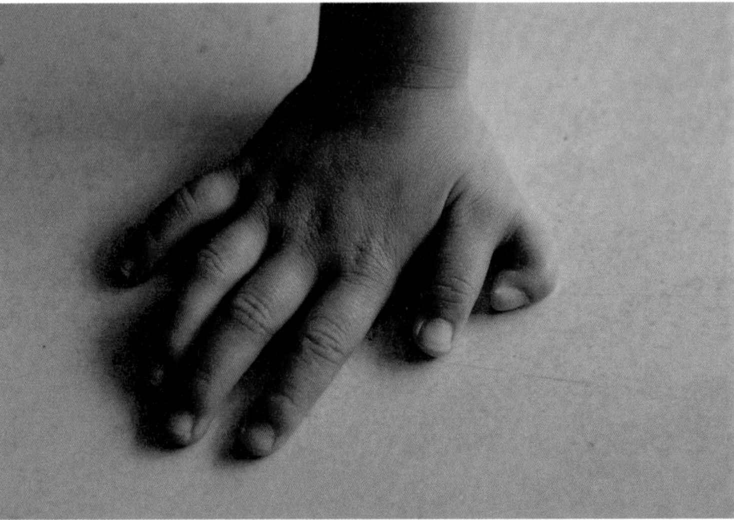

Figure 5

09.1 Give **two** possible genotypes of a person with polydactyly. **[2 marks]**

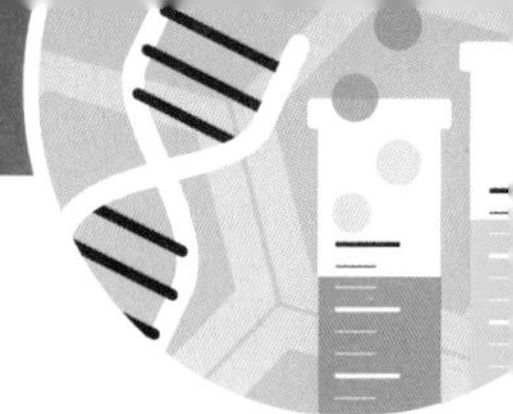

09.2 A person has the genotype **pp**.

Which **two** terms are used to describe the genotype of this person? **[2 marks]**

Tick **two** boxes.

dominant ☐
heterozygous ☐
homozygous ☐
phenotypes ☐
recessive ☐

09.3 Two parents with the genotypes **Pp** and **Pp** are expecting a child.

Complete the Punnett square and give the probability (chance) of the child having polydactyly. **[2 marks]**

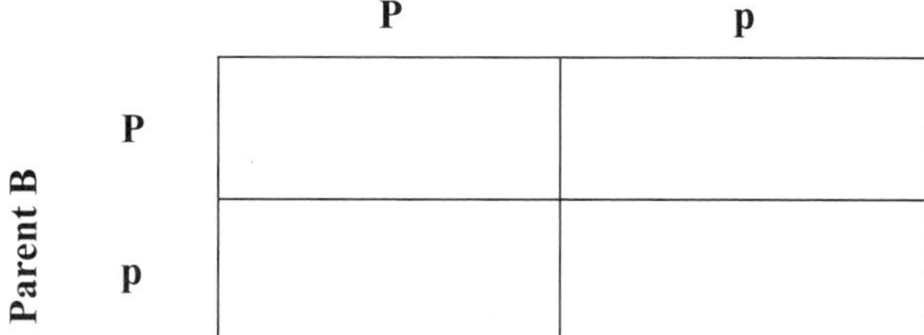

Parent A

		P	**p**
Parent B	**P**		
	p		

10 Measles is a communicable disease and is caused by a virus.

Figure 6 shows the number of measles cases reported by year.

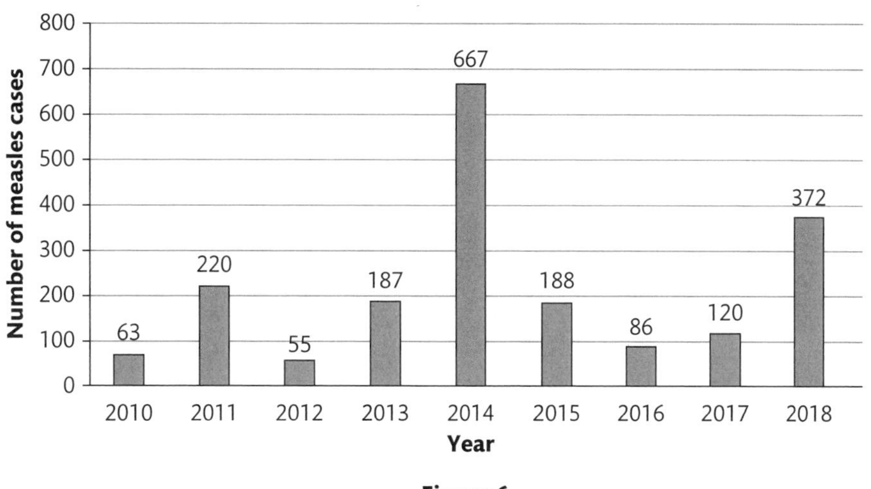

Figure 6

10.1 Give the year that the number of measles cases was highest. **[1 mark]**

10.2 Calculate the increase in numbers of measles cases between 2017 and 2018. **[1 mark]**

10.3 Vaccination is one reason for the decrease in number of cases of measles.

Describe the process of vaccination. **[3 marks]**

10.4 Describe **two** other ways to reduce the spread of communicable diseases. **[2 marks]**

11 Give **two** advantages and **two** disadvantages of the use of embryonic stem cells in medicine. **[4 marks]**

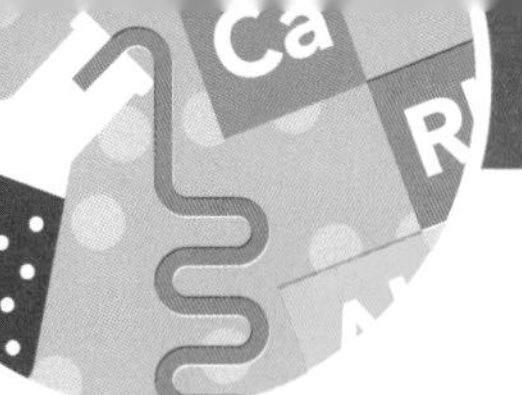

Practice paper: Chemistry

Time: 1 hour 15 minutes
You must have: ruler, calculator.
The total number of marks for this paper is 70.
Answer **all** questions.

01 Zinc reacts with sulfuric acid to form a salt and hydrogen. The equation is:

$Zn(\_\_\_\_) + H_2SO_4(aq) \rightarrow ZnSO_4(aq) + H_2(g)$

01.1 How many elements are in the formula $ZnSO_4$? Tick **one** box. **[1 mark]**

2 ☐
3 ☐
4 ☐
5 ☐

01.2 Complete the equation to show the state symbol for zinc. **[1 mark]**

01.3 Give the meaning of the state symbol (aq). **[1 mark]**

01.4 Name the salt formed in this reaction. **[1 mark]**

01.5 Describe **two** observations you would see during this reaction. **[2 marks]**

01.6 Describe a test to show that hydrogen is produced in the reaction. **[2 marks]**

02 Dmitri Mendeleev produced a periodic table of the elements in 1869. **Figure 1** shows part of this table.

B	Al	?	U

Figure 1

02.1 What are the names of the first two elements in **Figure 1**? Tick **one** box. **[1 mark]**

beryllium and aluminium ☐
beryllium and arsenic ☐
boron and aluminium ☐
bromine and arsenic ☐

02.2 There is a gap in the table between Al and U.
Give a reason why Mendeleev left this gap. **[1 mark]**

02.3 The modern periodic table is arranged in order of increasing atomic number.
In what order were the elements in Mendeleev's table? Tick **one** box. **[1 mark]**

atomic number ☐
atomic radius ☐
atomic weight ☐

02.4 Which of the following describes an element? Tick **one** box. **[1 mark]**

Its atoms have the same number of neutrons. ☐
Its atoms have the same number of protons. ☐
It can be broken down using chemical reactions. ☐
Its molecules always consist of one atom. ☐

02.5 Elements with similar properties are arranged in groups in the modern periodic table. Describe **one** feature that their atoms have in common. **[2 marks]**

03 Chlorine is placed in Group 7 of the periodic table.

03.1 Which of the following describes trends going down Group 7? Tick **one** box. **[1 mark]**

Relative molecular mass	Boiling point	
decreases	decreases	☐
decreases	increases	☐
increases	decreases	☐
increases	increases	☐

03.2 **Figure 2** shows a model of chlorine.

Cl–Cl

Figure 2

What does the line in **Figure 2** represent? Tick **one** box. **[1 mark]**

covalent bond ☐
intermolecular force ☐
ionic bond ☐
metallic bond ☐

03.3 Describe a test for chlorine. **[2 marks]**

Some students investigated the reactivity of three Group 7 elements.

They mixed solutions of each element with solutions containing their salts.

Table 1 shows what the students saw.

Table 1

Salt solution	Bromine solution	Chlorine solution	Iodine solution
sodium bromide	no change	turns orange	no change
sodium chloride	no change	no change	no change
sodium iodide	turns brown	turns orange	no change

03.4 Explain why a reaction happened when bromine solution was added to sodium iodide solution. **[2 marks]**

03.5 Write a word equation for the reaction that happens between chlorine and sodium bromide. **[2 marks]**

04 Dilute acids react with dilute alkalis.

04.1 Copy and complete this equation to show the reaction between an acid and an alkali. **[2 marks]**

____ + OH^- → ____

04.2 Describe how you could show that the reaction is an exothermic reaction. **[2 marks]**

05 Iron is extracted from iron oxide by heating with carbon.

05.1 Balance this equation for the reaction. **[2 marks]**

$Fe_2O_3 + 3C \rightarrow$ __ Fe + __ CO

05.2 Name the substance that is reduced in the reaction. **[1 mark]**

05.3 Graphite is a form of carbon. Describe the structure of graphite. **[2 marks]**

05.4 Iron and aluminium are good conductors of electricity. Explain why metals are good conductors of electricity. **[2 marks]**

05.5 Aluminium must be extracted by electrolysis instead of heating with carbon. Give a reason why. **[1 mark]**

05.6 Explain why a molten mixture of aluminium oxide and cryolite is used for the extraction of aluminium. **[3 marks]**

06 A student investigates the rate of reaction between an antacid tablet and dilute hydrochloric acid.
Figure 3 shows the apparatus used.

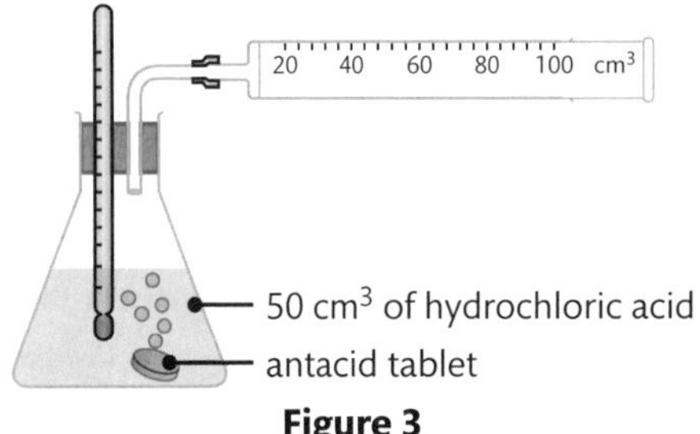

Figure 3

The student uses this method:

Add one antacid tablet to 50 cm³ of dilute hydrochloric acid.

Measure the total volume of gas in the syringe every 10 seconds.

Table 2 shows the results.

Table 2

Time in s	0	10	20	30	40	50	60
Total volume of gas in cm³	0	20	35	45	49	50	50

06.1 The reaction produces carbon dioxide gas.

Describe the test for carbon dioxide. **[2 marks]**

06.2 Calculate the mean rate of the reaction in cm³/s during the first 20 seconds of the reaction. **[2 marks]**

06.3 How do the results show that the reaction ended at 50 s? **[1 mark]**

06.4 Describe what happened to the rate as the reaction carries on. **[2 marks]**

07 When it is heated, ammonium chloride breaks down to form ammonia and hydrogen chloride:

ammonium chloride $\rightleftharpoons$ ammonia + hydrogen chloride

07.1 Describe how the equation shows that the reaction is reversible. **[1 mark]**

07.2 The reaction reaches equilibrium in a sealed container.
Compare the rate of the forward reaction with the rate of the reverse reaction. **[1 mark]**

07.3 Suggest a way to move the reaction in the reverse direction. **[1 mark]**

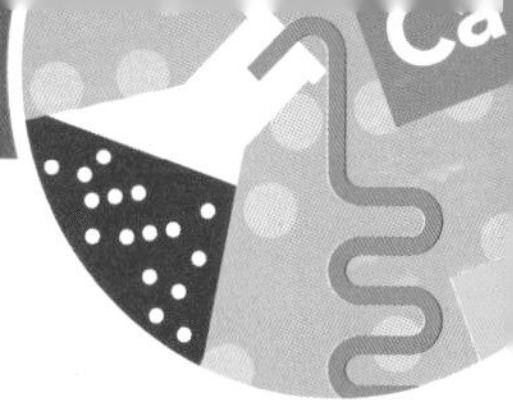

07.4 Ammonia dissolves in water. Describe a way to show that the ammonia solution is alkaline. **[2 marks]**

08 Alkanes are a family of hydrocarbons with the general formula C_nH_{2n+2}.

08.1 Which **two** organic molecules in **Figure 4** belong to the alkane family? **[2 marks]**

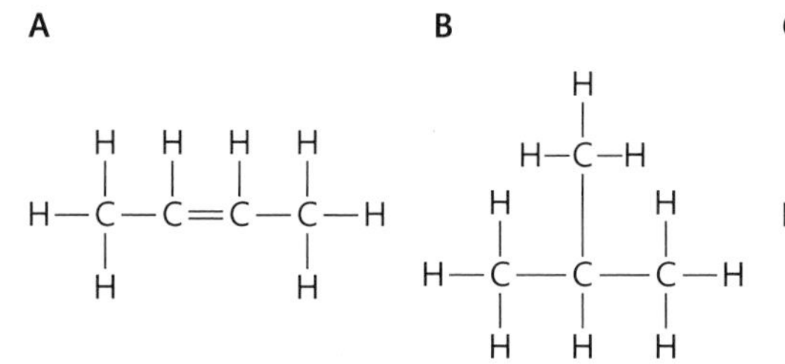

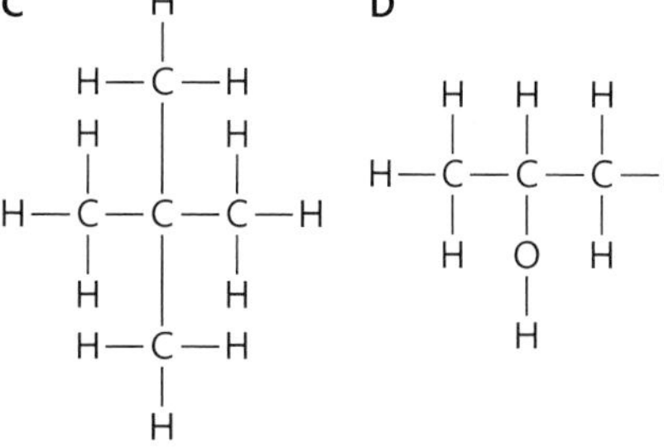

Figure 4

08.2 Crude oil is separated into useful mixtures by fractional distillation.

Copy and complete the sentence. Use words from the box. **[1 mark]**

condense	evaporate	freeze	melt

As hydrocarbon vapours rise through the column, they ______________.

08.3 Describe how the boiling point and viscosity of hydrocarbons change as their molecular size increases. **[1 mark]**

09 The Earth's atmosphere is a mixture of gases.

09.1 Complete **Table 3** to show the percentage of different gases in clean air today. **[2 marks]**

Table 3

Gas	Percentage in air
carbon dioxide and other trace gases	less than 1
	80
oxygen	

09.2 Describe how the early oceans formed. **[1 mark]**

09.3 Describe how the percentage of carbon dioxide changed over time. **[1 mark]**

09.4 Explain why the percentage of carbon dioxide changed. **[2 marks]**

10 A life cycle assessment (LCA) is carried out to assess the environmental impact of manufactured products.

10.1 Give **two** stages assessed in an LCA. **[2 marks]**

10.2 Describe **two** ways in which a metal can be recycled. **[2 marks]**

11 A student wants to make pure, dry magnesium chloride.

11.1 Name the acid that the student needs. **[1 mark]**

11.2 Suggest **two** insoluble substances that could be used to produce magnesium chloride. **[2 marks]**

11.3 The student is given the following apparatus: beaker, Bunsen burner, conical flask, evaporating basin, filter funnel and paper, spatula, stirring rod, tripod, gauze and mat.

Plan a safe method the student could use to make a pure, dry sample of magnesium chloride. **[6 marks]**

Practice paper: Physics

Time: 1 hour 30 minutes

You must have: ruler, calculator.

The total number of marks for this paper is 70.

Answer **all** questions.

01 **Figure 1** shows a circuit diagram containing two different resistors connected in series.

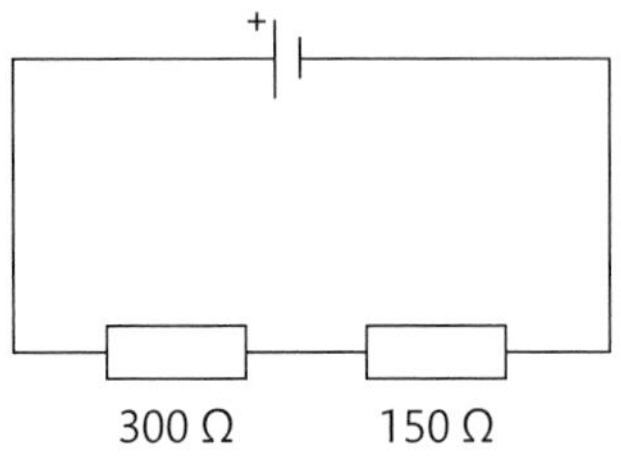

+

300 Ω 150 Ω

Figure 1

01.1 What is the other component in the circuit? **[1 mark]**
Tick **one** box.

a mains supply ☐

a battery ☐

a cell ☐

a switch ☐

01.2 Calculate the combined resistance of the resistors in **Figure 1** in ohms (Ω). **[2 marks]**

Figure 2 shows the same circuit as **Figure 1**, with components **A** and **B** added to make measurements.

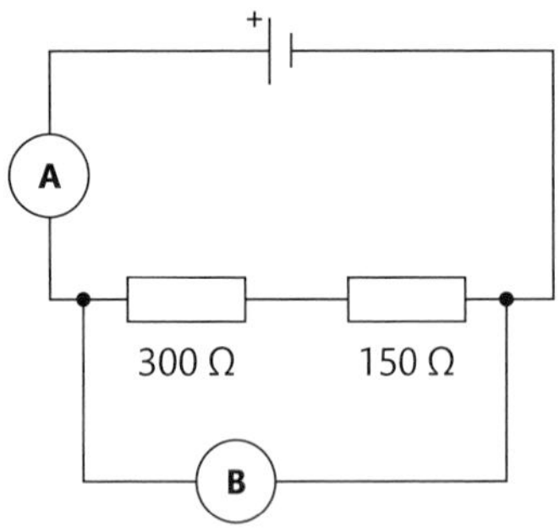

+

A

300 Ω 150 Ω

B

Figure 2

01.3 Which statement about **A** and **B** describes the correct way to connect measuring components? **[1 mark]**

Tick **one** box.

Component **A** is a voltmeter and component **B** is an ammeter. ☐

Component **A** is an ammeter and component **B** is a voltmeter. ☐

Components **A** and **B** are both voltmeters. ☐

Components **A** and **B** are both ammeters. ☐

01.4 The potential difference measured across both resistors is 1.35 V.

Use the following equation to calculate the current in the circuit in amps (A).

potential difference = current × resistance **[3 marks]**

Figure 3 shows the same components connected in a different way.

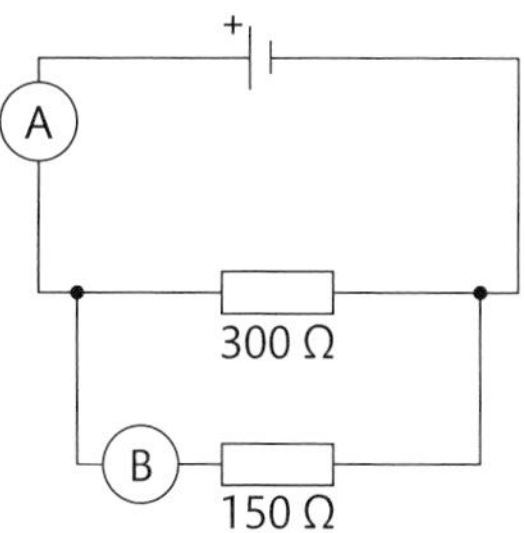

Figure 3

01.5 Name the type of circuit shown in **Figure 3**. **[1 mark]**

01.6 Which statement about the total resistance of the two resistors in **Figure 3** is true? **[1 mark]**

Tick **one** box.

The total resistance is greater than 300 Ω. ☐

The total resistance is 300 Ω. ☐

The total resistance is 150 Ω. ☐

The total resistance is less than 150 Ω. ☐

02 Some properties of atomic nuclei are shown by using symbols.

02.1 **Figure 4** shows the symbol for an isotope of magnesium.

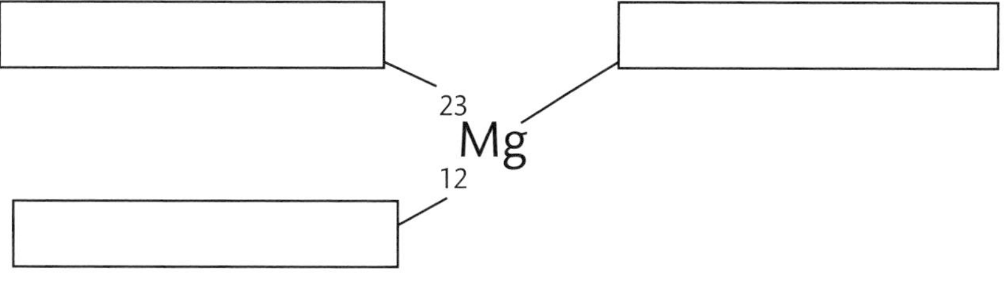

Figure 4

Complete the diagram labels. Use words from the box.

atomic number	neutron number	mass number	element

[2 marks]

Americium-241 is a radioactive isotope used in smoke detectors. **Figure 5** shows the symbol for americium-241.

$^{241}_{95}Am$

Figure 5

02.2 How many protons are there in a nucleus of americium-241? **[1 mark]**

Tick **one** box.

95 ☐

146 ☐

241 ☐

02.3 How many neutrons are there in a nucleus of americium-241? **[1 mark]**

Tick **one** box.

95 ☐

146 ☐

241 ☐

Americium-241 decays by emitting an alpha particle.

02.4 Which statement describes an alpha particle? **[1 mark]**

Tick **one** box.

a fast-moving electron ☐

a high-energy electromagnetic wave ☐

a nucleus of a helium atom ☐

02.5 Smoke detectors have a tough plastic casing.

Give the property of alpha radiation that means it is safe to use americium-241 in smoke detectors. **[1 mark]**

02.6 Americium does not occur in nature.

It must be made in nuclear reactors.

Suggest **one** reason why old smoke detectors should be returned to the manufacturer and not thrown away like normal waste. **[1 mark]**

03 A student investigates two cuboids made of different materials.

Figure 6 shows the cuboids. They are different sizes.

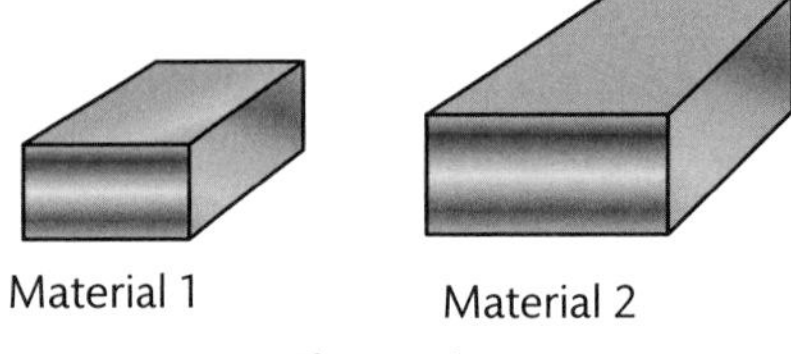

Figure 6

First, the student measures the sides of each cuboid using a ruler.

03.1 Name a piece of apparatus that could measure the sides more accurately than a ruler. **[1 mark]**

Table 1 shows the student's results.

Table 1

Cuboid	Length in cm	Width in cm	Height in cm	Volume in cm^3
1	3.2	2.0	1.0	6.4
2	5.0	2.5	1.4	

03.2 Calculate the volume of cuboid 2 in cm^3. **[2 marks]**

The student then measured the mass of each cuboid.

Table 2 shows the student's results.

Table 2

Cuboid	Mass in g
1	3.2
2	5.0

03.3 Use the following equation to calculate the density of cuboid 1 in g/cm^3.

density = mass/volume **[2 marks]**

Figure 7 shows a sample of rock.

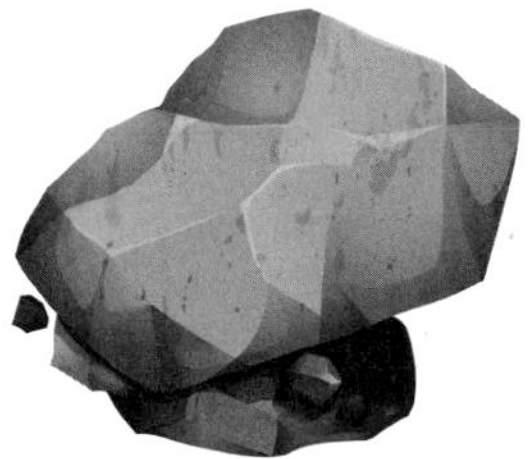

Figure 7

03.4 Describe a method for finding the density of the rock sample.

You should include a description of the apparatus and how it is used. **[6 marks]**

04 Speed and velocity are both used to describe how an object moves.

04.1 Describe the difference between speed and velocity. **[1 mark]**

A runner did a training run.

Figure 8 shows how the distance changed with time.

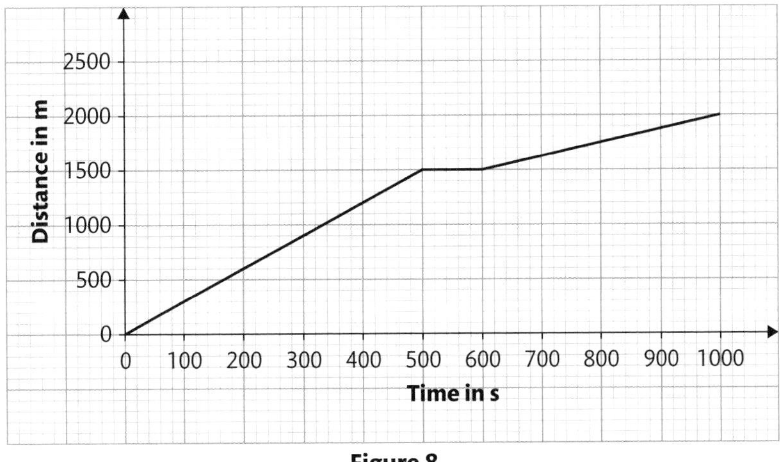

Figure 8

04.2 Give the time it took the runner to travel 1500 m in seconds (s). **[1 mark]**

04.3 Use the following equation to calculate the speed of the runner for the first 1500 m in m/s.

distance travelled = speed × time **[3 marks]**

04.4 Describe what the runner was doing between the times 500 s and 600 s. **[1 mark]**

04.5 Compare the speed of the runner over the last 500 m with their speed for the first 1500 m. **[1 mark]**

05 **Figure 9** shows apparatus used to investigate induced magnetism.

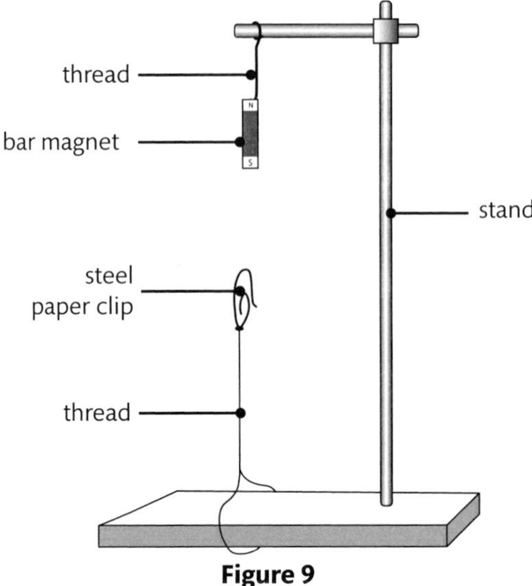

Figure 9

05.1 Describe the difference between permanent magnets and induced magnets. **[2 marks]**

As the bar magnet is lowered towards the paper clip, one end of the paper clip rises towards the magnet.

05.2 What type of magnet is the paper clip? **[1 mark]**

Tick **one** box.

permanent magnet ☐
induced magnet ☐
electromagnet ☐

Recycling facilities use electromagnets to separate steel cans from aluminium cans.

05.3 Describe the difference between steel and aluminium that makes this process work. **[1 mark]**

05.4 Suggest **one** reason why an electromagnet is better than a permanent magnet for this process. **[1 mark]**

06 **Figure 10** shows a diagram of a wave.

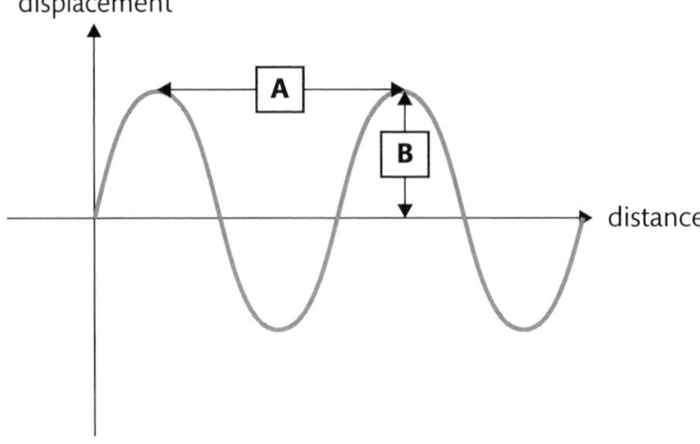

Figure 10

06.1 Draw **one** line from each quantity labelled on the diagram to its definition. **[2 marks]**

Quantity	**Definition**
	the number of waves passing a point each second
A	the maximum displacement of a point on a wave away from its undisturbed position
B	the rate at which energy is transferred through a medium
	the distance from a point on one wave to the equivalent point on the adjacent wave

06.2 Give **one** difference between transverse and longitudinal waves. **[2 marks]**

06.3 Which of the following waves is a longitudinal wave? **[1 mark]**

Tick **one** box.

water wave ☐

sound wave ☐

light wave ☐

Figure 11 shows a ripple tank used to measure the speed of water waves.

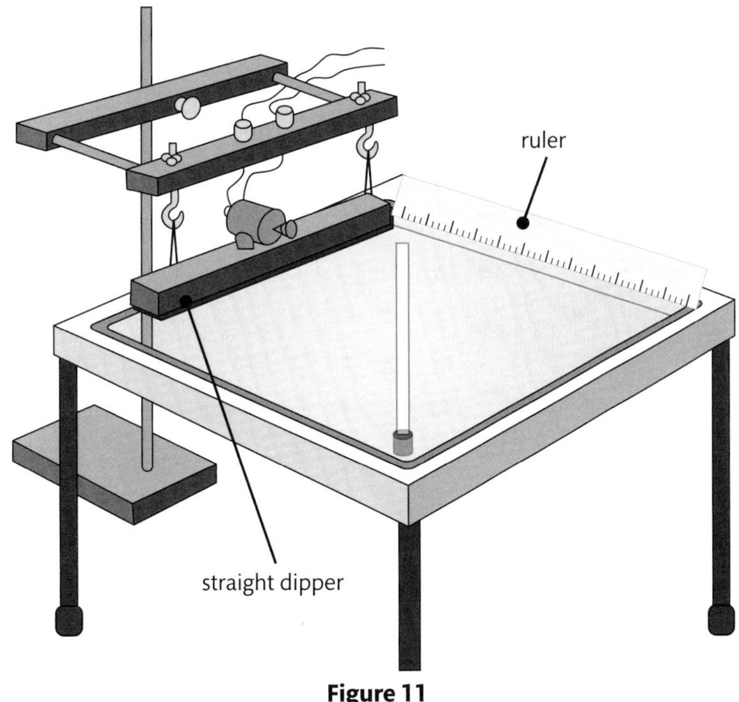

Figure 11

06.4 Write down the equation that links frequency, wavelength and wave speed. **[1 mark]**

The student counts the number of waves passing a point in 10 s. The measurement is repeated four times.

The results are shown in Table 3.

Table 3

Measurement	1	2	3	4
Number of waves passing a point in 10 s	21	27	20	19

06.5 One of the measurements is anomalous. Give the anomalous measurement. **[1 mark]**

06.6 Calculate the mean number of waves passing a point in 10 s. **[2 marks]**

06.7 The frequency of the waves is the number of waves passing a point in 1 s.

Calculate the frequency of the water waves in Hertz (Hz). **[1 mark]**

Another student estimates the wavelength using these steps:

1 Count the number of ripples seen in the tank at one time.

2 Divide by the length of the tank.

06.8 Suggest a reason why this student's estimate of wavelength is not very accurate. **[1 mark]**

06.9 Suggest **two** ways the student could estimate the wavelength more accurately. **[2 marks]**

07 In 1969, astronauts landed on the Moon for the first time. They found some differences compared to being on Earth.

07.1 Complete the sentences. Use words from the box. **[2 marks]**

energy	field	mass	weight

The force acting on an object due to gravity is called ....

The force of gravity close to the Moon is due to the Moon's gravitational ....

The force of gravity on an object can be measured using a newtonmeter.

Figure 12 shows the readings on a newtonmeter for the same object on Earth and on the Moon.

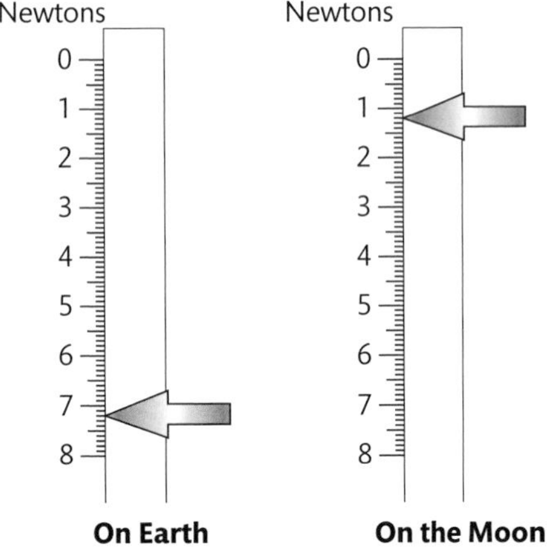

Figure 12

07.2 Write down the readings shown in **Figure 12** in Newtons (N) for the Earth and the Moon. **[1 mark]**

07.3 What can you conclude from these readings? Tick **one** box. **[1 mark]**

The mass of the object is smaller on the Moon than it is on Earth. ☐
The mass of the object is larger on the Moon than it is on Earth. ☐
The gravitational field strength on the surface of the Moon is weaker than on Earth. ☐
The gravitational field strength on the surface of the Moon is stronger than on Earth. ☐

For some visits to the Moon, astronauts took a 'buggy' with them.

Figure 13 shows a Moon buggy and the forces acting on it.

Figure 13

07.4 Forces **R** and **S** are equal and in opposite directions. Name forces **R** and **S**. **[2 marks]**

07.5 The astronaut can control the buggy.

Describe what happens if the astronaut makes force **P** larger than force **Q**. **[1 mark]**

07.6 The astronaut sees a rock ahead and applies the brakes to stop the buggy.

The braking distance of the buggy is 6 m.

The buggy travels 9 m from the astronaut seeing the rock to stopping.

Explain why. **[1 mark]**

08 This question is about energy transfers and renewable energy resources.

Figure 14 shows a hydro-electric power station.

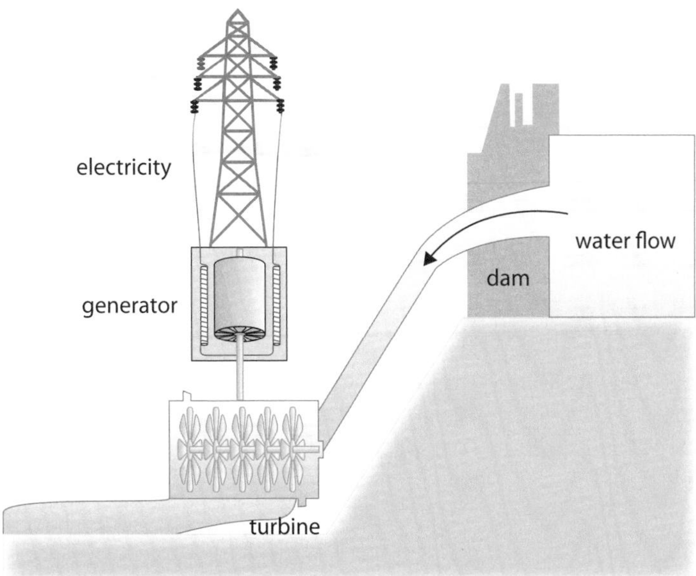

Figure 14

08.1 Write **three** sentences to describe the processes involving energy transfers that take place when the gate from the dam is opened. **[3 marks]**

The Netherlands produces electricity from solar panels and wind turbines.

Table 4 shows data about these two sources of electricity.

Table 4

Source	Total power input in MW	Cost to build in £	Cost to run per year in £
solar	6.5	750 000	1 500 000
wind	3.5	10 000	45 000

08.2 Write down the equation that relates efficiency, total power input and useful power output. **[1 mark]**

08.3 Show which source of electricity, solar or wind, is the most efficient. Use data from **Table 4** to support your answer. **[2 marks]**

08.4 Determine which source of electricity, solar or wind, is cheaper to build and run over a 25-year period. Use data from **Table 4** to support your answer. **[4 marks]**

Answers

Page 1 Levels of organisation

Quick quiz

cells → tissue → organ → organ system → organism

1. tissue – group of specialised cells with similar structures and functions

   organ – group of tissues that performs a specific job

   organ system – group of organs

[1 mark for 1 correct, 2 marks for 2 correct, 3 marks for 3 correct]

2. spinal cord **[1]**; brain **[1]**
3. lung **[1]**
4. Any two for one mark each from: circulatory system; human digestive system; respiratory system; reproductive system; nervous system; skeletal system; immune system
5.

Level of organisation	Example
cell	muscle cell
tissue	cardiac tissue
organ	heart
organ system	circulatory system

[1 mark for 1 or 2 correct, 2 marks for 3 correct, 4 marks for 4 correct]

Page 2 Eukaryotic and prokaryotic cells

Quick quiz

From top to bottom: false, false, true, true, true

1. centimetre – cm

   millimetre – mm

   micrometre – µm

   nanometre – nm

   [1 mark for 1 correct, 2 marks for 2 or 3 correct, 3 marks for 4 correct]

2. **(a)** 10 mm **[1]**

   (b) 0.5 m **[1]**

   (c) 15 cm **[1]**

   (d) 2.2 m **[1]**

   (e) 2×10^5 µm **[1]**

3. **(a)** plasmid **[1]**

   (b) flagella **[1]**

4. Any one each from similarity and difference for one mark each:

   Similarity: cytoplasm; ribosomes

   Difference: a cell wall, plasmids, a single loop of DNA, flagella

5. plasmid **[1]**

Page 3 Animal and plant cells

Quick quiz

(a)

Organelle	Animal cell	Plant cell
cell membrane	✓	✓
cell wall		✓
chloroplast		✓
mitochondria	✓	✓
nucleus	✓	✓

(b) cell membrane / mitochondria / nucleus

(c) cell wall / chloroplast

1. chloroplast **[1]**
2. (permanent) vacuole **[1]**
3. chloroplast – contains chlorophyll for photosynthesis

   cellulose cell wall – gives the cell protection, strength and structure

   cell membrane – controls what enters and exits the cell

   nucleus – contains the genetic material

   ribosome – where proteins are made

   [1 mark for 1 correct, 2 marks for 3 correct, 3 marks all correct]

4. **(a)** 80 ÷ 20 = 4 so 4 times larger **[1]**

   (b) Plant cells need to contain more types of cell organelles / chloroplasts / have a large permanent vacuole so are larger **[1]**.

Page 4 Microscopy

Quick quiz

magnification, resolution

1. **(a)** 10 × 40 = ×400 **[1]**

   (b) ×80 **[1]**

2. **(a)** $\times 100 = \frac{2000\,\mu\text{m}}{\text{size of real image}}$ **[1]** size of real image = $\frac{2000}{100}$ =

   20 **[1]** µm **[1]**

   (b) The scientist would be able to see the nucleus **[1]**. They wouldn't be able to see the chloroplasts **[1]**.

3. **(a)** Any three for three marks from: Light microscopes were invented before electron microscopes; Light microscopes have a lower magnification; Light microscopes have a lower resolution; Light microscopes use light (not electrons)
   OR Electron microscopes were invented more recently; Electron microscopes have a higher magnification; Electron microscopes have a higher resolution; Electron microscopes use electrons (not light)

   (b) Electron microscope **[1]**, because ribosomes are too small to see with a light microscope **[1]**

Page 5 Using microscopes

Quick quiz

Parts of microscope labelled correctly.

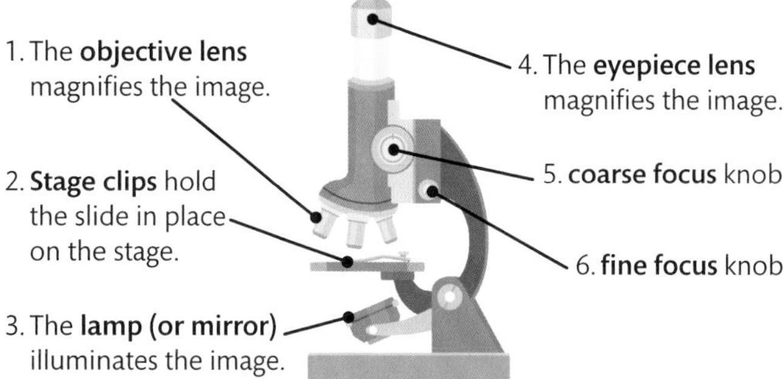

1. magnifies the image – eyepiece / objective lens

   adjusts the focus of the image – coarse focus knob

   illuminates the image – lamp

   [1 mark for 1 correct, 2 marks for 2 correct, 3 marks for three correct]

2.

Use the coarse focus knob to lower the low power objective lens to just above the slide.	2
Look through the eyepiece lens and raise the lens until the image is nearly in focus.	3
Place the prepared slide under the stage clips of the microscope.	1
Use the fine focus knob to get a clear sharp image.	4

[1 mark for 2 correct, 2 marks for 3 correct, 3 marks for all correct]

3. **(a)** Nucleus **[1]**
   (b) Cell membrane **[1]**
   (c) To be able to see parts of the cell more clearly / because the cell is transparent **[1]**

Page 6 Specialised cells

Quick quiz

Specialised cell	Animal or plant cell?
muscle cell	animal
nerve cell	animal
phloem	plant
root hair cell	plant

1. Nerve cells carry electrical impulses (around the organism). **[1]**
   Root hair cells absorb water and mineral ions from the soil. **[1]**
2. acrosome containing enzymes – digest the outer layer of the egg cell **[1]**
   haploid nucleus – to form a complete set of chromosomes after fertilisation **[1]**
   tail – to swim to the egg cell **[1]**
3. **(a)** water **[1]**; mineral ions **[1]**
   (b) lignin walls **[1]**
   hollow centre (lumen) **[1]**
   (c) phloem **[1]**
4. Mitochondria are the site of (aerobic) respiration **[1]**. Respiration releases energy **[1]**. Energy is required for muscle contraction **[1]**.

Page 7 Cell differentiation

Quick quiz

From top to bottom: specialised; stem; early in; throughout

1. Bone marrow **[1]**
   Embryos **[1]**
2. Any two for two marks from: muscle cells; nerve cells; epithelial cells; ciliated cells; skin cells; bone cells; egg cells; sperm cells
3. Any three for three marks from: healing broken bones; generating new red blood cells; healing skin cuts; hair growth; fingernail growth
4. Meristem **[1]**
5. Any one for one mark from: root hair cell; xylem; phloem
6. Cells in the meristems **[1]** can differentiate throughout a plant's life **[1]** and so divide and specialise into all the cell types needed to grow into a new / replacement branch **[1]**

Page 8 Chromosomes, mitosis and the cell cycle

Quick quiz

From top to bottom: true, false, false, true, true

1. gene → chromosome **[1]** → nucleus **[1]** → cell
2. The DNA inside the nucleus duplicates / replicates. **[1]**
   The number of subcellular structures increases. **[1]**
   There are now two copies of each chromosome. **[1]**
3. chromosomes are separating **[1]**
   nucleus is splitting **[1]**
4. Any two for two marks from: asexual reproduction; repair of cells; replacement of cells; growth
5. There is one parent cell and two daughter cells **[1]**. The cells are genetically identical / have same number of chromosomes **[1]**.

Page 9 Stem cells

Quick quiz

adult stem cell – bone marrow

embryonic stem cell – embryos

plant stem cell – meristem

1.

Feature	Adult stem cell	Embryonic stem cell
can form any type of cell		✓
when used, life is destroyed		✓
comes from living organisms	✓	✓
can be used to treat disease	✓	✓

[1 mark for each correct row]

2. A clone is an organism that is genetically identical to another organism. **[1]**
3. Taking cuttings produces cloned plants quickly and cheaply. **[1]**
   Rare plants can be grown to protect them from extinction. **[1]**
4. Brain tissue **[1]**; bone marrow **[1]**
5. Any one each from for and against for one mark each:
   For: no life is destroyed; adults can choose to donate; can be used to treat some diseases
   Against: is a painful procedure; not all diseases can be treated

Page 10 Diffusion

Quick quiz

Arrow drawn from left to right.

1. net; higher **[1]**; lower **[1]**
   [1 mark for 2 correct, 2 marks for 3 correct]
2. **(a)** One mark for calculation and one mark for correct answer for each cube **[4]**

Cube	Length of one side in cm = a	Area of one side in cm² = a × a	Number of sides	Surface area in cm² = b × c
1	2	4	6	24
2	3	9	6	54

   (b) One mark for calculation and one mark for simplification for each cube [4]

Cube	Surface area in cm^2	Volume in cm^3	Surface area to volume ratio
1	24	8	3 : 1
2	54	27	2 : 1

3. Any two for two marks from: concentration gradient; surface area of the membrane; temperature
4. well ventilated **[1]**
   efficient blood supply **[1]**
5. thin **[1]**; large surface area **[1]**

Page 11 Osmosis

Quick quiz

Diagram labelled correctly

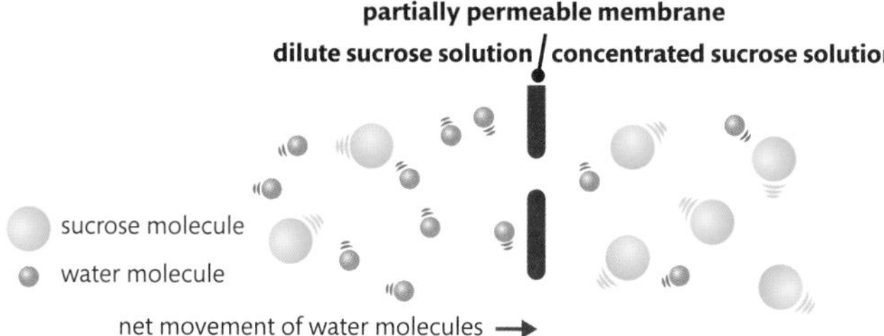

1. Any two for two marks from: water; oxygen; carbon dioxide
2. A dilute solution contains high concentrations of water molecules. **[1]**
   A concentrated solution contains low concentration of water molecules / higher concentrations of solute / sugar molecules. **[1]**
3. a more dilute solution – the cell increases in size
   a more concentrated solution – the cell decreases in size
   a solution with the same concentration – the cell stays the same size
   [1 mark for 1 or 2 correct, 2 marks for 3 correct]
4. Water moves into the red blood cell from a higher to a lower concentration (of water) by osmosis **[1]**. The red blood cell doesn't have a cell wall **[1]** so too much water causes it to swell and burst **[1]**.

Page 12 Investigating osmosis

Quick quiz

water

1. final mass – initial mass = 1.25 – 1.13 = 0.12 g **[1]**
   percentage change = $\left(\frac{0.12}{1.13\text{g}}\right) \times 100 = 10.6\%$ **[1]**
2. (a)

Variable	Independent variable	Dependent variable	Control variable
mass of potato		✓	
concentration of sugar solution	✓		
volume of sugar solution			✓

[1 mark for each correct column]

(b) (i) mass would decrease **[1]**

(ii) The sugar solution is more concentrated than the potato **[1]**. Water would leave the potato **[1]** by osmosis **[1]** from its higher concentration to its lower concentration **[1]**.

Page 13 Active transport

Quick quiz

From top to bottom: false, true, true, false

1. diffusion – the movement of particles from higher to lower concentration
   osmosis – the movement of water from a dilute to a more concentrated solution through a partially permeable membrane
   active transport – the movement of substances from a more dilute to a more concentrated solution using energy from respiration
   [1 mark for 1 correct, 2 marks for 3 correct]
2. **(a)** water **[1]**
   mineral ions **[1]**
   (b) Water – by osmosis **[1]**
   Mineral ions – by active transport **[1]**
3. Any four for four marks from: Glucose in the small intestine is a higher concentration than outside the cell. Active transport is used to absorb glucose. Active transport needs energy. Energy is released from respiration. Mitochondria are the site of respiration.

Page 14 Plant tissues

Quick quiz

Diagram correctly labelled

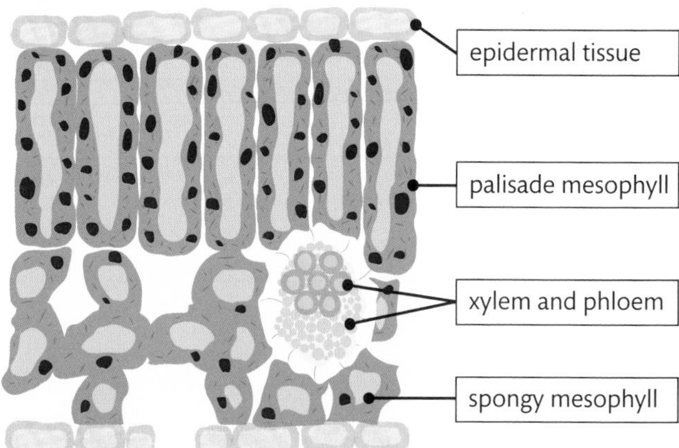

1. epidermal tissue – secretes a waxy cuticle for protections
   palisade mesophyll tissue – contains many chloroplasts for photosynthesis
   phloem tissue – transport of dissolved sugars
   spongy mesophyll tissue – has a large surface area for gas exchange
   xylem – transport of water and mineral ions
   [1 mark for 1 correct, 2 marks for 2 or 3 correct, 3 marks for all correct]
2. pores **[1]**; carbon dioxide **[1]**; water **[1]**; guard cells **[1]**; photosynthesis **[1]**
3. **(a)** to let light through **[1]** so can reach palisade mesophyll **[1]**
   (b) allow carbon dioxide in **[1]** and oxygen out **[1]**

Page 15 Plant transport

Quick quiz

	Phloem	Root hair cell	Xylem
dissolved sugars	✓		
mineral ions		✓	✓
water		✓	✓

1. **(a)** Transpiration is the movement of water from the roots up the plant and evaporation from the surface of the leaves. **[1]**
   (b) Water **[1]**; leaves **[1]**; stomata **[1]**
2. **(a)** As humidity increases the rate of transpiration decreases. **[1]**

(b) As air humidity increases the concentration gradient **[1]** between the water vapour inside the air spaces of the leaf and the outside air decreases **[1]** so the rate of diffusion decreases. **[1]**

(c) Temperature **[1]**; air movement / wind **[1]**; light intensity **[1]**

3. (a) hollow tubes or pits **[1]**

(b) Any two statements with reason for four marks from: large vacuole for increased absorption / osmosis; large surface area for increased absorption; lots of mitochondria for energy / for active transport

Page 16 Digestion in humans

Quick quiz

Diagram correctly labelled

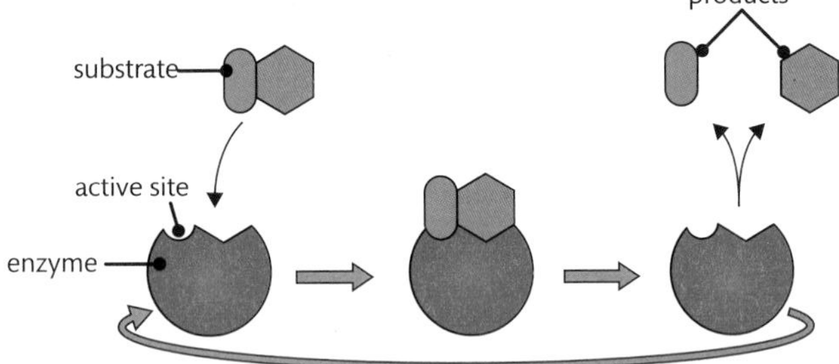

1.

Digestive enzyme	Substance	Products
lipase	fats and oils	fatty acids and glycerol
protease	proteins	amino acids
carbohydrase	starch	sugars

[1 mark for each correct row]

2. Digestion involves the use of digestive enzymes **[1]**. High temperatures affect the shape of an enzyme's active site **[1]**. So the enzyme and substrate (molecules) can no longer bind together **[1]**. So the food substances cannot be broken down / digested **[1]**.

3. **(a)** produced – liver

stored – gall bladder

released – small intestine

[2 correct = 1 mark, 3 correct = 2 marks]

(b) Neutralises stomach acid **[1]**; emulsifies fats **[1]**

Page 17 Food tests

Quick quiz

lipids – ethanol; proteins – biuret reagent; sugars – Benedict's solution; starch – iodine solution

1. lipids – forms a milky white emulsion

proteins – turns blue to purple

sugars – turns red-orange or green depending on the amount present

starch – turns from amber to black

[2 correct = 1 mark, 3 correct = 2 marks, 4 correct = 3 marks]

2. Add ethanol to the sample **[1]**. Shake the mixture **[1]**. Add a few drops of water to the mixture **[1]**.

3. **(a)** starch **[1]**

(b) red-orange / green **[1]**

(c) protein **[1]**

(d) No, the food was not tested with ethanol **[1]**. Ethanol is the reagent for testing for lipids / fats **[1]**.

Page 18 Investigating enzymes

Quick quiz

From top to bottom: iodine solution; black; yellow

1. **(a)** pipettes **[1]**

thermometer **[1]**

(b)

Pour one test tube of amylase into one test tube of starch.	4
Take a drop for each test tube every 30 seconds and add it to the iodine solution.	5
Add one drop of iodine solution to each well of the spotting tile.	1
Place beakers in the water bath.	3
Make up three beakers containing a test tube of starch, and three test tubes of amylase in different buffer solutions.	2

[1 mark for 3 correct, 2 marks for all correct]

2. **(a)** pH 6 **[1]**

(b) $\text{rate} \propto \dfrac{1}{\text{time taken for solution to turn black (s)}}$ **[1]**

(c) Any two for two marks from: difficult to tell when solution has changed colour completely; accuracy of the measuring equipment; temperature fluctuations; accuracy of stopwatch; different people doing the timing

Page 19 The blood

Quick quiz

Diagram correctly labelled

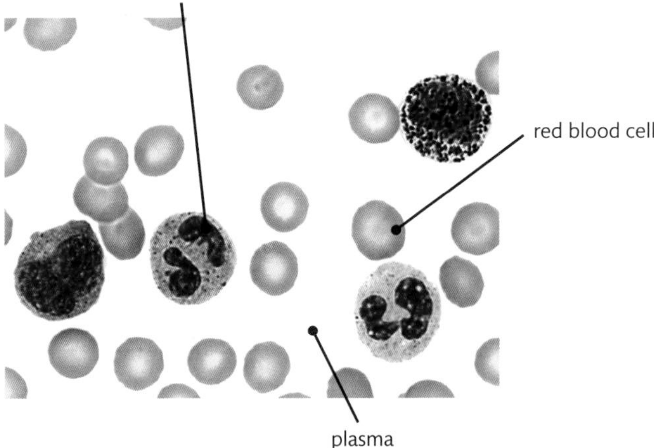

1. Any two for two marks from: carbon dioxide; urea; water; dissolved food; hormones; heat

2. Platelets help blood clot. [1]

3. **(a)** are small **[1]** have a biconcave shape **[1]**

(b) There is more room **[1]** for haemoglobin **[1]** to carry more oxygen **[1]**.

4. Phagocytosis / engulfing pathogens **[1]**; producing antibodies **[1]**; producing antitoxins **[1]**

Page 20 The heart and lungs

Quick quiz

From top to bottom: false, false, true

1. **(a)** trachea **[1]**; bronchus / bronchi / bronchiole(s) **[1]**

(b) They have thin membranes **[1]** so there is a short diffusion distance for gases **[1]**. There are millions of them **[1]** which provides a large surface area for gas exchange **[1]**.

2. **(a)** **(i)** B and C **[1]**
   (ii) A **[1]**
   (iii) right ventricle **[1]**

   (b) aorta – carries oxygenated blood away from the heart to the body

   pulmonary artery – carries deoxygenated blood away from the heart to the lungs

   pulmonary vein – carries oxygenated blood from the lungs to the heart

   vena cava – carries deoxygenated blood from the body to the heart

   [1 mark for 1 correct, 2 marks for 2 or 3 correct, 3 marks for 4 correct]

   (c) A thicker wall can squeeze harder / cause the blood to have a higher pressure **[1]** because the blood has to travel to all of the body **[1]**.

Page 21 Health issues

Quick quiz

Communicable diseases – HIV, flu, measles

Non-communicable diseases – cardiovascular disease, lung cancer

1. Health [1]
2. Any two for two marks from: diet; drinking; smoking; stress; autoimmune diseases; old age
3. bacteria **[1]**
4. **(a)** The number of cases of measles is highest in 2008. **[1]**

   There is a large decrease in the numbers of cases of measles between 2003 and 2005. **[1]**

   (b) People did not want their children to have autism **[1]**. The number of children getting vaccinated decreased **[1]**. Increased number of children catching measles (as it is a communicable disease) **[1]**.

Page 22 Coronary heart disease

Quick quiz

From top to bottom: heart; oxygen; valves

1.

Type of heart disease	Effects
blocked coronary artery	heart attack
faulty valves	harder for the heart to pump blood around the body.
heart failure	the heart is unable to efficiently pump blood around the body

[1 mark for each correct row]

2. There is a build-up of fat in the (walls of) coronary arteries. **[1]**

   This causes them to become narrow / blocked. **[1]**

   The heart muscle does not get any oxygen (or glucose). **[1]**

   So the heart stops beating. **[1]**
3. stents **[1]**; statins **[1]**
4. Any two each from advantages and disadvantages for two marks each:

   Advantages: normal quality of life; prolongs life; long-term solution

   Disadvantages: chance of rejection; risk of death during surgery; surgery is not always successful

Page 23 Effects of lifestyle

Quick quiz

Any three from: smoking; lack of exercise; unhealthy diet; excessive alcohol consumption; drug use

1. **(a)** BMI stands for body mass index. It is a measure of obesity. **[1]**

   (b) As BMI increases the risk of developing type 2 diabetes increases. **[1]**

   The data show there is a correlation between high BMI and type 2 diabetes **[1]**

   (c) If people are healthier they are less likely to develop illness / disease. **[1]**

   So they will not need to use doctors / the NHS / medication. **[1]**

   This means it will cost the government / NHS less money. **[1]**
2. **(a)** Patient B **[1]**

   (b) Patient A **[1]**
3. Baby might have poor growth **[1]**; baby might have poor development **[1]**

Page 24 Cancer

Quick quiz

From top to bottom: false, false, true, false

1. Two for two marks from: alcohol, smoking, UV radiation in sunlight, radon, asbestos
2.

Feature	Type of tumour	
	Benign	Malignant
are growths of abnormal cells	✓	✓
are cancerous		✓
grow slowly	✓	
produce secondary tumours		✓

[1 mark for each correct row]

3. **(a)** 79% greater (± 5%) **[1]**

   (b) Any two for two marks from: Genes are inherited. If there is a family history of breast cancer the person may have inherited the BRCA gene. They can be monitored more frequently. They may be treated more quickly. Early treatment is more successful. They may opt for mastectomy.

Page 25 Communicable diseases

Quick quiz

From top to bottom: true, false, true, false

1. Viruses enter cells and multiply. **[1]**

   The cells are damaged when they break open to release new viruses. **[1]**
2.

	Direct contact	Indirect contact
drinking contaminated water		✓
touching a diseased animal	✓	
breathing in pathogens in air droplets		✓

[1 mark for each correct row]

3. using surgical masks **[1]**

   washing hands **[1]**
4. Any three for three marks from: using gloves; using surgical masks; using hairnets; using aprons; sterilising equipment; cleaning patient skin to prevent skin pathogens invading body

Page 26 Viral diseases

Quick quiz

From top to bottom: humans; AIDS; antiviral drugs

1. (a)

	Ways measles is spread	Symptom
fever		✓
droplets in coughs sneezes	✓	
red skin rash		✓

[1 mark for each correct row]

(b) At a young age, children are given vaccinations / immunisations which provides immunity to measles. **[1]**

2. **(a)** the immune system **[1]**

   (b) sexual contact **[1]**

   sharing contaminated needles **[1]**

   (c) HIV attacked the immune system **[1]**. The body is no longer protected from pathogens / other diseases kill the person **[1]**.

3. **(a)** Tobacco mosaic virus **[1]**

   (b) Plants cannot photosynthesise **[1]**. Photosynthesis produces glucose **[1]**.

Page 27 Bacterial and fungal diseases

Quick quiz

gonorrhoea; salmonella

1. Gonorrhoea is a sexually transmitted disease. **[1]**

   Condoms are a barrier method of contraception. **[1]**

   If condoms are free more people will use them, preventing the spread of gonorrhoea. **[1]**

2. **(a)** 1997 **[1]**

   (b) The number of cases decreased. **[1]**

   (c) chickens were vaccinated **[1]**

   fewer people were eating undercooked meat **[1]**

3. **(a)** purple / black spots on the rose leaves **[1]**

   (b) fungicide **[1]**; remove infected leaves **[1]**

Page 28 Protist diseases

Quick quiz

A carrier of a disease

1. fever **[1]**
2. liver **[1]**; blood **[1]**
3. **(a)** protist **[1]**

   (b) Stops people being bitten by mosquitoes **[1]**; mosquitoes carry malaria / the protist **[1]**

4. **(a)** 2004 **[1]**

   (b) 15 000 000 – 5 000 000 = 10 000 000 people **[1]**

   (c) Mosquitoes are vectors / carry malaria **[1]**. Killing insects / mosquitoes will stop the spread of malaria **[1]**.

Page 29 Human defence systems

Quick quiz

skin; mucus

1. mucus **[1]**; hairs **[1]**
2. Cilia moves the mucus (with the trapped pathogens) out of the airways or into the stomach (where acid kills the pathogens). **[1]**

   Mucus traps pathogens **[1]**

3. **(a)** stomach **[1]**

   (b) hydrochloric acid **[1]**

   (c) in the food we eat **[1]**

4. phagocytes – white blood cells that engulf pathogens

   antibodies – proteins that target antigens and coat pathogens so they can be destroyed by white blood cells

   antitoxins – proteins that neutralise poisons produced by pathogens

   [1 or 2 correct = 1 mark, 3 correct = 2 marks]

5. A protein on a pathogen that causes an immune response **[1]**

Page 30 Vaccination

Quick quiz

communicable, specific, illness

1.

White blood cells produce antibodies and memory cells.	2
Memory cells rapidly produced antibodies.	4
The live pathogen is destroyed before you get ill.	5
A dead / inactive pathogen is injected into the body.	1
A live pathogen infects the body.	3

[1 mark for 3 correct, 2 marks for all correct]

2. **(a)** 1964 **[1]**

   (b) It decreases quickly / a lot **[1]**.

   (c) People have stopped having their children vaccinated (due to autism scare / false information about vaccinations). **[1]**

   (d) So that measles doesn't spread **[1]**. So that people that don't / can't have the vaccination don't get measles **[1]**.

Page 31 Antibiotics and painkillers

Quick quiz

antibiotic – drug that kills bacteria

antiviral – treats diseases caused by viruses

painkiller – medicine that relieves pain

1. foxglove; heart conditions, mould

   [1 mark for 1 correct, 2 marks for 3 correct]

2.

Feature	Antibiotics	Antiviral drugs	Painkillers
kill bacteria	✓		
treat symptoms of disease			✓
affects pathogens	✓	✓	
is a type of medicine	✓	✓	✓

[1 mark for each correct row]

3. **(a)** use of antibiotics **[1]**; improved cleanliness **[1]**

   (b) Bacterial infections are harder to treat. **[1]**

Page 32 Development of drugs

Quick quiz

Toxicity – how poisonous a drug is

Dose – how much drug to use safely at a time

Efficacy – how well the drug works

1. **(a)** 3–6 months **[1]**

   (b) Scientists find out what drugs are needed **[1]**. They find chemical compounds that have the same effect **[1]**. They test / modify the compounds **[1]**.

2. (a)

clinical trials	3
review and approval	4
research and development	1
pre-clinical studies	2

[1 mark for 1 correct, 2 marks for 2 or 3 correct, 3 marks for 4 correct]

(b) clinical trials - drugs are used on volunteers

pre-clinical studies - drug is tested on animals

research and development - drugs are made or discovered

review and approval - drugs are used on patients

[1 correct = 1 mark, 2 or 3 correct = 2 marks, 4 correct = 3 marks]

(c) in glass / (in a test tube / dish) **[1]**

(d) To check if it is toxic. **[1]**

(e) To monitor for any (long-term) side effects. **[1]**

(f) Advantage: their biology is similar so gives a good idea about how humans will react to the drug **[1]**

Disadvantage: people have ethical and moral objections to using animals for drug testing / people think that animals should have rights **[1]**

Page 33 Photosynthesis

Quick quiz

carbon dioxide; water; oxygen

1. light energy - from the Sun

carbon dioxide - from the air

water - from the soil

chlorophyll - in chloroplasts

[1 mark for 1 correct, 2 marks for 2 or 3 correct, 3 marks for 4 correct]

2.

Name of substance	Chemical formula
carbon dioxide	CO_2
glucose **[1]**	$C_6H_{12}O_6$
water	H_2O **[1]**
oxygen	O_2 **[1]**

3. Endothermic **[1]**
4. light **[1]**; chemical **[1]**
5. Any three for three marks from: Light is needed for photosynthesis / there is no light for photosynthesis. Photosynthesis produces glucose / so cannot make glucose. Glucose is used for other processes. Without those processes / the energy from respiration, the plant cannot live / function / grow.

Page 34 Rate of photosynthesis

Quick quiz

amount of chlorophyll; intensity of light; temperature; carbon dioxide concentration

1. (a) Initially, as light intensity increases the rate of photosynthesis increases. **[1]** As light intensity increases further, the rate of photosynthesis levels off / remains the same / does not increase any more / stabilises. **[1]**

(b) The rate of photosynthesis would decrease. **[1]**

2. (a) green as it contains chlorophyll / chlorophyll is needed for photosynthesis **[1]**

(b) (i) amber **[1]**

(ii) White part does not contain chlorophyll **[1]**; chlorophyll is needed for photosynthesis **[1]**; photosynthesis produces glucose **[1]**; glucose is stored as starch **[1]**

3. As temperature increases the rate of photosynthesis increases **[1]**. As temperature continues to increase the rate of photosynthesis decreases / reaches zero / photosynthesis stops **[1]**.

Page 35 Uses of photosynthesis

Quick quiz

From top to bottom: photosynthesis; respiration

1. (a) oil **[1]**

starch **[1]**

(b) cellulose - strengthens cell walls

glucose - used for respiration

amino acids - used to make proteins for growth and repair

(c) glucose **[1]**; nitrate **[1]**; soil **[1]**, root hair **[1]**

2. (a) 1pm (between 12 midday - 2pm is acceptable) **[1]**

(c) It is dark **[1]**. Light is needed for photosynthesis **[1]**.

(d) carbon dioxide **[1]**

Respiration releases carbon dioxide **[1]**.

Page 36 Investigating photosynthesis

Quick quiz

Any two from: temperature; carbon dioxide concentration; light intensity; chlorophyll; availability of water

1.

Record the number of bubbles released in one minute.	3
Place the lamp at a set distance from the plant.	2
Repeat the practical with the lamp at different distances.	4
Set up the apparatus.	1

[1 mark for 2 correct, 2 marks for all correct]

2. independent variable - distance of lamp from plant

dependent variable - number of bubbles produced

control variable - temperature; volume of water

[1 correct = 1 mark, 3 correct = 2 marks]

3. correctly drawn graph.

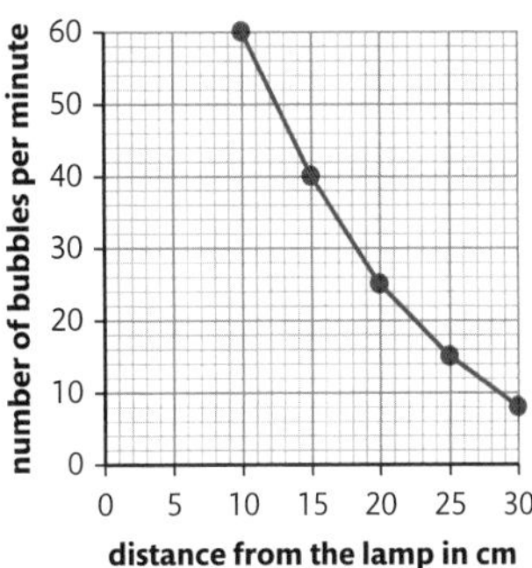

Correctly labelled axes (y is number of bubbles and x is distance from lamp) **[1]**; accurate plot points **[1]**; suitable scale (plot area should cover at least half of graph grid both ways) **[1]**; suitable line of best fit **[1]**

Page 37 Aerobic and anaerobic respiration

Quick quiz

From top to bottom: false, false, true, true

1. **(a)** glucose + oxygen **[1]** → carbon dioxide + water **[1]**
   (b) glucose **[1]** → lactic acid **[1]**
   (c) Any two for two marks from: muscle contractions; movement; keeping warm; nerve impulses; chemical reactions to build larger molecules
   (d) less **[1]**
2. **(a)** fermentation **[1]**
   (b) carbon dioxide **[1]**
   ethanol **[1]**
   (c) bread **[1]**; alcoholic drinks **[1]**

Page 38 Response to exercise

Quick quiz

From top to bottom: true, false, false, false

1. The rate of breathing increases. **[1]** The depth of breathing increases so the volume of each breath increases. **[1]**
2. Measure the volume of the breath before exercise **[1]**. Measure the volume of the breath after exercise **[1]**. Compare the two volumes **[1]**.
3. aerobic respiration **[1]**; anaerobic respiration **[1]**; lactic acid **[1]**, oxygen **[1]**

Page 39 Metabolism

Quick quiz

reactions; cell; molecules

1. From top to bottom: anaerobic respiration **[1]**; aerobic respiration **[1]**; fermentation **[1]**
2. cellulose – strengthen cell walls
   glycogen – storage in muscle cells
   starch – storage in plants
   [1 correct = 1 mark, 3 correct = 2 marks]
3. **(a)** storage **[1]**; insulation **[1]**
   (b) fatty acids – 3 **[1]**; glycerol – 1 **[1]**
4. **(a)** nitrate **[1]**
   (b) Any two for two marks from: keratin; enzymes; collagen
   (c) Proteins are broken down (in the liver) to form urea **[1]** which is then excreted in the urine **[1]** by the kidneys **[1]**.

Page 40 The human nervous system

Quick quiz

brain; spinal cord

1. **(a)** A stimulus is a change in the body or a change in the environment. **[1]**
   (b)

coordinator	3
effector	4
receptor	2
response	5
stimulus	1

[1 mark for 3 correct, 2 marks for all correct]

2. **(a)** motor neurone **[1]**
   (b) motor neurone – carry impulses from the CNS to effectors
   sensory neurone – carry impulses from receptors to the CNS
   synapse relay neurone – carry impulses from a sensory neurone to a motor neurone within the spinal cord
   [1 mark for 1 or 2 correct, 2 marks for 3 correct]
   (c) **(i)** A junction / gap between two neurones. **[1]**
   (ii) Information is passed as chemical neurotransmitters **[1]** by diffusion **[1]**.
3. **(a)** brain **[1]**
   (b) not using the brain speeds up reaction times **[1]** which increases chance of survival **[1]**

Page 41 Reaction times

Quick quiz

length; stimulus

1. **(a)** independent variable – person catching the ruler
   dependent variable – distance ruler dropped
   control variable – the ruler used
   [1 correct = 1 mark, 3 correct = 2 marks]
   (b) Any one for one mark from: the position the ruler is dropped from; the person dropping the ruler
   (c) $\frac{11.1 + 12.1 + 10.1}{3} = 11.1$ **[1]**
2. Answers could include the following points in a logical order for 4 marks.
   - One student drops a ruler.
   - The second student tries to catch the ruler as quickly as they can.
   - The distance the ruler falls is recorded.
   - One student drops a ruler again.
   - At the same time, a loud noise is made.
   - The second student tries to catch the ruler as quickly as they can.
   - The distance the ruler falls is recorded.
   - The distances with no sound and loud sound are compared.

Page 42 Homeostasis

Quick quiz

blood glucose concentration; water levels; body temperature

1. coordination centre – receives and processes information from receptors
   effector – brings about a response
   receptor – detects stimuli (changes in the environment or body)
   [1 or 2 correct = 1 mark, 3 correct = 2 marks]
2. glucose **[1]**; increases **[1]**; decreases **[1]**; hormone **[1]**
3. **(a)** Any two for two marks from: drinking; eating; respiration
   (b) kidney **[1]**
   (c)

Situation	How volume of urine changes
drinking lots of water	increases
a very hot day with no extra drink	decreases
lots of exercise with no extra drink	decreases

[1 mark for each correct row]

(d) Enzymes control many reactions in the body **[1]**. Enzymes get denatured if too hot so body reactions won't take place **[1]**.

Page 43 Human endocrine system

Quick quiz

glands; blood; slower; longer than

1. **(a)** thyroid gland **[1]**
   (b) D **[1]**
   (c) C **[1]**
2. **(a)** adrenal – adrenaline
   pancreas – insulin
   thyroid – thyroxine
   [1 or 2 correct = 1 mark, 3 correct = 2 marks]
   (b) controls growth **[1]**; controls metabolic rate **[1]**
   (c) The pituitary gland secretes lots of hormones **[1]** that stimulate hormonal glands to secrete their own hormones **[1]** when the hormone concentration is low **[1]**.

Page 44 Control of blood glucose

Quick quiz

respiration

1.

Insulin causes the cells to take glucose from the blood.	3
The pancreas releases insulin.	2
It also causes the liver and muscles to store glucose in the form of glycogen.	4
Blood glucose concentration increases.	1
This causes the blood glucose concentration to decrease.	5

[1 mark for 3 correct, all rest correct for 2 marks]

2.

Feature	Type 1 diabetes	Type 2 diabetes
controlled by insulin injections	✓	
controlled by diet		✓
pancreas does not produce enough insulin	✓	
body cells do not respond to insulin		✓

[1 mark for each correct column]

3. **(a)** 7% **[1]**
   (b) Any three for three marks from: Exercise reduces the amount of glucose in the blood; because it is used by muscle cells for respiration. People that exercise are less likely to be obese. Obesity is a risk factor for type 2 diabetes.

Page 45 Hormones in reproduction

Quick quiz

body; reproduction

1.

	Name of hormone	Where it is produced
men	testosterone	testes
women	oestrogen	ovary

[1 mark for each correct row]

2.

Hormone	Function
progesterone	builds up and maintains the uterus lining
follicle-stimulating hormone (FSH)	causes an egg to mature
oestrogen	secreted by the ovaries and causes only one egg to mature
luteinising hormone (LH)	triggers ovulation

[2 correct = 2 marks, 4 correct = 3 marks]

3. **(a)** Days 1 to 5 **[1]**
   (b) 14 **[1]**
   (c) the release of an egg **[1]** from the ovary **[1]**

Page 46 Contraception

Quick quiz

prevent pregnancy

1.

Non-hormonal	Hormonal
rhythm method condom IUD sterilisation	contraceptive pill contraceptive patch

[1 mark for each correct column]

2. condom – provides a physical barrier so sperm don't reach egg
   IUD – prevents fertilised egg from implanting in the uterus
   spermicide – kills sperm
   contraceptive pill – stops FSH being released
   [1 correct = 1 mark, 2 or 3 correct = 2 marks, 4 correct = 3 marks]
3. **(a)** protects against STIs **[1]**
   (b) IUD **[1]**; it is effective for a long time but not permanent **[1]**

Page 47 Asexual and sexual reproduction

Quick quiz

From top to bottom: asexual, sexual, sexual, asexual

1. **(a)** They are sex cells. **[1]**
   They are specialised cells. **[1]**
   (b) male – sperm **[1]**; female – egg / ovum / ova **[1]**
   (c) meiosis **[1]**
   (d) Sexual reproduction produces offspring that are genetically different **[1]**. This means they may be better adapted than the parents to the environment **[1]**.
2. bacteria – asexual reproduction
   cat – sexual reproduction
   budding yeast cells – asexual reproduction
   human – sexual reproduction
   potato producing potato tubers – asexual reproduction
   [1 mark for 2 correct, 2 marks for all correct]
3. **(a)** asexual **[1]**
   (b) clones **[1]**

Page 48 Meiosis

Quick quiz

From top to bottom: true, false, true, true

1. diploid – a cell containing two sets of chromosomes
   gametes – sex cells: sperm and egg cells
   haploid – a cell containing a single set of unpaired chromosomes
   [2 correct = 1 mark, 3 correct = 2 marks]
2.

Pairs of chromosomes divide.	4
Parent chromosomes make copies of themselves.	1
Cells divide into gametes.	5
Similar chromosomes pair up.	2
Chromosomes exchange genetic material.	3

[1 mark for 3 correct, all rest correct for 2 marks]

3. **(a) (i)** 46 **[1]**
   (ii) 23 **[1]**
   (iii) 46 **[1]**
   (b) The cell divides / grows **[1]** by mitosis **[1]**. Some of these cells differentiate **[1]**.

Page 49 DNA and the genome

Quick quiz

The total genetic material of an organism

1. gene; chromosome; nucleus; cell
   [1 mark for cell as largest, 2nd mark for all else correct]
2. DNA consists of two strands **[1]** twisted into a double helix. **[1]**
3. A polymer is a long chain made of repeating units. **[1]**
4. DNA **[1]**, chromosome **[1]**, amino acids **[1]**, protein **[1]**
5. A **[1]**
6. Any two for two marks from: find which genes are linked to diseases; understand inherited genetic disorders; treat inherited genetic disorders

Page 50 Genetic inheritance

Quick quiz

From top to bottom: gene, gene, phenotype

1. dominant – only one allele is needed for a characteristic to be expressed in the phenotype
   recessive – two of these alleles are usually needed for the characteristic to be expressed in the phenotype
   homozygous – both alleles for a gene are identical
   heterozygous – the alleles for a gene are different
   [1 mark for 1 correct, 2 marks for 2 correct, 3 marks for 4 correct]
2. **(a)** hh **[1]**
   (b) (i) heterozygous **[1]**
   (ii) 1 in 2 / 50% / 0.5 **[1]**
   (iii) Punnett square correct **[1]**

		Parent A	
		H	h
Parent B	H	HH	Hh
	h	Hh	hh

probability: 25% or 1 in 4 **[1]**

Page 51 Inherited disorders

Quick quiz

polydactyly – extra fingers and toes – one dominant allele

cystic fibrosis – production of thick sticky mucus – two recessive alleles

1. **(a) (i)** 1 **[1]**
   (ii) 1 **[1]**
   (b) Ff **[1]**; FF **[1]**
   (c) (i)

		Liam	
		F	f
Mia	F	FF	Ff
	f	Ff	ff

[1 mark for 1 row correct, 2 marks for all correct]
   (ii) 25% **[1]**

2. Any three for three marks from: genetic screening is expensive; embryo may be damaged during testing; people with the disorder may experience prejudice; ethical reasons, for example, potential abortion of embryo; religious objections

Page 52 Variation and mutation

Quick quiz

genes; environment

1.

Characteristics caused by genes	**Characteristics caused by environment**
blood group cystic fibrosis eye colour	language spoken tattoos

[1 mark for each correct column]

2. **(a)** A person may have inherited the genes for tallness. **[1]** However, environmental factors such as having a poor diet can lead to poor growth. **[1]**
   (b) Any one for one mark from: skin colour; weight; intelligence
3. A change in the genetic material / DNA **[1]**
4. Mutations occur all the time. **[1]**
   Mutations may cause genetic variation. **[1]**
5. Any one each from advantage and disadvantage for one mark each:
   Advantage: may improve chances of survival; increases genetic diversity
   Disadvantage: may lead to cancer; may lead to genetic disorders; may reduce chances of survival

Page 53 Sex determination

Quick quiz

From top to bottom: true, false, true, true

1. XX **[1]**, XY **[1]**, X **[1]**, X **[1]**, Y **[1]**
2. Meiosis **[1]**
3. male - sperm, female - egg / ovum / ova **[1]**
4. 50% **[1]**
5. **(a)** Genetic cross correct **[1]**

		male gametes X	male gametes Y
female gametes	X	XX	XY
	X	XX	XY

(b) (i) 1 : 1 ratio (2 girls : 2 boys) **[1]**

(ii) 50% **[1]**

Page 54 Evolution

Quick quiz

evolution - a change in the inherited characteristics of a population over time, leading to new species arising from ancestral species

natural selection - organisms that are the best suited to their environment are more likely to survive and reproduce

speciation - new species form; they can no longer interbreed to form fertile offspring

1. fossil record **[1]**; evolution of antibiotic resistance in bacteria **[1]**
2. The lighter coloured moths were more visible to predators and were eaten / died. **[1]**

   The dark coloured moths were not eaten / survived / were camouflaged. **[1]**

   The dark coloured moths bred, passing on their alleles. **[1]**

   This increased the number of dark coloured moths. **[1]**
3. **(a)**

Statement	Order
Passing on the alleles for long spikes.	4
Porcupines with longer spikes had an advantage.	2
There was variation in the length of porcupine spikes.	1
They survived and bred.	3
Eventually all the porcupines in the species had long spikes.	5

[1 mark for 1 and 5 in correct place, 2nd mark for all others correct]

(b) protection from being eaten / deters predators **[1]**

Page 55 Selective breeding

Quick quiz

dog - coloured markings on coat; cow - high milk yield; flower - sweet smell

1. **(a)** The horse breeder would choose the fastest horses and breed them. **[1]**

   The horse breeder would observe the offspring, select the fastest horses and breed them again. **[1]**

   The horse breeder would continue this over many generations. **[1]**

   (b) Any one for one mark from: temperament; coat colour; disease resistance
2.

Feature	Selective breeding	Natural selection
organisms' features can change	✓	✓
environment chooses features		✓
reduces variety of alleles	✓	

[1 mark for each correct column]

3. **(a)** produces more food for human consumption **[1]**

   (b) The wheat plants have little genetic variation **[1]**. The disease could wipe out the whole population **[1]** so less food available for humans **[1]**.

Page 56 Genetic engineering

Quick quiz

gene, genome, different

1.

Statement	Order
The gene is inserted into a bacterial plasmid.	2
The bacterial DNA is put into cells of the desired organism.	3
The required gene is removed from the cell.	1
The organism develops showing the desired characteristic.	4

[1 and 4 in the correct place for 1 mark, all others correct for the 2nd mark]

2. Any one for one mark from: medical drugs, fuel, human insulin, useful chemicals
3.

Feature	Artificial selection	Genetic engineering
humans choose desired features	✓	✓
involves inserting genes from other organisms		✓
interbreeding can occur	✓	

[1 mark for each correct row]

4. Any two each from benefits and risks for two marks each:

   Benefits: increased yield; increased pest resistance; increased nutritional content; drought or flood resistance; production of medicinal drugs, e.g. insulin; treatment for inherited diseases; improved characteristics of animals

   Risks: monoculture more likely to die from new disease; possible health risks; concerns that alleles will spread in the wild; ethical concerns over modification; religious concerns over modification; companies may control stocks of seeds

Page 57 Fossils

Quick quiz

remains, millions, rocks

1. **(a)** rocks **[1]**

   (b) Hard parts of the organism have not decayed, for example, bones / claws / shells **[1]**. Traces of the organism are preserved, for example, footprints / burrows / droppings / rootlet traces **[1]**

   (c) toxic gases **[1]**

   lack of moisture **[1]**
2. Some soft tissue and the hard parts / bones of the elk were preserved **[1]** because the peat bog was very acidic **[1]** and there was a lack of oxygen **[1]** so there was no decay **[1]**.
3. Any two for two marks from: fossilisation is rare; not all fossils have been found; some fossils have been destroyed (by geological changes)

Page 58 Extinction

Quick quiz

From top to bottom: true, false, false, true

1. **(a)** catastrophic event – e.g. an asteroid collision can wipe out a community

   mutations – a new species can evolve and be more successful than its competitor

   speciation – a new species evolves and the old one becomes extinct

   [1 mark for 1 or 2 correct, 2 marks for 3 correct]

   (b) Destruction of an organism's habitat **[1]** can leave it without food **[1]** or shelter. **[1]**

   (c) Any four for four marks from: new diseases, new predators, mutations, temperature change, catastrophic event, speciation

2. Humans hunt rhinos **[1]**. Humans destroy rhinos' habitats **[1]**. Increasing levels of pollution **[1]** affect rhinos' habitats. Rhinos lose food and shelter **[1]**.

Page 59 Resistant bacteria

Quick quiz

From top to bottom: pathogens, antibiotics, natural selection

1.

Bacteria that have the mutation survive longer and reproduce more.	3
Bacteria reproduce very rapidly and soon all the bacteria are resistant to the antibiotic.	4
Some bacteria have mutations which make them more resistant to an antibiotic.	1
Bacteria that do not have that mutation are killed when the antibiotic is used.	2
Resistant strains can then spread.	5

[1 mark for 1 and 5 in the correct place, 2nd mark for all others correct]

2. **(a)** 2005 **[1]**

   (b) 17 **[1]**

   (c) The number of deaths caused by MRSA increases between 1993 and 2005. **[1]**

   After the year 2005 (2006 in males), the number of deaths caused by MRSA decreases (sharply). **[1]**

   (d) Any two for two marks from: not taking antibiotics for viral infections; not taking antibiotics for non-serious diseases; completing a course of antibiotics if given them; reducing antibiotics use in healthy animals in agriculture

Page 60 Classification

Quick quiz

kingdom, phylum, class, order, family, genus, species

1. Any two for two marks from: fungi; protist; prokaryote
2. archaea – primitive bacteria that live in extreme environments

   bacteria – true bacteria

   eukaryota – protists, fungi, plants and animals

   [1 or 2 correct = 1 mark, 3 correct = 2 marks]
3. genus **[1]**

   species **[1]**
4. **(a)** fossil bones / teeth **[1]**

   (b) African elephant, steppe mammoth, Asian elephant **[1]**

   (c) Steppe mammoth **[1]** because it is most closely linked with the Asian elephant **[1]**.

Page 61 Communities

Quick quiz

organism, population, community, ecosystem

1. **(a)** community – all the populations of different species living in the same habitat

   ecosystem – the interaction of a community of all the living organisms with the non-living parts of their environment

   habitat – the environment where an organism lives

   population – all the organisms of one species in an ecosystem

   [1 correct = 1 mark, 2 or 3 correct = 2 marks, 4 correct = 3 marks]

   (b) Any two for two marks from: space; light; water; mineral ions

   (c) Any two for two marks from: mate(s); territory; food; water
2. **(a)** field mouse **[1]**

   (b) grass / food **[1]**

   (c) (i) The number of rabbits increases **[1]** because they are not being eaten **[1]**.

   (ii) The population of roe deer increases **[1]** because they have more food **[1]**.

Page 62 Abiotic factors

Quick quiz

From top to bottom: false, false, true

1. Any two for two marks from: temperature; mineral content of soil; pH of soil; wind intensity; moisture level; carbon dioxide level; light intensity; wind direction
2. **(a)** frogs **[1]**

   (b) clams **[1]**; snails **[1]**

   (c) pH 6.5 to pH 5.5 **[1]**

   (d) As the pH value decreases the number of species decreases **[1]**
3. As oxygen concentration decreases the number of species decreases **[1]**. Oxygen is needed for respiration **[1]** to release energy (for organisms to survive) **[1]**.

Page 63 Biotic factors

Quick quiz

From top to bottom: abiotic, biotic, abiotic, biotic, biotic

1.

	Increase the population?	Decrease the population?
introduction of disease		✓
decrease in food availability		✓
decrease in competition for mates	✓	
new predators		✓

[1 mark for each correct column]

2. **(a)** In 1998, the number of wolves was 0 **[1]**.
   Between 2000 and 2010, the number of wolves increased / increased from 177 to 501 **[1]**.

   (b) Wolf numbers increased **[1]** so the number of elk decreased **[1]** as they were eaten **[1]**.

   (c) Any one for one mark from: reduced availability of food; increased pathogens; increased competition for food; increased competition for mates; increased competition for territory

Page 64 Adaptations

Quick quiz

feature, grow

1. behavioural – ways the animal adjusts its behaviour
   functional – functions that an organism has to survive
   structural – physical features of the organism
   [1 or 2 correct = 1 mark, 3 correct = 2 marks]

2.

Feature	Behavioural	Functional	Structural
long eyelashes to keep sand out			✓
spitting to deter predators	✓		
shuts nostrils to keep sand out		✓	

3. **(i)** helps protect the bear from the cold **[1]**
   (ii) give a large surface area so that bear doesn't sink into the snow / can swim easily **[1]**
   (iii) help the bear to hunt efficiently / kill prey **[1]**
4. salt marshes **[1]** hot springs **[1]**

Page 65 Organisation of an ecosystem

Quick quiz

producer – usually a green plant or alga, which makes glucose during photosynthesis

consumer – organism that cannot make its own food; eats producers or other consumers

prey – animal that is hunted and killed by a predator

predator – kills and eats other animals

1. (a)

Organism	Producer	Predator	Prey	Primary consumer
grass	✓			
grasshopper			✓	✓
frog		✓	✓	
snake		✓		

[1 mark for each correct column]

(b) Producers use the process of photosynthesis **[1]** to produce biomass **[1]** which is eaten by other organisms **[1]**.

2. **(a)** The population of wolves increases when the population of moose increases **[1]**.
   (b) the population of moose will decrease **[1]** because there are more wolves to eat them **[1]**.

Page 66 Investigating population size

Quick quiz

a square frame used to sample the distribution of plants or animals

1.

Repeat these steps several times and record the results.	3
Multiply the average number per quadrat by the total number of quadrats that can fit into the garden.	5
Place a quadrat on the ground at a random point.	1
Calculate the mean number of squares per quadrat.	4
Count the number of snails in the quadrat.	2

[1 mark for 3 and 5 in the correct place, 1 mark for 4 and 2 in the correct place]

2. $21 + 4 + 12 + 7 + 3 = 47$ **[1]**

   $\frac{47}{5} = 9.4$ **[1]**

   $\frac{125\ m^2}{1\ m^2} = 125$ quadrats **[1]**

   $9.4 \times 125 = 1175$ daisies **[1]**

Page 67 Using a transect

Quick quiz

gradual, distribution

1. **(a)** Step 3: Move the quadrat a random distance along the tape and repeat step 2. **[1]**
   (b) Moss was found between 0 and 30 m **[1]**. There was no moss found beyond 30 m from the footpath **[1]**. The most moss was found at 15 m from the footpath **[1]**.
2. **(a)** 8 **[1]** m **[1]**
   (b) There is less light between 0 m and 4 m (because of the tree) **[1]**. Plants need light for photosynthesis **[1]**. Less light means less photosynthesis **[1]**.

Page 68 Cycling materials

Quick quiz

From top to bottom: carbon cycle, carbon cycle, water cycle

1. **(a)** A – evaporation
   B – condensation
   C – precipitation
   [1 mark for 1 or 2 correct, 2 marks for 3 correct]
   (b) Any two for two marks from: snow; rain; ice; hail
   (c) The plant absorbs water from the soil **[1]**. The water evaporates from the leaves of a plant into the air **[1]**. This is called transpiration **[1]**.
2. **(a) (i)** Any one for one mark from: decomposition; respiration
   (ii) photosynthesis **[1]**; respiration **[1]**
   (iii) combustion **[1]** respiration **[1]**
   (b) Trees remove carbon dioxide from the atmosphere **[1]**.
   They use carbon dioxide for photosynthesis **[1]**.
   The fewer trees there are, the less photosynthesis is carried out and the less carbon dioxide is removed from the air. **[1]**

Page 69 Biodiversity

Quick quiz

Biodiversity is the variety of species within an ecosystem

1. **(a)** Any two for two marks from: deforestation; pollution; global warming / climate change; landfill waste
   (b)

Situation	Increase biodiversity	Decrease biodiversity
farmers planting hedgerows between fields	✓	
farmers clearing forest to plant crops		✓
using a field to create a landfill site		✓
increase in plastic pollution in the ocean		✓

[1 mark for each correct column]

2. **(a)** Habitat A: 3 species; habitat B: 2 species **[1]**

   (b) Habitat A because there is a greater number of species **[1]**.

3. As the temperature increases the ice melts. **[1]**

   Fish migrate so there is no food for the penguins and other species. **[1]**

   Areas for the penguins and other species to shelter are reduced. **[1]**

   So the biodiversity decreases. **[1]**

Page 70 Waste management

Quick quiz

Any three from: sewage; smoke; gases; herbicides; pesticides; fertilisers; paper; cardboard; plastic; electricals; metals; organic waste

1. **(a)** Any two for two marks from: sewage; fertiliser; toxic chemicals

   (b) smoke **[1]**; toxic gases / acidic gases **[1]**

   (c) land **[1]**

2. Pollution destroys habitats **[1]** and kills animals and plants **[1]**. This leads to a decrease / reduction in biodiversity **[1]**.

3. **(a)** cardboard **[1]**

   (b) 69% (± 5%) **[1]**

   (c) The population is increasing **[1]**. The standard of living is increasing **[1]**. More resources are used **[1]**. More packaging is used **[1]**.

   (d) Waste materials would go to landfill **[1]** causing land pollution **[1]**. This reduces habitats / and decreases biodiversity **[1]**. If not recycled, many materials may run out or need to be extracted from the ground leading to loss of more habitats **[1]**.

Page 71 Land use

Quick quiz

increasing, more, agriculture, pollution

1. **(a)** Peat bogs are destroyed so that peat can be used for compost **[1]**. This is used for gardening / plant growth **[1]**.

   (b) Peat decays / is burnt **[1]**. It releases carbon dioxide **[1]** which is a greenhouse gas **[1]** and causes global warming **[1]**

2. **(a)** Any two for two marks from: quarrying; farming; landfill

   (b) Answers could include the following points in a logical order for 6 marks:

   - increasing population increases the food that needs to be produced
   - more land required for agriculture
   - increase in habitat destruction / deforestation / peat bog destruction
   - reducing biodiversity
   - increasing pollution from fertilisers / herbicides / pesticides
   - more building is required for housing / businesses, etc. for an increased population
   - more waste is produced
   - more land used for landfill of waste materials
   - more resources are required
   - more land is used for quarrying

Page 72 Deforestation

Quick quiz

removal of trees on a large scale

1. Any three for three marks from: clearing land for housing; providing land for cattle; providing land for rice; providing land for biofuels; cutting trees for paper; cutting trees for furniture; cutting trees for fuel; clearing land for coffee; clearing land for palm oil

2. sugar-rich crops **[1]**

3. Tree roots anchor soil. **[1]**

   Lack of tree roots leads to soil erosion. **[1]**

   Silt enters water sources which causes water pollution. **[1]**

4. **(a)** 1990 **[1]**

   (b) The total forested area is decreasing. **[1]**

   (c) Animals lose their habitat / shelter **[1]**. They lose their food source **[1]**. The animals die / migrate / become extinct **[1]**.

5. Trees remove carbon dioxide by photosynthesis **[1]**. Fewer trees means less carbon dioxide removed **[1]**. Carbon dioxide is a greenhouse gas **[1]** that contributes to global warming **[1]**.

Page 73 Global warming

Quick quiz

carbon dioxide; methane

1. An upward trend in temperature across the Earth. **[1]**

2. Flowering plants can be damaged. **[1]**

3. Increasing ocean temperature causes ice to melt and oceans to expand **[1]**. Sea levels rise and this causes flooding and loss of habitat **[1]**. Increasing ocean temperatures causes dissolved oxygen to decrease **[1]**. This causes organisms to die **[1]**.

4. **(a)** 50 **[1]** miles **[1]**

   (b) Birds get to breeding ground too early **[1]** so there may be a lack of food **[1]**.

Page 74 Maintaining biodiversity

Quick quiz

From top to bottom: false, true, false, true

1. Carbon dioxide is a greenhouse gas **[1]** and causes global warming **[1]**.

2. plant hedgerows **[1]** create field margins **[1]**

3. In breeding programmes, wild animals are bred in zoos / reserves / captivity **[1]**. This increases the population numbers **[1]**. The wild animals are then released back into the wild **[1]**.

4. **(a)** (The number of gorillas) decreases **[1]**

   (b) Any three for three marks from: habitat is conserved laws to ban hunting breeding programmes reintroduction of gorillas

Page 75 Atoms, elements and compounds

Quick quiz

atom – the smallest part of an element that can exist

element – made of only one type of atom

compound – consists of two or more different elements chemically combined

1.

Element name	Element symbol
sodium	Na
bromine	Br
lead	Pb
iron	Fe

[2 marks if all correct, 1 mark if 3 correct.]

2.

Substance	Element	Compound
oxygen	✓	
sodium chloride		✓
gold	✓	
water		✓
aluminium	✓	

[3 marks for all rows correct, 2 marks if four rows correct and 1 mark if three rows correct]

3. magnesium + oxygen → magnesium oxide **[1]**
4. **(a)** 2 **[1]**; **(b)** 5 **[1]**
5. barium chloride **[1]**
6. **(a)** hydrogen + oxygen → water **[1]**

   (b) Any two for two marks from: two hydrogen atoms; one oxygen atom; two different elements; three atoms

Page 76 Mixtures

Quick quiz

ethanol from a mixture of alcohols – fractional distillation

water from coal slurry – filtration

salts from seawater – crystallisation

pure water from seawater – simple distillation

coloured substances from leaves, dissolved in ethanol – paper chromatography

1. A mixture consists of two or more elements or compounds not chemically combined **[1]**.
2. **(a)** Correct order (top to bottom): 3, 4, 1, 5, 2 **[all five correct for 3 marks; 3 or 4 correct for 2 marks; 1 or 2 correct for 1 mark]**

   (b) Any one for one mark from: heat solution gently to prevent spitting; wear eye protection; tie long hair back
3. **(a)** filtration **[1]**

   (b) Sand is insoluble in water **[1]** so its particles are too large to pass through the filter paper **[1]**. The particles in seawater are small enough to pass through the filter paper **[1]**.

   (c) Any two for two marks from: use simple distillation; heat the seawater so that the water evaporates / boils; cool the water vapour so that it condenses to the liquid state.

Page 77 The model of the atom

Quick quiz

Order from top to bottom: 3, 4, 2, 1

1.

Feature	Plum pudding model	Nuclear model
Protons in a nucleus		✓
Contains electrons	✓	✓
Contains positive charges	✓	✓
Electrons at fixed distances		✓

[1 mark for each correct row]

2. **(a)** Bohr / Niels Bohr **[1]**; **(b)** 20 **[1]**
3. Most alpha particles passed straight through. – Most of the atom is empty space. **[1]**

   Some alpha particles were deflected. – The nucleus is positively charged. **[1]**

   A very small number of alpha particles were deflected backwards. – The nucleus has most of the atom's mass. **[1]**

Page 78 Subatomic particles

Quick quiz

(a) x = electrons; y = neutrons; z = protons

(b) nucleus

1.

Name of subatomic particle	Electrical charge
proton	positive / +1
neutron	neutral
electron	negative / –1

[2 marks for all correct rows, 1 mark if only two rows correct]

2. proton **[1]**
3. They have equal numbers of protons and electrons **[1]**.
4. In shells / energy levels **[1]** around the nucleus **[1]**
5. 6 **[1]**
6. 11 **[1]**
7. 0.000 000 000 1 m **[1]**

Page 79 Size and mass of atoms

Quick quiz

Subatomic particle	Relative mass
proton	1
neutron	1
electron	very small or $\frac{1}{1840}$

1. **(a)** 79 **[1]**; **(b)** 197 **[1]**; **(c)** 197 – 79 = 118 **[1]**
2. Mass number is the sum of the protons and neutrons **[1]**.
3. Protons = 12 **[1]**; neutrons = 13 **[1]**; electrons = 12 **[1]**
4. 17 + 1 = 18 **[1]**
5. Protons = 4 **[1]**; neutrons = 9 – 4 = 5 **[1]**
6. Neutrons = 39 – 19 = 20 **[1]**; electrons = 19 – 1 = 18 **[1]**

Page 80 Isotopes and relative atomic mass

Quick quiz

They have the same chemical properties.

They can have different percentage abundances.

1. B and D **[both needed for 1 mark]**
2. relative atomic mass = $\frac{[(63 \times 69.2) + (65 \times 30.8)]}{100}$ **[1]**

   = 63.616 **[1]**

   relative atomic mass of copper = 63.6 to 3 sig fig **[1]**
3. **(a)** protons 2 **[1]**; neutrons 1 **[1]**; electrons 2 **[1]**

   (b) Isotopes with a greater mass are in more abundance / this isotope is in low abundance / other isotopes contribute more to the relative atomic mass **[1]**

Page 81 Electronic structure

Quick quiz

Electron shell	Maximum number of electrons
first	2
second	8
third	8

1. (a)

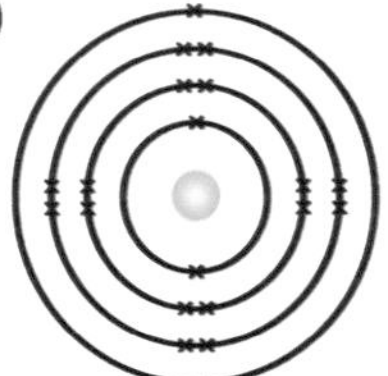

[1 mark for the correct number of electrons in the correct shells]

(b) There are 19 electrons **[1]**, because this is equal to all the numbers in the electronic structure added together **[1]**.

2. They both have full outer electron shells **[1]**.

3. **(a)** 4 **[1]**; **(b)** 2,8,4 **[1]**

4. **(a)** 2,8,2 **[1]**

(b)

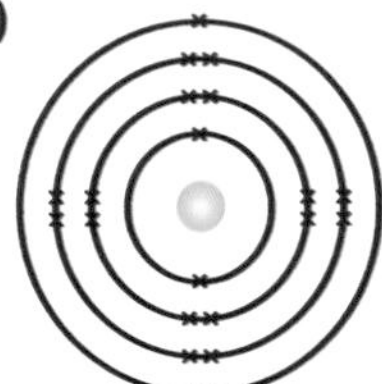

[1 mark for the correct number of shells; 1 mark for correct numbers of electrons in the correct shells]

Page 82 The periodic table

Quick quiz

(a) alkali metals – Group 1; halogens – Group 7; noble gases – Group 0

(b) Elements with similar properties occur at regular intervals in the periodic table.

The position of an element in the periodic table lets you predict its possible reactions.

1. **(a)** groups **[1]**

(b) The elements are arranged in order of increasing **[1]** atomic number **[1]**.

(c) Their atoms all have the same number of electrons in their outer shells **[1]**.

2. It will form an alkaline solution **[1]** because both elements are in Group 1. This means they have similar chemical properties / reactions **[1]**.

3. **(a)** 4 **[1]**; **(b)** 6 **[1]**

4. **(a)** 2,8,7 **[1]**; **(b)** Group 7 **[1]**

Page 83 Developing the periodic table

Quick quiz

From top to bottom: true, false, true, false

1. **(a)** Group 6 **[1]**

(b) Po and some other elements are missing **[1]**, but there are extra elements such as Fe / Ro / Ru / Au / Th **[1]**.

2. **(a)** Increasing atomic weight **[1]**

(b) Mendeleev changed the order of some elements **[1]**, and he left gaps for elements not discovered then **[1]**.

3. **(a)** Some elements were not in the correct group **[1]** (unless their order was reversed).

(b) He grouped elements with similar properties together **[1]** and left gaps where elements did not fit the pattern **[1]**.

Page 84 Metals and non-metals

Quick quiz

Metals – On the left, Towards the bottom;

Non-metals – On the right, Towards the top

1.

Property	Metals	Non-metals
poor conductor of electricity		✓
good conductor of heat	✓	
strong	✓	
brittle when solid		✓
dull		✓
malleable when solid	✓	

[3 marks for all correct rows, 2 marks for 4 or 5 correct rows, 1 mark for 1 or 2 correct rows]

2. Metals lose electrons to form positively charged ions **[1]**. Non-metals gain electrons to form negatively charged ions **[1]**.

3. **(a)** Metal, because it has three electrons in its outer shell **[1]**

(b) Helium is a non-metal **[1]** but it has fewer than 4 electrons in its outer shell **[1]**.

4. Non-metals do not usually conduct electricity **[1]**. Non-metals usually have low boiling points **[1]**.

Page 85 Group 0

Quick quiz

The size of the atoms increases as you go down Group 0.

1. −190 **[1]**; answer in the range −175 to −205 **[1]**.

2. **(a)** They both have eight electrons in their outer shells **[1]**, so they both have full outer shells / stable arrangements **[1]**.

(b) It only has two electrons in its outer shell (rather than eight) **[1]**.

(c) They all have full outer shells / stable arrangements **[1]**.

3. **(a)** Their atoms have full outer shells / stable arrangements **[1]**.

(b) Molecules form when atoms share electrons **[1]**. (Full outer shell) means noble gases cannot easily share electrons **[1]**.

Page 86 Group 1

Quick quiz

(a) metals

(b) Any two for two marks from: sodium, potassium, rubidium, caesium, francium

(c) alkali metals

1. **(a)** They all fizz in the water. **[1]**

The water turns universal indicator purple after all the reactions. **[1]**

(b) potassium + water ⟶ potassium hydroxide + hydrogen **[1]**

2. **(a)** lithium + oxygen ⟶ lithium oxide **[1]**

(b) red **[1]**

3. **(a)** Their outer shells both have one electron **[1]**.
   (b) +1 **[1]**
   (c) It increases **[1]** going down the group **[1]**.

Page 87 Group 7

Quick quiz

(a) Non-metals
(b) Any two from: chlorine, bromine, iodine, astatine, tennessine
(c) Halogens

1. They have low melting and boiling points **[1]**.
   They exist as molecules with pairs of atoms **[1]**.
2. **(a)** Their outer shells both have seven electrons **[1]**.
   (b) –1 **[1]**
   (c) It decreases **[1]**.
3. Correct order: Z, X, Y **[2 marks for all correct, 1 mark for 1 or 2 correct]**

Page 88 Chemical bonds

Quick quiz

Ionic bonding occurs between a metal and a non-metal element.
Covalent bonds form in non-metals only.

1. **(a)** A bond formed when two atoms share a pair of electrons. **[1]**
   (b) Both hydrogen and oxygen are non-metals **[1]** and so can only share electrons between them. **[1]**
2. ionic: sodium chloride, iron sulfide, magnesium oxide
   covalent: water, carbon dioxide, methane **[1 mark for each correct column]**
3. Missing words, in order: an electrostatic; attraction; electrons **[1 mark for each correct word]**
4. The electrostatic force of attraction **[1]** between oppositely charged ions. **[1]**
5. Metal atoms **[1]** sharing delocalised electrons **[1]**.

Page 89 Ionic bonding

Quick quiz

magnesium Mg^{2+}; oxygen O^{2-}; sodium Na^{+}; aluminium Al^{3+}; fluorine F^{-}; calcium Ca^{2+}

1. **(a)** Non-metals gain electrons to form negative ions. **[1]**
   (b)

Group number	1	2	6	7
Charge on ions formed	1+ **[1]**	2+ **[1]**	1– **[1]**	2– **[1]**

2.

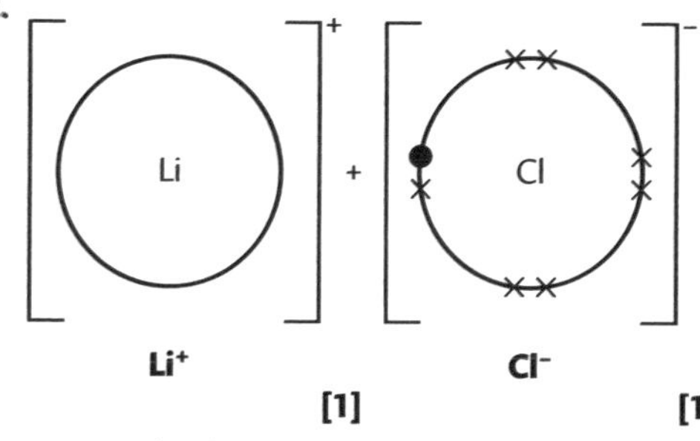

You can also draw two dots or two crosses on the lithium ion provided you only draw one circle.
[1 mark for each circle]

3. Each magnesium atom transfers / loses **[1]** its two outer electrons **[1]**.
   Each oxygen atom gains / receives **[1]** two electrons (in the outer level).

Page 90 Ionic compounds

Quick quiz

two-dimensional; three-dimensional; ball and stick; dot and cross

1. **(a)** giant **[1]**
   (b) ions **[1]**
   (c) It is strong electrostatic forces of attraction **[1]** between oppositely charged ions **[1]**.
   (d) Ratio of ions is 6 : 6 which simplifies to 1 : 1 **[1]** so the empirical formula is CaS **[1]**.
2. One advantage for one mark from: the different ion sizes can be seen; gives an idea of the position of the ions
   One disadvantage for one mark from: does not show the bonds between the ions; the internal structure cannot be seen
3. **(a)** Any one for one mark from: models are not to scale; size of ions is incorrect
   (b) Any one for one mark from: only a two-dimensional representation; cannot see the actual arrangement of ions

Page 91 Covalent bonding

Quick quiz

(a) electrons
(b) small molecules; polymers; giant covalent structures

1. **(a)** A bond formed by a shared pair of electrons **[1]**
   (b) outer shell **[1]**
   (c) The number of bonds equals eight minus the group number **[1]**.
2.

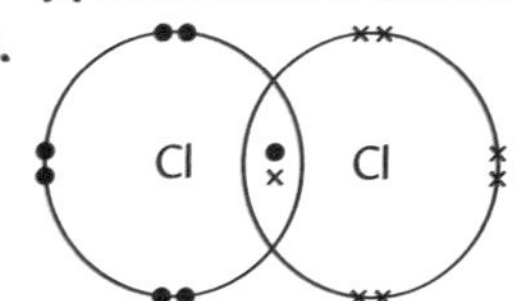

Correct number of bonding electrons (one dot and one cross) **[1]**; correct number of non-bonding electrons (seven dots and seven crosses) **[1]**

3.

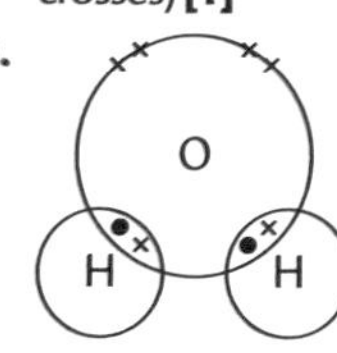

Correct number of bonding electrons (one dot and one cross) in each O-H bond **[1]**; correct number of non-bonding electrons (four dots or crosses) **[1]**

Page 92 Metallic bonding

Quick quiz

(a) Large circle labelled 'metal ion'; small circle labelled 'electron'
(b) Negative / – / –1

1. delocalised / random **[1]**
2. **(a)** electrostatic **[1]**
   (b) positive **[1]**
3. They are free to move between atoms. **[1]**
   They are free to move in the outer shells of atoms. **[1]**

4. They have strong (metallic) bonds **[1]**.
5. electrons **[1]**
6. a giant structure of atoms **[1]** arranged in a regular pattern **[1]**

Page 93 States of matter

Quick quiz

(a) solid, liquid, gas

(b) freezing, melting

1. **(a) [1 mark for each correct row]**

	Closeness		Arrangement	
	Close together	**Far apart**	**Regular**	**Random**
solid	✓		✓	
liquid	✓			✓
gas		✓		✓

(b) Missing words in order: solid **[1]**; quickly **[1]**; all **[1]**

2. As the strength of the forces increases **[1]**, the boiling point increases **[1]**.
3. liquid **[1]**
4. **(a)** (s) solid **[1]**, (l) liquid **[1]**, **(g)** gas **[1]**
   (b) (aq) **[1]**

Page 94 Properties of ionic compounds

Quick quiz

sodium chloride, magnesium oxide, copper sulfate

1. **(a)** in a giant structure with a regular pattern **[1]**
   (b) Missing words in order: electrostatic **[1]**; oppositely **[1]**; ions **[1]**
2. Their ions are free to move **[1]**.
3. Connect the lamp to the battery **[1]**; place the wires in a beaker of sodium chloride **[1]**; dissolve the sodium chloride in water **[1]**; the lamp should light in the solution (but not in the solid) **[1]**
   [you can draw a suitable diagram for the first two marks]

Page 95 Properties of small molecules

Quick quiz

water, chlorine, methane

1. **(a)** low, weak **[1]**
   (b) intermolecular **[1]**
2. **(a)** fluorine **[1]**
   (b) iodine **[1]**
   (c) As the relative formula mass increases **[1]** the boiling point increases. **[1]**
3. Simple molecules do not have an overall electric charge / mobile charged particles / electrons **[1]** so they cannot carry electric charge from place to place **[1]**.

Page 96 Polymers

Quick quiz

ethene – poly(ethene)

tetrafluoroethene – poly(tetrafluoroethene)

chloroethene – poly(chloroethene)

1. **(a)** Polymer molecules are very large **[1]**.
   (b) covalent bonds **[1]**.
   (c) They are strong **[1]**.
2. **(a)** Both have three hydrogen atoms **[1]** and one chlorine atom **[1]**.
   (b) The repeat unit has a C–C bond but the substance has a C=C bond **[1]**.
3. **(a)** repeat unit with brackets **[1]**; part of a molecule with bonds at each end **[1]**
   (b) The bonds between the molecules are strong **[1]** so need a lot of energy to break **[1]**.

Page 97 Giant covalent structures

Quick quiz

From left to right: small molecule; small molecule; small molecule; giant covalent

1. **(a)** covalent bond **[1]**
   (b) in a giant structure with a regular pattern **[1]**
   (c) To conduct electricity, a substance needs charged particles that can move about **[1]** but silica does not have particles like these **[1]**.
2. **(a)** Covalent bonds **[1]** joining atoms together in a giant structure **[1]** with a regular pattern **[1]**
   (b) Any two for two marks from: high melting / boiling point; does not conduct electricity; hard

Page 98 Properties of metals and alloys

Quick quiz

A mixture at least one metal and another element

1. high, strong **[1]**
2. The layers of atoms **[1]** can slide over each other **[1]**.
3. **(a)** They are different **[1]**.
   (b) They are in layers in the pure metal but not in the alloy **[1]**.
4. The alloy has different-sized particles **[1]** so the atoms / layers cannot slide over one another easily **[1]**.
5. Pure metal was too soft to be used for coins **[1]**.

Page 99 Metals as conductors

Quick quiz

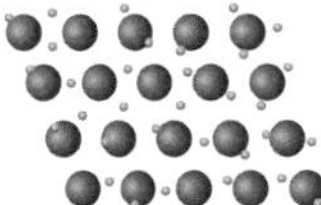

1. **(a)** negative / – / –1 **[1]**
   (b) Electrons are free to move between atoms. **[1]**
   (c) They are in a giant structure **[1]** with a regular arrangement **[1]**.
2. **(a)** They vibrate faster **[1]**.
   (b) They move more quickly **[1]**.
   (c) It will be transferred to the atoms **[1]**.
3. Metals have delocalised / free electrons **[1]** which can move through the metal carrying charge **[1]**.

Page 100 Diamond

Quick quiz

Any two from: jewellery, drilling tools, cutting tools, polishing tools

1. **(a)** 4 **[1]**
   (b) covalent **[1]**
   (c) Missing words in order: giant **[1]**; regular **[1]**
2. high; strong **[1]**
3. It has a giant structure **[1]** where its atoms are joined together by strong (covalent) bonds **[1]**.

4. No, because it has no free electrons / ions **[1]** and these are needed for substances to conduct electricity **[1]**.

Page 101 Graphite

Quick quiz

Any two from: pencils, lubricants, electrodes

1. **(a)** 3 **[1]**
   (b) covalent **[1]**
   (c) hexagonal **[1]**
2. **(a)** Missing words in order: free **[1]**; between **[1]**
   (b) one / 1 **[1]**
   (c) metals **[1]**
3. It has weak forces between its layers **[1]** so these can easily slide past each other **[1]**.
4. Yes, because it has delocalised / free electrons **[1]** and these are needed for substances to conduct electricity **[1]**.

Page 102 Graphene and fullerenes

Quick quiz

From top to bottom: true; false; true; false

1. **(a)** three / 3 **[1]**
   (b) Both have high melting and boiling points so are solid at room temperature **[1]**. Both conduct electricity **[1]**.
2. Graphene has a giant structure **[1]** with covalent bonds **[1]**. These bonds are very strong / need a lot of energy to break **[1]**.
3. high tensile strength, very high length to diameter ratios **[1]**
4. Any two for two marks from: nanotechnology; electronics; in drug delivery systems; reinforcing structures
5. Yes, because they have delocalised / free electrons **[1]** and these are needed for substances to conduct electricity **[1]**.

Page 103 Conservation of mass

Quick quiz

sodium hydroxide + hydrochloric acid → <u>sodium chloride</u> + <u>water</u>

1. The atoms are rearranged / no atoms are lost or made. **[1]**
2. **(a)** The mass of products is equal to the mass of reactants. **[1]**
   (b) 3 g **[1]**
3. 24 + 16 = 40 g **[1]**
4. 50 – 28 = 22 g **[1]**
5. **(a)** 1.70 + 1.03 = 2.73 g **[1]**
   (b) 2.73 – 0.85 = 1.88 g **[1]**

Page 104 Relative formula mass

Quick quiz

From top to bottom: true, false, false

1. **(a)** 2 × 1 = 2 **[1]**
   (b) 28 **[1]**
   (c) 32 **[1]**
   (d) 71 **[1]**
2. **(a)** 36.5 **[1]**
   (b) (2 × 1) + 16 = 18 **[1]**
   (c) 17 **[1]**
   (d) 134.5 **[1]**
   (e) 40 **[1]**
   (f) 159.5 **[1]**
3. **(a)** 40 + 32 + 2 = 74 **[1]**
   (b) 97.5 **[1]**
   (c) 164 **[1]**

Page 105 Balancing equations

Quick quiz

$2Ca + O_2 \rightarrow 2CaO$; $CH_4 + 2O_2 \rightarrow CO_2 + 2H_2O$

1. **(a)**

	Magnesium	Oxygen	Magnesium oxide
magnesium atoms	1	0	1
oxygen atoms	0	2	1

   [1 mark for each correct row]
   (b) There is one Mg atom on the left but two on the right **[1]**.
   (c) $2Mg + O_2 \rightarrow 2MgO$ **[1]**
2. **(a)** $BaO + 2HCl \rightarrow BaCl_2 + H_2O$ **[1]**
   (b) $2Na + Br_2 \rightarrow 2NaBr$ **[1]**
   (c) $N_2 + 3H_2 \rightarrow 2NH_3$ **[1]**
   (d) $4Al + 3O_2 \rightarrow 2Al_2O_3$ **[1]**
   (e) $2NaOH + H_2SO_4 \rightarrow Na_2SO_4 + 2H_2O$ **[1]**
   (f) $Li_2CO_3 + 2HNO_3 \rightarrow 2LiNO_3 + H_2O + CO_2$ **[1]**
3. **(a)** $4Na + TiCl_4 \rightarrow 4NaCl + Ti$ **[1]**
   (b) $2SO_2 + O_2 \rightarrow 2SO_3$ **[1]**
   (c) $Fe_2O_3 + 3CO \rightarrow 2Fe + 3CO_2$ **[1]**

Page 106 Mass changes

Quick quiz

No atoms are lost or made during a chemical reaction so the mass of the products equals the mass of the reactants.

1.

Description of system	Closed	Non-enclosed
Two solutions reacting in a beaker to form an insoluble solid	✓	
An evaporating basin containing a boiling liquid		✓
A reaction mixture in a stoppered flask	✓	
A solid being heated in an open boiling tube		✓

   [1 mark for each correct row]
2. **(a)** 6.22 g – 5.79 g = 0.43 g **[1]**
   (b) Some of the oxygen is not collected / it escapes **[1]**.
3. **(a)** It increases **[1]**.
   (b) Oxygen from the air combines with iron in the nails **[1]**.
4. **(a)** copper + iodine → copper iodide **[1]**.
   (b) It increases **[1]** because iodine combines with copper **[1]**.

Page 107 Chemical measurements

Quick quiz

$1.0 + 1.2 + 1.3 + 1.1 + 1.4 = \frac{6}{5} = 1.2\,g$

1. mean – the total of the values divided by the number of values
   accuracy – a measure of how close a value is to its true value
   range – the difference between the highest and lowest values
   anomalous results – results that do not fit the pattern
   [2 marks if 4 correct, 2 marks if 2 correct]

2. **(a)** Mean = 88 cm^3 **[1]**
   (b) Range = 9 cm^3 **[1]**
   (c) Uncertainty of the mean = 88 cm^3 ± 4.5 cm^3 **[1]**

3.

Feature of the type of error	Systematic	Random
error is reproducible	✓	
can be reduced by taking the mean of several results		✓
gives values above and below the true value		✓
the inaccurate reading is the same each time	✓	

[1 mark per correct row]

Page 108 Concentrations of solutions

Quick quiz

(a) solute – substance that is dissolved in a liquid
solvent – liquid that a substance can dissolve in
solution – mixture of a liquid and a dissolved substance
(b) concentration in g/dm^3 = mass in g/volume in dm^3

1. 0.25 dm^3 **[1]**
2. **(a)** 0.1 dm^3 **[1]**
   (b) $\frac{3.7}{0.1}$ = 37 g/dm^3 **[1]**
3. 40 × 0.5 **[1]** = 20 g **[1]**
4. 50 cm^3 = 0.05 dm^3 **[1]**
   concentration = $\frac{2}{0.05}$ **[1]** = 40 g/dm^3 **[1]**
5. 125 cm^3 = 0.125 dm^3 **[1]**
   4 × 0.125 **[1]** = 0.5 g **[1]**

Page 109 Metal oxides

Quick quiz

(a) to the left / towards the bottom left
(b) non-metal

1. **(a)** calcium oxide **[1]**
   (b) iron oxide **[1]**
   (c) magnesium oxide **[1]**
2. **(a)** lead oxide **[1]**
   (b) sodium oxide **[1]**
   (c) zinc oxide **[1]**
   (d) aluminium oxide **[1]**
3. **(a)** aluminium + oxygen → aluminium oxide **[1]**
   (b) In the reaction, aluminium gains oxygen **[1]**.
4. Copper oxide is reduced because it loses oxygen **[1]**. Hydrogen is oxidised because it gains oxygen **[1]**.
5. Iron oxide is reduced because it loses oxygen **[1]**. Carbon is oxidised because it gains oxygen **[1]**.

Page 110 The reactivity series

Quick quiz

potassium, sodium, lithium
calcium, magnesium, zinc
zinc, iron, copper

1. **(a)** Metal Z **[1]** because it reacted the most vigorously **[1]**
   (b) Z, X, Y **[1]**
   (c) Metal Z **[1]**
2. **(a)** (Most reactive to least reactive) Y, Z, X **[1]**.
   (b) Because metal Y reacted with two metals (X and Z) **[1]**; metal Z reacted with X but not with Y **[1]**; metal X did not react with Y or Z **[1]**

Page 111 Extraction of metals and reduction

Quick quiz

1, 3, 2, 4 (aluminium, iron, copper, gold)

1. **(a)** A naturally occurring rock **[1]** that contains a sufficient amount of metal or metal compounds **[1]**
   (b) gold **[1]**
2. Any one for one mark from: zinc; copper
3. **(a)** iron oxide + carbon → iron + carbon dioxide **[1]**
   (b) Iron is less reactive than carbon **[1]**.
   (c) Oxidised: carbon because it gains oxygen **[1]**. Reduced: iron oxide because it loses oxygen **[1]**.

Page 112 Reactions of acids with metals

Quick quiz

(a) From top to bottom: 3, 1, 2
(b) hydrogen

1.

Metal	Hydrochloric acid	Sulfuric acid
magnesium	magnesium chloride **[1]**	magnesium sulfate **[1]**
zinc	zinc chloride **[1]**	zinc sulfate **[1]**
iron	iron chloride **[1]**	iron sulfate **[1]**

2. iron + hydrochloric acid → iron chloride + hydrogen
   [1 mark for correct reactants; 1 mark for correct products]
3. zinc + sulfuric acid → zinc sulfate + hydrogen
   [1 mark for correct reactants; 1 mark for correct products]
4. $Ca + H_2SO_4 \rightarrow CaSO_4 + H_2$
   [1 mark for correct formulae; 1 mark for correctly balanced]
5. sulfuric acid **[1]**
6. zinc chloride **[1]**
7. iron + sulfuric acid → iron sulfate + hydrogen
   [1 mark for correct reactants; 1 mark for correct products]
8. Hydrogen is produced **[1]**; this is a gas **[1]**

Page 113 Salt production

Quick quiz

hydrochloric acid – chloride; nitric acid – nitrate; sulfuric acid – sulfate

1.

Reaction	Product		
	Salt	Water	Carbon dioxide
acid + metal hydroxide	✓	✓	
acid + metal oxide	✓	✓	
acid + metal carbonate	✓	✓	✓

[1 mark for each correct row]

2. **(a)** sodium chloride **[1]**
   (b) copper sulfate **[1]**
   (c) zinc nitrate **[1]**

3. (a) $NaCl$ **[1]**
   (b) $Mg(NO_3)_2$ **[1]**
   (c) $CuSO_4$ **[1]**
   (d) $CuCl_2$ **[1]**
4. (a) zinc oxide + hydrochloric acid → zinc chloride + water

[1 mark for correct salt; 1 mark for remaining substances]

   (b) calcium carbonate + nitric acid
   → calcium nitrate + water + carbon dioxide

[1 mark for correct salt; 1 mark for remaining substances]

Page 114 Soluble salts

Quick quiz

From top to bottom: true; false; true

1. Missing words in order: filtering **[1]**; crystallising **[1]**
2. (a) It is too reactive / it would be unsafe to use **[1]**.
   (b) Silver does not react with dilute acids **[1]**.
3. (a) The magnesium ribbon would become smaller or disappear **[1]**, and the student would see bubbling / fizzing **[1]**.
   (b) Filter the mixture **[1]**.
4. (a) zinc **[1]**; zinc oxide **[1]**; zinc carbonate **[1]**
   (b) Any one for one mark from:
   zinc + hydrochloric acid → zinc chloride + hydrogen
   zinc oxide + hydrochloric acid → zinc chloride + water
   zinc carbonate + hydrochloric acid → zinc chloride + water + carbon dioxide

Page 115 Making salts

Quick quiz

From left to right: evaporating basin, filter funnel, beaker, tripod, Bunsen burner

1. Correct order (top to bottom): 3, 4, 6, 1, 2, 7, 5 **[5 or more correct for 5 marks; 4 correct for 4 marks; 3 correct for 3 marks; 2 correct for 2 marks; 1 correct for 1 mark]**
2. Warm some nitric acid gently in a beaker with a Bunsen burner **[1]**; add zinc oxide until no more reacts, stirring gently **[1]**; filter to remove unreacted zinc oxide **[1]**; heat the zinc nitrate solution gently and leave to crystallise in an evaporating basin **[1]**; pat the crystals dry with filter paper **[1]**.

Page 116 The pH scale and neutralisation

Quick quiz

left-hand end, 1–6, labelled 'acidic', 7 labelled 'neutral', right-hand end, 8–14, labelled 'alkaline'

1. It is a measure of the acidity or alkalinity of a solution **[1]**.
2. (a) battery acid **[1]**; vinegar **[1]**; tomato juice **[1]**
   (b) shampoo **[1]**; baking soda **[1]**
3. (a)

	Acidic solutions	Alkaline solutions
Name of ion	hydrogen **[1]**	hydroxide **[1]**
Formula of ion	H^+ **[1]**	OH^- **[1]**

   (b) $H^+ + OH^- \rightarrow H_2O$ **[1]**
4. Add a small spot of the solution to the paper / dip the paper in the solution **[1]**; (leave for 30 seconds) and record the colour **[1]**; match the colour to the nearest colour on a pH colour chart **[1]**.

Page 117 Electrolysis

Quick quiz

(a) electrode – a solid electrical conductor
electrolysis – using electricity to decompose a compound
electrolyte – a liquid or solution that can conduct electricity
(b) ions

1. (a) cathode **[1]**
   (b) anode **[1]**
2. They become free to move about / around **[1]**.
3. (a) carbon / graphite **[1]**
   (b) Dissolve it in water **[1]**; Melt it **[1]**
4. Missing words, in order: positive; positive; ions; elements **[1 mark for each correct word]**
5. (a) Place two copper electrodes **[1]** in a solution of copper sulfate **[1]**; connect to a dc power supply or battery **[1]**; if copper ions are positively charged, the negative electrode will gain copper / get heavier **[1]**.

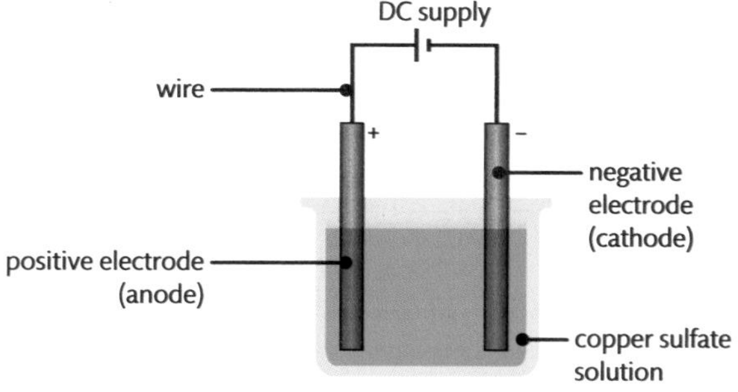

Page 118 Electrolysis to extract metals

Quick quiz

3, 4, 1, 2 (potassium, zinc, iron, copper)

1. Any one for one mark from: sodium; magnesium
2. When the compound is dissolved in water **[1]** and when it is molten **[1]**.
3. (a) Aluminium oxide is insoluble / it does not dissolve in water **[1]**.
   (b) Cryolite melts at a lower temperature than aluminium oxide **[1]**, so this reduces the energy needed to produce an electrolyte **[1]**.
4. (a) A large amount of electricity is needed **[1]**.
   (b) oxygen **[1]**
   (c) Hot carbon reacts with oxygen to produce carbon dioxide **[1]** which uses up the anodes **[1]**.

Page 119 Electrolysis of aqueous solutions

Quick quiz

(a) anode; (b) cathode; (c) a liquid or solution that is able to conduct electricity

1. (a) hydrogen **[1]**
   (b) copper **[1]**
   (c) hydrogen **[1]**
   (d) silver **[1]**
2. (a) chlorine **[1]**
   (b) oxygen **[1]**
   (c) bromine **[1]**
   (d) oxygen **[1]**

3. **(a)** hydroxide ions, OH^-, **[1]** and hydrogen ions, H^+ **[1]**
   (b) hydroxide ions / OH^- ions **[1]**
4. **(a)** cathode: hydrogen; anode: oxygen **[1]**
   (b) cathode: hydrogen; anode: iodine **[1]**

Page 120 Electrolysis of copper(II) chloride

Quick quiz

Hydrogen is produced at the cathode if the metal is more reactive than hydrogen.

Oxygen is produced at the anode unless the solution contains halide ions.

1.

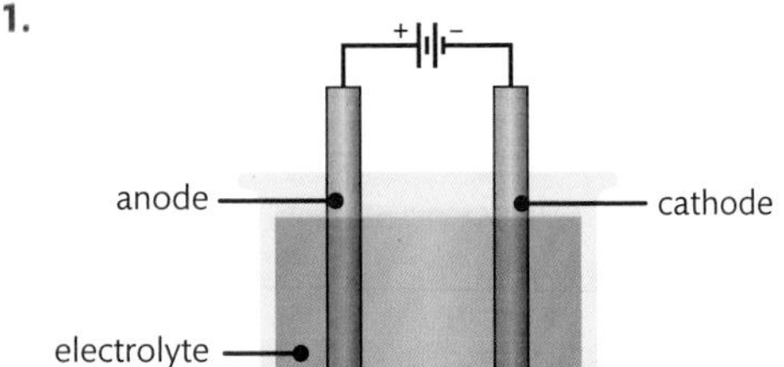

[1 mark for correctly labelled anode and cathode, 1 mark for correctly labelled copper (II) chloride solution and electrolyte.]

2. **(a)** copper **[1]**
   (b) chlorine **[1]**
   (c) Inert electrodes will not react with the substances in the electrolysis cell **[1]** so copper metal is obtained **[1]**.
3.

Aqueous solution	Product at cathode	Product at anode
sodium chloride	hydrogen	chlorine
copper sulfate	copper	oxygen
sodium sulfate	hydrogen	oxygen

[1 mark for each correct row]

Page 121 Exothermic and endothermic reactions

Quick quiz

In endothermic reactions – energy is transferred from the surroundings, – which get colder.

In exothermic reactions – energy is transferred to the surroundings, – which get warmer.

1.

Type of reaction	Exothermic	Endothermic
combustion	✓	
electrolysis		✓
neutralisation	✓	
oxidation	✓	
thermal decomposition		✓

[3 marks if all correct, 2 marks if 3 or 4 correct and 1 mark if 1 or 2 correct]

2. Endothermic because the temperature goes down **[1]**
3. **(a)** A = 17 °C **[1]**; D = 12 °C **[1]**
   (b) C, A, D, B **[1]**
   (c) The more exothermic the reaction, the greater the increase in temperature / the greater the increase in temperature, the higher the reactivity **[1]**.

Page 122 Temperature changes

Quick quiz

exothermic – oxidation, combustion, metal displacement

endothermic – electrolysis, photosynthesis, thermal decomposition

1. **(a)** There is an air gap between the polystyrene cup and the beaker. **[1]**
   The reaction mixture is in an insulating polystyrene cup. **[1]**
   There is a lid on the polystyrene cup. **[1]**
   (b) (i) Any two for two marks from: same volume of solution / acid / alkali; same type of acid / alkali; same concentration of acid
   (ii) The reaction is exothermic **[1]**; the greater the concentration **[1]**, the greater the temperature increase **[1]**.
2. Measure some acid into a polystyrene cup using a measuring cylinder **[1]**; put the cup in a beaker to stop it falling over / to insulate it more **[1]**; record the starting temperature using a thermometer **[1]**; add some zinc and record the maximum / end temperature **[1]**; the temperature should increase **[1]**.

Page 123 Reaction profiles

Quick quiz

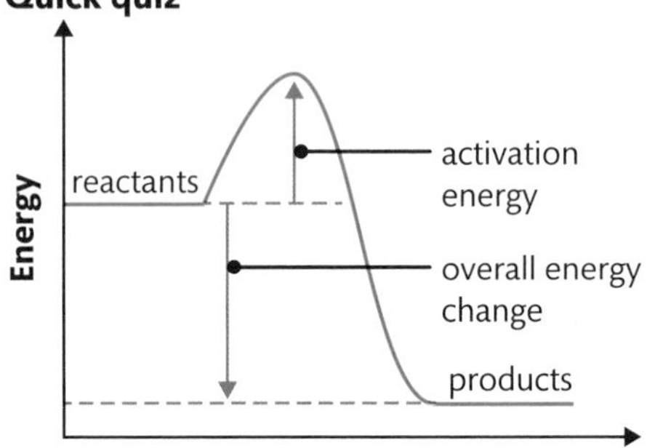

1. **(a)** The products have less energy than the reactants. **[1]**
   (b) X is the overall energy change of the reaction / the difference between the energy of the reactants and the energy of the products. **[1]**
   (c) The energy needed for a reaction to happen. **[1]**
2.

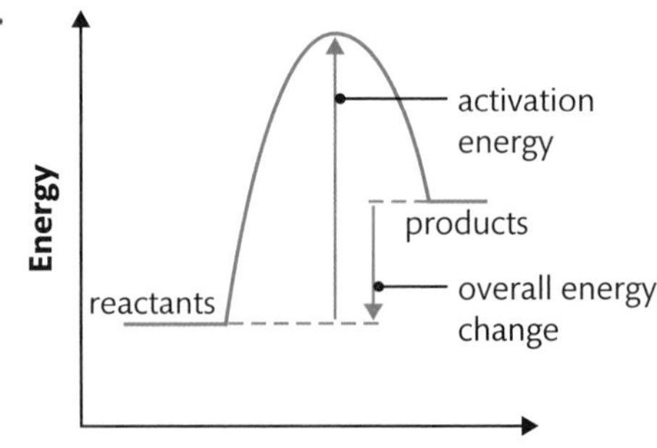

Both axes drawn and correctly labelled **[1]**; on a correct profile line, labelled relative energies of the reactants and products, and the overall energy change **[1]**; activation energy correctly identified **[1]**.

Page 124 Calculating rate of reaction

Quick quiz

g/s; cm^3/s

1. $\frac{0.12}{50}$ = 0.024 (2.4×10^{-3}) **[1]** g/s **[1]**

2. **(a)** The line becomes horizontal / the volume of gas stays the same **[1]**.

   (b) Tangent drawn at 10 s **[1]** (red line on graph)

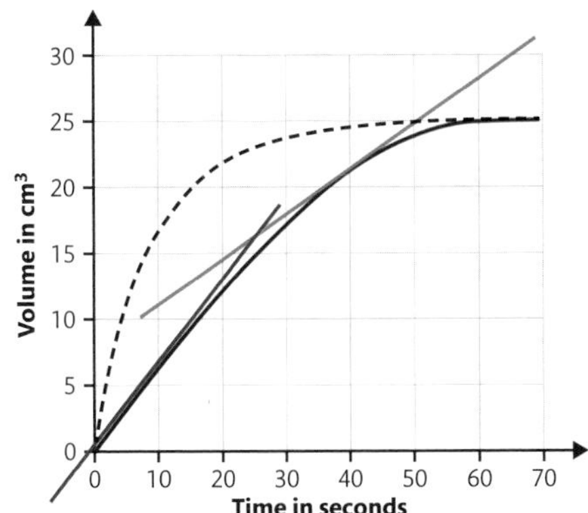

   (c) The slope decreases, for example, from 10 s to the end of the reaction. **[1]** This means that the rate decreases as the reaction goes on **[1]**.

3. **(a)** 25 / 60 = 0.42 **[1]** cm^3/s **[1]**

   (b) Tangent drawn at 40 s **[1]** (green line on graph above)

   (c) Curve shown should be steeper initially **[1]** then level off at the same volume of gas **[1]** to show the rate of reaction has speeded up (dashed black line on graph).

Page 125 Factors affecting rate of reaction

Quick quiz

Measure the volume of a gas; measure the change in mass; look for a colour change

1.

Change in factor	Increases rate	Decreases rate
increase in temperature	✓ **[1]**	
increase in concentration of a reactant in solution	✓ **[1]**	
decrease in the pressure of reacting gases		✓ **[1]**

2. Particles collide more often **[1]** and with more energy **[1]**.
3. It reduces the activation energy **[1]**.
4. **(a)** The larger the chips, the smaller the mass lost **[1]** so the lower the rate of reaction **[1]**.

   (b) size / surface area of the chips **[1]**

   (c) change the temperature **[1]**; change the concentration of the acid **[1]**

Page 126 Rate of reaction

Quick quiz

Any four from: concentration; pressure; surface area; temperature; catalysts

1. **(a)** Replace the gas jar with a measuring cylinder / burette / gas syringe **[1]**.

   (b) the mass of magnesium **[1]**; the volume of acid **[1]**; the temperature **[1]**.

   (c) The rate of reaction will increase / hydrogen will be produced more quickly **[1]**.

2. **(a)** As the concentration increases **[1]** the time taken decreases **[1]**.

   (b) The rate of reaction increases **[1]**.

Page 127 Catalysts

Quick quiz

(a) Enzymes; **(b)** different catalysts

1. **(a)** A substance that changes the rate of a chemical reaction **[1]** but is not used up during the reaction **[1]**

   (b) Manganese dioxide does not appear in the word equation **[1]**.

   (c) The reaction starts after the manganese dioxide is added **[1]**.

2. **(a)**

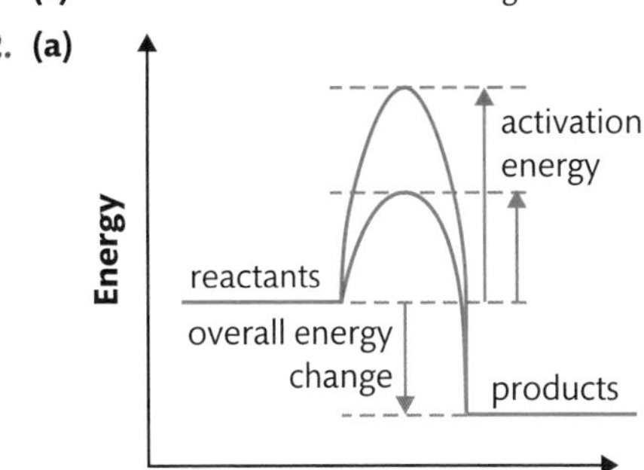

   On a correct profile line, labelled relative energies of the reactants and products, and the overall energy change **[1]**; activation energy correctly identified (red line) **[1]**

   (b) The activation energy would be lower with a catalyst **[1]**.

   (c) Top of activation energy curve is lower, with no change to positions of line for reactants and products (green line) **[1]**

   (d) The catalyst provides a pathway with a lower activation energy **[1]**; more particles have the activation energy / enough energy to react **[1]**.

Page 128 Reversible reactions

Quick quiz

The reversible symbol is used instead of a single arrow.

1. **(a)** It will turn from pink **[1]** to blue **[1]**.

   (b) blue cobalt salt + water **[1]** $\rightleftharpoons$ **[1]** pink cobalt salt **[1]**

2. change in pressure **[1]**; change in temperature **[1]**; change in concentration **[1]**
3. Cool them down / reduce the temperature / increase the pressure **[1]**
4. They are the same **[1]**.

Page 129 Energy changes in reversible reactions

Quick quiz

In endothermic reactions, - energy is taken in - and the reaction mixture cools down.

In exothermic reactions, - energy is released - and the reaction mixture warms up.

1. **(a)** It goes up / increases **[1]**.

   (b) Energy is transferred from the reaction mixture **[1]** to the surroundings **[1]**.

2. **(a)** sulfur dioxide + oxygen $\rightarrow$ sulfur trioxide **[1 mark for correct reactants and product; 1 mark for using the ordinary arrow]**

   (b) Endothermic **[1]**, because if the reaction is exothermic in one direction, it is endothermic in the other direction. **[1]**

   (c) The amount of energy is the same **[1]**.

3. **(a)** carbon monoxide + hydrogen $\rightleftharpoons$ methanol

   [1 mark for correct reactants and product; 1 mark for using the reversible arrow]

   (b) 2800 J **[1]**

Page 130 Crude oil, hydrocarbons and alkanes

Quick quiz

Missing words in order: finite; biomass; millions; mixture

1. A compound **[1]** of hydrogen and carbon only **[1]**
2. non-renewable **[1]**
3. **(a)**

Number of carbon atoms	Name of alkane
1	methane **[1]**
2	ethane **[1]**
3	propane **[1]**
4	butane **[1]**

(b) C_4H_{10}

4. **(a)** C_nH_{2n+2} **[1]**

(b) $(2 \times 1) + 2 = 4$ **[1]**

5. **(a)** propane **[1]**

(b) 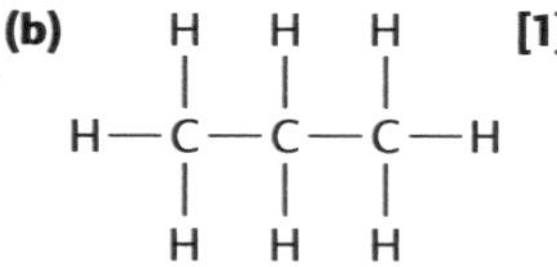 **[1]**

Page 131 Fractional distillation

Quick quiz

solvents; detergents; polymers

1. **(a)** Top to bottom: petrol, diesel oil, heavy fuel oil

[2 marks for all three in correct order; 1 mark for one correct]

(b) Turned into a liquid **[1]**

(c) Any three for three marks from: petrol; kerosene; diesel oil; heavy fuel oil

2. **(a)** the bottom **[1]**

(b) They evaporate / boil **[1]**.

(c) They condense **[1]**.

3. **(a)** They have a similar number of carbon atoms **[1]**.

(b) The molecules in a fraction have different numbers of carbon atoms **[1]**. Each fraction boils over a range of temperatures **[1]**.

Page 132 Hydrocarbons

Quick quiz

C_3H_8, $C_{12}H_{24}$, $C_{100}H_{202}$, $CH_3CH_2CH_3$, CH_2CHCH_3

1. **(a)** $CH_4 + 2O_2 \rightarrow CO_2 + 2H_2O$ **[1]**

(b) carbon dioxide **[1]**; water **[1]**

(c) oxidised **[1]** because they gain oxygen in the reaction **[1]**

(d) exothermic **[1]**

2. **(a) (i)** thick rather than runny **[1]**

(ii) easy to ignite / easily set alight **[1]**

(b) Viscosity increases **[1]**; flammability decreases **[1]**.

3. They increase **[1]**.
4. $C_3H_8 + 5O_2 \rightarrow 3CO_2 + 4H_2O$

[1 mark for formulae on correct sides; 1 mark for balancing]

Page 133 Cracking and alkenes

Quick quiz

Steam cracking; catalytic cracking

1. Large hydrocarbons are broken down to form smaller more useful molecules. **[1]**
2. Missing words in order: high **[1]**; small **[1]**; cracking **[1]**; starting **[1]**
3. **(a)** $C_8H_{18} \rightarrow C_4H_{10} + C_4H_8$ **[1]**

(b) $C_{10}H_{22} \rightarrow C_8H_{18} + C_2H_4$ **[1]**

(c) $C_5H_{12} \rightarrow C_3H_8 + C_2H_4$ **[1]**

(d) $C_4H_{10} \rightarrow CH_4 + C_3H_6$ **[1]**

4. **(a)** no change / stays orange **[1]**

(b) changes from orange to colourless / it is decolourised **[1]**

Page 134 Pure substances

Quick quiz

A, B, D

1. orange squash **[1]**

milk **[1]**

2. Oxygen is a single element and carbon dioxide is a single compound, **[1]** but air is a mixture of gases / contains different gases / atoms / molecules and so it is not pure **[1]**.
3. **(a)** decreases the melting point **[1]**

(b) increases the boiling point **[1]**

4. A pure substance melts and boils at a specific temperature **[1]**. but petrol boils over a range of temperatures **[1]**.
5. **(a)** melting points **[1]**; boiling points **[1]**

(b) Orange juice is a mixture of different substances **[1]**.

Page 135 Formulations

Quick quiz

Missing words in order: two; compounds; combined; unchanged

1.

Feature	Tick if correct
Each component has a particular purpose.	✓ **[1]**
It has components in random amounts.	
It is a natural substance.	
It is a complex mixture.	✓ **[1]**
It is designed to be useful.	✓ **[1]**

2. alloys **[1]**

fertiliser **[1]**

medicine **[1]**

3. Cow's milk does not have all the substances human babies need / substances are in the wrong amounts **[1]**; baby milk powder has these in the right amounts **[1]**.
4. **(a)** It contains substances in measured amounts **[1]**; each with a particular purpose **[1]**.

(b) To make it smell nice **[1]**; to make it look nice **[1]**.

(c) It would not remove oil / remove grease / clean the dishes **[1]**.

Page 136 Chromatography

Quick quiz

From top to bottom: true; false; false

1.

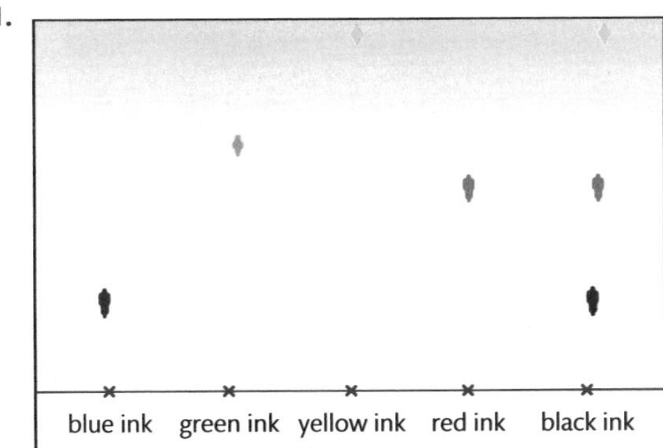

[2 marks for all correct, 1 mark if two correct, as long as green dot not included]

2. R_f = 0.506849 **[1]** = 0.51 (2 sig fig) **[1]**
3. Answers could include the following points in a logical order for 5 marks:
   - the paper contains the stationary phase
   - the mobile phase / solvent moves through the paper
   - the substances in the sample are attracted to the two phases
   - the separation depends on how the substances distribute between the two phases
   - a substance travels further if it is more strongly attracted to the mobile phase than to the stationary phase
   - different substances travel different distances on the paper.

Page 137 Paper chromatography

Quick quiz

R_f value – the distance a substance travels relative to the solvent

mobile phase – the liquid solvent

solvent front – the level reached by the solvent

stationary phase – the chromatography paper

1. Correct order (top to bottom): 5, 3, 6, 1, 4, 2
   [all correct for 5 marks; 4 or 5 correct for 4 marks; 3 correct for 3 marks; 2 correct for 2 marks; 1 correct for 1 mark]
2. **(a)** Both contain a (green) spot at the same height **[1]**.
   (b) The original has 3 spots but the forgery has 2 spots **[1]**; the original has a yellow spot but the forgery only has green spots **[1]**.
3. The sample of powder contained a spot at the same height as the pure cocaine **[1]**; but it also contained another spot **[1]**.

Page 138 Testing for gases

Quick quiz

chlorine, oxygen, hydrogen, carbon dioxide

1. **(a)** Place damp litmus paper near the mouth of a test tube of the gas **[1]**. If chlorine is present the paper turns white **[1]**.
   (b) Place a lighted splint near the mouth of a test tube containing the gas **[1]**. If hydrogen is present, the gas ignites with a squeaky pop **[1]**.
2. Place a glowing splint in the gas **[1]**. If oxygen is present it will it relight **[1]**.
3. **(a)** carbon dioxide **[1]**
   (b) Bubbling **[1]**; the limewater turns milky / cloudy (white) **[1]**
4. Place damp litmus paper in the gas **[1]**; if it turns white the gas is chlorine **[1]**; place a lighted splint in the gas **[1]**; if it re-ignites, the gas is oxygen **[1]**.

Page 139 Gases in the atmosphere

Quick quiz

(a) nitrogen; **(b)** oxygen; **(c)** carbon dioxide / water vapour

1. **(a)** argon – Ar; oxygen – O_2; carbon dioxide – CO_2; nitrogen – N_2; water – H_2O
   [4 marks if all correct, 3 marks if 4 correct, 2 marks for 3 correct and 1 mark for 2 correct]
   (b) (i) Any two for two marks from: argon; oxygen; nitrogen
   (ii) carbon dioxide **[1]**; water **[1]**
2. **(a)** 80% **[1]**
   (b) one-fifth / $\frac{1}{5}$ / 20% **[1]**
   (c) Any one for one mark from: argon; carbon dioxide; water
3. **(a)** oxygen **[1]**; nitrogen **[1]**
   (b) 200 million years **[1]**

Page 140 Earth's early atmosphere

Quick quiz

nitrogen – increased; oxygen – increased; carbon dioxide – decreased

1. The Earth formed over four billion years ago. **[1]**
2. volcanic activity **[1]**
3. As the Earth cooled, **[1]** water vapour condensed **[1]**.
4. CH_4 – methane **[1]** NH_3 – ammonia **[1]**
5. Nitrogen is (relatively) unreactive **[1]**.
6. Any three for three marks from: the percentage of nitrogen is less; the percentage of oxygen is less; the percentage of carbon dioxide is greater; the percentage of other gases is greater

Page 141 Oxygen and carbon dioxide levels

Quick quiz

(a) 4.6 billion years; **(b)** 2.7 billion years

1. **(a)** carbon dioxide + water $\rightarrow$ glucose + oxygen
   [1 mark for correct reactants; 1 mark for correct products]
   (b) They are the same **[1]**
2. Carbon dioxide is absorbed when **[1]** algae / plants carry out photosynthesis **[1]**
3. **(a)** calcium carbonate **[1]**
   (b) carbon **[1]**
4. **(a)** photosynthesis **[1]**
   (b) It reduces carbon dioxide levels **[1]** because plants absorb carbon dioxide for photosynthesis **[1]**
   (c) It prevented carbon dioxide returning to the atmosphere / coal contains the carbon **[1]**

Page 142 Greenhouse gases

Quick quiz

infrared radiation; ultraviolet light

1. **(a)**

Name of gas	Formula	Number of atoms	Number of elements
carbon dioxide	CO_2	3	2
nitrogen	N_2	2	1
oxygen	O_2	2	1
water vapour	H_2O	3	2

[1 mark for each correct row]

(b) (i) Any one for one mark from: carbon dioxide; water vapour

(ii) Any one for one mark from: nitrogen; oxygen

(iii) Its molecules contain two different elements **[1]**.

2. Missing words in order: ultraviolet **[1]**; Sun **[1]**; surface **[1]**; infrared **[1]**; atmosphere **[1]**

Page 143 Human contribution to greenhouse gases

Quick quiz

Any two from: farming; use of fossil fuels; industry

1. **(a)** methane + oxygen → carbon dioxide + water

   [1 mark for correct reactants; 1 mark for correct products]

   (b) (i) Methane is a greenhouse gas **[1]**.

   (ii) Burning natural gas releases carbon dioxide **[1]**; which is a greenhouse gas **[1]**.

2. **(a)** rice farming **[1]** and cattle farming **[1]**

   (b) Fuels / petrol / diesel oil / kerosene release carbon dioxide when they burn **[1]**.

3. **(a)** 412 - 302 = 110 (parts per million) **[1]**

   (b) $\frac{110}{100}$ 110 / 100 = 1.1 (parts per million) **[1]**

Page 144 Global climate change

Quick quiz

From top to bottom: true, true, true

1. Missing words in order: short **[1]**; hours **[1]**; weather **[1]**; long **[1]**; years **[1]**
2. Global warming is a cause of climate change. **[1]**
3. **(a)** The volume increases **[1]**.

   (b) They will increase **[1]**.

   (c) Increasing temperatures will cause ice to melt **[1]**. The water will run into the sea in rivers **[1]**.

   (d) It decreases **[1]**.

   (e) As the temperature increases, the mass of dissolved oxygen decreases. **[1]** Fish will have less oxygen for respiration **[1]**

4. Any two for two marks from the following: reduced crop yields; farmers have to plant different crops

Page 145 The carbon footprint

Quick quiz

Gas	Contains carbon?	Greenhouse gas?
carbon dioxide	✓	✓
methane	✓	✓
nitrogen		
water vapour		✓

1. **(a)** the total amount of carbon dioxide and other greenhouse gases emitted over its full life cycle **[1]**

   (b) services **[1]**; events **[1]**

2. Carbon dioxide **[1]**; methane **[1]**
3. **(a)** 14% **[1]**

   (b) (i) transport **[1]**

   (ii) Any one sensible way of reducing transport emissions for one mark, e.g: reducing the use of cars / aeroplanes; taking the bus / train instead of a car; using fuel-efficient vehicles; using electric vehicles; cycling; walking

4. **(a)** Any two for two marks from: switch things off when not in use; recycle and compost rather than discarding into landfill; reuse; purchase less; use energy-efficient appliances; buy local produce; use transport less; have showers rather than baths

   (b) Any one for one mark from: some of the family may not want to do these things; people may forget to do something, e.g. turn off the lights; the family may already be doing some / all of these things; the family may not be able to do some / all of these things; no public transport available in area

Page 146 Atmospheric pollutants

Quick quiz

particulates	global dimming
nitrogen oxides	respiratory problems
carbon monoxide	toxic gas

1. **(a)** hydrocarbon + oxygen → carbon dioxide **[1]** + water **[1]**

   (b) (i) carbon monoxide **[1]**; **(ii)** soot / carbon **[1]**

2. sulfur + oxygen → sulfur dioxide

   [1 mark for correct reactants; 1 mark for correct product]

3. **(a)** nitrogen + oxygen → oxides of nitrogen **[1]**

   (b) acid rain **[1]**

4. It is colourless and does not have a smell. **[1]**
5. oxides of nitrogen **[1]**; sulfur dioxide **[1]**

Page 147 Earth's resources

Quick quiz

All circled

1. finite resource – It is not being made any more, or is being made very slowly. **[1]**

   non-renewable resource – It is being used up faster than it can be replaced. **[1]**

   renewable resource – It can be replaced after it has been used. **[1]**

2. **(a)** It is synthetic **[1]** because it has been made using a chemical reaction **[1]**.

   (b) manure **[1]**

   (c) Manure is produced naturally by animals. **[1]**

3. Missing words in order: needs **[1]**; harming **[1]**; future **[1]**
4. Any one for one mark from: wool; leather; cotton; linen
5. 700 / 20 **[1]** = 350 years **[1]**

Page 148 Potable water

Quick quiz

(a) Lakes, rivers, ground water

(b) Seawater

1. **(a)** It is water that is safe to drink **[1]**.

   (b) It contains dissolved substances / salts / microbes **[1]**.

2. Box 1 – sedimentation **[1]**; box 2 – filtration **[1]**; box 3 – sterilisation **[1]**
3. Ultraviolet light **[1]**; chorine **[1]**; ozone **[1]**
4. **(a)** desalination **[1]**

   (b) a membrane **[1]**

   (c) distillation **[1]**

Page 149 Purifying water

Quick quiz

purification - removing contaminants

condensation - water changing from the gas state to the liquid state

evaporation - water changing from the liquid state to the gas state

pH - a measure of how acidic or alkaline a solution is

1. **(a)** to remove insoluble / undissolved solids **[1]**
   (b) Heat the water in a flask so that it boils **[1]**. Cool the water vapour **[1]** so that it condenses / turns back to the liquid state **[1]**.
2. **(a)** nothing / a clean watch glass **[1]**
   (b) solid / powder left on the watch glass **[1]**
3. **(a)** 7 **[1]**
   (b) sample C **[1]** because its pH is closest to that of pure water **[1]**
   (c) It will contain dissolved substances (that affect its pH) **[1]**.
4. **(a)** 100 °C **[1]**
   (b) Sample X **[1]** because its boiling point is closest to the boiling point of pure water **[1]**

Page 150 Waste water treatment

Quick quiz

Sewage; agricultural waste; industrial waste

1.

	Main contaminant		
Type of waste water	**Organic matter**	**Harmful microbes**	**Harmful chemicals**
Sewage	✓ [1]	✓ [1]	
Agricultural waste	✓ [1]	✓ [1]	
Industrial waste	✓ [1]		✓ [1]

2. aerobic biological treatment - breaks down effluent, releasing carbon dioxide
   anaerobic digestion - breaks down sludge, releasing methane
   sedimentation - lets solids settle out to produce sludge and effluent
   screening - removes rubbish and grit
   [3 marks if 4 correct, 2 marks for 2 correct]
3. **(a)** Fuel **[1]**
   (b) global warming / climate change **[1]**
4. **(a)** Any two for two marks from: organic matter; harmful microbes; harmful chemicals
   (b) Clean seawater only needs distillation / reverse osmosis (but the other sources need several stages) **[1]**.

Page 151 Life cycle assessment

Quick quiz

Any three from: use of water; use of resources; use of energy sources; production of some waste / pollutants

1. **(a)** Correct order: 4, 1, 3, 2
   [3 marks for all correct; 2 marks for 2 or 3 correct; 1 mark for 1 correct]
   (b) distributing the product **[1]**; transporting resources and the product **[1]**
2. To assess the environmental impact of the product **[1]**
3. Any three for three marks from: the mass of natural resources used; the volume of water used; the amount of energy used; some of the wastes produced
4. **(a)** paper cup **[1]**
   (b) (Plastic cup because) any two of the following two marks: it uses the least energy; it produces the least carbon dioxide; it uses the least volume of water
   (c) The paper cup may be least harmful overall **[1]**; because it is made from a renewable resource **[1]**.

Page 152 Reducing the use of resources

Quick quiz

Reduce our use of them; reuse materials; recycle materials

1.

Product	Made from a limited raw material
cotton	
glass	✓ [1]
metal	✓ [1]
plastic	✓ [1]
wood	

2. **(a)** reforming into different products **[1]**; melting and recasting **[1]**
   (b) Use a magnet **[1]**; steel is attracted to a magnet but aluminium is not **[1]**
   (c) Any one for one mark from: it reduces the amount of iron ore needed; it increases the amount of iron produced from the same amount of ore
3. **(a)** crushing **[1]**; melting **[1]**; cooling / moulding **[1]**
   (b) Any one for one mark from: use less glass use other materials instead of glass; reuse glass
   (c) Any one for one mark from: it is difficult to reuse them; it is expensive to reuse them; they cannot be reused safely

Page 153 Energy transfers in a system

Quick quiz

gravitational potential, kinetic, electrical, heating

1. Energy can be transferred usefully, stored or dissipated, but cannot be created or destroyed **[1]**
2. **(a)** chemical **[1]**
   (b) gravitational potential energy **[1]**, kinetic energy **[1]**
   (c) gravitational potential energy **[1]**
3. elastic potential energy to kinetic energy **[1]**

Page 154 Gravitational potential energy

Quick quiz

potential, mass, field, height

1. $E_p = mgh$ = 65 × 9.8 × 1090 **[1]** = 694 330 **[1]** = 694 000 J **[1]** (to 3 sf)
2. **(a)** 2600 × 9.8 × 40 **[1]** = 1 019 200 J / 1 020 000 J **[1]**
   (b) it would be half / halved / 509 600 J / 510 000 J **[1]**
3. **(a)** 65 × 9.8 × 4000 **[1]** = 2 548 000 J / 2 550 000 J **[1]**
   (b) gravitational potential energy → kinetic energy **[1]**

Page 155 Kinetic energy

Quick quiz

From top to bottom: true; false; true; false

1. proportional to its (speed)^2 **[1]**
2. **(a)** kinetic energy = 0.5 × 10 000 × (10)^2 **[1]** = 500 000 J **[1]**
   (b) 500 000 J **[1]**
3. **(a)** 4.0 g = 0.004 kg **[1]**; kinetic energy = 0.5 × 0.004 × (1000)^2 **[1]** = 2000 J **[1]**
   (b) Any one for one mark from: energy dissipated as heat, energy transferred as sound (eventually dissipated as heat), energy transferred as kinetic energy of part of target that flies off

Page 156 Energy in a spring

Quick quiz

spring constant – k – N/m

extension – e – m

elastic potential energy – E_e – J

1. elastic potential energy **[1]**
2. 20 J = 0.5 × spring constant × $(0.1)^2$ **[1]**

   spring constant = 2 × (20) / $(0.1)^2$ **[1]** = 4000 **[1]** N/m
3. Spring stretched by 10 cm has 4 times more energy stored as spring stretched by 5 cm. **[1]**

Page 157 Using energy equations

Quick quiz

ball dropping from a height of 5 m – gravitational potential to kinetic

battery-powered model car moving – chemical to kinetic

spring that is stretched then released – elastic potential to kinetic

1. **(a)** elastic potential energy = 0.5 × 200 × $(0.25)^2$ **[1]** = 6.25 J / 6.3 J / 6 J **[1]**

   (b) elastic potential energy → kinetic energy **[1]**

   (c) (i) gravitational potential energy **[1]**

   (ii) gravitational potential energy = mass × gravitational field strength × height **[1]**
2. **(a)** At its highest point **[1]**

   (b) Any one for one mark from: dissipated; temperature / thermal store of surroundings / water; kinetic energy of water

Page 158 Power

Quick quiz

power = $\frac{\text{work done}}{\text{time}}$, time = $\frac{\text{work done}}{\text{power}}$

1. time = 3600 seconds **[1]**

   Power = $\frac{198000}{3600}$ **[1]** = 55 W **[1]**
2. 2.5 kW = 2500 W **[1]**

   2500 = energy transferred / 120 s **[1]**

   Energy transferred = 2500 × 120 **[1]** = 300 000 J **[1]**
3. **(a)** Change in gravitational potential energy = 80 × 9.8 × 7.5 **[1]** = 5880 J **[1]**

   (b) Power = $\frac{5880}{15}$ **[1]** = 392 W / 390 W **[1]**

Page 159 Efficiency

Quick quiz

The closer to 1 (or 100%), the more efficient the device.

If a device is 40% efficient, 40% of the energy is usefully transferred and 60% is wasted.

1. **(a)** Lamp A: 15 / 60 = 0.25 **[1]**, Lamp B: 15 / 30 = 0.5 **[1]**

   (b) Lamp A: 25%, Lamp B: 50% **[1]**

   (c) Lamp B (is more efficient) **[1]**
2. **(a)** 2000 – 1500 = 500 W **[1]**

   (b) efficiency = 1500 / 2000 **[1]** = 0.75 / 75% **[1]**

Page 160 Renewable energy resources

Quick quiz

sunlight – light energy is used to generate electricity using solar panels

geothermal – heat energy from rocks underground is used to generate electricity

wind – air movement forces turbines to rotate, generating electricity

tides – daily movement of the ocean is used to generate electricity

1. Any two for one mark each from both advantages and disadvantages:

   Advantages: Can be placed in isolated locations; Free energy but some maintenance costs; Requires no fuel / combustion

   Disadvantages: Some people think they spoil the landscape / are an eyesore; They may be a danger to birds; They can be noisy for people living nearby; In light or no winds, they do not generate power
2. *Tidal barrage*: Any one for one mark each from advantage and disadvantage for two marks:

   Advantage: Reliable; High power output; Free energy once installed, but has maintenance costs; Easier to connect to National Grid than offshore wave power or wind power; Requires no fuel or combustion; Little or no pollution

   Disadvantage: Flooding river estuaries can destroy habitats (for birds, fish, shellfish, invertebrates and mammals); Very expensive; Has major effect on local shoreline / natural erosion and deposition processes; Not attractive to look at

   Hydroelectric dam: Any one for one mark each from advantage and disadvantage for two marks:

   Advantage: Reliable; High power output; Small waterwheels work in some isolated locations; Free energy once installed, but some maintenance costs; Easier to connect to National Grid than offshore wave power or wind power; Requires no fuel or combustion; Little or no pollution

   Disadvantage: Building dams can flood valleys, which destroys habitats (for local plants and wildlife); Has major effect on local area / permanently affects whole river and valley; May involve flooding villages / relocating people; Often very expensive; Not attractive to look at
3. Solar panels are expensive to install although they have low running costs. **[1]**

   Solar panels do not produce constant electricity; other sources of power or very expensive storage batteries are needed. **[1]**

Page 161 Non-renewable energy resources

Quick quiz

Any three from: coal, oil, (natural) gas, kerosene, petrol, diesel

1. **(a)** renewable and non-renewable **[1]**

   (b) Hybrid cars can travel further than electric cars without having to stop for fuel or to recharge. **[1]**

   There are more fuel stations for hybrid cars than there are charging stations for fully electric cars. **[1]**
2. **(a)** A resource that cannot be naturally replenished as it is used. **[1]**

   (b) Any two for two marks from: Carbon dioxide, a greenhouse gas, is produced; Carbon dioxide contributes to global warming; Sulfur dioxide and smoke can cause breathing problems; A large amount of fuel needs to be transported with coal.
3. Non-renewable. **[1]** The nuclear fuel is used up and cannot be replaced. **[1]**

Page 162 Circuit diagrams

Quick quiz

cell – E, variable resistor – F, lamp – A, LED – B, ammeter – D, thermistor – C

1. **(a)**

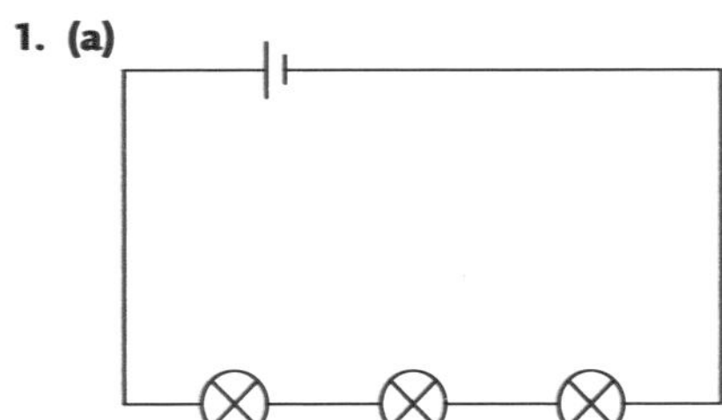

Correct components (1 power supply, 3 lamps) **[1]**; all components in series **[1]**

(b)

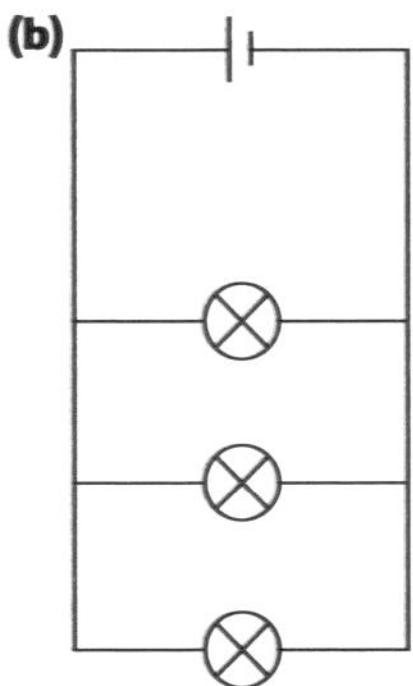

Correct components (1 power supply, 3 lamps) **[1]**; all components in parallel **[1]**

(c) The lamps in the parallel circuit would be brighter **[1]**

2.

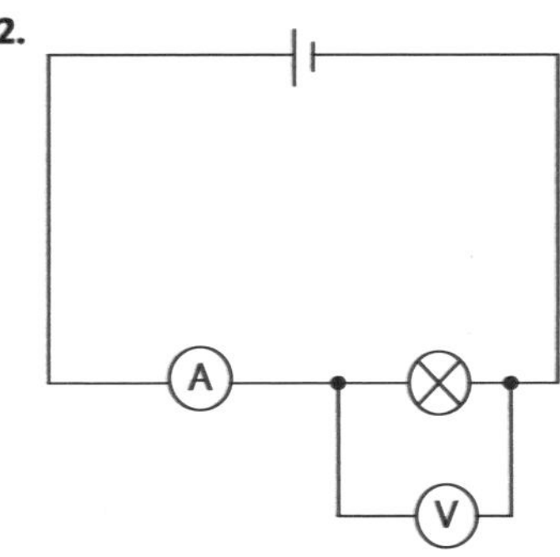

Complete circuit with power supply and lamp **[1]**, ammeter connected in series **[1]**, voltmeter connected in parallel across lamp **[1]**

3. **(a)**

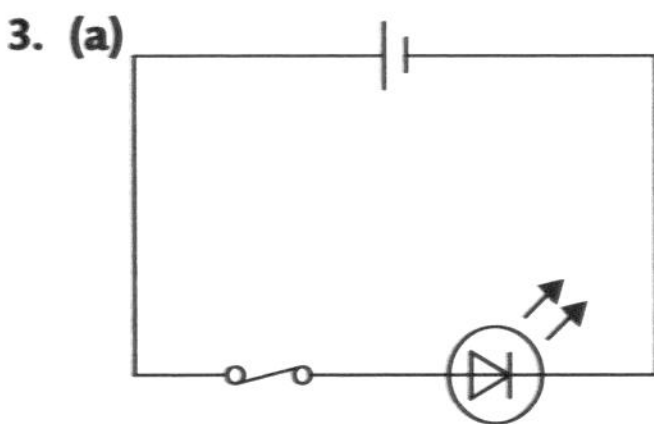

Complete circuit with cell, switch and LED. **[1]**

(b) Any one for one mark from: car lights; home lights; remote controls; low energy bulbs; street lights; displays in appliances; some flat panel televisions

Page 163 Current, resistance and potential difference

Quick quiz

current – The flow of charge, measured in amps (A).

potential difference – the energy given to a charge as it flows; measured in volts (V).

resistance – opposes the flow of charge, caused by electrons colliding with metal ions inside wires; measured in ohms (Ω).

1. **(a)** The reading will be 2 V **[1]** because the potential difference is 'split' three equal ways across the three resistors **[1]**.

(b) 6 = current × (3 × 10) **[1]**

$$\text{current} = \frac{6}{(3 \times 10)} \textbf{[1]} = 0.2\,\text{A} \textbf{[1]}$$

(c) The current will be halved **[1]** to 0.1 A **[1]**

2. $$\text{resistance} = \frac{\text{potential difference}}{\text{current}} \textbf{[1]} = \frac{12}{5} \textbf{[1]}$$

$$= 2.4\,\Omega \textbf{[1]}$$

Page 164 Electrical charge

Quick quiz

Current is produced when a cell causes the electrons in a wire to move. The electrons have a negative charge. They are attracted to the positive terminal on the battery and repelled by the negative terminal.

1. **(a)** 30 minutes = 30 × 60 = 1800 seconds **[1]**

charge flow = current × time = 10 A × 1800 s **[1]** = 18 000 C **[1]**

(b) energy transferred = charge flow × potential difference = 18000 × 230 **[1]**

= 4140000 J **[1]**

2. complete **[1]**; potential difference **[1]**

3. **(a)** 0.75 A **[1]**

(b) charge flow = current × time = 0.75 × 120 **[1]** = 90 C **[1]**

Page 165 Resistance

Quick quiz

It opposes the flow of electrical current in a circuit.

1. **(a)** The wire needed to be cleaned to improve the connection / remove any resistance due to dirt **[1]**.

(b) Resistance will increase at higher temperatures **[1]**

(c) Any two for two marks from:

Keep the length of the wire long

Keep the current low

Have the circuit switched on for the shortest possible time

Switch off between tests to allow cooling

2. **(a)** Resistance of a thermistor decreases as the temperature increases **[1]**.

(b) Answers should include the following points in a logical order for 6 marks.

- Circuit set up with thermistor in series with ammeter and in parallel with voltmeter
- Heat thermistor and allow to cool slowly
- At regular intervals measure temperature of thermistor along with potential difference and current
- Calculate resistance for each measurement using $R = V/I$
- Repeat individual measurements or experiment at least once
- Plot graph of resistance against temperature
- Graph not a straight line
- Not an ohmic resistor / component

Page 166 Resistors

Quick quiz

X = diode, Y = ohmic conductor, Z = filament lamp

1. **(a)** For an ohmic conductor, the current is proportional to the potential difference at a constant temperature. **[1]**
   (b) The steeper / larger the gradient, the lower the resistance **[1]**. So the resistance of X is lower / less than the resistance of Y **[1]**.
   (c) The conductor is non-ohmic **[1]**. The resistance is not proportional to the potential difference **[1]**.
   (d) The current through a diode flows in one direction only. **[1]**
2. **(a)**

current
potential difference

Correct axis labels **[1]**
Curved line **[1]** but with positive gradient through origin **[1]**

   (b) As the current increases, (the wire heats up so) the resistance increases (at a faster rate than the current increases) **[1]**.

Page 167 Series and parallel circuits

Quick quiz

From top to bottom: series; parallel; parallel; series; series

1. **(a)** total resistance = 10 + 3 **[1]** = 13 Ω **[1]**
   (b) less than **[1]**
2. **(a)** B **[1]**
   (b) **(i)** Switch open: lamp 1 off, lamp 2 on **[1]**
   (ii) Switch closed: both lamps on **[1]**
   (c) Add a switch **[1]** to the second lamp loop **[1]**

Page 168 *I-V* characteristics

Quick quiz

Step	Order
Plot potential difference on the *x*-axis and current on the *y*-axis.	5
Measure the current passing through the component for a particular potential difference.	2
Change the potential difference across the component using a variable resistor and repeat the measurements.	3
Set up a circuit with an ammeter to measure the current through the component and a voltmeter to measure the potential difference across it.	1
Change the direction of the current and potential difference by swapping the connections on the power supply.	4

1. **(a)**

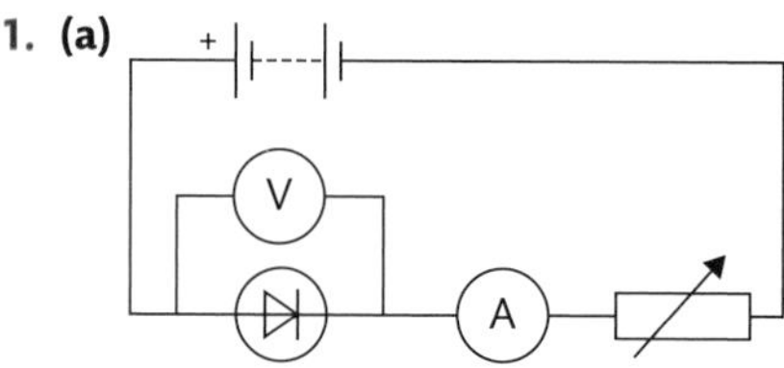

Complete circuit with cell, switch and diode **[1]**, ammeter connected in series **[1]** and voltmeter connected across diode in parallel **[1]**

   (b)

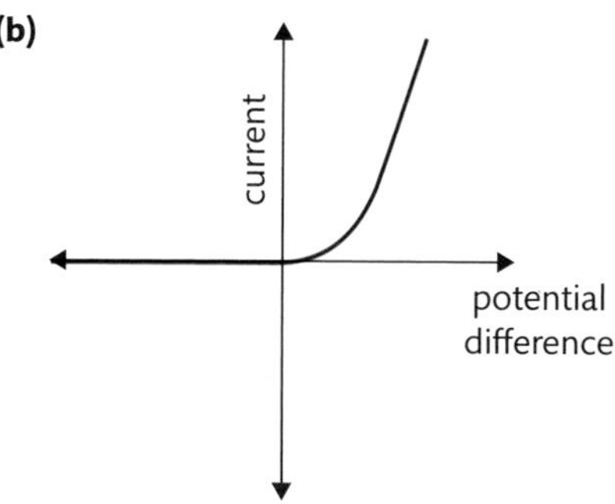

Graph shows zero current for negative potential difference **[1]** and a sharp increase in current at a particular positive potential difference **[1]**

2. **(a)** graph C **[1]**
   (b) Current is proportional to potential difference **[1]**. Doubling the potential difference doubles the current in the circuit **[1]**.

Page 169 Mains electricity

Quick quiz

From top to bottom: false; true; true; true; false

1. **(a)** Touching the live wire is dangerous because you complete a circuit / connection **[1]** between the live wire / the mains supply and earth / ground **[1]**.
   (b) Metal case is connected to earth / ground by the earth wire. **[1]**
2. It carries the (ac) voltage **[1]**
3. **(a)** Mains electricity is alternating current / ac **[1]** and battery is direct current / dc **[1]**.
   (b) 50 Hz **[1]**
4. Graph A **[1]**

Page 170 Energy transfers in appliances

Quick quiz

From top to bottom: useful; wasted; wasted

1. thermal energy transferred to surroundings / environment **[1]**
   thermal energy used to warm water **[1]**
   kinetic energy of spinning drum **[1]**
   sound is kinetic energy of surroundings **[1]**
2. **(i)** thermal, kinetic **[1]**
   (ii) sound **[1]**
3. **(a)** sound / kinetic energy of surroundings **[1]**, light **[1]**, thermal energy of surroundings **[1]**
   (b) sound and light = useful **[1]**; thermal = wasted **[1]**
   (c) wasted = 500 J **[1]**
   (d) transfers to the thermal energy store of surroundings **[1]**

Page 171 Electrical power

Quick quiz

power – watts (W)
energy – joules (J)

time – seconds (s)

current – amps (A)

potential difference – volts (V)

resistance – ohms (Ω)

1. **(a)** Power is the rate **[1]** at which energy is transferred **[1]**.

   (b) power = $\frac{\text{energy transferred [1]}}{\text{time [1]}}$

   (c) $P = I^2 \times R$ **[1]**; $P = V \times I$ **[1]**

2. **(a)** energy transferred = power × time

   or power = $\frac{\text{energy transferred}}{\text{time}}$

   or time = $\frac{\text{energy transferred}}{\text{time}}$ **[1]**

   (b) 3 minutes = 180 seconds **[1]**

   power = $\frac{\text{energy transferred}}{\text{time}} = \frac{200\,000}{180}$ **[1]**

   = 1100 W **[1]**

3. current = $\frac{\text{power}}{\text{potential difference}}$ **[1]** = $\frac{800}{250}$ **[1]** = 3.5 A (to 2 sig figs) **[1]**

Page 172 Transformers and the National Grid

Quick quiz

From top to bottom: false; true; false; false

1. The input is 230 V and the output is 10 V, so the potential difference goes down **[1]**. This means it is a step-down transformer **[1]**.

2. **(a)** increases the potential difference at which the electrical power is transmitted **[1]**

   (b) reduces the energy wasted in the transmission cables **[1]**

Page 173 Density

Quick quiz

mass – kg, volume – m^3, density – kg/m^3.

1. **(a)** density = $\frac{2025}{750}$ **[1]** = 2.7 g/cm^3 **[1]**

   (b) Steel is more dense than aluminium **[1]**.

   (c) The same volume of steel would have (about three times) more mass than the same volume of steel / aluminium is less dense than steel / an aluminium aircraft requires much less fuel to fly / an aluminium aircraft is a much lighter aircraft that flies more easily. **[1]**

2. **(a)** Cooking oil is less dense **[1]**, so the oil will rise to the surface and sit on top of the water surface **[1]**.

   (b) $0.915 = \frac{\text{mass}}{10}$ **[1]**

   mass = 10 × 0.915 **[1]** = 9.15 g **[1]**

3. The cork is less dense than water **[1]**

Page 174 Density of materials

Quick quiz

Find the mass of the object.	1
This is the volume of the irregular shape.	5
Fill a displacement can to the spout.	2
Place the object in the can.	3

Use density = mass / volume to determine the density. 6

Collect the water that runs out into a measuring cylinder. 4

1. **(a)** Use a ruler / metre rule / tape to measure **[1]** the length, width and height of the cuboid **[1]**.

   Use the formula length × width × height to calculate the volume **[1]**.

   (b) Vernier callipers **[1]**, micrometer **[1]**

   (c) In step 1, the student says to 'partly fill' a displacement can. This will cause an error in the measurement of volume. **[1]** The student should fill the can right up to the level of the spout **[1]**.

2. **(a)** measuring cylinder **[1]**; displacement can **[1]**

   (b) mass **[1]**

   (c) mass balance / digital balance **[1]**

   (d) density = $\frac{\text{mass}}{\text{volume}}$ **[1]**

Page 175 State changes

Quick quiz

The temperature a substance condenses at is called the boiling point. The temperature a substance freezes at is called the melting point. The density and volume of a substance can change during a change of state but the mass stays the same. As a substance is heated, the particles gain kinetic energy.

1. **(a)** The ethanol is a liquid so the particles are touching **[1]**. They move faster as more energy is taken in **[1]**.

   (b) 78 °C **[1]**

   (c) The particles of ethanol separate from each other to move more freely. **[1]**

2. 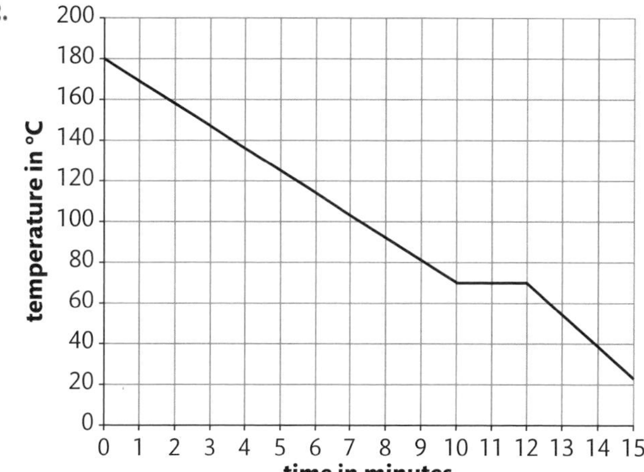

   General trend of straight line downwards from 180 °C at 0 minutes before. **[1]**

   Horizontal line at about 70 °C for a short time. **[1]**

   Another straight line downwards to 20 °C at 15 minutes. **[1]**

Page 176 Specific heat capacity

Quick quiz

ΔE	change in energy
m	mass
c	specific heat capacity
$\Delta\theta$	change in temperature

1. The specific heat capacity of a substance is the amount of energy required **[1]** to raise the temperature of 1 kg of the substance by 1 °C **[1]**.

2. **(a)** change in temperature = 100 – 20 = 80 °C **[1]**

   (b) 1500 g = 1.5 kg **[1]**

   change in thermal energy = 1.5 × 4200 × 80 **[1]** = 504 000 J **[1]**

3. **(a)** The insulation reduces heat / energy loss to the surroundings **[1]**.

   (b) change in thermal energy = 1 × 900 **[1]** × (32 – 20) **[1]** = 10 800 J **[1]**

Page 177 Specific heat capacity

Quick quiz

From top to bottom correct words are: higher; high; low

1. Answer could include the following points in a logical order for 6 marks.
   - Measure the start temperature of the aluminium block using the thermometer.
   - Switch on the electric heater
   - and record its power output rating.
   - Measure the highest temperature reached after a measured amount of time.
   - Calculate the energy input using the equation energy input = power rating of heater × time
   - Calculate the specific heat capacity using the equation change in thermal energy = mass × specific heat capacity × temperature change
   - rearranged to give specific heat capacity = $\frac{\text{change in thermal energy}}{(\text{mass} \times \text{temperature change})}$
2. **(a)** 12.5 °C **[1]**

   (b) 10 °C **[1]**

   (c) change in thermal energy = 2 × 2200 × 10 **[1]** = 44 000 J **[1]**

Page 178 Specific latent heat

Quick quiz

From top to bottom: False; True; True; True

1. **(a)** The particles in the solid ice are starting to move apart **[1]** so that the ice melts to form a liquid **[1]**.

   (b) energy for a change of state = 5.2 × 336 000 **[1]** = 1 747 200 J / 1 750 000 J **[1]**
2. **(a)** mass of iced water = 30 g = 0.030 kg **[1]**

   energy for a change of state = 0.030 × 336 000 **[1]** = 10 080 J **[1]**

   (b) To check the temperature stays constant **[1]**

Page 179 Particle motion in gases

Quick quiz

When a gas is heated, the particles gain kinetic energy.

An increase in kinetic energy causes the particles to move more and spread apart.

1. **(a)** The balloon would have reduced in size. **[1]**

   (b) Particles in cooler gases have less kinetic energy so they move slower / more slowly. **[1]** This means the particles exert a lower pressure **[1]**, causing the balloon to become smaller.
2. **(a)** The kinetic energy store of the particles in the gas increases **[1]** so the particles move around faster **[1]** (and collide more often).

   (b) to cope with the high pressure of the gas **[1]**

Page 180 The structure of an atom

Quick quiz

Correct labels: nucleus contains 6 protons and 6 neutrons; 1 electron – there are 6 of these arranged outside the nucleus

1.

Particle	Location in atom	Relative electric charge (+, – or 0)
proton	inside the nucleus	+
neutron	inside the nucleus	0
electron	outside the nucleus	–

[1 mark for each correct row]

2. 1×10^{-14} m **[1]**
3. A proton has a positive charge while a neutron has zero / no charge **[1]**.

   Both are found in the nucleus **[1]**.

   Both have a similar / relative mass of 1 **[1]**.
4. **(a)** The electron moves to a higher energy level. **[1]**

   (b) Any two for two marks from: mass of electron; charge of electron; number of electrons

Page 181 Mass number, atomic number and isotopes

Quick quiz

From top to bottom: true; false; true; true; false

1. **(a)** Isotopes are atoms with the same number of protons **[1]** but a different number of neutrons **[1]**.

   (b) Carbon-12 has 6 neutrons but carbon-14 has 8 neutrons **[1]**.
2. **(a)**

Property	Atom A	Atom B	Atom C
number of protons	5	4	5
number of neutrons	5	5	6
atomic number	5	4	5
mass number	10	9	11

[1 mark for each correct column]

(b) Atom A, Atom C **[1]**. They have the same number of protons / same atomic number **[1]**.

3. **(a)** protons 20 **[1]**, neutrons 20 **[1]**, electrons 20 **[1]**

   (b) ion **[1]**

   (c) 18 **[1]**

   (d) + **[1]** 2 **[1]**

Page 182 Development of the atomic model

Quick quiz

in the nucleus

1.

Statement	Order
James Chadwick discovered that neutrons existed inside the nucleus of an atom.	5
The plum pudding model was suggested by scientists who thought that the atom was a positively charged 'pudding' with negatively charged electrons ('plums') stuck inside it.	2
Niels Bohr suggested that electrons travel in orbits around the nucleus.	4
Rutherford's scattering experiment suggested that atoms were mostly empty space with a tiny, massive nucleus in the centre.	3
The Ancient Greeks thought that atoms were tiny spheres that could not be divided.	1

[1 mark for 1 or 2 statements numbered correctly, 2 marks for 3 or 4 statements numbered correctly, 3 marks for all statements numbered correctly]

2. **(a)** The plum pudding model suggested that the atom is a ball of positive charge **[1]** with negative charge / electrons embedded in it **[1]**.

   (b) The positive charge is found in a small nucleus at the centre **[1]**.

   The negative charge is found spread out on orbiting electrons. **[1]**

3. **(a)** alpha particles **[1]**
   (b) They passed (straight) through **[1]**.
   (c) Most of an atom is empty space **[1]**.

Page 183 Radioactive decay and nuclear radiation

Quick quiz

random; which, when

1.

Radiation	Description	Ionising power	Penetrating power	Range in air
alpha	2 proton and 2 neutrons (helium nucleus)	high	skin / paper	less than 5 centimetres
beta	fast-moving electron	low	3 mm aluminium foil	about 1 metre
gamma	electromagnetic wave	very low	lead / concrete	more than 1 kilometre

[1 mark for each correct row]

2. paper **[1]**; less **[1]**; be stopped by **[1]**
3. gamma radiation **[1]**

Page 184 Half-lives

Quick quiz

half-life; time; rate; half, time; atoms

1. random **[1]**
2. **(a)**

Time in years	0	30	60	90	120
Activity in Bq	1600	800	400	200	100

[1 mark for each correct column]

   (b) 75 years **[1]**
3. A **[1]** and D **[1]**

Page 185 Nuclear equations

Quick quiz

alpha – helium nucleus – 2 – 4

beta – fast-moving electron – –1, 0

1. **(a)** The number 14 represents the mass number of carbon-14. **[1]**
   The number 6 represents the atomic number of carbon-14. **[1]**
   (b) ${}^{0}_{-1}e$ **[1 mark for each correct value for the electron.]**
   (c) beta (decay) **[1]**
2. **(a)** atomic number decreases by 2, mass number decreases by 4 **[1]**
   (b) ${}^{198}_{86}Rn \rightarrow {}^{194}_{84}Po + {}^{4}_{2}He$
   [1 mark for 194, 1 mark for 84, 1 mark for both 4 and 2 correct]
3. beta decay **[1]**

Page 186 Radioactive contamination

Quick quiz

radioactive decay – a random process in which unstable nuclei give out radiation

radioactive contamination – the unwanted presence of materials containing radioactive atoms

irradiation – the process of exposing an object to radiation, but the object does not itself become radioactive

1. contamination **[1]**; irradiation **[1]**
2. **(a)** Gamma radiation can penetrate skin and cause damage / harm / cancer **[1]**. Standing in another room means that the doctor is protected from / receives less gamma radiation **[1]**.
   (b) The amount of radiation a patient receives depends on the time they are exposed to the source **[1]**. A longer time means a larger dose **[1]**.
3. **(a)** peer review **[1]**
   (b) Any two for two marks from: Avoid direct contact with radioactive sources; Keep sources in sealed containers; Clean off immediately any contamination that does occur; Wear protective clothing

Page 187 Scalar and vector quantities

Quick quiz

Scalar: distance, time, speed, mass, temperature

Vector: weight, displacement, force

1. Velocity tells us the speed of an object and its direction of movement. **[1]**
2. Velocity is 40 m/s in the north / northerly direction **[1]**.
3. **(a)** Arrow labelled 300 N parallel to 150 N force, twice the length of the 150 N force **[1]**
   (b) resultant force = 300 N + 150 N = 450 N **[1]**
4. **(a)** 1500 N **[1]**
   (b) forwards **[1]**

Page 188 Forces

Quick quiz

Contact: tension, friction, air resistance

Non-contact: weight, magnetic force, electrostatic force

1. **(a)** One arrow labelled 'weight' starting from centre of box pointing vertically downwards **[1]**, one further arrow labelled 'friction' pointing horizontally backwards **[1]**
   (b) normal contact force; pushing force; friction **[1]**
2. **(a)** arrow labelled 'weight' pointing vertically downwards **[1]**
   (b) arrow labelled 'lift' pointing vertically upwards **[1]** and same length as weight arrow **[1]**
   (c) Weight = non-contact; Lift = contact **[1]**
3. **(a)** Both the poles near to each other are north OR both are south **[1]**.
   (b) Magnets are not touching **[1]**.

Page 189 Gravity

Quick quiz

mass – the amount of matter in an object – kg

weight – the force acting on an object due to gravity – N

gravitational field strength – the strength of gravity at any point – N/kg

1. **(a)** gravitational force **[1]**
   (b) A mass balance only measures the mass, which is the same **[1]** on different planets. A newtonmeter measures weight, which changes **[1]** on different planets.
2. **(a)** The weight of an object depends on the gravitational field strength **[1]** of the planet or moon the object is near.
   The gravitational field strength on the Moon is less than / weaker than **[1]** than on Earth.
   (b) weight = 8.0 × 1.6 **[1]** = 12.8 N **[1]**
3. **(a)** the centre of mass of the shape **[1]**
   (b) Measure from one or more further hanging points **[1]**.

Page 190 Resultant forces

Quick quiz

From top to bottom: 2, 3, 1.

1. **(a)** Resultant force = 400 – 300 **[1]** = 100 N to the left **[1]**
   (b) Extra force = 100 N **[1]** to the right **[1]**
2. **(a)** The velocity of an object falling through a fluid / the air when the drag force / force due to air resistance is equal and opposite to its weight (making the resultant force zero) **[1]**
   (b) Weight does not change **[1]**. The force due to air resistance increases **[1]**.

Page 191 Work done and energy transfer

Quick quiz

From top to bottom: false; true; false; false

1. Work done = energy transferred when a force moves an object through a distance. **[1]**
2. gravitational potential energy store **[1]**
3. **(a)** work done = 2500 × 12 **[1]** = 30 000 J **[1]**
   (b) 60 000 J = 2500 N × braking distance **[1]**
   braking distance = $\frac{60\,000}{2500}$ **[1]** = 24 m **[1]**

Page 192 Forces and elasticity

Quick quiz

From to top bottom: true; true; false; true; true

1. If the mass is removed from the end of the rubber band, the band should return to its original shape. **[1]**
2. 10 cm = 0.1 m **[1]**
   Elastic potential energy = 0.5 × 100 **[1]** × 0.1^2 = 0.5 J **[1]**
3. **(a)** force = spring constant × extension **[1]**
   (b) 2.0 = spring constant × 0.1 **[1]**; spring constant = 2.0 / 0.1 **[1]** = 20 N/m **[1]**

Page 193 Force and extension

Quick quiz

From top to bottom: false; true; true; false

1. Plot a graph of force against extension **[1]** that should produce a straight line through the origin. Force should increase in proportion to extension **[1]**.
2. **(a)** Reading of 10 cm against 3 N **[1]**
   (b) 12 cm **[1]**
   (c) (Spring constant = 6.0 / 0.24 =) 25 N/m **[1]**
   (d) Any two for two marks from:
   Repeat each reading one or two more times and take an average.
   Measure the spring length from the same point on the spring each time.
   Make sure the spring is at eye level when measuring it.

Page 194 Distance and displacement

Quick quiz

true; false; false; true

1. **(a)** distance = 20 + 20 = 40 km **[1]**
   (b) 0 km **[1]**
2. 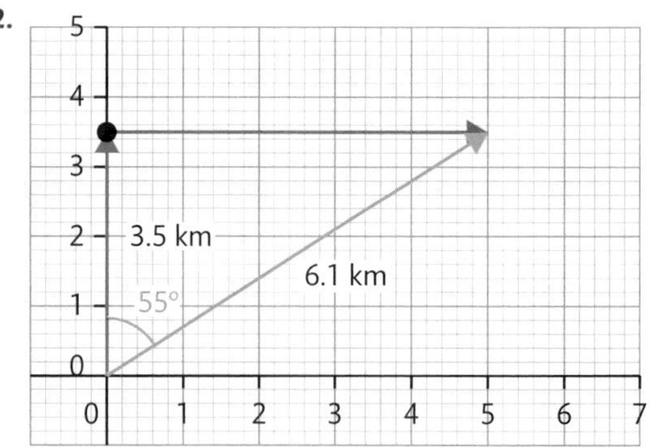

   Scale diagram that shows 3.5 km north then 5.0 km east **[1]** magnitude of displacement = 6.1 km **[1]**; direction 55° to north **[1]**
3. **(a)** 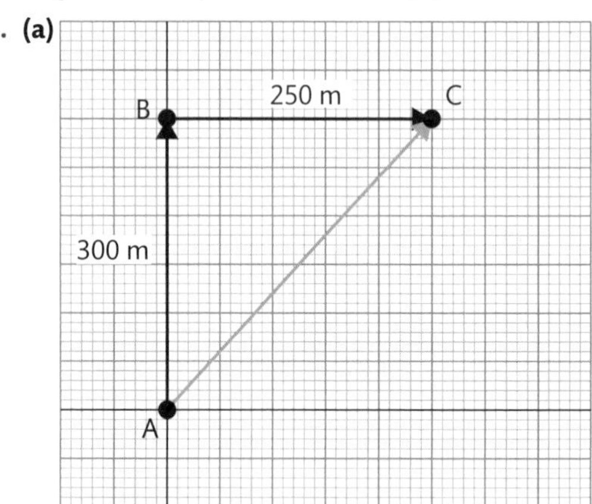

   Scale diagram that shows A to B 300 m north then B to C 250 m east **[1]**
   (b) total distance = 300 + 250 = 550 m **[1]**
   (c) Displacement is between 0° and 90° (between north and east) **[1]**

Page 195 Speed and velocity

Quick quiz

speed; direction; distance; time

1. distance = speed × time **[1]**
2. **(a)** 3.6 × 1000 m = 6.0 m/s × time **[1]**
   time = 3.6 × 1000 / 6.0 **[1]** = 600 s **[1]**
   (b) The person was cycling **[1]**, because a speed of 6 m/s is closest to the approximate speed of that activity over that distance **[1]**.
3. **(a)** Average speed = 50 / 1.5 **[1]** = 33.3 km/h / 33 km/h **[1]**
   (b) 20 km in a direction west **[1]**
   (c) The distance travelled by the bus is a scalar quantity / includes bends in the roads **[1]** but the displacement is a vector quantity / is a straight line. **[1]**

Page 196 Distance-time relationships

Quick quiz

the gradient of the line increases – the object is accelerating
the gradient of the line decreases – the object is decelerating
the gradient of the line is zero – the object is stationary
the gradient of the line is constant – the object travels at a constant speed

1. **(a)** A–B: The cyclist travels 30 km in 3 hours **[1]** at a constant speed **[1]**.
   (b) speed = distance / time = 30 / 3 **[1]** = 10 km/h **[1]**
   (c) The cyclist travels faster in part C to D than in part A to B **[1]**

2. **(a)** 250 m **[1]**
   (b) constant speed **[1]**
   (c) stationary / stopped moving / 0 m/s **[1]**
   (d) The bus is accelerating **[1]**

Page 197 Uniform acceleration

Quick quiz

s – distance – m

u – initial velocity – m/s

v – final velocity – m/s

a – acceleration – m/s^2

t – time – s

1. **(a)** 0 m/s **[1]**
   (b) acceleration = $\frac{(18-0)}{6}$ **[1]** = 3 m/s^2 **[1]**
2. **(a)** acceleration = $\frac{(90-0)}{9}$ **[1]** = 10 m/s^2 **[1]**
   (b) time taken = change in velocity / acceleration **[1]**
   time taken = $\frac{(0-90)}{-36}$ **[1]**
   = 2.5 s **[1]**
3. (final velocity)^2 – (10)^2 = 2 × 0.8 × 3 × 1000 **[1]**
   (final velocity)^2 = 2 × 0.8 × 3 × 1000 + (10)^2 **[1]**
   final velocity = $\sqrt{4900}$ **[1]** = 70 m/s **[1]**

Page 198 Velocity-time graphs

Quick quiz

gradient of a downward sloping line – deceleration

gradient of an upward sloping line – acceleration

a horizontal line – constant speed

1. **(i)** gradient = distance / time so tells us the speed **[1]**
   (ii) gradient = speed / time so tells us the acceleration **[1]**
2. **(a)** The graph starts at the origin, where velocity is 0 when the time is 0 **[1]**.
   (b) For the first 20 seconds of the journey, the cyclist accelerates **[1]** from rest to a velocity of 6 m/s **[1]**. The cyclist continues travelling at 6 m/s for a further 30 seconds **[1]**.

(c)

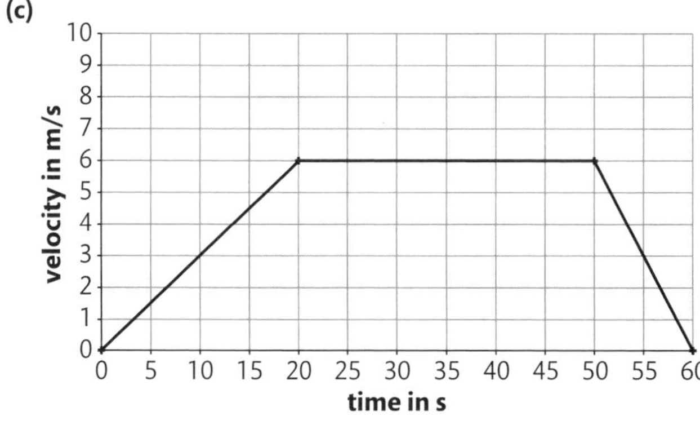

Straight line with negative gradient **[1]** passing through (50 s, 6 m/s) and (60 s, 0 m/s) **[1]**

Page 199 Newton's laws of motion

Quick quiz

Newton's first law – An object will continue to move in the same direction at the same speed unless acted upon by a resultant force.

Newton's second law – The acceleration of an object is proportional to the resultant force and inversely proportional to the mass of the object.

Newton's third law – When two objects interact, they exert an equal and opposite force on each other.

1. **(a)** force = mass × acceleration **[1]**
   (b) If mass is increased, a larger / bigger force **[1]** is needed to produce the same acceleration **[1]**.
2. equal **[1]**, opposite **[1]**
3. **(a)** Travelling at a constant speed **[1]** in a straight line **[1]**
   (b) The weight of the car / the gravitational force due to the Earth **[1]**

Page 200 Newton's second law

Quick quiz

From top to bottom: true; true; true; false

1. **(a)** resultant force = 1200 – 800 **[1]** = 400 N **[1]**
   (b) force = 1500 × acceleration **[1]** acceleration = $\frac{400}{1500}$ **[1]**
   = 0.27 m/s^2 / 0.266 m/s^2 **[1]**
2. **(a)** resultant force = 75 × 2 **[1]** = 150 N **[1]**
   (b) forwards force needed = resultant force + backwards force
   = 150 + 30 **[1]** = 180 N **[1]**

Page 201 Investigating acceleration

Quick quiz

speed – m/s, mass – kg, acceleration – m/s^2, force – N

1. **(a)** The independent variable is the force / masses producing force **[1]**.
   (b) The dependent variable is the acceleration **[1]**.
   (c) Newton's second law states that force = mass × acceleration. **[1]** So if the force is increased and the mass stays the same, **[1]** the acceleration must increase **[1]**.
2. force **[1]**

Page 202 Stopping distance

Quick quiz

From top to bottom: False; False; True; False

1. **(a)** distance = speed × time **[1]**
   (b) distance = 13.4 × 1.3 **[1]** = 17.4 m **[1]**
   (c) stopping distance = 17.4 + 14 = 31.4 m **[2]**
2. **(a)** 38 m (any value in range 25 to 54 m) **[1]**
   (b) Any two for two marks from: tiredness; drugs / medicine; alcohol; distractions; poor visibility

Page 203 Braking distance

Quick quiz

thinking distance – the distance a car travels between something happening and the driver reacting to it

braking distance – the distance it takes a car to stop after brakes are applied

stopping distance – the total distance it takes for a car to stop

1. **(a)** Worn brakes **[1]**; Any sensible change that affects braking distance, such as slippery road, wet road, icy road, snow on road **[1]**
   (b) When a car brakes, work is done by the force of friction between the brakes and the wheels. **[1]**
   The kinetic energy of the car reduces. **[1]**
   The temperature of the brakes increases. **[1]**
2. **(a)** work done = 10 000 × 40 **[1]** = 400 000 J **[1]**
   (b) Energy transfer from kinetic energy of van **[1]** to temperature of brakes **[1]**
3. thinking distance stays the same **[1]**, braking distance increases **[1]**

Page 204 Types of waves

Quick quiz

The vibrations are parallel to the direction the wave is travelling. - longitudinal wave

The vibrations are perpendicular to the direction the wave is travelling. - transverse wave

Ripples on water are an example of this type of wave. - transverse wave

Sound waves are an example of this type of wave. - longitudinal wave

1. **(a)** Longitudinal sound wave **[1]**
   (b) A compression **[1]**; B rarefaction **[1]**
2. **(a)** Water wave - transverse **[1]**
   Sound wave - longitudinal **[1]**
   (b) light wave **[1]**
3. energy **[1]**

Page 205 Properties of waves

Quick quiz

amplitude - the maximum displacement of a point on a wave away from its undisturbed position

frequency - the number of waves passing a point each second

wavelength - the distance from a point on a wave to an identical point on an adjacent wave

1. **(a)** frequency = $\frac{1}{\text{period}}$ **[1]**
   (b) hertz **[1]**
   (c) frequency = $\frac{1}{\text{period}}$ **[1]** = $\frac{1}{0.02}$ **[1]** = 50 Hz **[1]**
2. B - wavelength **[1]**, C - amplitude **[1]**
3. **(a)** wave speed = frequency × wavelength **[1]**
   (b) 5.0 × 0.10 **[1]** = 0.5 **[1]** = 0.50 m/s (to 2 sf) **[1]**

Page 206 Investigating waves

Quick quiz

Measure the distance the wave travelled.	2
Calculate the wavelength of the wave using wave speed = frequency × wavelength.	6
Time how long it takes for one wave to travel from the paddle to the edge of the ripple tank.	1
Calculate the wave speed using speed = distance / time.	3
Time 10 rotations of the motor and divide by 10 to get the time period of the wave.	4
Calculate the frequency of the wave using frequency = 1 / period.	5

1. **(a)** half the wavelength **[1]**
   (b) Find the wavelength by measuring the length of string and doubling it. **[1]** Use the frequency from the generator. **[1]** Calculate the speed using the equation:
   wave speed = frequency × wavelength **[1]**
   (c) Any two for two marks from: weight used; same string material; same length of string
2. It is difficult to get an accurate value by measuring just one wave **[1]**. Taking an average over a longer amount of time gives a more accurate value **[1]**.

Page 207 Types of electromagnetic waves

Quick quiz

EM: light, infrared, X-rays, radio, microwaves

Not: water waves, sound, waves on a string, ultrasound

1. **(a)** Any two for two marks from: transverse; electromagnetic; travel in straight lines; all travel at the same speed (in a vacuum)
   (b) Similarity: The wave speed is the same for light and ultraviolet radiation. **[1]**
   Difference: Any one for one mark from: The frequency is different. The wavelength is different.
2. A - microwaves **[1]**, B - infrared **[1]**, C - ultraviolet waves **[1]**, D - X-rays **[1]**
3. **(a)** nucleus **[1]**
   (b) Ionising radiation is radiation / electromagnetic waves **[1]** that can change the electric charge on an atom **[1]**.
   (c) Any one for one mark from: gene damage; mutation; cancer

Page 208 Properties of electromagnetic waves

Quick quiz

refraction - Light changes direction at a boundary between two different materials.

reflection - Light bounces back from a surface.

emission - Light is produced by an object.

absorption - Light is taken in by an object.

1. angle of incidence - A
   angle of refraction - D
   refracted ray - B
   normal - C
   incident ray - E

[3 marks all correct; 2 marks 3 or 4 correct; 1 mark 1 or 2 correct]

2.

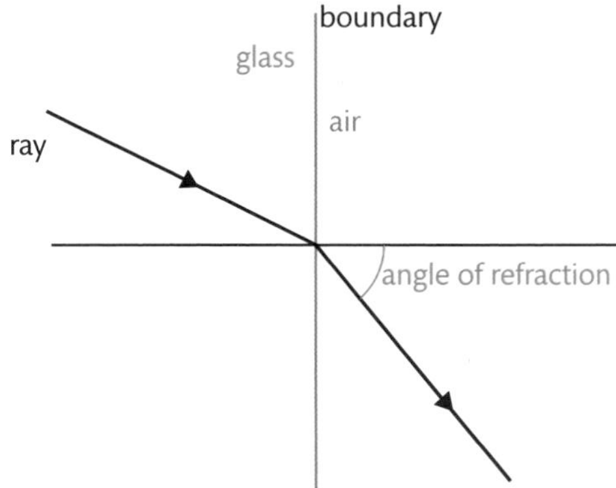

Straight line starting at meeting point of normal, incident ray and boundary, labelled with an arrow **[1]** at a greater angle than the incident ray **[1]** with angle of refraction labelled **[1]**

3. **(a)** refraction **[1]**
   (b) The light (reflected) from the straw travels more quickly through air than through water **[1]** so the light bends at the boundary between air and water **[1]**.

Page 209 Infrared radiation

Quick quiz

thermal, electromagnetic, hot

1. **(a)** independent; dependent; control
   [1 mark for 1 or 2 correct; 2 marks for all 3 correct]
   (b) material the surface is made from **[1]**
   (c) Any two for two marks from: Amount of energy transferred by source; Distance of object from source; Time source is switched on / after which temperature is measured; Starting temperature

2. **(a)** matt black **[1]**
   (b) shiny silver **[1]**

Page 210 Applications of EM waves

Quick quiz

light waves – viewing objects through microscopes

X-rays – medical imaging

ultraviolet – skin tanning

gamma rays – sterilising food

1. energy **[1]**
   satellite communications **[1]**
2. **(a)** information **[1]**
   (b) Any two for two marks from: (broadcast) radio / music / sound; television; walkie talkies
3. **(a)** skin – pass through **[1]**; bone – absorbed **[1]**
   (b) Any two for two marks from: Ionising radiation; May damage tissues / skin after a long exposure; Penetrating so may damage cells

Page 211 Magnetic fields

Quick quiz

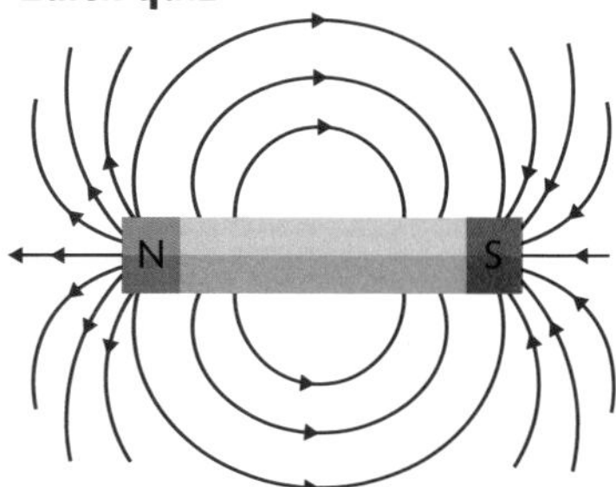

1. **(a)** The north pole of magnet 1 repels the north pole of magnet 2, and attracts the south pole of magnet 2 **[1]**. Magnet 2 will rotate until the attracting poles are close to each other **[1]**.
   (b) There will be a force pushing magnet 3 away **[1]** from magnet 2 because the south pole of magnet 2 repels the south pole of magnet 3 **[1]**.
2. Use a bar magnet where the poles are known **[1]** and then find which pole of the unknown magnet is repelled by the south pole of the known magnet **[1]** OR Use a north-seeking magnetic compass. **[1]** The north-seeking needle end will point away from the south pole of the unknown magnet. **[1]**
3. **(a)** (Fix the bar magnet under a sheet of paper and draw its outline on the paper.) Place the compass near to one pole of the magnet **[1]**. Use a pencil to plot a point where the end of the compass needle furthest away from the magnet comes to rest **[1]**. Move the compass so the end of the needle pointing towards the magnet points towards the plotted point. Now plot a new point where the other end of the compass needle comes to rest **[1]**. Continue until you reach the other end of the magnet, and join the points to produce a magnetic field line **[1]**.
   (b) The closer the field lines are together, the stronger the field / The further the field lines are apart, the weaker the field. **[1]**

Page 212 Electromagnetism

Quick quiz

From top to bottom: D; A; A ; D

1. A coil of wire **[1]** that produces a magnetic field when a current flows through it **[1]**.
2. **(a)**

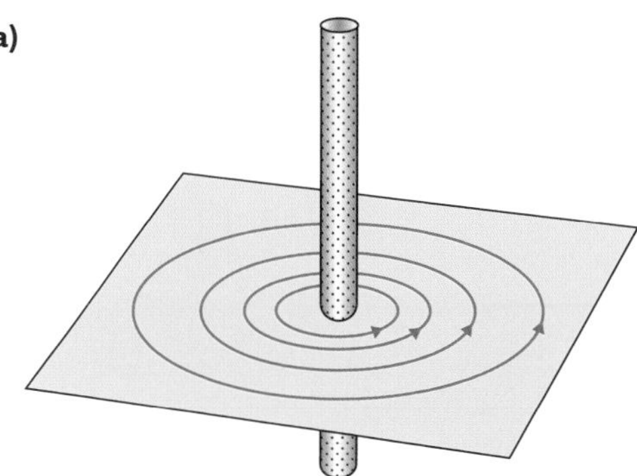

   Circles centred on wire, getting gradually further apart when moving away from wire **[1]** with direction of field indicated by arrows **[1]**
   (b) current in the wire **[1]**; distance from the wire **[1]**
3. **(a)** Any two for two marks from: Current in the solenoid; Whether an iron core is placed inside the solenoid; Distance from the solenoid
   (b) current in the circuit **[1]**
   (c) solenoid A because it has more turns **[1]**

Practice paper: Biology

01.1 protein synthesis **[1]**

01.2 cell membrane **[1]**
mitochondria **[1]**

01.3 0.05 **[1]** mm **[1]**

01.4 arrow drawn left to right **[1]**

01.5 Any one for one mark from: temperature; surface area; length of diffusion pathway

02.1

Organism	Producer	Secondary consumer	Prey
grass	✓		
grasshopper			✓
mouse		✓	✓
owl			

[1 mark for each correct row]

02.2 more competition for food **[1]**
number of owls would decrease **[1]**

02.3 Any two for two marks from: new disease; mutations; temperature change; environmental change, e.g. loss of habitat; catastrophic event; speciation

03.1 Male – any one for one mark from: voice breaks; pubic hair growth; facial hair growth; underarm hair growth; sexual organs grow; shoulders broaden
Female – any one for one mark from: breasts grow; menstruation; hips widen; pubic hair growth; underarm hair growth

03.2 contraceptive pill **[1]**
implant **[1]**

04.1 Any five marks from:
use a quadrat
place quadrat randomly
count the number of buttercups in the quadrat
repeat
calculate the mean number of buttercups per quadrat
calculate how many quadrats in the field / area of field
multiply the mean number of buttercups per quadrat by the number of quadrats in the field

04.2 Abiotic – any one for one mark from: light intensity / mineral content / moisture

Biotic – any one for one mark from: predators / competition

05.1 carry out repeats **[1]**

05.2 measure the reaction time without sugar **[1]**

get (the same) student to take some sugar **[1]**

measure the reaction time again **[1]**

06.1 plasma – transport heat and other substances

platelets – help blood clotting

red blood cells – transport oxygen

white blood cells – help protect the body from disease

[1 mark for 1 correct; 2 marks for 2–3 correct; 3 marks for all 4 correct]

06.2 Answers should include the following points in a logical order for 6 marks.

- stents can be used to keep arteries open
- statins are drugs that can be used to lower blood cholesterol
- biological / mechanical valves used to replace faulty valves
- heart transplant where a healthy organ is used to replace a diseased organ
- artificial heart can use used to replace a damaged heart
- risk of death from surgery
- transplants can sometimes be rejected
- shortage of donors
- artificial hearts need a power source so inconvenient
- statins may have side effects
- risk of blood clots forming with stents / valves
- mechanical valves can wear out

07.1 A and C **[1]**

07.2 B **[1]**

07.3 two **[1]**

07.4 add ethanol and shake **[1]**

add water / pour ethanol into water **[1]**

white emulsion / cloudiness **[1]**

07.5 276 + 277 + 286 = 839 **[1]**

839 / 3 = 279.67 = 280 **[1]**

07.6 pH 6 **[1]**

08.1 Any one for one mark from: distance of lamp; light intensity

08.2 Any one for one mark from: temperature of the water; volume of water; concentration of carbon dioxide

08.3 oxygen **[1]**

08.4 the closer the lamp the greater the number of bubbles released (per minute) **[1]**

08.5 Any one for one mark from: respiration; stored as starch; used to make cellulose; used to make fats; used to make oils; used to make proteins

09.1 PP **[1]**

Pp **[1]**

09.2 homozygous **[1]**

recessive **[1]**

09.3 Punnett square completed **[1]**

		Parent A	
		P	p
Parent B	P	PP	Pp
	p	Pp	pp

Probability of the child having polydactyly: 75% / 3 in 4 / 0.75 **[1]**

10.1 2014 **[1]**

10.2 372 – 120 = 222 **[1]**

10.3 Any three for three marks from:

dead / inactive pathogen injected / given

white blood cells produce antibodies

antibodies destroy pathogen

white blood cells produce memory cells to protect the body in the future

10.4 Any two for two marks from:

antibiotics

physical barriers such as gloves / mask

vaccination

isolating those infected

hygiene / example of good hygiene

better housing / less overcrowding

ventilation

better sanitation

correct disposal of medical waste / dressings

11 Any two for two marks from advantages: can replace damaged cells; can treat nerve / spinal / brain injuries; can treat degenerative disorders; can cure / treat genetic diseases

Any two for two marks from disadvantages: embryos are destroyed in the process; people have religious / ethical objections; stem cells could contain viruses

Practice paper: Chemistry

01.1 3 **[1]**

01.2 s **[1]**

01.3 aqueous solution / dissolved in water **[1]**

01.4 zinc sulfate **[1]**

01.5 bubbling **[1]**; zinc gets smaller / disappears **[1]**

01.6 Place a lighted splint in the gas **[1]**; it will ignite with a pop if hydrogen is present **[1]**.

02.1 boron and aluminium **[1]**

02.2 for an element he thought had not been discovered **[1]**

02.3 atomic weight **[1]**

02.4 Its atoms have the same number of protons. **[1]**

02.5 They have the same number of electrons **[1]** in their outer shell **[1]**.

03.1 increases, increases **[1]**

03.2 covalent bond **[1]**

03.3 Place damp litmus paper in the gas **[1]**; it will bleach / turn white if chlorine is present **[1]**.

03.4 Bromine is more reactive than iodine **[1]**; a more reactive halogen can displace a less reactive halogen **[1]**.

03.5 chlorine + sodium bromide $\rightarrow$ sodium chloride **[1]** + bromine **[1]**

04.1 H^+ **[1]** + $OH^- \rightarrow H_2O$ **[1]**

04.2 Measure the temperature before and after **[1]**; it will increase **[1]**.

05.1 $Fe_2O_3 + 3C \rightarrow 2Fe$ **[1]** + $3CO$ **[1]**

05.2 iron / iron oxide **[1]**

05.3 carbon atoms joined in hexagonal rings **[1]**; in layers **[1]**

05.4 Metals contain free / delocalised electrons **[1]**; which can move through the metal **[1]**.

05.5 Aluminium is more reactive than carbon **[1]**.

05.6 (Aluminium) ions must be free to move for electrolysis **[1]**; this happens in a molten substance **[1]**; cryolite lowers the melting point **[1]**.

06.1 Bubble through limewater **[1]**; this will turn milky / cloudy white **[1]**

06.2 35 / 20 **[1]** = 1.75 **[1]** cm^3/s

06.3 No more gas was produced after 50 s **[1]**.

06.4 It decreases **[1]**; until it becomes zero **[1]**.

07.1 The reversible symbol is shown in the equation **[1]**.

07.2 They are the same / equal **[1]**.

07.3 Cool the reaction down **[1]**.

07.4 Use universal indicator paper / solution **[1]**; if the colour turns blue / purple, the solution is alkaline **[1]**. OR Use a pH meter **[1]**; if the pH is greater than 7, the solution is alkaline **[1]**.

08.1 [B and C]

08.2 evaporate **[1]**

08.3 Boiling point and viscosity both increase. **[1]**

09.1 Table completed:

Gas	Percentage in air
carbon dioxide and other trace gases	less than 1
nitrogen **[1]**	80
oxygen	20 **[1]**

09.2 Water vapour condensed. **[1]**

09.3 Carbon dioxide decreased. **[1]**

09.4 Two for two marks from: carbon dioxide dissolved in the oceans; carbonates were precipitated; limestone / sedimentary rock formed; fossil fuels formed

10.1 Two for two marks from: extracting / processing raw materials; manufacturing and packaging; use during its lifetime; disposal at the end

10.2 Melt and recast **[1]**; reform into a different product **[1]**.

11.1 hydrochloric acid **[1]**

11.2 Two for two marks from: magnesium; magnesium oxide; magnesium hydroxide; magnesium carbonate

11.3 Answers should include the following points in a logical order for 6 marks.

Method:

add (excess) solid / named solid to the acid

heat the mixture

filter the mixture

evaporate about half the water, e.g. using a water bath

let solution cool so crystals form

dry crystals, e.g. with filter paper

Safety points: wear eye protection; avoid skin contact with the acid; warm but not boil the mixture during evaporation

Practice paper: Physics

01.1 a cell **[1]**

01.2 300 + 150 **[1]** = 450 (Ω) **[1]**

01.3 Component A is an ammeter and component B is a voltmeter. **[1]**

01.4 1.35 V = current × 450 **[1]** so current = 1.35 / 450 **[1]** = 0.003 A **[1]**

01.5 parallel **[1]**

01.6 The total resistance is less than 150 Ω. **[1]**

02.1 23 mass number; Mg - element; 12 atomic number

[2 marks for all three correct, 1 mark for two correct]

02.2 95 **[1]**

02.3 146 **[1]**

02.4 a nucleus of a helium atom **[1]**

02.5 Any one for one mark from: low penetration / penetrating power; short / low range in air

02.6 Any one for one mark from:

radioactive materials are hazardous / unsafe

americium can be recycled

03.1 Vernier callipers / micrometer **[1]**

03.2 5.0 × 2.5 × 1.4 **[1]** = 17.5 cm^3 **[1]**

03.3 3.2 / 6.4 **[1]** = 0.5 g/cm^3 **[1]**

03.4 Answers should include the following points in a logical order for 6 marks.

Find mass:

measure the mass of the rock using a mass balance or balancing scales

Find volume:

fill a displacement can with water to just below the spout

place / submerge the rock in the water in the displacement can

take care not to let water splash out of the top

collect the water displaced in a measuring cylinder to determine the volume

Find density:

calculate the density

use the equation density = mass / volume

04.1 Velocity is a vector; speed is a scalar / velocity includes direction; speed does not **[1]**.

04.2 500 (s) **[1]**

04.3 1500 m = speed × 500 s **[1]** so speed = 1500 / 500 **[1]** = 3 m/s / 3.0 m/s **[1]**

04.4 stationary / standing still / not moving **[1]**

04.5 The speed is less / The gradient is less steep so the runner has a lower speed / Slower than initial speed **[1]**.

05.1 Permanent magnet produces its own magnetic field **[1]**.

Induced magnet (only) becomes magnetic when placed in another magnetic field **[1]**.

05.2 induced magnet **[1]**

05.3 Steel is a magnetic material, aluminium is not **[1]**.

05.4 Any one for one mark from:

electromagnet can be switched off (to release cans)

electromagnet can be switched on when in position (to attract cans)

electromagnet can be made easier to control

06.1 A – the distance from a point on one wave to the equivalent point on the adjacent wave

B – the maximum displacement of a point on a wave away from its undisturbed position

[2 marks for both correct, 1 mark for one correct]

06.2 In transverse waves, vibrations are at right angles / perpendicular to the direction of wave travel / there is no compression and rarefaction in transverse waves **[1]**

In longitudinal waves, vibrations are parallel to / in same direction as the direction of wave travel / there is compression and rarefaction in longitudinal waves **[1]**

06.3 sound wave **[1]**

06.4 wave speed = frequency × wavelength or v = f × λ **[1]**

06.5 Measurement 2 **[1]**

06.6 (21 + 20 + 19) / 3 **[1]** = 20 **[1]**

((21 + 27 + 20 + 19) / 4 = 21.75 / 22 for 1 mark only as it includes anomalous measurement)

06.7 20 / 10 = 2 Hz **[1]**

06.8 The wave crests are difficult to see on the water surface / the waves (wave crests) are moving all the time so are difficult to count / the length of the tank may not be an exact multiple of wavelength / difficult to measure the length of the tank accurately **[1]**

06.9 Any two for two marks from:

shine a light through the top of the tank to produce shadows of the waves (wave crests) under the tank that are easier to see / count

count the number of waves at different times and calculate the mean

take a photograph of the waves (or the image of the waves under the tank

adjust the frequency of the vibrating bar to make the waves easier to see

make the length of the tank a whole multiple of wavelengths

07.1 weight **[1]**; field **[1]**

07.2 On Earth: 7.2, On the Moon: 1.2 **[1]**

07.3 The gravitational field strength on the surface of the Moon is weaker than on Earth. **[1]**

07.4 R: (normal) reaction **[1]**; S: weight / force due to gravity **[1]**

07.5 the buggy accelerates (forwards) / speeds up **[1]**

07.6 total stopping distance is the sum of thinking distance and braking distance **[1]**

08.1 Gravitational potential energy of water stored by dam is transferred to movement (kinetic energy) of water **[1]**

Movement (kinetic energy) of water is transferred to movement (kinetic energy) of turbine **[1]**

Movement of turbine drives / turns electrical generators **[1]**

08.2 $\text{efficiency} = \frac{\text{useful power output}}{\text{total power input}}$ **[1]**

08.3 wind, **[1]** because efficiency = 1 / 3.5 which is greater than solar efficiency = 1 / 6.5 **[1]**

08.4 Answers should include the following points in a logical order for 6 marks.

Wind costs £750 000 more to build / twice as much

Solar costs £250 000 to run over 25 years

Wind costs £1 125 000 to run over 25 years

Total cost of solar = £1 000 000 over 25 years

Total cost of wind = £2 625 000 over 25 years

So solar is cheaper / wind is more expensive overall

OR

Solar:

10 000 × 25 = £250 000

Total cost = 750 000 + 250 000 = £1 000 000

Wind:

45 000 × 25 = £1 125 000

Total cost = 1 500 000 + 1 125 000 = £2 625 000

So solar is 2 625 000 – 1 000 000 = £1 625 000 cheaper overall

Physics equation sheet

(final velocity)^2 – (initial velocity)^2 = 2 × acceleration × distance	$v^2 - u^2 = 2\,a\,s$
elastic potential energy = 0.5 × spring constant × (extension)^2	$E_e = \frac{1}{2}\,k\,e^2$
change in thermal energy = mass × specific heat capacity × temperature change	$\Delta E = m\,c\,\Delta\theta$
$\text{period} = \frac{1}{\text{frequency}}$	
thermal energy for a change of state = mass × specific latent heat	$E = m\,L$

Periodic table

Key

relative atomic mass atomic symbol name atomic (proton) number

1	2											3	4	5	6	7	0
							1 H Hydrogen 1										4 He Helium 2
7 Li Lithium 3	9 Be Beryllium 4											11 B Boron 5	12 C Carbon 6	14 N Nitrogen 7	16 O Oxygen 8	19 F Fluorine 9	20 Ne Neon 10
23 Na Sodium 11	24 Mg Magnesium 12											27 Al Aluminium 13	28 Si Silicon 14	31 P Phosphorus 15	32 S Sulfur 16	35.5 Cl Chlorine 17	40 Ar Argon 18
39 K Potassium 19	40 Ca Calcium 20	45 Sc Scandium 21	48 Ti Titanium 22	51 V Vanadium 23	52 Cr Chromium 24	55 Mn Manganese 25	56 Fe Iron 26	59 Co Cobalt 27	59 Ni Nickel 28	63.5 Cu Copper 29	65 Zn Zinc 30	70 Ga Gallium 31	73 Ge Germanium 32	75 As Arsenic 33	79 Se Selenium 34	80 Br Bromine 35	84 Kr Krypton 36
85 Rb Rubidium 37	88 Sr Strontium 38	89 Y Yttrium 39	91 Zr Zirconium 40	93 Nb Niobium 41	96 Mo Molybdenum 42	98 Tc Technetium 43	101 Ru Ruthenium 44	103 Rh Rhodium 45	106 Pd Palladium 46	108 Ag Silver 47	112 Cd Cadmium 48	115 In Indium 49	119 Sn Tin 50	122 Sb Antimony 51	128 Te Tellurium 52	127 I Iodine 53	131 Xe Xenon 54
133 Cs Caesium 55	137 Ba Barium 56	139 La Lanthanum 57	178 Hf Hafnium 72	181 Ta Tantalum 73	184 W Tungsten 74	186 Re Rhenium 75	190 Os Osmium 76	192 Ir Iridium 77	195 Pt Platinum 78	197 Au Gold 79	201 Hg Mercury 80	204 Tl Thallium 81	207 Pb Lead 82	209 Bi Bismuth 83	[210] Po Polonium 84	[210] At Astatine 85	[222] Rn Radon 86
[223] Fr Francium 87	[226] Ra Radium 88	[227] Ac Actinium 89	[261] Rf Rutherfordium 104	[262] Db Dubnium 105	[266] Sg Seaborgium 106	[264] Bh Bohrium 107	[277] Hs Hassium 108	[268] Mt Meitnerium 109	[271] Ds Darmstadtium 110	[272] Rg Roentgenium 111	[285] Cn Copernicium 112	[286] Uut Ununtrium 113	[289] Fl Flerovium 114	[289] Uup Ununpentium 115	[293] Lv Livermorium 116	[294] Uus Ununseptium 117	[294] Uuo Ununoctium 118

* The Lanthandies (atomic numbers 58 – 71) and the Actinides (atomic numbers 90 – 103) have been omitted.
Relative atomic massses for Cu and Cl have not been rounded to the nearest whole number.

Notes

Notes

Notes

Notes

Notes